FROM THESE
BEGINNINGS

VOLUME ONE

FROM THESE BEGINNINGS

*A Biographical Approach
to American History*

SEVENTH EDITION

Roderick Nash
Gregory Graves

University of California, Santa Barbara

New York   San Francisco   Boston
London   Toronto   Sydney   Tokyo   Singapore   Madrid
Mexico City   Munich   Paris   Cape Town   Hong Kong   Montreal

Vice President and Publisher: Priscilla McGeehon
Assistant Editor: Jacob Drill
Executive Marketing Manager: Sue Westmoreland
Managing Editor: Valerie Lynn Zaborski
Project Coordination, Text Design, and Electronic Page Makeup:
  Stratford Publishing Services
Cover Design Manager: Wendy Ann Fredericks
Cover Designer: Kay Petronio
Cover Art: Frederick Douglass: © MPI/Getty Images Inc.—Hulton Archive Photos; and
  Tecumseh: (c. 1768–1813) (oil on canvas). Arthurs, Stanley Massey (1877–1950),
  Delaware Art Museum, Wilmington, USA/Bridgeman Art Library
Photo Researcher: Photosearch, Inc.
Senior Manufacturing Buyer: Dennis J. Para

Cover Printer: Coral Graphic Services, Inc.

For permission to use copyrighted material, grateful acknowledgment is made to the
copyright holders on p. 256, which is hereby made part of this copyright page.

Library of Congress Cataloging-in-Publication Data

Nash, Roderick.
    From these beginnings : a biographical approach to American history / Roderick Nash
and Gregory Graves.—7th ed.
        p.   cm.
    Includes bibliographical references and index.
    ISBN 0-321-21640-7 (v.1) — ISBN 0-321-21639-3 (v.2)
    1. United States—History.   2. United States—Biography.   I. Graves, Gregory.
II. Title.
  E178.N18   2005
  973'.09'9—dc22   2004011058

Please visit our website at http://www.ablongman.com

ISBN 0-321-21640-7

2 3 4 5 6 7 8 9 10—HT—07 06 05

Preface

There is properly no history; only biography.

—Ralph Waldo Emerson

That *From These Beginnings: A Biographical Approach to American History* has gone to a seventh edition provides continuing evidence for the old adage that the proper study of people is people. Certainly the proper study of the historian is humanity, more than laws, treaties, elections, or eras. History is about people who loved, hated, achieved, failed, and shared with us a fascinating complexity of thought and feeling. Like its predecessors, this seventh edition is dedicated to the proposition that teaching and learning about history lose significance and fun when they are divorced from human beings.

The biographical approach is one way to enliven the study of history. The logic behind this choice is obvious: People are interested in people. History concerns, or should concern, people. Historical writing can be made as exciting as life itself if we think of it as a series of biographies. These assumptions underlie the novel structure of this book.

This is hardly a radical approach. Much of our best historical writing is in the form of biography or family history. Motion pictures and television programs have included docudramas, historical fiction, and straight biographies of such famous Americans as Malcolm X, Jimmy Hoffa, Harry Truman, Jacqueline Kennedy Onassis, Woody Guthrie, Janis Joplin, and Jim Morrison. Documentary-style biographies are regularly broadcast on several cable television networks. The success of all these ventures serves as a challenge to professional historians. Why should history be as "dry as dust"? Why shouldn't history have all the drama of life itself, which, after all, is what it is? Yet, surprisingly, no textbook used a biographical form of organization before the first edition of *From These Beginnings* (1973).

It has been our experience in teaching undergraduate history at several universities that biography is an effective lecturing tool. Whether in short vignettes or hour-long lectures, telling the story of people who affected and were affected by their times remains a reliable way of maintaining student interest. The standard textbook method of dividing the past into periods, eras, or ages has been discarded in *From These Beginnings*. Nineteen often-overlapping lives provide the organizational framework, and the larger story of the American experience is woven around these lives. In this way, broad concepts are tied to specific examples. The frontier, slavery, and industrialization, for instance, acquire a sharper focus when viewed from the perspective of a pioneer, a slave, and an industrialist. At the same time, the narrative of national events deepens one's understanding of the nineteen individuals profiled.

The greatest problem in using a biographical approach is finding a happy compromise between "straight" biography and "straight" American history. This is not difficult, of course, when an individual life impinges directly on the course of national events. Thomas Jefferson writing the

Declaration of Independence, Henry Ford revolutionizing transportation, and Martin Luther King Jr. leading the civil rights movement are good examples. But frequently, even a famous person sinks back into the general citizenry, and his or her life becomes typical rather than unusual. On such occasions we have used a life-and-times approach, consisting of a description of the historical context surrounding the individual. The technique is justifiable, we believe, on the grounds that any life is in large part shaped by the stream of events in which it floats.

Given the success of the sixth edition, biography replacements proved to be a challenge. For months we discussed who and why between ourselves and among our friends, colleagues, students, and families. Our decision to add a new biography of Kit Carson in Volume 1 reflects our desire to assess recent interpretations of so-called frontier heroes. The addition of Ted Turner to Volume 2 affords an opportunity to analyze the impact of television—news, sports, talk—through the life story of one of the nation's great media entrepreneurs. The most extensive additions to the existing biographies are in Thomas Jefferson and Robert E. Lee in Volume 1, and in Richard Nixon in Volume 2.

Although none of these nineteen individuals may be completely satisfactory as the subject for a chapter in a history book, there is some comfort in the realization that the choice is not all-important. A surprising amount of information about the course of national events can be tied to *any* American life. Try it, for example, with your own life. *From These Beginnings* could feature any of the approximately half billion people who have called themselves Americans. As Americans, they all have affected and have been affected by American history.

We would like to acknowledge the help of our reviewers and thank them for their efforts: Stanley Adamiak, University of Central Oklahoma; Ken Bindas, Kent State University; Jack M. Holl, Kansas State University; Stephen Middleton, North Carolina State University; G. David Price, Santa Fe Community College; John David Smith, North Carolina State University.

Roderick Nash
Gregory Graves

FROM THESE
BEGINNINGS

Chapter 1

Christopher Columbus

With a rising moon and a strong east wind behind them, the three ships sailed headlong into history. It was shortly before 2 A.M. on October 12, 1492, but most hands were on deck. The usual signs of a landfall—a green branch, a carved stick, many birds—had made the crews eager, desperate, for their first sight of land in thirty-three days. The tall, gray-haired captain braced himself on the sterncastle of the *Santa María.* His face showed the strain of a twenty-year dream on the brink of realization. Suddenly, a muffled shot from the lead ship, *Pinta,* broke the rhythmic hiss of the waves. It was the signal for land ahead, and the *Pinta* fell off the wind, waiting for the flagship. As the *Santa María* approached, its captain, too, could see the pale gleam of limestone cliffs. Christopher Columbus had reached a new world for Europeans.

The son and grandson of humble weavers in the Republic of Genoa, north and west of Rome, Christopher Columbus, one might imagine, had little reason to anticipate a life of discovery and exploration. But the Europe into which he was born in 1451 simmered with the forces that eventually propelled him across the Atlantic. Some were already centuries old. Beginning in 1095, the several crusades to free Jerusalem from Turkish control had opened European eyes to new worlds. Nobles and fighting men who had journeyed to the Holy Land had encountered a whole new standard of living at this crossroads where East met West. For the first time, the crusaders saw luxurious silk cloth, which contrasted sharply with their rough woolen garments, such as those Columbus's family wove. And there were heavy, colorful tapestries that made ideal wall hangings for dark, drafty European castles and Oriental spices to preserve as well as flavor food. The Europeans also saw fabulous quantities of gold and gems. They heard about still more, especially in the late thirteenth century, when Marco Polo reported his overland journey to China, Japan, and the Spice Islands. Columbus's copy of Marco Polo's book was underlined where the author mentioned "pearls, precious stones, brocades, ivory, or pepper, nuts, nutmeg, cloves and an abundance of other spices." He also noted the reference to the palace of the king of Japan, "which is entirely roofed with fine gold, just as our churches are roofed with lead." Such tales of Asia whetted the appetite of Columbus's generation and lifted its eyes to far horizons.

Traders could satisfy European desire for the treasures of the East. After goods from Asia arrived at eastern Mediterranean ports such as Constantinople and Alexandria, merchants from Genoa, along with those from Venice, Florence, and Pisa, distributed them throughout Europe.

Prices, however, were exceedingly high. As a result, Europe was soon faced with an unfavorable balance of trade: Money flowed to the East and goods to the West. Asia had no use for Europe's bulky agricultural products. The economic situation was bad, and, to make matters worse, in 1453 the Turks captured Constantinople and thus closed to the Christian Europeans the key link in the route to the East. Columbus's Europe desperately needed cheap and direct access to the Orient. The vast highway of the sea promised both.

The Renaissance also played an important role in readying Christopher Columbus and his society for the exploration and colonization of the Americas. The term *renaissance* suggests a rebirth. To be sure, the so-called Dark Ages were not all that dismal, except by contrast to the accomplishments of Greece and Rome. But around the twelfth century, Arab and Jewish scholars alerted their European counterparts to the cultural brilliance of the classical civilizations. A shiver of excitement spread north from Italy. A society long accustomed to the Christian emphasis on the afterlife, the next world, now glimpsed the potential of the present. The idea of improving the human condition on earth—the idea of progress—gained momentum. A passion for fame, for glory, for achievement, for mastery gained a foothold in the European mind. Individualism flourished. It spread from the arts and letters to politics and business and fed the development of capitalism. Columbus and his contemporaries were restless, increasingly dissatisfied with the status quo. Understandably, this dissatisfaction created an urge for new lands and new beginnings.

Columbus had the restlessness, confidence, and ambition of a Renaissance man, and the sea offered a perfect outlet for his energies. It also provided an outlet for a man who was instilled with Christian mission and the fulfillment of prophecy. Although there are many ambiguities and mysteries surrounding his life and times, it is certain that Columbus met the sea in the harbor of his native Genoa and may well have transported woolen cloth along the Italian coast. In his twenties he made his first extensive voyages in the Mediterranean as a common seaman. In 1476 Columbus sailed in a large Genoese convoy bound for Portugal, England, and the North Sea ports. Just outside the Strait of Gibraltar, however, a war fleet from France and Portugal descended on the convoy. In the furious battle that followed, Columbus was wounded and his ship sunk. Grasping an oar for support, he struggled six miles to the southern coast of Portugal. As he crawled onto the beach of an unknown country, his chances of ever commanding an expedition to the New World seemed remote. But Columbus was an unusual man with a knack for persevering in the face of adversity.

The country Columbus reached in such unpromising circumstances was then the European leader in maritime discovery. Much of the credit for Portugal's eminence goes to Dom Henrique, better known as Prince Henry the Navigator. This talented prince, who died in 1460, personified the spirit of the age of European expansion. From his headquarters on the Atlantic Ocean, he sent expeditions into the unknown, funding them with his personal fortune. Some went north and developed a brisk trade with England and Iceland. Others pushed west, a thousand miles into the open ocean, to find the Azores. But Prince Henry reserved his keenest enthusiasm for those who sailed south to coast along the continent of Africa. At first, the Portuguese were satisfied to take part in the lucrative trade in gold, ivory, and slaves—the Guinea trade of West Africa. Soon, however, they began to believe that sailing down the west coast of Africa might provide a way to circumvent the Italian monopoly on trans-Mediterranean trade with Asia and India. Driven by a desire for trade and wealth, Prince Henry's captains had, at the time of his death in 1460, reached within ten degrees of the equator.

The Portuguese also achieved preeminence in developing the sciences of sailing and navigation. Not only exploration but the entire colonization movement depended on establishing safe and

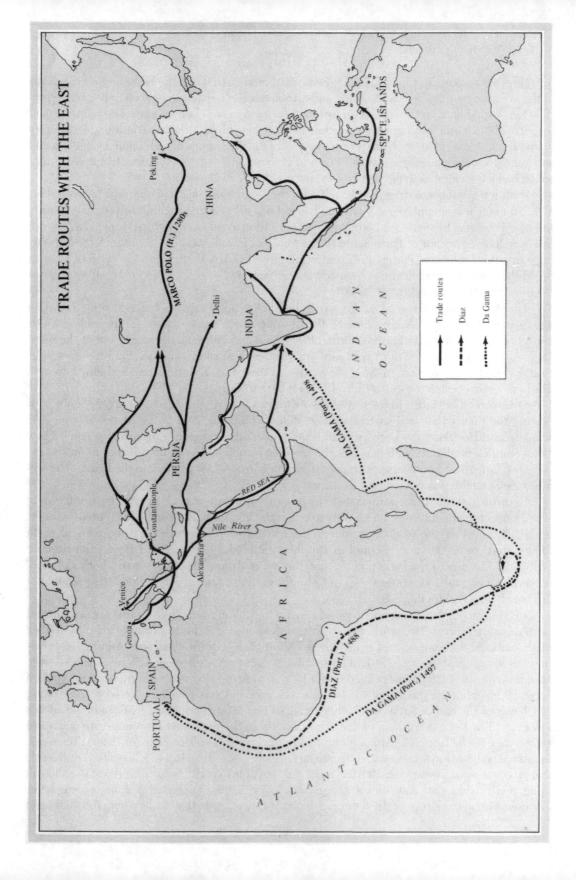

TRADE ROUTES WITH THE EAST

Peking

CHINA

SPICE ISLANDS

MARCO POLO (It.) 1280s

Delhi

INDIA

INDIAN OCEAN

Constantinople

PERSIA

DA GAMA (Port.) 1498

RED SEA

Venice

Alexandria

Nile River

Genoa

A F R I C A

PORTUGAL SPAIN

DIAZ (Port.) 1488

DA GAMA (Port.) 1497

A T L A N T I C   O C E A N

Trade routes

Diaz

Da Gama

reliable sea transport. To this end, Prince Henry gathered around him the best navigational minds in the Western world. The charts, tables, and astronomical observations they compiled made possible long expeditions on the open ocean without the need to stay close to shore. The refinement of the astrolabe, for example, permitted a captain to determine his latitude with considerable accuracy on the basis of star sightings. Equally important were the institutions of early capitalism, the banks and joint-stock companies that enabled Portugal to finance far-flung exploration. Ironically, a shipwreck had left Columbus in the best place to pursue the life of an explorer.

Within six months of dragging himself onto the Portuguese beach, Columbus recovered his health and once again put to sea. This time Iceland was the goal and trading the purpose. During the next few years he mastered Latin and Spanish and married Dona Felipa Moniz, daughter of the hereditary governor of Porto Santo in the Madeira Islands west of Gibraltar. After his marriage into this prominent Portuguese family, Columbus lived on Porto Santo for a year or more in the early 1480s. During that time, he made at least one voyage around the hump of West Africa to Guinea and the Gold Coast.

The African experience added greatly to his skill as a sea captain, but it also produced an unexpected dividend. Columbus noticed that south of the Canary Islands, the prevailing winds always blew from the east. Farther north, off England and Portugal, they came out of the west. It gradually dawned on him that to sail west into the North Atlantic winds was foolish. A far better course would be to sail south to the trade winds and then west. To return, one had simply to set a northerly course, catch the west wind, and ride it back to Europe.

Driftwood that storms frequently cast on European shores provided exciting evidence supporting the theory that land lay to the west. When Columbus lived in the Madeiras, he could scarcely avoid noticing the huge tropical canes, seedpods, and tree trunks that we now know came from Central and South America. Even carved wood had been found, and, on one occasion, two human bodies of an appearance strange to Europeans washed onto the beach. The significance of all this was not lost on Columbus.

Returning from Africa with knowledge about wind patterns, Columbus gave increasing attention to the possibility of sailing west to reach the Far East. The roots of this idea lay in his understanding that the world was round. Educated Europeans had taken a spherical earth for granted for 2,000 years; Columbus simply attempted a feat that had been discussed for centuries. The size of the earth and the distribution of its landmasses were still hotly debated, however, among the foremost scholars of Columbus's time. "Knowledge" tended to be a blend of fact, myth, and wishful thinking.

In constructing his conception of world geography, Columbus drew on a variety of ancient and contemporary sources. He owned an early fifteenth-century translation of the work of the Greek mathematician Ptolemy, whose calculations fell short of the earth's actual size. Adding reinforcement to his concept was the standard geography of the late Middle Ages—Pierre d'Ailly's *Imago Mundi*, written in 1410 but not printed until 1480. Columbus pored over his copy, making marginal notations on almost every page. "The earth is round and spherical," he jotted at one point, ". . . between the end of Spain and the beginning of India lies a narrow sea that can be sailed in a few days." Further confirmation of this error came from the renowned Florentine physician and geographer Paulo Toscanelli. Although trained in medicine at the University of Padua, Toscanelli found science, math, astronomy, and cosmography more fascinating. In 1474, he stated confidently that an ocean voyage west to reach Asia "is not only possible to make, but sure and certain, and will bring inestimable gain and utmost recognition." Presumably through his wife's connections, Columbus obtained a copy of the letter in which Toscanelli made that declaration. Toscanelli had

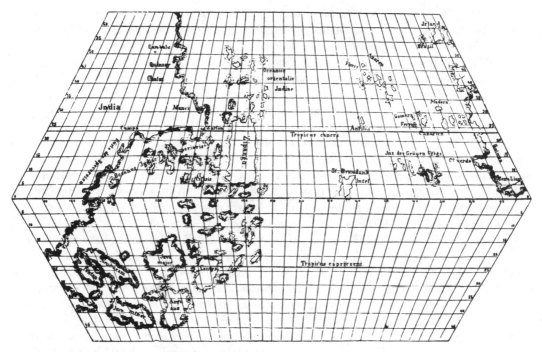

Columbus received this map from the geographer Paul Toscanelli and used it as evidence of the feasibility of sailing west to reach the Far East. The map accurately portrays this possibility, but it contains two glaring errors. According to the grid-shaped pattern of measurement, "Zipangu" (Japan), the other Spice Islands, and the Asian mainland are actually located more than 9,000 miles closer to Europe. The second error is the complete omission of North and South America. The large island in the center of the map existed only in European legend.

also drawn a map that Columbus used to calculate the distance from Portugal to Marco Polo's gold-roofed Japan as 3,000 miles. This was only 9,200 miles short!

Toscanelli also perpetuated another fallacy by postulating that only a small island group, Antilla, lay to the west between Portugal and Japan. Most fifteenth-century Europeans agreed that at least an island or a group of islands lay between these limits of geographical knowledge. No one, however, had conceived of a continent dividing the sea into the Atlantic and Pacific oceans. Even if Columbus and his contemporaries knew of the Irish and Viking contacts with North America, dating possibly from the sixth century and certainly from the eleventh, they did not realize that it was a continent. Yet ignorance, in this case, proved advantageous. Had he been correctly informed, Columbus would more than likely never have ventured west.

Myth also played an important role in his motivation. In company with all Europeans since the Greeks, Columbus believed in an earthly paradise. Life was good in paradise, really good. Ripe fruit hung heavy on every bough. The climate was delightful, and flowers perfumed the air. Precious stones and quantities of gold could be picked up at will. In some paradise traditions, these sensual joys were subordinated to spiritual ones. Paradise became a place where sin was unknown and people lived in accord with God's commandments. Those lucky enough to enter paradise, it was thought, left behind all worry, fear, and discomfort—even death was unknown there.

According to the Christian tradition, people once occupied paradise, but somewhere along the way they had become separated from it, as when an angry God drove Adam and Eve from the Garden of Eden. Later generations remembered, however—or at least they dreamed. Almost every culture in Western history has subscribed to the idea that paradise still exists, that somewhere there is an island or a mountain or an enchanted valley, and if they could only find it, the good life could be regained. The thought is irresistible, and it was particularly so when parts of the earth were yet unknown. It was tempting and easy to believe that paradise lay around the next bend, over the known horizon.

The idea of going *west* to find the lost paradise had existed for centuries before Columbus's venture. The Jews, wandering in the desert after fleeing Egypt, traveled back in that direction to find Canaan, their promised land of milk and honey. The Greeks, Romans, and Phoenicians had had similar traditions of an earthly paradise to the west. These mythical places even appeared on maps, set in the middle of the Atlantic under the names of Antilla, Atlantis, the Islands of the Blest, Elysium, and the Isle of Fair Women. In the sixth century an Irish monk, St. Brendan, supposedly sailed west in an attempt to reach the paradisiacal Fortunate Isles. According to the legend that grew up around this voyage, Brendan crossed the North Atlantic to Newfoundland, struck south to Bermuda, and then west to Florida. When he arrived, he found a settlement of Irish monks already enjoying the luxuriance of the tropics. True or not—and there is some evidence that Europeans of this time really did reach North America, if not paradise—the prospect of finding a Garden of Eden continually fired imaginations. In Columbus's time serious discussions of the location and characteristics of paradise were common in every European port. *Imago Mundi,* for example, declares "the Earthly Paradise is an Elysian spot . . . far distant from our inhabited world both by land and sea." To be the discoverer of this place was reason enough to motivate a man like Columbus.

To implement his plans for a westward voyage to the East and perhaps to paradise, Columbus needed financial backing. He turned first to King John II of Portugal. In 1484 Columbus enthusiastically unfolded his plan to the king's advisory committee, but this distinguished group of mathematicians and astronomers was not impressed. In particular, they doubted Columbus's calculation of the distance to Japan and China, contending, correctly, that it was closer to 10,000 than to 3,000 miles. The committee favored a course around Africa. Portuguese mariners were continuing the explorations to the south begun under Prince Henry, and it seemed only a matter of time before they would round Africa and open a sea route to India. Therefore, the advisory committee dismissed Columbus's plan as unnecessary and as based on imagination more than fact. At about the same time, Columbus received news that his wife had died in Porto Santo.

At this low point in his life, Columbus became the beneficiary of Europe's changing political structure. Before the fifteenth century, an endless series of nobles, barons, earls, and dukes had vied for dominance within particular regions. The abundance of leaders had scattered wealth and power into small and relatively weak units. From this feudal chaos, however, kings and nations began slowly to emerge. By the late fifteenth century, a few families had proved superior in the political struggle for existence. Forcing subservience on what became the lesser nobility, they created a series of hereditary monarchies. Extremely competitive and ambitious, these emerging national rulers aspired to the Roman example of world domination. Discovery and expansion appealed to them as avenues to glory. The nation that could find an easy route to Asia and establish lucrative trading colonies would have an immense advantage over its rivals.

For Columbus, the emerging new order presented an opportunity. After his rejection by the Portuguese monarchy, Columbus traveled to Palos, Spain. Arriving in this seaport city in southern Spain in 1485, Columbus studied cosmography with a Franciscan friar whose knowledge and library restored the explorer's spirit. A year later, Columbus presented his ideas to the Spanish monarchs Ferdinand and Isabella, who were enmeshed in a struggle to unite Spain under their banner and to expel the Moors.

Primarily because of their preoccupation with this struggle, Ferdinand and Isabella paid Columbus little attention when he first approached them. But Columbus also made things difficult for himself by his attitude. Ambitious and conceited, he insisted—as a prerequisite for any voyage—on a guarantee of three fully equipped ships, one-tenth of all the treasures he might find, an appointment as governor and viceroy of the lands discovered, and a place in the Spanish nobility with the title Admiral of the Ocean Sea. Detractors raised the old question of distance, and Columbus was again accused of unwarranted optimism. After months of deliberation, the Spanish court rejected his proposal.

But this rejection, based on scientific doubt, was premature. Other voices in the Spanish court, impressed by his brash confidence and aware of the need to compete with Portugal, continued to debate the idea. Skepticism vied with desire. At some point Columbus probably played his trump card: the pattern of the winds. He explained how to reach Asia by following the northeast winds in the South Atlantic. Even if the trip proved longer than anticipated, it would be easy to turn north and ride the west winds home.

As the debate continued into the 1490s, events became Columbus's ally. Portuguese explorer Bartholomeu Diaz had rounded the southern tip of Africa in 1488, giving that nation a commanding lead in reaching Asia by sea. Ferdinand and Isabella's treasurer, Luis de Santángel, believed it was time to act. He pointed out that the recent surrender of Granada, the last stronghold of African Moors in Spain, on January 2, 1492, had freed the nation's resources for discovery. The voyage just might prove a bonanza in the wake of Spanish unity. Moreover, Columbus could be Spain's vehicle for spreading Christianity to heathen peoples. Considerations of gold, God, and glory, Santángel concluded, lent Columbus's proposal irresistible appeal.

Many Europeans of Columbus's time believed that along with the economic, political, and scientific opportunities inherent in discovering new lands went a religious responsibility. Christianity had to be extended to the heathens. In this sketch from a 1500 map of the world, Columbus is shown wading ashore in the New World with an infant Christ on his shoulders. Appropriately, Columbus's first name was Christopher, meaning "Christ bearer." Some recent scholarship suggests that Columbus may have had Jewish ancestry.

At last, the monarchs agreed. Columbus, on his way to France to make his proposal there, was recalled by royal messenger. Ferdinand and Isabella accepted his terms in a formal agreement of April 17, 1492, and with ample money and connections, Columbus, his energy pent up, exploded into action. Less than three months after arriving in the port of Palos, Columbus was ready to begin his quest.

Two of the three ships in his expedition, the *Pinta* and the *Niña*, were caravels. These vessels, light and narrow and approximately seventy-five feet long, had been designed for extended voyages. They were swift and could sail almost directly into the wind. Columbus's flagship, the *Santa María*, was longer, bulkier, and slower. Perhaps the ship owners of Palos were unwilling to risk a third caravel on so dubious a venture. Still, ninety men volunteered for the crew. Of course, as a foreigner in Spain, Columbus needed the assistance of local residents who were also interested in the voyage. The most important among these were members of one of the leading shipping families of Palos: the Pinzóns. In addition to helping Columbus select an able crew, one Pinzón brother, Martin, commanded the *Pinta* and chose as his first mate a younger brother, Francisco. Still another Pinzón brother, Vicente, was captain of the *Niña*. The Pinzóns provided the expert seamanship and strong moral support that Columbus badly needed. On August 3, 1492, the three ships left Palos, bound for the unknown.

Just as he had proposed, Columbus led his expedition on a southwest slant to the Canary Islands, then due west along the twenty-eighth parallel of latitude. The winds proved favorable, as predicted, and the ships made good time. Of course, there were misgivings. Columbus continually had to restrain the crew from altering course to search for islands that seemed just out of sight. As the days stretched into weeks and no land appeared, whispers and then open complaints spread among the men. The sailors did not fear a sudden drop off a flat earth or sea monsters; they were simply a long way from home on an open ocean.

Responding to these challenges, Columbus offered reminders of the riches that lay ahead in Asia. He may have deliberately falsified his log to make the distance back to Spain seem shorter. Ultimately, however, it was a question of will. Columbus was committed. Only death or mutiny could have forced him to turn around in midpassage. His spirit, and the continued support of the Pinzón brothers, sustained the crew. It was Martin Pinzón who, aided by a flock of migratory birds obviously bound for land, persuaded Columbus to turn southwest and, miraculously, in the direction of the shortest distance to land. When San Salvador (as they named the landmass) loomed in sight on the morning of October 12, 1492, the Captains Pinzón and their proclaimed Admiral Columbus prepared to disembark on what they were convinced was a remote corner of the Asian continent.

Although recent scholarship suggests that the actual landfall site was not Watling Island but Caicos or Samana Cay, there is still no conclusive proof about where Columbus and his men first set foot on land. Whether they landed on one of these islands—or on Crooked Island, Rum Cay, Grand Turk, Mayaguana, Plana Cay, or Cat Island (all of these have been identified as the true landfall at one time or another)—Columbus did sight one of the Windward Islands of the Lesser Antilles. And he and his crew disembarked, came ashore, and explored.

It was surely one of history's dramatic moments when a native of the island, walking the beach at dawn, glanced up to see three ships approaching from the east. By the time the ships anchored, many natives had gathered. Columbus's journal notes their nakedness and describes them as "very well built, with handsome bodies and fine faces." These people had occupied the islands of the Caribbean for only a century. Their ancestors had come to the area from mainland South America, conquering a more primitive race of islanders in the process. Ultimately, their

It took extreme bias to have regarded the North American Indians encountered by the first Europeans as wild animals. Many did so, however, in spite of the sophistication of Indian villages such as this one in North Carolina.

roots went back to the Mongoloid hunters who had crossed the Bering Strait to Alaska at least 10,000 and perhaps 40,000 years before Columbus appeared. Fanning out over a continent newly released from the grip of the glaciers (see Chapter 6, pages 138–139), their descendants were on hand to challenge the Vikings when they landed in the eleventh century. European contact with the New World before then is probable, if not fully substantiated. Like Columbus, early mariners could have sailed the trade winds from the Canary Islands to the West Indies. Rock inscriptions from New England and inland sites as distant as the Mississippi Valley date from

The whole age of discovery and exploration depended on a device as simple as a compass. This reconstruction of a later fifteenth-century model, similar to the one Columbus used, consists of a wooden bowl, an iron needle, and a thin directional "rose" made of wood or paper. The rose could be turned to compensate for magnetic variation.

1000 B.C., and are written in scripts known only to the Celts, Basques, Libyans, and Egyptians. If these people did establish permanent settlements in the New World, what happened to them? Where were the members of this first wave of European pioneers when Columbus touched on San Salvador? The answer among scholars who hold to the early-contact theory is that they were still present, having been absorbed into the tribes of the still earlier immigrants from Asia.

When Columbus termed the San Salvador people "Indians," he was, unknowingly, partly right. Their most distant ancestors had come from India (a term loosely applied in the fifteenth century to Asia generally). But Columbus's conscious use of the term was strictly a product of wishful thinking and erroneous geography. As a twentieth-century Sioux put it, commenting on the history of the subjugation of the Native American, "Even the name Indian is not ours. It was given to us by some dumb honky who got lost and thought he'd landed in India."

European arrogance toward the so-called Indians began with Columbus. From the start he regarded them as inferior, even as he noted their good looks and idyllic environment. Nonchalantly he took possession of a land they occupied. And while gathering specimen flowers, fruits, and birds to take back to Europe, he also collected seven natives. In his mind they were just another type of animal, and his journal contains frank speculations on the ease with which they could be enslaved. "These people," he noted on October 14, "are very unskilled in arms . . . with fifty men they could all be subjected and made to do all that one wished." The statement proved to be a grim prophecy.

The first island disappointed Columbus. There were no treasures of the Orient. But he saw what he wished to see, what he felt must be there. The Indians wore small gold ornaments. By signs, they gave the strangers to believe that much more gold could be found elsewhere. Columbus assumed that Japan was close at hand. On the afternoon of October 14 he left San Salvador, intending to island-hop to Asia. The Spaniards cruised among several smaller islands and then, following natives' directions, pushed on to Cuba. When its high blue mountains appeared to the south, their goal once more seemed on the brink of realization. But again disappointment followed exaggerated expectation. No Grand Khan, wallowing in gold, could be located. Parties sent on inland explorations of Cuba returned with the same depressing story of poor natives and forbidding jungle.

Lisbon, Portugal, was one of the most exciting places in fifteenth-century Europe. It was a jumping-off place—a Cape Canaveral of its time. This 1590 engraving shows Columbus's fleet returning from its first voyage to the New World. The ships are caravels, about seventy-five feet long.

The island of Hispaniola, to which the explorers sailed next, proved to be more promising. The Indians had considerable gold and told Columbus of rich mines in the interior. But just when success seemed imminent, the *Santa María* ran aground on a reef and was abandoned on Christmas Day 1492. Columbus made a quick decision. He would plant a colony, called Navidad, and leave forty men on Hispaniola to find the gold and ascertain the location of Asia. On January 16, 1493, the *Pinta* and the *Niña* began the voyage home.

Columbus's arrival in Lisbon almost three months later, on March 4, triggered a surge of excitement. People debated whether he had found the outskirts of Asia, or islands midway between Europe and Asia, or a whole new continent, but few remained indifferent. Hunger for the Oriental trade and Renaissance curiosity and political ambition combined to create a climate in which Columbus's reports ignited imaginations. Europe was ripe for the news he brought. This had not been true at the time of the earlier discoveries of the New World. When the Vikings, for example, made contact in the eleventh century, Europeans were not straining impatiently at their physical and intellectual bounds. Asia and its riches were unknown. The Crusades had not begun. Neither capitalism nor nationalism had appeared. Open-ocean navigation was a risky, hit-or-miss operation. Consequently, the Viking feat had little impact on history. Christopher Columbus, on the contrary, had the good fortune to sail at a time when Europe was ready. His "discovery" began the continuous European expansion that led directly to the formation of the United States. Not literally, then—but significantly—Columbus discovered America.

After completing his first round trip to the Caribbean, Columbus could have retired on his laurels, but for a man of his temperament, the first voyage could be only a prelude. Ferdinand and Isabella were similarly inclined. Their Admiral of the Ocean Sea had come to Barcelona and astounded them with his collection of strange fish, wood, and fruit. Columbus spread gold before the monarchs, assuring them that it was but a token of what existed. The Indians Columbus displayed to the court provided additional incentive. On command, they recited the Ave Maria and crossed themselves. In the eyes of fervent Catholics like Ferdinand and Isabella, who had organized Spain around Christianity, this was reason enough to continue the Western exploration. A whole civilization of heathens seemed to be waiting for conversion to Christianity. And by a Papal Bull of May 4, 1493, which set a line of demarcation 100 leagues west of the Azores, Spain was given the exclusive right to exploit and colonize the new lands.

With the stakes so high, Columbus found little difficulty in assembling the men and means to support his return to the Caribbean. On September 25, 1493, seventeen ships and between 1,200 and 1,500 men left the Spanish port of Cádiz. Once again the ocean crossing caused no problem, but the expedition failed to fulfill expectations. Neither the Asian mainland nor Japan materialized, although the search was much more extensive. The amount of gold found was far smaller than Columbus had expected. The Indians, moreover, proved as poor as subjects for missionary work as the Spaniards proved as missionaries. Columbus fought the cannibals of the Leeward Islands and made them slaves and concubines. The Indians had turned the tables at Hispaniola, however. When Columbus returned to his Navidad colony, he found nothing but bones and charred timbers. Every Spaniard had been killed or carried off into the jungle.

Columbus's fortunes went from bad to worse. He attempted to start another colony, called Isabella, on Hispaniola, but his men suffered from sickness, dissension, and apathy. When they realized that gold could not be picked up on the beaches, they quickly became disenchanted with the New World. Actually, their situation was a symptom of the more general failure of the trading-post colony in the Americas. In wealthy and sophisticated societies like those of India and coastal Africa, Europeans simply set up shop and traded for valuable goods. Amid the comparatively poorer and more primitive people of the Caribbean and North America, however, there was little for which to trade. Europeans would have to work for wealth in these places; they would have to invest time, effort, and money before they could expect returns. Columbus unconsciously realized this in one of his official reports. Hispaniola, he declared, "is a wonder, with its hills and mountains, plains and meadows, and a land so rich and fertile for planting and sowing, for raising livestock of all sorts, for building towns and villages." But for over a century, neither he nor his followers proved capable of translating this vision into reality. The lure of quick, easy wealth blinded them to the real abundance of the new land.

Troubled by discontent among his men, Columbus had to face the additional problem of full-scale war with the Indians. The missionary ideal broke down completely. Headstrong men, thousands of miles from home, often did not respect Ferdinand and Isabella's directive that their new subjects be treated gently. Between 1494 and 1496, all of the natives of Hispaniola, who numbered in the millions before Columbus's arrival, were killed, died of European-borne diseases, or were put to work in the gold mines. Columbus himself implemented draconian

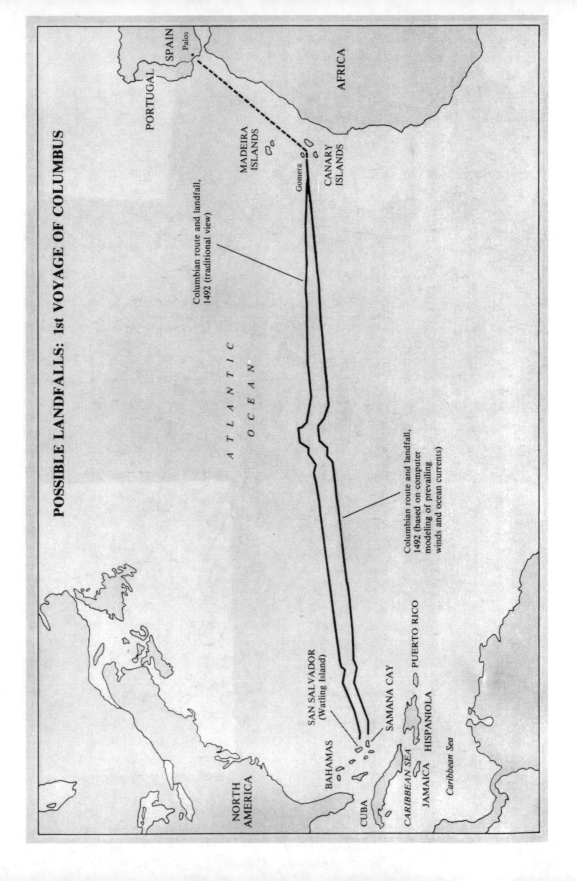

POSSIBLE LANDFALLS: 1st VOYAGE OF COLUMBUS

SPAIN

Palos

PORTUGAL

AFRICA

MADEIRA ISLANDS

Gomera

CANARY ISLANDS

Columbian route and landfall, 1492 (traditional view)

A T L A N T I C   O C E A N

Columbian route and landfall, 1492 (based on computer modeling of prevailing winds and ocean currents)

NORTH AMERICA

BAHAMAS

SAN SALVADOR (Watling Island)

SAMANA CAY

PUERTO RICO

CUBA

HISPANIOLA

CARIBBEAN SEA

JAMAICA

Caribbean Sea

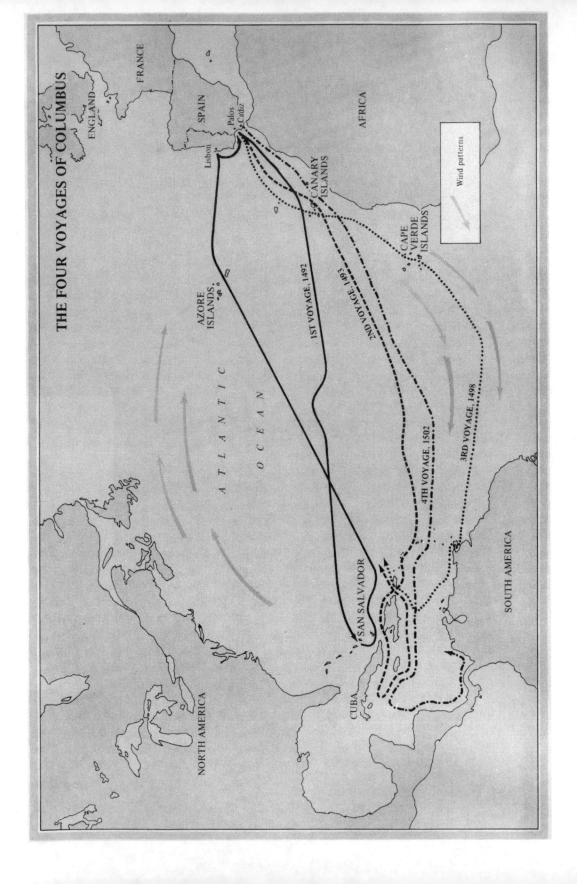

THE FOUR VOYAGES OF COLUMBUS

ENGLAND
FRANCE
SPAIN
Palos
Cadiz
Lisbon
AFRICA

Wind patterns

CANARY
ISLANDS

CAPE
VERDE
ISLANDS

AZORE
ISLANDS

1ST VOYAGE, 1492

2ND VOYAGE, 1493

A T L A N T I C

O C E A N

4TH VOYAGE, 1502

3RD VOYAGE, 1498

NORTH AMERICA

SAN SALVADOR

CUBA

SOUTH AMERICA

measures for working the Indians and inflicted harsh punishment on those who failed to bring in sufficient amounts of gold.

As a colonial governor, Columbus proved to be almost a total failure. The very traits that made him a good navigator—vision, confidence, and courage—worked against him as an administrator. Yet for a time he retained the confidence of Ferdinand and Isabella. In 1498 and 1502 the admiral led new expeditions west, but he no longer pioneered. He had shown the way, and now others followed. His authority continued to dwindle, and at one point he was actually arrested and sent back to Spain in chains. Eventually he lost his position as governor.

Even Columbus's own assurance that he had found the edge of Asia began to waver. On his third voyage in 1498 he made the first recorded sighting of the South American continent and the Amazon River. At first, he supposed the land ahead was another island, but there was disconcerting evidence to the contrary. Far from the coast, Columbus was amazed to find the seawater fresh and suitable for drinking. He concluded, correctly, that the flow of a river had temporarily overcome the salinity of the ocean. But what a river! Columbus knew that only large landmasses could produce rivers of this size. The experience forced him to admit that this land might be a continent—"another world," as his journal expressed it. But the old dream died hard. Perhaps, Columbus desperately reasoned, he had found a magic island not far from Asia that was none other than the earthly paradise. Future expeditions continued to seek out what the Spaniards began calling the Straits of Anian, a presumed opening somewhere in the landmass, with the Orient just on the other side.

Apart from such thoughts, there was little to cheer Columbus's declining years. Queen Isabella, whose faith in him had been instrumental in making his first voyage possible, died in 1504, and the Spanish court thereafter denied the admiral's pleas for restoration of his former incomes and positions. And then his health failed. Embittered and disappointed, yet still proud, Columbus gave up the struggle on May 20, 1506, in Valladolid, Spain. The cruelest slight came a few years later, however. Martin Waldseemüller, a renowned German geographer, drew a map and wrote a book in which he attributed the discovery of South America to Amerigo Vespucci, an Italian explorer who sailed for Spain. Vespucci, a vain and deceitful man, widely publicized his "discovery" of South America in 1500. Years later, Waldseemüller tried to change the name on his map, but it was too late. Europeans were using America, not Columbia, to refer to the entire New World.

Christopher Columbus opened the door for further European discovery and exploration of the Americas. In 1497 Giovanni Caboto (better known as John Cabot), an Italian like Columbus, carried England's flag along the northern route of the Vikings to claim Newfoundland for King Henry VII. With a crew of eighteen, Cabot set out from the English port of Bristol and, sailing along the Atlantic coast of North America, may have reached as far south as Maine before returning. A year later Cabot was back, searching for Japan and the Spice Islands. But disaster befell this journey; four of five ships, including John Cabot's, were lost at sea. Cabot's death discouraged further English navigation efforts for several decades. Whereas Cabot set the foundation for English claims to North America, Francis Drake helped steer England along its way to ruling the seas. A favorite of Henry VIII's successor, Queen Elizabeth I, Drake could boast a long career of seafaring during the late sixteenth century, including slaving, privateering (attacking Spanish gold ships), circumnavigating the globe in 1579, and participating in the defeat of the Spanish Armada in 1588—an event more than symbolic in contributing to Spain's decline as a world power.

French contact with the New World began with fishing expeditions to Newfoundland's Grand Banks as early as 1504, but a formal effort at exploration awaited the appointment by Francis I of Giovanni da Verrazano, another Genoese mariner. In 1524 Verrazano became the

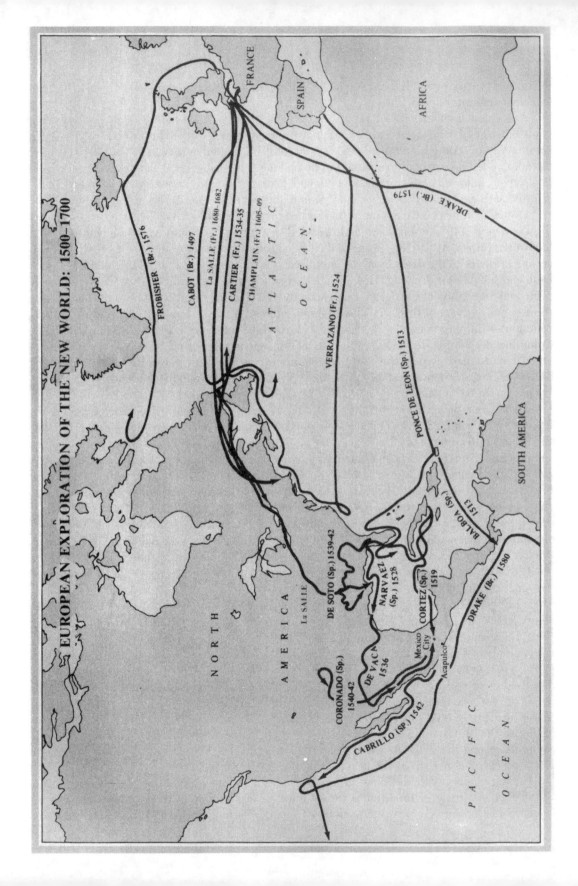

EUROPEAN EXPLORATION OF THE NEW WORLD: 1500–1700

first to sail the whole coast of North America from Florida to Newfoundland, but he found no northwest passage to Asia. Jacques Cartier tried again in 1534, leaving from Saint Malo and sailing as far as the first rapids on the Saint Lawrence River. He solidified the French claim to Canada. As in the Caribbean, the northland spawned rumors of fabulous golden kingdoms that vanished like mist as the explorers penetrated the wilderness. And despite the extensive seventeenth-century expeditions into the Saint Lawrence River region by Samuel de Champlain and the exploration of the Mississippi River by René-Robert Cavalier Sieur de La Salle (both of them seeking gold and a northwest passage to Asia), the French ultimately had to be satisfied with fish, furs, and land.

For the Portuguese, the urge to explore the New World lessened considerably when, in 1498, Vasco da Gama actually reached India after rounding Africa. But the Spanish successors to Columbus continued to search for the elusive passage through the Americas. The pace of this quest increased after 1513, when Vasco Nuñez de Balboa struggled across the narrow isthmus of Panama and became the first European to see the Pacific Ocean from its eastern coast. The unlucky Columbus had spent the entire winter of 1502–1503 sailing up and down the Panamanian coast, unaware that he was only forty miles away from a clear passage to India.

Despite the failure to find India, Spain lost no time in improving on the opportunities that Columbus had created in the Caribbean and the adjacent mainlands. Juan Ponce de León, a member of Columbus's second expedition, found little except mangrove swamps in Florida in 1513, but Hernan Cortés in Mexico (1519) and Francisco Pizarro in Peru (1531) struck it rich. The exploits of these two conquistadors in many ways typify the history of encounters between the Europeans and the Native Americans. Lust for gold and conquest compelled Cortés to lead an expedition with some 600 soldiers into the Aztec empire of Mexico with its five million inhabitants. For two years the Spaniards besieged the magnificent Aztec capital city of Tenochtitlán.

Fighting was often fierce, but Cortés and his men had time on their side. The Aztecs themselves had conquered many other people in Mexico and proved to be tyrannical rulers. They used the conquered as a labor force for building temples and palaces and also sacrificed thousands atop the temples in religious rites. Cleverly, Cortés turned those he liberated into willing belligerents against the Aztecs. But even more important, the same diseases that had decimated indigenous populations in the Caribbean—smallpox, measles, and diphtheria—also wreaked havoc in Mexico. In 1521 Cortés marched into Tenochtitlán. The Spanish crown then divided the conquered Indians into groupings called *encomiendas* and distributed them among Cortés and his lieutenants. In the *encomienda* system, which the Spaniards employed widely in New Spain, Indians served their masters with labor and servitude. The *encomenderos,* or holders of the *encomiendas,* promised the crown protection of the Indians and their eventual conversion to Christianity. In its best form, the system served the desires of the Spaniards to live off the work of others; at its worst, *encomiendas* were a brutal form of slavery.

Ten years after the conquest of the Aztecs, Francisco Pizarro secured King Charles V's assent to launch a conquest of northwestern South America. Reliable sources had told of a fabulous kingdom on the other side of the Andes Mountains, and Pizarro and his band of 150 conquistadors were assured of a percentage of the take if their conquest was successful. The Incas were an advanced people in art and culture and, through their own military conquests, had forged a huge empire of some twelve million people. Yet they, too, were susceptible to European diseases. Smallpox had made its way southward from Panama after Balboa's expedition. Moreover, their religious prophecies foretold of the coming of gods who traveled on strange animals. When Pizarro and his bearded and helmeted men arrived on horseback, clad in armor and wielding steel swords and lances, many Incas (like the Aztecs before them) believed they were the gods of prophecy. Pizarro's treachery, however, soon dispelled such beliefs. Killing the Inca king, Atahuallpa, Pizarro declared himself ruler and began to consolidate power over the vast but disease-ridden empire. Finally, the Incas watched in disbelief as the Spaniards melted down the golden walls of the imperial palace and then loaded the cooled ore onto their ships. Such bonanzas for Spain were unmitigated disasters from the viewpoint of the Aztecs and the Incas.

The gold that Cortez and Pizarro took from the Aztecs and Incas made Spain the foremost power in Europe. It also sustained the New World treasure hunt through a succession of wild goose chases. In 1527–1528, for example, Pánfilo de Narváez led 400 men through present-day Florida and Georgia and along the Gulf Coast to Texas. Disaster piled on disaster until only two men remained. They staggered into Mexico City in 1536, having traveled great distances with Native American tribes. One of the survivors, Cabeza de Vaca, returned with an incredible pack of lies about the Seven Cities of Cibola, where kings bathed in gold dust. The governor of Cuba, Hernando de Soto, could not resist. In 1539 he landed on the Florida coast with 600 men. In the next four years de Soto, one of Pizarro's conquistadors in Peru, marched north to the Appalachian Mountains, then west through the Mississippi Valley, and finally as far as present-day Oklahoma. Depressed by his failure to find the Seven Cities, despised by his men, and stalked by hostile Indians, de Soto died somewhere on the frontier of present-day Arkansas during the winter of 1542.

At the same time, Francisco Vásquez de Coronado sought the mythical Seven Cities from the west. He traveled north from Mexico into Arizona, discovered the Grand Canyon, and pushed east into Kansas, only to return empty-handed in 1542. The accompanying sea voyage by Hernando de Alarcón up the Gulf of California and into the Colorado River was similarly unrewarding.

The Spaniards were also motivated by other mythology regarding California. In 1510, Garcí Ordóñez de Montalvo of Seville published a romantic narrative entitled *The Exploits of Esplandián.* "On the right hand of the Indies," Montalvo wrote, "there is an island called California, very near to the Terrestrial Paradise." The island was inhabited by its queen, Califia, and many dark-skinned women with arms full of gold. After conquering much of central and South America, the Spaniards sent conquistadors west to find California. In 1535 Hernan Cortés found nothing but hostile Indians and desert along the coast of Baja California. In 1542 Juan Rodríguez Cabrillo sailed up the California coast past San Francisco Bay. Cabrillo died in the aftermath of an Indian attack on one of the islands in the Santa Barbara Channel, and his crew returned to Mexico starving and sick with scurvy.

The false expectations of Columbus lived on in men like de Soto, Coronado, and Cabrillo. In spite of their courage and persistence, however, they failed to see the real potential of the New World. They fixed their sights entirely on gold. They did not understand that in their disappointment, they had walked over and sailed along some of the most fertile land in the world—land capable of sustaining a great Western-style civilization. The problem, of course, was that, beginning with Columbus, the Spaniards were conquistadors, not farmers and settlers. Their purpose was the collection of treasure, not the extension of Western culture. Even when souls, not gold, were the objective and priests rather than soldier-adventurers the agents, the early Spaniards proved to be inept colonizers. Their idea of a settlement was a virtual prison that cruelly forced both labor and religion down the throats of bewildered Native Americans. The primary concern of Spanish conquistadors in the Americas was, like the French preoccupation with furs, a triumphant return to the Old World, not a permanent place in the New. The ultimate cost of such conduct was the loss of North America to the English latecomers, who, after a few false starts, learned to accept the land for what it was. Eventually Spanish colonists would come in the form of Jesuit, Dominican, and Franciscan missionaries and, along with civil government officials, establish the vast empire of New Spain. But Christopher Columbus and the first Spanish explorers never even tried. Their dreams stood in the way, yet their acts paved the way for the settlement of America.

Selected Readings

The Person

Amler, Jane Francis: *Christopher Columbus's Jewish Roots* (1991). Makes the case for Columbus's Jewish ancestry.

°Cohen, John M. (ed.): *The Four Voyages of Christopher Columbus* (1769). A shorter collection than the Jane collection, below.

Davidson, Miles H.: *Columbus Then and Now: A Life Re-Examined* (1997). New interpretations of Columbus based on sources unavailable before 1990, and based on the author's extensive personal library.

Deagan, Kathleen, and Jose Maria Cruxent: *Columbus's Outpost among the Tainos: Spain and America at La Isabela, 1493–1498* (2002). Pathbreaking study of the Spaniards' early settlements on Hispaniola, land of the Tainos.

De Vorsey, Louis, Jr. (ed.): *In the Wake of Columbus: Islands and Controversies* (1985). A collection of essays expressing various theories on the Columbus landfall.

Jane, Lionel Cecil (ed.): *Select Documents Illustrating the Four Voyages of Columbus* (2 vols., 1930–1933). A comprehensive collection of letters, dispatches, log books, and journals.

Landström, Björn: *Columbus* (1966). A biography embellished with dozens of magnificent full-color drawings and maps.

Least Heat-Moon, William: *Columbus in the Americas* (2002). Succinct account of the four voyages only, reflecting recent interpretations.

Morison, Samuel Eliot: *Admiral of the Ocean Sea: A Life of Christopher Columbus* (2 vols., 1942). A thorough and vivid biography based on contemporary knowledge of Columbus. Abridged as °*Christopher Columbus, Mariner* (1955).

Schnaubelt, Joseph C., and Frederick Van Fleteren (eds.): *Columbus and the New World* (1998). Edited series that includes essays on cartography and European myths about a New World.

Smith, Bradley: *Columbus in the New World* (1962). A spectacular photographic record of the lands and seas Columbus saw.

°Wilford, John Noble: *The Mysterious History of Columbus: An Exploration of the Man, the Myth, the Legacy* (1992). A comparison of various writings on Columbus, demonstrating many ambiguities and contradictions in his biography.

The Period

Axtell, James: *Beyond 1492: Encounters in Colonial North America* (1992). Perspectives from both sides of the Atlantic on the legacy of Columbus.

°Bakeless, John: *The Eyes of Discovery: America as Seen by the First Explorers* (1950). A unique description of the environment the first Europeans encountered in the New World.

°Available in paperback

Brebner, John B.: *The Explorers of North America, 1492–1800* (1933). A thorough, general account.

°Crone, G. R.: *The Discovery of America* (1969). The best short account of the background and aftermath of Columbus's feat.

°Crosby, Alfred: *The Columbian Exchange: Biological and Cultural Consequences of 1492* (30-Year Commemorative Edition, 2002). A far-reaching study of the changes initiated by Columbus and other explorers of the New World. New edition is expanded from the 1972 edition.

°Gibson, Charles: *Spain in America* (1966). A good general treatment of Spanish discovery and colonization of the New World.

Holand, H. R.: *Explorations in America before Columbus* (1956). A review of the numerous claims of North American contact by Europeans before 1492.

°Jones, Howard Mumford: *O Strange New World* (1964). The impact of North America on the European imagination.

Materassi, Mario, and Maria Santos (eds.): *The American Columbiad: "Discovering" America, Inventing the United States* (1996). Collection of essays exploring the impact of Columbus at the quincentennial of the first voyage.

Meinig, D. W.: *The Shaping of America: A Geographical Perspective on 500 Years of History* (Vol. 1, 1988). A fascinating blend of history and geography, demonstrating how the land shaped the European settlement of the Americas.

Morison, Samuel Eliot: *The Great Explorers: The European Discovery of America* (1978). Detailed, scholarly accounts of voyages to both North and South America.

Parry, J. H.: *The Age of Reconnaissance* (1963). A survey of European expansion and empire-building into the seventeenth century.

Pennington, Piers: *The Great Explorers* (1977). Illustrated biographies of explorers from ancient times to the present.

°Penrose, Boies: *Travel and Discovery in the Renaissance, 1420–1620* (1952). A competent survey that puts Columbus's voyages in the perspective of an expanding Europe.

Quinn, David B.: *Explorers and Colonies: America, 1500–1625* (1990). Focuses on English explorers, including Hakluyt and Drake.

°Sale, Kirkpatrick: *The Conquest of Paradise: Christopher Columbus and the Columbian Legacy* (1990). An indictment of Columbus as the embodiment of a decadent and brutal culture.

Todorov, Tzetvan: *The Conquest of America: The Question of the Other* (1984). A study of the tragic confusion that resulted when Spaniards and natives confronted each other in Mexico.

°Turner, Frederick: *Beyond Geography: The Western Spirit against the Wilderness* (1980). A sweeping synthesis of Western estrangement from the land, which includes accounts of Columbus and Cortés.

Tyler, S. Lyman: *Two Worlds* (1988). An analysis of Spanish attitudes toward the natives encountered in the Caribbean, based on contemporary accounts.

Waldman, Carl, and Molly Braun: *Atlas of the North American Indian* (1985). An illustrated encyclopedia of Native Americans, with extensive maps.

For Consideration

1. In what ways did the Renaissance and the Turkish occupation of Constantinople compel overseas exploration?

2. What role did mythology about unexplored parts of the world play in inspiring men like Columbus?

3. Conquistadores like Columbus were driven by God, gold, and glory. Explain each of these motivations.

4. It has been said that Columbus was in the right place at the right time with the right idea. What historical factors give credence to this statement?

5. Explain the biases inherent in the Europeans when they first encountered the people of the Americas. What were some immediate consequences of these biases for the native people?

Chapter 2

John Winthrop

It was a Sunday morning in the spring of 1630, and the faithful were gathered for worship. Being in the middle of the North Atlantic on the *Arbella* made little difference to Puritans. Religion came first, always. The preacher was a layman, but governor of the migrating band, and they quieted as he mounted the forecastle. Pausing, John Winthrop looked out at the expectant faces and beyond to the open ocean. These people had cast their lots with the New World. Unlike the Spanish gold seekers, they were coming as settlers, hoping to find freedom to live according to their ideals. These involved nothing less than the continuation of the Protestant Reformation and the creation of a godly society. Winthrop fully appreciated the obstacles in their way, and as he began to speak his tone was grave. He tried to show his followers how the very freedom that made the North American wilderness attractive could also prove to be a liability. It would be easy to forget high purposes. Discipline and unity were consequently cardinal virtues. If the colonists weakened, he warned, God's special protection would be replaced by the full measure of His special wrath. Near the end of the shipboard sermon, Winthrop repeated a striking metaphor that has reverberated through American history. "For we must consider," he shouted against the sound of waves and wind, "that we shall be as a city upon a hill, the eyes of all people are upon us." Here was recognition of the unprecedented opportunity as well as the awesome responsibility that went with a fresh start in a New World. While he lived, the force of John Winthrop's conviction and character played a major role in sustaining the Puritans in this self-conceived mission. Inevitably, that zeal waned and, with it, the tight social control Winthrop prized, but not before Puritanism made a deep impression on the American character.

The year of John Winthrop's birth, 1588, proved exceptionally exciting for his native England. Queen Elizabeth had occupied the throne for three decades, and under her guidance the nation had become the most powerful in Europe. English "sea dogs," notably John Hawkins and Francis Drake, had brazenly pirated Spanish galleons in Caribbean and South American waters. In 1580 Drake had returned with a cargo of Spanish gold after circumnavigating the globe. A proud Elizabeth promptly knighted him. Spain was furious, however, and in 1588 sent a mighty fleet against the upstart English. But the quick English warships, with help from the weather, the tides, and dysentery aboard the Spanish fleet, demolished the Spanish Armada. Now England ruled the seas and, armed with a different philosophy of colonization, prepared to replace Spain as the dominant power in North America.

At home, England's economy was flourishing under the influence of a burgeoning capitalism. The effects were at once invigorating and dislocating. Prices and profits soared during the sixteenth century. With the woolen industry leading the way, manufacturing became a large-scale enterprise. To supply the mills with raw material, fields once used for crops were fenced (the sixteenth-century term was *enclosed*) for sheep pastures. Some farmers suffered, but for others change created opportunity. John Winthrop's grandfather Adam, for example, quit farming early in the sixteenth century to try his luck in commerce. He did well, entering the clothworkers' guild, or union, as an apprentice. He subsequently became a journeyman and then a master clothier. Adam also became rich enough to purchase the manor of Groton in Suffolk, acquire a coat of arms, and join the landed gentry.

John Winthrop grew up in the comfortable, rustic setting of Groton. As his parents' only son and heir, John seemed destined for a life devoted to the gentlemanly art of estate management. At fifteen he journeyed to Cambridge for the traditional two years of polishing at that university's Trinity College. In 1605, at the age of seventeen, Winthrop married Mary Forth, a bride carefully selected by his father for her economic assets and social connections. Ten months later there was a baby, and the Winthrops appeared ready to settle down in Suffolk. At this point, North America seemed totally irrelevant to Winthrop's life, but he was soon to encounter an influence that ultimately transformed the country gentleman into a wilderness colonizer. The new force was the Protestant Reformation, and it led John Winthrop to the New World, just as the Renaissance spirit of discovery and glory had led Christopher Columbus.

The Reformation began in Germany in 1517 with the work of Martin Luther. Fed as well by the ideas of the French theologian John Calvin, it spread rapidly throughout northern Europe. Numerous variations in doctrine existed, but, in general, Protestants favored reducing the elaborate organizational structure that Catholicism placed between the individual believer and God. Their goal was recovery of the simplicity and sincerity of the original Christian faith.

In England, the Reformation quickly acquired political as well as theological importance. Henry VIII, king since 1509, had little sympathy for Protestant ideas, but he coveted power and property. The Catholic Church in England had both in plenty. And Henry harbored personal grounds for resentment: The Pope refused to grant him a divorce. Finally, in the 1530s, Henry made his move. Defying Rome, he appointed himself head of the Church in England, granted himself a divorce, and confiscated all the property of the Catholic Church, which amounted to about a quarter of the entire kingdom. One beneficiary of the confiscation was John Winthrop's grandfather, who bought the old monastic estate of Groton from Henry in 1544.

It remained for Henry's daughter, Elizabeth, to pursue the Reformation in England. In 1559, at the beginning of her reign, Elizabeth established Anglicanism (the Church of England) as the nation's official religion and proceeded to define what and how the English could worship. The penalty for disobedience was a fine and imprisonment. For most Protestants this arrangement proved to be satisfactory, since the Church of England did eliminate some of the hierarchy and ritual of Roman Catholicism. But the more radical regarded Anglicanism as little better than what it replaced. Many of these dissenters joined hands after 1560 under the banner of Puritanism, with the intent of purifying Christianity. In terms of doctrine, this meant accepting the Bible as the sole source of authority and eliminating the hierarchy of church officials in favor of government by local congregations. Because the king headed the church under Anglicanism, Puritans tended to oppose monarchical authority. Here lay the seeds of strife—and also the beginnings of New England.

Puritanism was a central part of John Winthrop's life by 1606, when he was eighteen and just settling down as squire of Groton. His diary gives the details. On February 2, "a seacret desire after pleasures & itchinge after libertie & unlawfull delightes" on Winthrop's part coincided with his wife's illness. The latter, he assumed, must be a warning to him from the Lord. But his "sinnes" continued, and he himself fell ill. Finally, on April 20, John Winthrop made an agreement (Puritans called it a *covenant*) with God. Winthrop would undertake to purge himself of "pride, covetousnesse, love of this worlde, vanitie of minde, unthankfulnesse [and] slouth . . . both in His service & in my callinge." The Lord's contribution, Winthrop continued, was the provision of "a new heart," strength to resist the temptations of the "Divell," and forgiveness in case Satan temporarily triumphed. "God give me grace to performe my promise," the entry for April 20 concluded, "& I doubt not but he will performe His. God make it fruitfull. Amen."

Winthrop's personal covenant, painstakingly set down as a constant reminder, reflected the core of the Puritan mind. Following Calvin, he assumed that original sin predestined all people to eternal damnation. All, that is, but an undeserving few whom God regenerated and granted salvation. These heaven-bound "elect" or "saints," as Winthrop frequently called them, did not in any sense earn their pardon. The best anyone could do was to accept the covenant, have faith, and seek in the course of life some sign of the Lord's predetermined decision respecting eternal fate. Good deeds, a godly life, and success in one's career were such signs—the evidence, not the cause, of salvation. As a saying popular in Winthrop's time went, "A good man does good works, but good works do not make a good man." Living with this paradox was part of being a Puritan.

Once planted in Winthrop, Puritanism took root rapidly. Even as he became absorbed in a career of law and the management of Groton, his concern with religion increased. His central problem was how to live in the real world without loving worldly pleasures too much. This is not to say that Puritans had to be the solemn, gloomy, self-righteous killjoys of the stereotype. The important thing was to love God above all. If a man like Winthrop could enjoy a tankard of ale, a good dinner, a pipe, and his wife without lessening his enjoyment of God, fine. The danger lay in forgetting one's first duty. John Winthrop, who was by his own admission strongly drawn to the lusts of the flesh, teetered between secular and spiritual delights for most of his early life. The pattern was cyclical: After a bout of sensuality, Winthrop's conscience drove him to a period of monastic abstinence. But his resolve always weakened, and the cycle continued. After thirty years of struggle with himself, Winthrop concluded that the key virtue was discipline. Because sinful man could not be continually good, he had to learn to deal with his lower desires and channel their energies upward whenever possible.

While the individual soul dominated the attention of English Puritans, the condition of society also concerned them deeply. Winthrop and his fellows believed it their duty to make the world as godly as possible. The welfare of a nation depended on a social or group covenant between God and its people. As in the case of the individual covenant, God was thought to protect and sustain an entire people who endeavored to live according to His laws. Conversely, if society broke those laws, a wrathful God was expected to dispense lethal punishment. Government, then, was crucial as a way of ensuring godliness.

With the stakes so high, Puritans like Winthrop looked with growing uneasiness at the course of English political history in the early seventeenth century. In 1603 James I succeeded Queen Elizabeth, and religious dissenters hoped the change would mean greater sympathy for their cause. King James, however, was determined to crush dissent and also to put women back in their place after the tremendously successful reign of Elizabeth I (1558–1603). Declaring himself "Almighty Father of England," the Scottish king admonished his own son, Crown Prince Henry, to "teach your wife that it is your office to command and hers to obey." The Elizabethan era, when a tolerant woman sat on the throne, providing a powerful inspiration for all women, was decidedly over.

King James I was no more tolerant toward religious separatists like the Puritans. In January 1604, at Hampton Court, James made his position clear: "I shall make them conform themselves," he declared in reference to the Puritans, "or I will harry them out of this land, or else do worse." Winthrop was only sixteen at the time, but Puritanism had entered his life during his days at Cambridge. News of James's pronouncement must have sent cold chills along his spine. As his involvement with Puritanism grew, he knew he was inviting royal displeasure or, as James had said, "worse." The cells in the Tower of London and the executioner's block provided vivid illustrations of the king's meaning. Yet Winthrop could not think of abandoning his covenant with God. Almost as distasteful was the prospect of watching his country forget the Reformation and perhaps slip back to Roman Catholicism. What could be done?

The alternatives were not hard to discover, and Winthrop surely weighed them on the long, solitary rides from Groton to his law duties in the Court of Wards in London. For decades, separatists like the Puritans had attempted to purify the church by setting an example in England, and such actions would continue despite King James. Another possibility was revolt. In the seventeenth century, however, kings cast awesome shadows. One did not dismiss their authority lightly. Even when Charles I, James's successor, married a Catholic and dissolved Parliament in 1629, Winthrop could not entertain revolutionary thoughts. Two decades later, bolder and more desperate English Puritans, led by Oliver Cromwell, would overthrow the throne, but by that time Winthrop had found a different solution.

The alternative Winthrop considered was separating from England and leaving that unhappy country to the bitter fruits of its own ungodliness. Many precedents existed in the Christian past for this kind of response to evil. Hermits and monks had repeatedly fled to lonely retreats to make their separate peace with God. Occasionally an entire group of people, following the example of the Israelites, escaped from persecution. After James's ominous pronouncement at Hampton Court, some radical Puritans from the village of Scrooby in Nottinghamshire organized under the leadership of William Brewster, William Bradford, and John Robinson. Extremely dissatisfied with the incomplete purification of the Anglican Church, they determined to reject it entirely.

Although these Separatists desired only to be left alone, the Anglicans harassed them unmercifully. In the winter of 1608–1609 they left England for the more permissive climate of Holland, but their troubles continued. The materialistic Dutch culture offered many temptations, and Catholic Spain threatened to conquer the country and crush all forms of Protestantism. The Separatists finally decided that their best hope for freedom was a complete break with Europe. They would seek the wilderness of the New World. Securing a grant of land from the settler-hungry Virginia Company, thirty-five Separatists and sixty-seven other colonists (we have come to call them all Pilgrims) sailed for New England in the fall of 1620 on the *Mayflower.*

The Pilgrims proved the feasibility of separation, but John Winthrop remained unconvinced. He could not escape a sense of responsibility to his fellow man. No matter how ungodly society had become, the true Christian, as Winthrop defined him, could not turn his back. The goal, after all, was the reformation of Christendom. The purification of a tiny part of it had no meaning. On a more fundamental level, Winthrop perceived that all human beings were united by original sin. People could not escape from evil in the world any more than they could flee from evil in themselves. Both had to be confronted. Winthrop knew that in this respect the Separatists on the *Mayflower* had failed. They had simply deserted England, and in quest of the perfection of their little group, they had forgotten the meaning of purification.

Yet Winthrop could not but envy the Pilgrims their opportunity to build a society according to their understanding of God's wishes. Musing on this apparent dilemma in the 1620s, he gradually formulated a solution. Suppose he left England in order to create a model Christian community that by its very godliness would command the attention and admiration of the rest of the world? Eventually, Winthrop reasoned, other societies would follow the New England example in their own homelands. Surely this would be a contribution to the Reformation. Leaving in order to lead and ultimately to save all humanity—here was an alternative he could support.

Although Winthrop had found good grounds to justify migration, he remained uncommitted at the beginning of 1629. The events of the next ten months, however, forced a decision. During this time the New World became an increasingly familiar subject of conversation around the Winthrop table. England's Virginia plantations were beginning to take root, with 3,000 new settlers arriving between 1619 and 1622. There were settlements on Bermuda and on several Caribbean islands. In fact, Henry Winthrop—a son whose wayward ways disappointed his father—had already tried and failed to grow tobacco on Barbados in the late 1620s. Of course the Pilgrims' experiment in New England was a subject of constant interest to a religious household like the Winthrops'. A group of Puritan merchants, well known to Winthrop, had formed the New England Company and in 1629 already had an outpost at Salem in what was being called Massachusetts Bay. On March 4 its leaders renewed their royal charter and renamed themselves the Massachusetts Bay Company. Winthrop was unimpressed, but six days later Charles I dissolved Parliament. Now there was nothing to stand between the Puritans and the hostility of the king. Suddenly, New England acquired much greater interest for John Winthrop. On May 15, 1629, he wrote Margaret, his third wife (his first two wives had died), that he soon expected the Lord to "bringe some heavye Affliction upon this land." Winthrop hoped that before that time "a shelter and a hidinge place" might appear to the faithful. Almost certainly, Winthrop had begun to think seriously of New England as a sanctuary from impending persecution.

With the English political climate chilled for men of his persuasion, Winthrop resigned his position as a royal attorney. Returning to Groton, he contemplated an uncertain future. His friends in the Massachusetts Bay Company, however, knew exactly what Winthrop should do. A man of his substance and experience, they pointed out, was needed in the colonial enterprise. He might well become its leader. And thousands of miles from Charles I and the Anglican Church, such a leader could use his own ideals to shape society. The prospect appealed to Winthrop, as did the argument that his participation was crucial to the success of the entire effort. He was told, probably with some truth, that many Puritans were reserving judgment about America until after John Winthrop decided. For someone with his sense of social responsibility, this situation generated considerable pressure.

But for Winthrop, the central question was how the Massachusetts Bay Company would be governed. He knew what had happened in the case of the Virginia Company's colony on Chesapeake Bay. In 1624, after seventeen years of existence, James I had simply voided its charter, disbanded its representative assembly (the House of Burgesses), and placed a royal governor in control. If this could happen in Virginia, Winthrop reasoned, then there was no point in proceeding further with plans for a Puritan community in Massachusetts Bay that could be dissolved by the crown. He was right, of course, but in July of 1629 those interested in securing his support made a telling bid. A careful reading of the March 4 charter, they explained, revealed no provision regarding the location of the company's government. Normally, the directors were Englishmen who remained at home under the watchful eye of the king. Yet it appeared that the Massachusetts Bay Company had the option of directing itself from a New World location far removed from royal scrutiny. Winthrop relished this prospect. Here was assurance of the independence he considered essential for the success of a spiritual experiment. In August 1629 Winthrop cast his lot with the New World and began preparations for departure.

The enormity of Winthrop's decision cannot be overemphasized. He had not just opted for another nation but for another "world." Despite the achievements of the explorers as reported in Richard Hakluyt's *Principall Navigations, Voiages and Discoveries of the English Nation,* published a year after Winthrop's birth in 1589, North America was still terra incognita—a wilderness peopled by savages, its vague western boundaries fading into the mists of the unknown. And Winthrop was not just taking a trip or, in the manner of the conquistadors, planning a lucrative junket of one or two years followed by a triumphant return home. He was migrating, permanently, with the understanding that in all likelihood he would never set foot in the British Isles again.

On October 20, 1629, the General Court, or membership, of the Massachusetts Bay Company elected John Winthrop to be governor. Since this was the Lord's work, he found the responsibility somewhat overwhelming. "So it is," he wrote to Margaret, "that [it] hath pleased the Lorde to call me to a further trust in this business of the plantation, than either I expected or finde my selfe fitt for."

Despite this initial lack of confidence, Winthrop proved an extremely able governor in the busy months before the Puritan exodus. He understood that his first task was to recruit colonists for the holy experiment. Turning to the pen, Winthrop wrote down the reasons for migrating. Widely circulated among Puritans, these "Conclusions," combined with Winthrop's prestige, proved to be highly persuasive. He began by pointing out that the New World offered few temptations to the younger generation, whereas England was full of "evil examples." Indeed, the corruption of church and society in Europe invited an unfavorable judgment from the Lord. Perhaps the Old World was doomed. New England, Winthrop argued, might be the refuge God provided for those "He means to save out of the generall callamity." Elsewhere in his "Conclusions" he relied on the rivalry between religions in the seventeenth century to drive home the point that if Protestants did not colonize the New World, Catholics would.

Worldly considerations also figured in Winthrop's inducements. He emphasized the depressed English economy and how a man could scarcely earn a living, even with hard work. Better to seek new fields where success—that sign of God's pleasure—might crown one's efforts. Moreover, in the New World land was abundant and free. For those who argued that the land belonged to Indians, Winthrop replied according to Scripture. He interpreted Genesis 1:28, the first commandment of God to those who followed Him, to sanction the right to conquer and subdue those parts of the world that "lie waste without any improvement." The North American wilderness, in Winthrop's mind, was intended by God to be colonized, civilized, and made fruitful by people like himself. The heathen Indians did not count as human beings. Finally, Winthrop answered the charge that he was deserting Europe with the assertion that the Puritans were actually spearheading the Reformation.

In addition to recruiting colonists, he was responsible for provisioning and partly financing the expedition. Like Noah, he had to think of everything necessary to begin civilization anew. Seeds, livestock, tools, books, and even limes to ward off scurvy went onto his careful lists and into the holds of the ships. Also needed were representatives of the various crafts and professions, and Winthrop chose his colleagues with this in mind. As a result, the thousand English men and women who gathered in April of 1630 at Cowes to board the eleven ships of the Massachusetts Bay Company were a society in miniature.

Thus far, John Winthrop's energy and idealism had been equal to the task of leaving England. But when the Puritan fleet left Cowes on April 8, his challenge had only begun. In quiet moments, gazing over the ocean, thinking of Groton and of Margaret, who remained behind for the moment, eight months pregnant, misgivings crowded in on him. Given the uncertainties of transoceanic travel in the seventeenth century and of life in the New World wilderness, there was no assurance his family would ever be together again.

Winthrop also knew of the difficulties encountered in previous efforts to colonize North America. The complete disappearance of the "Lost Colony," Sir Walter Raleigh's 1587 settlement on Roanoke Island, was an extreme example, but subsequent English outposts in the New World had fared only slightly better. The Virginia Company's colony at Jamestown had been started in May 1607, when 105 survivors of a voyage that had claimed thirty-nine lives landed on the north bank of the James River about thirty miles upstream from Chesapeake Bay. Their troubles had begun at once. The site chosen for the colony was a tidal marsh characterized by foul water and malaria-bearing mosquitoes. Tied as they were to ships, the colonists hesitated to move inland to better locations. But attitude as well as environment produced the nightmare of the next several years. Self-styled gentlemen and adventurers in the conquistador mold, the first Virginians balked at performing tasks such as farming that were essential for survival. Their supplies dwindled. Disease swept the colony. By January of 1608, only thirty-eight of the original contingent remained.

At this point, realistic, hard-boiled John Smith engineered a temporary improvement with his insistence that Jamestown make crops and livestock, rather than gold, its principal concern. But in 1609 Smith was ousted and sent back to England. Now exposed to the full force of their ignorance, the settlers entered on a "starving time." The winter of 1609–1610 reduced them to a diet of rats, snakes, horsehide, and even human flesh. Of approximately 500 colonists, only sixty survived, and they were en route back to England when they met a relief expedition entering the mouth of the James. Conditions improved slowly, but only because the London Company pumped a stream of new settlers into Virginia to replace the discouraged and the dead. By the 1620s people no longer starved and tobacco production flourished, but the settlement still clung tenuously to the edge of the wilderness.

As he sailed for America, John Winthrop was keenly aware of the difficulties in Virginia. Indeed, one of the "Objections" in his 1629 argument for migrating had been that "the ill success of other Plantations may tell us what will become of this." But his "Answer" pointed out that most of Virginia's problems "happened through . . . slouth." The Puritans, never forgetful of their duty to God and the rest of humanity, would avoid these perils, Winthrop hoped. Yet only a fool would make light of the immense obstacles associated with New World colonization. A wilderness environment demanded radically different skills and temperaments from those particular to rural England. English country squires did not immediately become American frontiersmen. Acknowledging this in his "Conclusions," Winthrop faced the fact that the Puritan endeavor "is attended with many and great difficulties." But his answer to this objection went right to the point: "Soe is every good action." This frame of mind gave promise of the physical and mental toughness necessary for survival.

The record of earlier settlement north of Virginia likewise offered little cheer. Winthrop knew that in 1607 English merchants had sent colonists to Maine, only to see them straggle back after a few miserable months. The story of the Pilgrims in 1620 was almost as discouraging. The *Mayflower* had transported William Bradford's little group to New England at the worst possible time of the year—November. With snow already on the ground and a slate-gray sky promising more, Bradford described the New World as "a hideous and desolate wilderness." Half the Pilgrims had died that first winter. Summer brought crops and the assistance of Indians such as Squanto, but the precariousness of their hold on the land gave the celebration of the first Thanksgiving in 1621 a hollow ring. From such experiences, Winthrop learned the full price of religious freedom.

THE INCONVENIENCIES
THAT HAVE HAPPENED TO SOME PER-
SONS WHICH HAVE TRANSPORTED THEMSELVES

from *England* to *Virginia*, vvithout prouisions necessary to sustaine themselues, hath greatly hindred the *Progresse of that noble Plantation:* For preuention of the like disorders heereafter, that no man suffer, either through ignorance or misinformation; it is thought requisite to publish this short declaration: wherein is contained a particular of such necessaries, as either priuate families or single persons shall haue cause to furnish themselues with, for their better support at their first landing in Virginia; whereby also greater numbers may receiue in part, directions how to prouide themselues.

Whosoeuer transports himselfe or any other at his owne charge vnto Virginia, shall for each person so transported before Midsummer 1625. haue to him and his heires for euer fifty Acres of Land vpon a first, and fifty Acres vpon a second diuision.

Imprinted at London by FELIX KYNGSTON. 1622.

Modern campers can choose from a variety of what-to-take lists and guides designated to facilitate their stay in the wilderness. But the first settlers in the New World wilderness had none until this 1622 broadside was printed in London for the Virginia Company. We can suppose that John Winthrop provided similar information to prospective colonists a decade later.

After the frantic months of preparation, the slow Atlantic crossing afforded him an opportunity to meditate on the problems ahead. But Winthrop would not have been on the *Arbella* without a sense of the bright promise of new beginnings. The concept of mission, so central to Puritan thought, captured both these moods. In Winthrop's mind, mission resulted from a covenant with God. It meant the responsibility of performing special work for Him and the opportunity of receiving His special protection. Winthrop and the migrating Puritans believed they were a chosen people. God, they thought, had singled them out to lead humanity. And He had given them an almost incredible opportunity. The New World was a vacuum, a clean slate on which humanity could write a fresh and, perhaps, a better record. None of the mistakes of the past need be made again. For John Winthrop in the seventeenth century, the New World was analogous to another habitable planet for people in the twentieth century. But in Winthrop's mind, the most logical comparison to the New World was the Garden of Eden—and he was a latter-day Adam. As his son, John Winthrop Jr., put it later, the Puritan venture to America was like "the beginninge of the world." The New World gave them and all of the human race another chance.

Winthrop expounded the theme of mission and some of its consequences in a mid-Atlantic sermon, "A Modell of Christian Charity," on board the *Arbella*. He began by enumerating the purposes of the migration: to serve the Lord, to preserve themselves from "the common corruptions of this evil world," and to "work out our salvation." The core of the sermon was the covenant struck between the America-bound Puritans and God. If God brought them safely across the Atlantic, then they had the obligation to keep the faith. For Puritans this was no casual agreement—it was a solemn promise that touched every aspect of their lives. "Thus stands the cause between God and us," thundered Winthrop. "We are entered into covenant with Him for this work; we have taken out a commission." Every aspect of Puritan policy was directed to this end. Again and again Winthrop stressed the importance of discipline and unity if the mission was to be accomplished. "We must be knit together in this work as one," he insisted. "We must delight in each other, make others' conditions our own, rejoice together, mourn together, labor and suffer together; always having before our eyes our commission." Of paramount importance, Governor Winthrop continued, was the need for the people to obey their governors and for the governors to obey God. If they did, God would adopt and protect the wilderness colony as He had the ancient Jews. The result would be a model society, "a city upon a hill."

No one knew better than John Winthrop that the extraordinary opportunity of the New England Puritans also meant extraordinary responsibility. Because of this chance to build a godly society, failure would be especially loathsome in the eyes of the Lord. Winthrop felt certain that breaking the covenant and ignoring the mission would bring divine wrath crashing down on their colony. If we "embrace this present world," he warned, "and prosecute our carnal intentions," an angry God will "be revenged of such a perjured people" by stranding them without protection in a wilderness.

As the *Arbella* drew near New England, such considerations became increasingly real. On June 6, 1630, Winthrop's shipmates enjoyed their first sight of land in almost two months. They struck the coast well north of their destination and for the next several days sailed southwest along the coast of Maine. On June 12 the ship anchored off John Endicott's Puritan outpost at Salem, and the passengers feasted on venison and wild strawberries. In time, the other vessels straggled into port, and by the end of the summer the population of New England had more than doubled. The previous occupants were only a few Pilgrims under William Bradford at Plymouth, a scattering of survivors from the unsuccessful fishing and trading settlements of Sir Ferdinando Gorges's Council for New England, and gentlemen of wealth and independence like Samuel Maverick and William

Blackstone. Winthrop's initial problem as governor was to keep up morale. The long ocean voyage had sapped the Puritans' physical strength and the vigor of their ideals. Face-to-face contact with the New England wilderness further eroded their resolve. Was the migration a huge mistake, the "city upon a hill" a sorry joke? When strong leadership was imperative, Winthrop took command.

His first decision was to find a better location than Salem. Exploration southward into Massachusetts Bay revealed the land around the mouth of the Charles River to be rich, flat, well watered, and abounding with good harbors. Winthrop approved, and the Puritans quickly spread out around the bay. After a few false starts, the governor located himself immediately south of the Charles on a narrow-necked peninsula he called Boston. Though death claimed eleven of Winthrop's servants and some 200 other Puritans the first winter, compared to the "starving times" of earlier settlers, this survival rate was good. Not being first had some great advantages. Older New England hands, some with ten years of pioneering under their belts, helped with advice and gifts of food.

The Puritans were also relatively rich and could buy supplies from England. The arrival of a ship bearing reinforcements of goods and people in February 1631, for instance, contributed a great deal to maintaining the settlement through the first winter. Even so, by spring some of the Puritans were weary of being God's guinea pigs and booked passage back home. Winthrop stood firm. He believed that merely surviving the winter signified God's pleasure with New England. "I would not have altered my course," he wrote to his much loved wife, Margaret, "though I had foreseen all these Afflictions: I never fared better in my life, never slept better, never had more content of minde." Only Margaret herself was missing, and on November 4, 1631, she arrived in Boston harbor with the rest of the Winthrop family. The reunion was a joyous time of feasting for the entire colony—the Puritan equivalent of the Pilgrim Thanksgiving ten years earlier.

Margaret Winthrop arrived in Boston as part of a growing stream of Puritans fleeing political adversity in England. Throughout the 1630s Charles I ruled without Parliament, while William Laud, the powerful archbishop of Canterbury, harassed Puritans relentlessly. The combined oppression of state and church drove about 20,000 Englishmen to America before 1640. John Winthrop was glad to see them come. The newcomers not only brought sorely needed supplies and skills, but they also reinforced the cherished city-upon-a-hill concept. In the 1630s, with immigrants continuously arriving, Massachusetts nearly approached Winthrop's vision of it as a

John Winthrop and his Massachusetts Bay contemporaries had an obsession about orderly existence. When a new town was "planted" in the wilderness, an elaborate survey preceded settlement. Each settler was assigned a designated parcel of land. Other parcels were reserved for the church, schools, and the "commons" that everyone shared. This was the plan for Wethersfield, Connecticut.

refuge and an example. Yet the growth of Massachusetts Bay created problems for a leader like Winthrop. He found that ideals and realities, theory and practice, did not often correspond in the New World. European plans shattered on the rocks of American circumstances.

Winthrop learned this lesson quickly in regard to government. The charter of the Massachusetts Bay Company gave him and a few other "freemen" full authority to legislate for the colony and to choose its governor. In theory, this oligarchic arrangement suited the purposes of the holy experiment quite well. Puritans believed that among the several covenants ordering their lives was one respecting the relationship of people and their governors. It held that God's laws could be enforced among imperfect men only if they agreed to submit to political leaders who could best interpret divine will. Governors, in Puritan thought, were like Old Testament prophets, but chosen by ballot. Though the people elected them, their authority, drawn from God, was unquestionable.

The first years of Massachusetts Bay revealed the presence of forces working against this political arrangement. First, the New World situation gave individuals potential, no matter what their previous status. With the clean slate of the American wilderness, they had opportunities unimagined in the older, established European society. Pioneering placed a premium on performance. On the New England frontier, success was measured by ambition and ability. Under such circumstances, the successful—and mere survivors were successful at first—gained self-respect. These individuals began to chafe under ideas and institutions that stifled initiative. The wilderness also tended to blur the social distinctions so carefully maintained in European civilizations and to increase democratic impulses. Equality meant more in the New World than it did in the Old. It was easy to sense the difference as soon as the settlers landed, and the impact on politics came almost immediately.

On October 19, 1630, Governor John Winthrop opened the first meeting of the General Court of the Massachusetts Bay Company. Seven other "assistants" attended. Under the terms of the company's charter, these few prepared to conduct the business of the colony. But other men also came, and rivalries among church members quickly arose. Some individuals drew Winthrop aside and let him know their desire to have a voice in the affairs of the plantation. It was difficult to refuse. These people, after all, were Winthrop's colleagues in colonization. They had dared together. Many had come as a direct result of his encouragement. They were partners in performing God's work on earth. Moreover, Winthrop realized, the Massachusetts Bay Company was not just a joint-stock company but, in the New England context, a civil government. Still, he was no democrat. The saints were chosen from the congregation, which consisted of residents of the community, both elect and nonelect. The saints in turn chose the elders, who led the entire society. Sovereignty rested with God through the eyes of the elders, not the people. Strong, theocratic leadership, based on a correct reading of God's will, must continue. This was the covenant theology.

The solution, Winthrop decided, was to broaden the base of government by creating a new political category, the *freeman*. Any adult male, indentured servants excepted, who was a member of the Puritan church could apply for such status. As a consequence, the second meeting of the General Court in May 1631 included 118 freemen. They had no legislative authority, but they could, along with the saints and elders, elect the assistants who did. Election of the assistants also indirectly influenced the choice of governor. Thus, less than a year after its beginnings, the Massachusetts government had moved in a republican direction.

The new arrangement pleased Winthrop, who remained governor, but his liberalism soon received a harder test. In 1632 various communities in Massachusetts Bay launched a protest against a tax assessed by Winthrop and his fellow assistants. According to the disgruntled colonists, taxation without some form of representation was contrary to the tradition of English liberties. Winthrop gave ground grudgingly. He finally agreed to consult with two representatives from every town before imposing the next tax. He also consented to the direct election of the governor by the freemen instead of by the assistants.

The drift toward republicanism from oligarchy continued in 1634, when Thomas Dudley, a political opponent of Winthrop, concluded that the wording of the Massachusetts Bay charter gave all freemen, not just the assistants, the power to make laws. Winthrop balked at this idea. God's will, not the public's, he believed, should determine policy. The people might select their leaders, but once selected, the leaders must answer only to God. The laws of men were not acceptable substitutes, in Winthrop's opinion, for the laws of God.

Respected as he was in Massachusetts, Winthrop could not prevent the continued erosion of his political ideas. Most of those who migrated to New England had come in search of freedom from the power of a king or an archbishop. Their deep-rooted aversion to arbitrary authority did not end with the transatlantic crossing. Indeed, the lack of restraints inherent in a wilderness situation encouraged an even more passionate dedication to liberty. God's authority went unquestioned, of course, but increasing numbers felt that they, too, could discern His will, and they demanded a role in translating it into law. This attitude, in fact, was part of the priesthood of all believers of the Protestant Reformation—one that especially influenced the congregational theory to which the American Puritans subscribed. Even Winthrop's repeated assurances that he and the other assistants best knew God's desires did not placate popular suspicion. There seemed to be too much arbitrary power in an arrangement under which a small group ruled at their own discretion.

In 1634 Winthrop was pressured into permitting each of the ten towns to send two deputies to the General Court. These deputies actually made laws along with the assistants in a semi-representative assembly. That same year Thomas Dudley, the beneficiary of political criticism of John Winthrop, replaced him in the governor's chair. For the next three years, Winthrop was merely one of the assistants.

During this time the freemen took steps to reform the government of Massachusetts Bay. Nathaniel Ward of Ipswich prepared the Body of Liberties, which spelled out the rights and obligations of citizenship. In the manner of the English Magna Carta (1215), it reflected the idea that a government of laws offered better protection for popular liberties than a government of men. Winthrop, who regained the governorship in 1637, fought the Body of Liberties doggedly. It was not that he quarreled with its substance; rather, he believed that such rules should result from the slow accumulation of the magistrates' interpretation of the Bible. Time and place were against him, however. In December 1641 the General Court adopted Ward's code of laws.

The government that was developing in Massachusetts Bay was neither a theocracy nor a democracy. The ministers had no official political authority, but the elected magistrates usually served their interests. Although elected, the magistrates did not believe they served the voters or the people at large. Instead, their role was to interpret the will of God. The town was the other foundation of Puritan society. The town built the meetinghouse where the congregations met for church services and civic gatherings. All townspeople were expected to obey the laws set down by the town governments, including serving in the local militia, paying taxes, and building houses in designated areas. In addition, townspeople were expected to give financial support to the local minister. Even though the ministers had no official authority, with their influence in the towns, they and the magistrates, working together, wielded considerable power.

Continued sparring between leaders and followers in Winthrop's New England resulted in the division of the General Court into two houses—that is, into a bicameral legislature—in 1644. Winthrop and the other assistants in the upper chamber benefited from this arrangement because they secured a veto over laws made by the deputies in the lower house. The following year, however, the deputies struck back, and again the controversy revolved around Winthrop. The trouble began in the town of Hingham, when the people refused to accept the militia officer appointed by Winthrop and the assistants. In his place they nominated another man. Feelings ran hot on both sides. One citizen of Hingham vowed to "die at the sword's point, if he might not have the choice of his own officers." Another simply rejected the idea that the Boston officials had anything to do with the affairs of Hingham. This was the beginning of frontier independence. But for Winthrop, it was a serious breach of the covenant and merited the strongest punishment. The men of Hingham responded by accusing Winthrop of overreaching the powers granted him in the Body of Liberties, whereupon the lower house of the General Court impeached John Winthrop! A remarkable trial followed. Those who feared concentrated and continuous power hoped to clip Winthrop's wings. Others believed that the kind of authority he represented was essential to the Puritan mission. The stormy trial sessions, therefore, went far beyond the Hingham mutiny. Finally, on July 3, 1645, the General Court was ready with its verdict: not guilty. Winthrop must have anticipated this verdict, because he was ready with what he termed a "little speech." It was one of his greatest moments.

"I entreat you to consider," he began, "that when you choose magistrates, you take them from among yourselves, men subject to like passions as you are." Of course assistants, or "magistrates" as Winthrop called them, could make mistakes. Winthrop even implied that he regretted some of his own recent actions. But, he quickly countered, "When you see infirmities in us, you should reflect upon your own." It was the Puritan mind at its best and worst. Winthrop then advised the people that once they had selected a leader, the terms of the social covenant obliged them to "run the hazard of his skill and ability," as long as he tried to follow God's law.

The second part of Winthrop's speech took up the vexing problem of liberty. In Winthrop's view, there were two kinds. "Natural" liberty belonged to man as it did to "beasts and other creatures" and simply meant to do as one pleased. Good might result, Winthrop conceded, but more frequently evil triumphed, because no restraint stood between desire and action. Natural liberty, then, left imperfect human nature uncontrolled and in time made men "worse than brute beasts." Such considerations were not academic in the wilds of America. The other kind of liberty, which Winthrop called "civil or federal," meant the freedom to do what is "good, just and honest." The definition of "good, just and honest" came from God through the medium of those who could best discern His purposes—that is, magistrates like John Winthrop. In accepting this more restricted form of liberty, people showed their ability to rise above the animals, restrain evil tendencies, and fulfill the terms of their covenant with God. "So shall your liberties be preserved," Winthrop concluded, "in upholding the honor and power of authority amongst you." Thus rebuked, the Hingham radicals subsided.

European feudal and monarchical tradition figured more prominently in Winthrop's 1645 speech than did the currents of individualism and popular sovereignty already percolating through New World society. But, of course, all but the children in Massachusetts Bay in 1645 were Europeans. Coupled with Winthrop's personal prestige and the unifying concept of mission, this fact served to delay social and political change in New England.

Elsewhere in North America, however, Old World expectations and institutions collapsed more quickly. Indeed, in the light of the experience of other plantations, Winthrop had reason to be encouraged by the Massachusetts record. The original plans of the Virginia Company, for instance, had called for a military dictatorship combined with feudal landholding policies. In 1619, however, the London-based directors of the company, hoping to create an environment for higher profits in Virginia, created a representative assembly, the House of Burgesses. That same year, local political authority was removed from Jamestown and given to the several counties. The change indicated a trend; Virginians desired autonomy and continued to resist European directives. By 1624, the Virginia Company had been stripped of its charter, and the colony had reverted back to the king. But royal agents proved no more successful. From their wilderness environment, the Virginians derived a passion for independence and a driving ambition. From their English background as ambitious country gentry, they inherited a persistent localism, a casual religion—at least when compared to Winthrop's—and an emphasis on the liberties and privileges of a landholding aristocracy. Both tendencies led them to question any authority other than their own and contributed to stamping the American character at the outset with its primary traits: making money and getting ahead.

Further north on Chesapeake Bay, Sir George Calvert, Lord Baltimore, and his son had launched Maryland at the same time Winthrop founded the Puritan colony. The colonies' early histories differed sharply. The Calverts held complete power and intended Maryland to be a feudal estate on the European model, complete with a landed gentry, serfs, and feudal dues. The scheme existed only on paper, however. The proprietors and their agents were first simply ignored, then defied, and at length made to concede the rights of landownership and meaningful political representation to most of the settlers.

Economic and social aspirations remained aristocratic in Maryland and Virginia, but they were not limited to an aristocracy. Everyone wanted to skim the cream off the top. Settlers had not crossed 3,000 miles of ocean merely to change masters. Political authority that stood in the way of individual ambition was among the first casualties of the American experience. Winthrop would have preferred it otherwise, but he understood the mood of the people. This realism, coupled with the spiritual commitment of the Puritans, allowed him to retain the essence of his authority in Massachusetts long after it had faded elsewhere.

There is evidence of this in Winthrop's high-handed treatment of Robert Child. In 1645, while Winthrop was lecturing the General Court on the meaning of liberty, Child, a physician, wrote a "Remonstrance and Humble Petition" that challenged the basis of the entire Puritan political system. It spoke for the rights of those who were not church members and therefore not voting freemen. Either suffrage or church membership ought to be expanded, Child argued. And for good measure he challenged the right of the General Court to legislate without regard to Parliament. He even threatened to return to London and tattle on the colony. Winthrop lost no time in clamping down on the upstart. Arbitrary seizures, fines, and imprisonment were the colony's answers to Child. Before being sent back to England in 1647, he was thoroughly discredited. Time and America were on Child's side, to be sure, but in the 1640s his challenge to authority brought the conservatism latent in Puritan political theory crashing down on his defenseless head. Winthrop found the result immensely satisfying. The Lord's will had been upheld, the unity of the New England way preserved.

Despite the attention paid to politics, the dominant concern of Winthrop's Massachusetts Bay was religion. Churches were the core of New England intellectual and social life and consisted of the saints and their ministers. Others might worship in the congregation, hoping for that awakening revelation of regeneration that would qualify them to sit among the elect. Yet membership in the church was restricted to those who succeeded in convincing themselves and their peers that they had been regenerated or saved. One consequence was an intense intolerance in Puritan minds. They believed, quite literally, that they and they alone knew God's will. Anyone who disagreed with Puritan theology was not only wrong but actually in league with evil. As Nathaniel Ward put it in 1645, "Poly-piety is the greatest impiety in the world." Those who tolerated other faiths could not be sincere in their own. Toleration was thought to be particularly

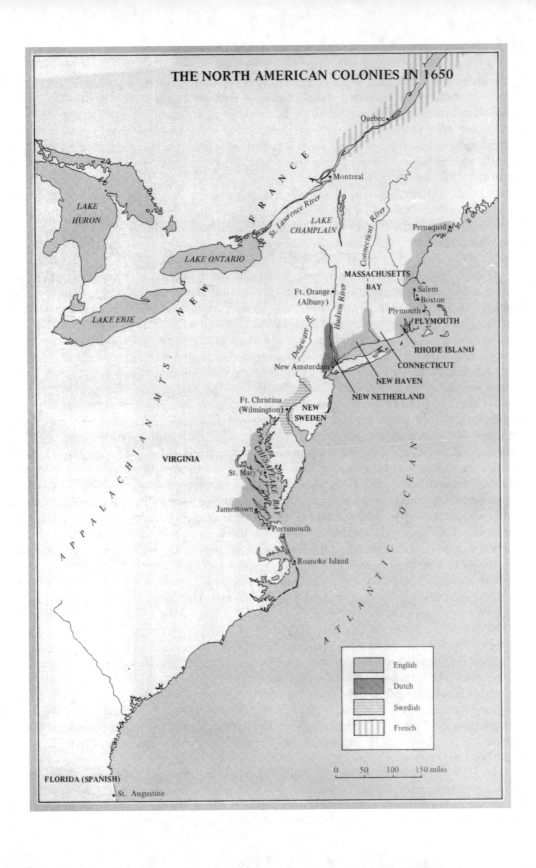

THE NORTH AMERICAN COLONIES IN 1650

Quebec

LAKE HURON

NEW

FRANCE

Montreal

St. Lawrence River

LAKE ONTARIO

LAKE CHAMPLAIN

Connecticut River

Pemaquid

LAKE ERIE

MASSACHUSETTS BAY

Ft. Orange (Albany)

Hudson River

Salem
Boston

Plymouth

PLYMOUTH

A P P A L A C H I A N   M T S.

Delaware R.

New Amsterdam

RHODE ISLAND

CONNECTICUT

NEW HAVEN

NEW NETHERLAND

Ft. Christina (Wilmington)

NEW SWEDEN

VIRGINIA

CHESAPEAKE BAY

St. Mary's

Jamestown

Portsmouth

Roanoke Island

A T L A N T I C   O C E A N

	English
	Dutch
	Swedish
	French

0   50   100   150 miles

FLORIDA (SPANISH)

St. Augustine

unbecoming in a society that regarded itself as God's chosen, a city upon a hill. This attitude left dissenters from Puritan orthodoxy with little choice but to leave. In Massachusetts, religion was far too weighty a matter for variations to be allowed.

As governor, Winthrop carried the responsibility of preserving the colony's piety, a task that brought some of his most trying moments. The first crisis involved a personal friend, the brilliant and charismatic Roger Williams. Only twenty-seven years old when he came to Massachusetts Bay in 1631, Williams fused the intense idealism of youth with a religious fervor exceptional even among Puritans. His conflict, in fact, resulted from his high standards. Williams began by refusing to associate with those who would not denounce and separate from the Church of England. These included Winthrop and most of the colonists in Massachusetts Bay. Displeased as they were with Anglicanism and Archbishop Laud, they took pains to make clear that in leaving for New England, they were not abandoning the church back home. They preferred to think of themselves as good examples, not deserters. Williams could not live with this compromise, and his zeal led him to other unorthodox stands. He declared that a saint must not even pray in the company of unregenerate people and thus challenged the structure of all New England churches. Scrupulous in every ethical matter, Williams even went so far as to question the legitimacy of taking land from the Indians; perhaps the whole political edifice of the New World colonies rested on the sands of injustice. Before leaving England, Winthrop had attempted to bury such doubts. Roger Williams had a disconcerting knack for unearthing them.

On several occasions in the early 1630s Winthrop attempted to moderate his idealistic young friend. Experience had taught the governor that people must live with and try to correct the evil they find in the world and in themselves. Removal to America in search of a clean slate was all right, but ultimately a man had to take a stand. The holier-than-thou attitude of Williams, Winthrop argued, might result in personal salvation, but the proper concern of the godly man should be world reformation. Williams, in turn, advised Winthrop to "abstract yourselfe with a holy violence from the Dung heape of this Earth." Winthrop balked. His style was to clean dung heaps, not flee them.

Williams first tried Boston but found that settlement cool to his ideas. Next he moved to Plymouth, where the Pilgrims had at least fully separated from the Church of England. But in time, predictably, Williams found imperfections there, too. He moved on to Salem, and here he made his strongest impression. Captivated by the charm and sincerity of the young zealot, the citizens of Salem chose him as their minister. Winthrop's eyebrows must have risen at the news. One dissenter was bad enough, but now Williams threatened to convert an entire congregation. In 1635, Winthrop and the General Court ordered Salem to dismiss Williams. The town exploded over the firing of the popular minister. Salem prepared to elicit sympathy for its cause in other communities, and the fate of Massachusetts Bay hung in the balance. In fact, Williams explicitly called for those who agreed with him to withdraw from Massachusetts Bay into a purer, independent organization. The self-styled leaders of the Reformation were themselves to be reformed. For most Puritans, this was too much. Williams lost support even in Salem.

At this juncture the General Court chose to have it out with Roger Williams. No one, especially not Winthrop, wanted to punish this sweet-tempered visionary, if only he would retract his extreme statements and work for the colony. But Williams was unyielding: Massachusetts, he insisted, should work with him. This left the General Court with no choice. In October 1635 Roger Williams was banished and given six weeks to leave the colony.

The Williams decision pained John Winthrop. He knew firsthand the passion that impelled the man. He, too, had been young and idealistic—sufficiently so to migrate 3,000 miles to the New World. He, too, had dreamed of a city upon a hill. In Winthrop's eyes, Williams was not a sinner; his error was an excess of virtue. So while Winthrop the magistrate sternly banished the young upstart, Winthrop the man privately suggested where he might go to find a sanctuary: the shore of Narragansett Bay, in what would become Rhode Island. Moreover, Winthrop may have been instrumental in blocking a move on the part of his more conservative colleagues in the General Court to send Williams back to England. Part of Winthrop wanted to see Williams succeed—as long as he left Massachusetts. Besides, in the 1630s there was sufficient wilderness in North America for a variety of Zions. So it happened that in January of 1636, Roger Williams and four followers trudged through the snow toward Narragansett Bay in pursuit of perfection. They bought, rather than took, land from the Indians and founded Providence, a town that attracted a steady flow of refugees from the northern colonies. Even Winthrop, whom Williams still greatly admired, was invited to join. He refused, of course.

Winthrop followed the history of Providence with considerable interest. For a time, Williams spiraled into even narrower circles of perfectionism and intolerance; at one point he found himself conscience-bound to worship with no one except his wife. But time taught him that absolute purity was, after all, unattainable, and tolerance accompanied this realization. In the end, Williams's capacity for toleration far surpassed that of the Puritans.

Even as Winthrop was breathing a sigh of relief over the departure of Roger Williams, another religious tempest loomed on the horizon. Anne Marbury had been born in England in 1591, when John Winthrop, who would come to loathe her, was three. Her father was a strong-minded clergyman who dared to challenge church doctrine. Anne managed to become well read in theology and adept at conversation at a time when education for women was thought to be an unnecessary adornment. In 1612 she married William Hutchinson, a promising and already well-to-do merchant. Fifteen children resulted from the union, but Anne found time to become an enthusiastic follower of John Cotton, an Anglican theologian who had begun a systematic debunking of traditional liturgical proceedings in services at his parish in Boston, England. The charismatic preacher attracted many listeners with his elegant sermons, in which he espoused the spiritual aspects of Christianity. Even more important, Cotton revived the beliefs of John Calvin (1509–1564). From Geneva, Calvin had led the Protestant world to his way of thinking, particularly as it concerned the relationship between human beings and God. In reality, Calvin had merely reopened an age-old debate among theologians and philosophers dating back to the time when people began to wonder about abstract issues such as an afterlife. Did God preordain all things on earth and in the hereafter? Or could humans, through their own free will, control whether they went to heaven or hell after death? In Calvin's view, similar to that of the apostle Paul in the first century A.D., the human condition was depraved, and all but a few predetermined souls were condemned to eternal damnation. Only through God's saving grace would the few, the elect predestined for salvation, have everlasting life. All was preordained; human beings could not, by free will, gain salvation, no matter what they did on earth.

John Cotton followed St. Paul and Calvin in this extreme line of thought. Cotton's sermons warned people against performing the rituals of Anglicanism and deluding themselves into believing that such "works" were signs of salvation. It was impossible to know truly whether one was predestined for salvation. But if a person were so ordained, according to Cotton, God would instill faith in and bestow grace on that individual. As a result, Cotton required from his congregation a complete submission to God's omnipotence and an evangelical adherence to biblical Scripture. During the 1610s and 1620s, popular demand for his words of religious purity compelled him to give additional weekday sermons. Although the Anglican hierarchy was impressed by his ability to increase church attendance, Cotton's message troubled them. He created a religious fervor among his parishioners that eventually threatened the staid traditions of Anglicanism. The Anglican ministers believed that the congregations at large should not bandy about such weighty questions of theology.

Consequently, in 1633, Cotton was obliged, or was forced, to join his fellow Puritan dissenters in Massachusetts Bay.

While a parishioner in old Boston, Anne Hutchinson had listened faithfully to Cotton's message. Her own intellectual background and Cotton's individualistic interpretation of religion had led her to develop a philosophy more egalitarian, but also more mystical, than Anglican conservatives could abide. Hutchinson's experience as a midwife in London early in the century had served to bolster her self-confidence—and her willingness to assert her opinions in the male-dominated realm of Christian theology. During congregational meetings in her home, she wondered aloud about the nature of salvation and the practices of Anglicanism. Through personal communication with God, she asked, could not a person know the Almighty more surely than through the rigid ritual of Catholicism or Anglicanism?

Meanwhile, John Cotton had established himself in New England. His movement away from Anglican ritual and reliance on church hierarchy was a basic tenet of Puritanism and had found favor with people like John Winthrop. And Cotton's message of strict Calvinistic predestination warned New Englanders of their own depravity—and of their tendency to slip toward "Arminianism." Jacobus Arminius, a Dutch Protestant theologian who died in 1609, had rejected Calvinistic predestination in favor of the individual's ability to accept or reject salvation through free will. Arminianism had gained a considerable following in continental Europe and in the Anglican Church as well. Its acceptance by King Charles I and Archbishop Laud had influenced the Puritans' decision to leave England.

Even though Puritans did not know if they were among those predestined to be saved, they intended to be ready for the "covenant of grace" with God—if and when it came—through the preparation of piety and good works. This preparation included searching for signs of grace and studying and quoting Scripture, which would please the saints and elders. But such preparation, Cotton reminded his New England congregation, became itself an Arminian trap by inviting lethargy and allowing ritual to interfere with true worship. Cotton's teachings, from which Winthrop and other Bostonians drew inspiration, identified a more intimate and spiritual relationship with God. People must humble themselves completely before God and spare Him no exaltation. After listening to Cotton, John Winthrop himself exclaimed that he had awakened from "twenty yeares" of slumber in his relationship with God.

But Cotton's revival of Calvinism was not without problems for New England. Among other things, it led to a general questioning of the New England covenant theology. Had the religious experiences of Puritans over the past years been genuine or not? And if not, what value did preparation and good works have in the overall scheme of things? No theologian himself, John Winthrop had less trouble squaring such metaphysical abstractions of the afterlife with the present than did more intellectual people. Spiritual concerns aside, Winthrop had a colony to run, and earthly "covenants"—the basis of Puritan society—were agreements designed in part to maintain order. For Winthrop, good citizenship was an integral part of religion. Although theological debate was not discouraged, it could not be permitted to compromise the supremacy of Winthrop and the elders. On a practical level, religion in New England was a means of enforcing strict social control. Whatever threatened Puritan efforts to build a "Christian Sparta" in the New World could not, in Winthrop's view, be tolerated. Too much spirituality and evangelism, Winthrop soon learned, was as dangerous to the colony as the lethargy of Arminianism that John Cotton decried.

For John Cotton and his brightest protégé, Anne Hutchinson, however, metaphysical interpretations were the only important religious matters. Hutchinson's bold interpretations of Cotton's sermons continued when, for economic more than spiritual reasons, she and William moved their family to New England in the summer of 1634. Anne was certainly pleased by their mutual decision to go to the New World. She was convinced that she would find greater tolerance for her religious beliefs—and that women would have more equality than they did in Stuart-dominated England. However, as she soon discovered, John Winthrop, her neighbor across the street, was tolerant on neither issue.

While William Hutchinson was quick to set up a profitable merchant business, Anne tended to housekeeping and regularly attended the Boston parish of John Cotton. But Cotton had changed. His intellectual interests had led him to become more of a scholar than a preacher. By the time the Hutchinsons arrived, Cotton was delivering few sermons. He shunned outside discussion whenever possible in favor of reading the great works of antiquity. Denied intellectual discourse with Cotton, Anne Hutchinson resumed the practice of holding religious discussions in her home. Taking spiritualism in bold new directions, she began to doubt openly that simply because a person broke no laws of God—or was "sanctified" in Puritan terms—this was a sign of salvation. In fact, argued Hutchinson, "sanctification," which included loyalty and obedience to the colony, offered no evidence at all of "justification," or salvation. Rather, justification came only when the Holy Spirit, or Holy Ghost, offered through God's free grace, entered the human soul. Thereafter, the Holy Ghost directed the earthly life of the saved person. For Hutchinson the mystical process surrounding God's implantation of the Holy Spirit in human souls became the crux of true Christianity.

The New England Puritan orthodoxy frowned in displeasure at Anne Hutchinson's interpretations of religion. Winthrop and others believed in the doctrine of God's free grace, but they were unwilling to concede that sanctification had no bearing on justification. In fact, an individual's good works might indeed be the result of salvation. Hutchinson's denial of this relationship troubled them, but even more troubling was the growing popularity of her biweekly fireside chats, which, by 1636, were attracting sixty to eighty Bostonians. Winthrop was aware of both the impressive attendance and the subject matter of the gatherings. By the autumn of 1636 he was regularly sending observers to her meetings.

Anne Hutchinson remained undaunted. She began to attack the basic premises of original sin; refusing to accept the doctrine that woman (Eve) was responsible for the fall of man (Adam) and his subsequent banishment from the Garden of Eden. Instead, she argued, men and women shared the blame for the Fall. She also believed that men had for centuries used original sin to control women. And men such as Winthrop and the conservative minister of nearby Roxbury, Thomas Weld, continued that practice in the New World. In the words of historian Selma R. Williams, the Puritan man regarded woman "as nothing more than a necessary evil—necessary only because she supplied children to ensure the future, evil because she was the incarnation of Eve." Because Eve had tempted Adam to sin—and the results were banishment from paradise and animalistic procreation—it followed that all women were descendants of, and the same as, Eve. And each time a woman gave birth, God reminded her of her contribution to original sin.

Anne Hutchinson, who had given birth to fifteen children, was repulsed by this interpretation of original sin. Moreover, she found the belief that a stillborn child was a sign from God of the mother's wickedness to be equally absurd. As an experienced midwife who had delivered hundreds of babies, as well as an expert herbalist who successfully practiced a form of prenatal care, Hutchinson dismissed the orthodox point of view on childbearing as merely another means of keeping women in their place. Delivering her emotional message with a powerful, hypnotic voice, Hutchinson struck a blow at the rigid oligarchy of the colony. John Winthrop himself felt her impact when he lost the governorship in 1635 to a Hutchinson supporter, Henry Vane. At the same time, Hutchinson's brother-in-law, John Wheelwright, became minister in Boston.

With her friends in power, Hutchinson's mysticism took a new turn. She began to argue that only those who had received the Holy Spirit could look into the souls of others and determine whether they were "truly saved." When she accused all of the Massachusetts ministers, with the exception of Wheelwright and Cotton, of being deluded under "a covenant of works," not saved, and therefore not fit to preach the gospel, Winthrop knew he must act before she destroyed the colony. Although he recognized her "ready wit and bold spirit," Winthrop viewed her as a dangerous and wicked woman who had cajoled her husband into bringing her to Massachusetts to spread heresy. He condemned the beliefs of Hutchinson and her followers, branding them as "antinomians" (meaning literally, in Greek, "against law"). Winthrop's ally, the Reverend Thomas Weld, borrowed the orthodoxy's original sin analogy to condemn Hutchinson when he correlated Eve's role in the Fall with "Mistress Hutchinson's opinions," which were beginning "to raise sedition among us." The orthodoxy had to draw the line before Anne Hutchinson could do more damage.

Retribution was quick. In May 1637 the general elections returned Winthrop to the governorship. Henry Vane returned to England, and Winthrop determined to crush antinomianism

This lithograph depicts the trial of Anne Hutchinson in 1637. Winthrop and other magistrates are interrogating her on charges of heresy.

completely. John Wheelwright was the first target. Called before Winthrop's General Court in November 1637, Wheelwright was convicted of sedition and contempt and banished to New Hampshire. A few days later Anne Hutchinson was summoned to appear before the magistrates. It was a dramatic moment. The quick-witted woman repeatedly parried the charges of Winthrop and his colleagues or trapped them in their own logic. But the court was not interested in weighing evidence, only in passing a predetermined judgment. And then, as the relentless examination continued, Hutchinson lost her poise. In a hysterical flood of words, she told the court that God had spoken to her directly and informed her that if she were punished, He would "ruine you and your posterity, and this whol State."

That was the last straw for Winthrop. He called the court into private session; its verdict: banishment. No reasons were given. When Hutchinson asked, "Wherefore am I banished?" Winthrop replied, "Say no more, the court knows wherefore and is satisfied." Of course, the real reason Anne Hutchinson could not remain in Massachusetts Bay was the threat she posed to order, unity, and authority and, ultimately, to covenant and mission. Winthrop allowed Hutchinson and her family to leave for Rhode Island. After her husband's death in 1642, Anne moved to the Dutch colony of New Netherland, settling along a river that now bears her name just north of New York City. In 1643 Anne and all her children, with the exception of the youngest daughter, were killed in an Indian raid. To his discredit, Winthrop commented on the murder that "God's hand is . . . seen herein."

But the specter of Anne Hutchinson refused to die. Another manifestation of her impact presented a new threat to John Winthrop's conception of a covenant community in the form of Robert Keayne. A genuinely self-made man, Keayne had overcome his beginnings as a poor London butcher's helper to become one of the wealthiest men in New England. His trade was the importing business. The colonists were desperate for manufactured goods such as cloth, pots, glass, guns, and saws. Keayne had these items in stock, and he knew the laws of the marketplace. He charged high prices and made high profits. It was good business, but unfortunately for Keayne, Massachusetts Bay was not primarily a business venture. It was not that Puritans opposed material success; rather, they insisted that all such worldly accomplishments be subordinated to spiritual ones.

In regard to business, John Calvin and other leaders of the Reformation in Europe had carefully instructed the faithful with a doctrine later labeled the Protestant ethic. Keayne, Winthrop, and their colleagues believed that worldly success was related to virtue, diligence, and the blessing of the Lord. They also knew that a man might strive to succeed in his calling provided he did so for the glory of God and not his personal gain. The Protestant ethic also required that a businessman observe fair "rules for trading," as Winthrop called them. The first was restraint: One must not press an economic advantage to the utmost but should rest content with a "just" price and profit. To ensure "just" profits, Winthrop and other Puritan leaders imposed a system of wage-and-price controls. Many merchants, however—including Keayne and William Hutchinson—were fully aware that Winthrop's restraints limited their profits. Anne Hutchinson agreed; before her banishment, her meetings had begun to attract an increasing number of disgruntled businessmen. Many had left England primarily to escape the heavy duties on business activities exacted by the crown. But in Massachusetts Bay they found themselves likewise dominated by Winthrop and his magistrates. Anne Hutchinson's refusal to link sanctification with salvation was a popular stance among businessmen. Accordingly, defiance of the colony's laws might not lead to defiance of God. If the public obedience that Puritan leaders viewed as sanctifying was, in reality, religious hypocrisy, as Hutchinson argued, then the colony's businessmen had reason enough to oppose the economic controls. Indeed, businessmen were largely responsible for Winthrop's gubernatorial defeat in

1635. Although he successfully banished the Hutchinsons in 1637, Winthrop still had to attend to unfinished business with the "new converts . . . infected with her opinions."

The Keayne case first came to John Winthrop's attention in 1639, just as the colony appeared to be relaxing from the tension of the Hutchinson controversy. Various reports reached the governor that the merchant was reaping too large a profit. Word had it that he went so far as to double his own cost in pricing an item. One Boston widow accused Keayne of seizing her prize pig when she could not meet his exorbitant charges. Winthrop responded by calling Keayne before the General Court and conducting a full inquiry into his business practices. At its conclusion, according to Winthrop, the merchant "did, with tears, acknowledge and bewail his covetous and corrupt heart." Nonetheless, he was severely reprimanded and fined.

In Winthrop's eyes, Robert Keayne was a frightening example of how the New World's economic opportunities could lure even a member of a holy experiment away from godliness. Keayne put personal considerations ahead of the commonwealth. He was so severely rebuked, one suspects, because Winthrop wanted to make him an example to those who might be tempted to imitate his enterprising practices. Still, the economic individualism Keayne represented was not easily suppressed. New England merchants proved increasingly unmanageable and invariably took a stand against Puritan authority and the repressive authoritarianism it represented. All but the most devout had taken the side of Anne Hutchinson in 1637 because they thought her doctrine promised less centralized control of economic life. And in the late 1680s, when the structure of New England government underwent reorganization, the merchants initially sided with English royal authority in preference to that of the American Puritans. By that time, of course, it was becoming clearer that for better or for worse, the Robert Keaynes of the New World would prevail over the John Winthrops.

Different as they were, Winthrop's experiences with Roger Williams, Anne Hutchinson, and Robert Keayne taught a common lesson: Individualism—or "separatism" in seventeenth-century terms—posed the greatest threat to New England's covenanted purposes. Winthrop had anticipated this on board the *Arbella* when he underscored the need for keeping "knit together" in Massachusetts. But the separatist and atomizing tendencies of Puritanism, strong in Europe, grew even stronger in the frontier of the New World. In a wilderness, he quickly discovered, there was no order except that which the newcomers established. And the structure was always tenuous. It was easy for someone to spin off the approved track. Total freedom, unprecedented in the Old World, lay only a few miles away in the forest. Consequently, the American Puritans worked at maintaining standards with an urgency born of desperation.

One result of this mentality was the rigid supervision Winthrop and the General Court gave the process of westward expansion. Town "planting" involved a series of careful steps. First, the area to be settled was selected and the boundaries were laid out. Sites for homes and, most important, a church were designated, and construction was begun. Then an entire community moved into the wilderness. To do this, however, often required the removal of Indian tribes who currently occupied the land. In the eyes of Winthrop and his colleagues, Indians were not human beings but savages.

The Pequot tribe, occupying much of the land west of Boston, bore the brunt of the Puritans' divine justification in the 1630s. Since the Pequots had not subdued the land by cultivating it, the Puritans invoked biblical Scripture from Genesis, declaring the region a jurisdictional vacuum to which the Indians had no legitimate claim. The Indians disagreed. Winthrop called the removal policy of 1637, which became known as the Pequot War, "a divine slaughter," based on the right of God's chosen people to take the land they needed to subdue and make fruitful. With muskets and swords, the Puritan militiamen marched on the confused Pequots, who did not understand that white men waged war for keeps. And after the relentless attack, in which virtually every Pequot man, woman, and child was killed or captured, John Winthrop observed, "The Lord delivered up the heathen to the sword of his chosen people." The refusal of Anne Hutchinson and her followers to support what they believed to be atrocities against fellow human beings enraged Winthrop and ensured Hutchinson's banishment. Ironically, her death in 1643 was at the hands of Indians in New Netherland who sought retribution for white incursions into their land.

In numbers, Puritans thought, lay the strength to resist barbarism. Nonetheless, the pioneers were carefully instructed "to carry and behave yourselves as good and sober men" and reminded that "you are in this voyage concerned not only for a worldly interest but . . . for the translating of Christ's ordinances and worship into that country." Here was an extension of the mission idea that had applied originally to the planters of the seaboard towns. Puritan pioneering was a controlled group effort. The Daniel Boone type of frontiersman, whom later generations of Americans celebrated, was definitely not heroic to John Winthrop and his contemporaries. On the contrary, such men appeared to have forgotten the holy mission, followed their own conception of liberty, and become, in Winthrop's words, "worse than brute beasts."

After 1640 when the Puritan Revolution in England caused Massachusetts to lose its appeal as the cutting edge of world Protestantism, orderly settlement of the frontier became even more important. The transformation of wilderness into civilization became the core of the concept of a new mission. And such a restatement was sorely needed. Winthrop himself felt the pangs of uncertainty. In the 1630s, the most important English Puritans, including Oliver Cromwell, had at least contemplated moving to New England. But in the next decade the action shifted to England, and it was Winthrop who contemplated a move. That he remained in the New World was due in part to his ability to redefine the Massachusetts mission in terms of westward expansion. Replaced as a "city upon a hill" by events in England, Americans could still take satisfaction from their expansion of the boundaries of Christendom.

While doing so, however, Puritans still considered it essential to regulate the lives of individuals in the older towns. Winthrop's journal history of Massachusetts Bay is full of entries describing the General Court's efforts to stamp out sin. Its tool was a body of regulations on personal conduct known retrospectively as blue laws. Perhaps the most interesting of them stipulated that every person in the colony had to be a member of a family. It was illegal to live alone. If people lacked a spouse or relatives with whom they could live, they were obliged to join a family as serving men or maids. The theory behind the law was that the family would provide an excellent means of social control. Other laws regulated sexual practices, the use of alcohol, and recreation on the Sabbath. Winthrop's Puritans simply felt that their situation and purpose made it imperative not to relax their guard. Against the dark background of the wilderness, the flame of civilization seemed tiny and fragile. Unpoliced frivolity could lead to the abandonment of standards, and individuals could not be entirely trusted with their own policing. The blue laws provided an incentive to preserve order in a potentially chaotic environment.

The struggle against barbarism also entailed reconstructing the full range of civilizing and humanizing institutions known in Europe. Simple survival, even prosperity, was not enough. A city upon a hill required more. As a 1643 tract explained, "After God had carried us safe to New England, and wee had builded houses, provided necessarries for our livelihood, rear'd convenient places for Gods worship, and setled the Civill Government: One of the next things we longed for, and looked after was to advance Learning and perpetuate it to Posterity." One of the first results of this determination was the founding of Harvard College in 1636. Retrospectively,

Colleges ranked high on the list of early American priorities. They were regarded as evidence that civilized standards could and would be maintained in the New World wilderness. Harvard College, founded across the Charles River from Boston in the community of Cambridge in 1636, was the showpiece of seventeenth-century Massachusetts Bay. This view of the college in 1726 reveals buildings that must have been among the most imposing in the colony. They were tangible evidence of New Englanders' determination to succeed in their colonizing endeavor.

it is astonishing that only six years after Winthrop and the bulk of New England's settlers came to the wilderness, they created a college. No better indication exists of the Puritan temperament. Virginia, in contrast, did not found a college (William and Mary) until 1693. Massachusetts's first press was operating in 1639; Virginia's did not come until 1729. The Puritans also prized elementary and secondary education. A grammar school began in Boston in 1636, and eleven years later a Winthrop-led General Court required every town of 100 families to establish a school. With such institutional support, lofty purposes and the discipline essential for their achievement could be maintained.

John Winthrop's beloved Margaret died in 1647, after three decades of married life that in its joyous warmth belies much of the Puritan stereotype. A year after her death, the lonely governor married for the fourth time and, at the age of sixty, fathered his sixteenth child. But the driving energy that had carried Winthrop so far was running low. A six-week bout with fever preceded his death on March 26, 1649. It was a timely end. The great age of Puritan mission was gradually fading, while the mystical, self-styled religion inspired by John Cotton and Anne Hutchinson was on the rise. Cotton's sermons and Hutchinson's evangelical message anticipated the fiery grass roots preaching of such eighteenth-century Great Awakening ministers as Jonathan Edwards. Following the Great Migration of the early 1640s and thereafter, the first-generation Puritan oligarchy was forced to make ever-increasing concessions to the second generation, many of whom proved to be less devout than their elders. Their unwillingness to make public testimonial of having embraced the covenant of grace precluded them from church membership. According to the Cambridge Platform of 1649, the children of nonchurch members could not be baptized and thus cleansed of original sin. As a result, New England church membership declined to less than 50 percent during the 1650s, much of the colony lived in original sin, and the majority of the population had no covenant with the church.

The founders' brand of Puritanism, with its exclusive church membership, could no longer withstand the pressures of mass migration and westward expansion without considerable change. Their efforts to restrict church membership threatened to undermine church control of the colony. They had to find a way to keep the church pure and still ensure that the popular will would defer to church authority. The solution was the Halfway Covenant of 1662, which allowed for the baptism of third-generation children if their parents assented to the "faith" of the church and conformed to God's holy word. Many nonmembers took advantage of the compromise, in which they essentially agreed to acknowledge church doctrine in hopes of guaranteeing their own conversion and to accept church authority. The Halfway Covenant preserved the strength of the Puritan community for a time. It included residents who did not meet all of the tests of Puritanism in the covenant of the local congregation. But at the same time, it did not dilute the purity of the church with unregenerate full members.

Over the next half century the Puritan experiment grew to include more than 500 towns in New England. Although the rigid church-based local governments had to yield gradually to increasing secularization, the communities nonetheless maintained the religious character that Winthrop and his fellow Puritans had brought to the new land. Signing covenants to obey the town laws, residents retained a belief in their mission and their form of government.

Fear and paranoia over lost control sometimes led to gruesome excesses, however; Salem Village during the 1690s was a case in point. When the daughter of a Puritan minister and several other women claimed to be possessed by demons, a "witch hunt" ensued throughout the region. Governor William Phips oversaw the trials of more than 150 people (mostly women) who were charged with practicing witchcraft. At least twenty people were executed for being witches. The executions had the support of leading Puritan ministers such as Cotton Mather, who believed that witchcraft was an "Assault of the evil Angels upon the Country." Although Mather's father, Increase, persuaded Governor Phips to stop the executions on behalf of those who were perhaps innocent, the witch trials clearly damaged the credibility of Puritan ministers.

Despite the inequities and intolerance of John Winthrop's Massachusetts, the Puritan ethos made an indelible stamp on American history. Second-generation New Englanders such as John Winthrop Jr., who allowed both science and industry to rival religion as the dominant concern of their lives, still believed in the holy experiment that their fathers' generation had brought from England. Carving a civilization from a "howling wilderness" required, in Winthrop's mind, strict control. Creating a society that was to be a shining light to the whole world necessitated that civil and religious authority come from the select leaders of God's chosen people. This concept of mission, transformed into literature, education, and government, spearheaded the colonial movement toward republicanism. The habits of discipline, hard work, and piety and the desire for perfection and purity—so much a part of John Winthrop's society—proved a lasting legacy for many generations of Americans.

Selected Readings

The Person

°Dunn, Richard S.: *Puritans and Yankees: The Winthrop Dynasty of New England, 1630–1717* (1962). Traces the lives of John, John Jr., Fitz, and Wait Winthrop.

°Dunn, Richard S., and Laetitia Yandel: *The Journal of John Winthrop: 1630–1649* (1996). An abridged version of Winthrop's journal, with modern punctuation and annotations.

°Morgan, Edmund S.: *The Puritan Dilemma: The Story of John Winthrop* (1958). The most satisfying (and succinct) biographical study.

°Morison, Samuel Eliot: *Builders of the Bay Colony* (rev. ed., 1946). Contains chapters on Winthrop, on John Winthrop Jr., and on other leaders of early Massachusetts.

Moseley, James C.: *John Winthrop's World* (1992). A new assessment of Winthrop's role in the Puritan experiment.

Rutman, Darrett: *Winthrop's Boston* (1965). An excellent life and times.

Rutman, Darrett: *John Winthrop's Decision for America: 1629* (1975). Primary documents and interpretation concerning Winthrop's personal and public struggle over whether to remain in England or move to the New World.

The Winthrop Papers (5 vols., 1929–1947, published by the Massachusetts Historical Society). The most authoritative edition of John Winthrop's journal, which records the main events of New England's early history.

The Period

Ahlstrom, Sydney E.: *A Religious History of the American People* (1972). A clarifying textbook on religion throughout American history.

°Bailyn, Bernard: *The New England Merchants in the Seventeenth Century* (1955). Documents the tension between secular and spiritual success in early New England society.

Baltzell, E. Digby: *Puritan Boston and Quaker Philadelphia: Two Protestant Ethics and the Spirit of Class Authority and Leadership* (1979). Comparative history of the dominant religion, dissent, and tolerance in the two colonies.

Battis, Emery: *Saints and Sectaries: Anne Hutchinson and the Antinomian Controversy in the Massachusetts Bay Colony* (1962). A Freudian interpretation of the most remarkable woman in seventeenth-century America.

°Boorstin, Daniel: *The Americans: The Colonial Experience* (1964). An interpretive study of American history in the seventeenth century.

Breen, Timothy: *Puritans and Adventurers: Change and Persistence in Early America* (1980). Insightful essays on life and government in colonial Massachusetts and Virginia.

Bremer, Francis J.: *The Puritan Experiment: New England Society from Bradford to Edwards* (1976). Excellent social history of Winthrop's generation and after.

Bremer, Francis J. (ed.): *Anne Hutchinson: Troubler of the Puritan Zion* (1981). Collects the best scholarship concerning Hutchinson's challenge to Winthrop's intellectual and political leadership of Massachusetts Bay.

Conroy, David W.: *In Public House: Drink and the Revolution of Authority in Colonial Massachusetts* (1995). Lively glimpse of New England society as the Puritan oligarchy began to lose power.

°Available in paperback.

Gura, Philip F.: *A Glimpse of Sion's Glory: Puritan Radicalism in New England, 1620–1660* (1984). A look at New England Puritan radicalism, with case studies of Anne Hutchinson, Samuel Gorton, and William Pynchon.

Jennings, Francis: *The Invasion of America: Indians, Colonialism and the Cant of Conquest* (1975). Reexamination of traditional writings about relations and conflicts between Indians and European colonists, including the Puritans.

°McGiffert, Michael (ed.): *Puritanism and the American Experience* (1969). An excellent collection of primary and secondary writings.

°Miller, Perry: *Errand into the Wilderness* (1956). The essence of the ideas of this foremost scholar of Puritan thought in the New World. See especially Chapter 1, "Errand into the Wilderness," and Chapter 3, "The Marrow of Puritan Divinity."

°Nash, Roderick: *Wilderness and the American Mind* (1982). Attitudes toward the New World environment at the time of colonization.

Notestein, Wallace: *The English People on the Eve of Colonization* (1954). A concise, readable text on English government and society during the seventeenth century.

Petit, Norman: *The Heart Prepared: Grace and Conversion in Puritan Spiritual Life* (1966). A revisionist study (primarily with regard to Perry Miller's work) that deals with matters of central importance to Winthrop and his peers.

°Powell, Sumner Chilton: *Puritan Village: The Formation of a New England Town* (1963). A study of everyday Puritan life.

Rosenbaum, Stuart (ed.): *Pragmatism and Religion* (2003). Primary documents tracing the history of American religion. Includes Winthrop's "A Model of Christian Charity."

Rowse, Alfred L.: *The Expansion of Elizabethan England* (1955). The background of English expansion to New England.

Stiles, T. J. (ed.): *The Colonizers: Early European Settlers and the Shaping of North America* (1998). Primary accounts of prominent Europeans like Winthrop who colonized North America.

Stone, Lawrence: *The Causes of the English Revolution: 1529–1642* (1972). Explains the religious and political context in which Winthrop made his decision to move to New England.

Stout, Harry S.: *The New England Soul: Preaching and Religious Culture in Colonial New England* (1986). Extensive analysis of the importance of religion during the seventeenth and eighteenth centuries.

Williams, Selma R.: *Divine Rebel: The Life of Anne Marbury Hutchinson* (1981). An insightful perspective on Hutchinson and her dealings with Winthrop.

For Consideration

1. Puritanism in England was a separatist movement away from Anglicanism. What did Puritans oppose regarding the Anglican faith?

2. What factors led to the Great Migration of John Winthrop and other Puritan faithful?

3. Describe what Winthrop envisioned when he called the Massachusetts Bay Colony settlement "a city upon a hill."

4. Discuss the challenges for Puritan governance of the Massachusetts Bay Colony. How did Winthrop and the Puritan leadership respond to environmental, political, and economic challenges to their authority?

5. What were some of the lasting legacies of Winthrop's New England to future generations of the nation?

Chapter 3

Benjamin Franklin

Busying himself in the rear of his brother's printing shop, the sixteen-year-old apprentice kept an ear cocked to the conversation in the front of the store. Some literary gentlemen were excitedly leaning over a lengthy letter he had secretly slipped under the door the previous night as a contribution to the *New England Courant*. The letter purported to be the work of a Mrs. Silence Dogood, but in the early eighteenth century every satirist used a pseudonym. Guesses as to the identity of the author ranged over the most talented writers in Boston, and with each name mentioned, the apprentice's amusement and pride increased. Yet his understanding of human nature kept him silent. On April 2, 1722, "Mrs. Dogood's" first letter appeared in the *Courant*. The practical apprentice, Benjamin Franklin, was on his way to becoming an American legend.

In origin, station, and ambition, the Franklin family typified much of American society at the beginning of the eighteenth century. Their nationality was English; Franklins have been traced back to the 1550s in the parish records of Northamptonshire. Their religion was Protestant but stopped short of the purifying zeal of people such as John Winthrop. The Franklins had accepted Anglicanism and remained in England while the first waves of settlers began New England's history. The decision to stay did not involve much strain of conscience, for the Franklins as a rule were more artisans and farmers than theologians. But near the end of the long reign of Charles II (1660–1685), Josiah Franklin, Benjamin's father, experienced religious conversion and began to attend illegal meetings of dissenters from the Anglican church. In 1683 he opted for America and moved his family to Boston in pursuit of the goals of religious freedom and economic opportunity. He found a measure of both, establishing a soap and candle shop on Boston's Milk Street and, in 1694, gaining admission to the Puritan Old South Church.

Although Benjamin Franklin later wrote in the manner of the English demographer and parson Thomas Robert Malthus about the danger of a population explosion, the circumstances of early eighteenth-century America encouraged large families. There was, after all, a continent to fill, and there was work for many hands. Josiah had seven children by his first wife and ten by his second. Benjamin, born in 1706, was the youngest son of the second union. Franklin later recalled that his father intended him to be "the tithe . . . to the service of the church," a kind of human offering. So while the other Franklin boys were apprenticed to various tradesmen in Boston, Benjamin received instruction in reading at home. "I do not remember," he declared in later life, "when I could not read." At a time when literacy was a luxury, this ability was a great advantage. At the age of eight, Franklin attended the Boston Grammar School, an institution founded in the 1630s in informal association with Harvard College and concerned chiefly with the intricacies of Latin. The year at Boston Grammar proved profitable. Franklin noted, characteristically, how he had "risen gradually from the middle of the class . . . to be at the head." But lack of money obliged Josiah to end Benjamin's formal schooling almost before it had begun. At the age of ten, he entered the family business. A refined hatred of the mindless work with wax and tallow was the immediate result. At twelve, seeking an avenue of rebellion, Benjamin threatened to go to sea. Josiah reacted intelligently. His son's apprenticeship was transferred to the printing business of an older brother, James.

It was a brilliant solution. A self-styled "bookish lad," Benjamin thrived in an environment of words. As part of a campaign of self-education, he read voraciously—often, with the aid of his father's candles, far into the night. Franklin also tried his hand at writing. Obtaining a copy of Joseph Addison and Richard Steele's satiric London periodical, *The Spectator,* he tried to imitate its pithy style. Taking notes on the essays, he reconstructed them in his own words and then compared his efforts with the originals. After some weeks of practice, Franklin could report that he "sometimes had the pleasure of fancying that in certain particulars of small import I had been lucky enough to improve the method or the language." The deceptively unassuming language hid pride and ambition of colossal proportions. Coupled with enormous energy and considerable talent, these traits led both to his success and, in certain quarters, to his unpopularity. The same might be said about his nation.

Occupied by his apprenticeship, Franklin had to steal the time for self-improvement. The principal victims were his sleep and his religion. Although raised by strict Puritan principles, he found it tempting to cut corners. On Sundays, while his family worshiped at the Old South Church, Franklin read and wrote in the quiet of the closed printing shop. It was not that he denied or despised religion, simply that new goals arose to challenge the old ones. In Franklin's words, "I still thought [public worship] a duty, though I could not . . . afford the time to practice it."

As horrifying as this attitude would have been to John Winthrop's generation, Benjamin Franklin spoke for growing numbers of his contemporaries. The ninety years that separated Winthrop's Boston from Franklin's had witnessed a gradual erosion of spiritual energies. The initial New England ideal of a closely knit, covenanted community proved difficult to maintain in the face of economic growth. The Puritan old guard, fearful of worldliness, tried to bridge the gap between the sacred and the secular with the Protestant ethic and the idea of a Christian calling. But glorifying God with worldly success did not provide a clear means for choosing between God and success, as Franklin's experience demonstrated. If one could get ahead by skipping church, why not do it? Was this kind of diligence in one's work evil?

The tendency to answer in the negative was apparent even in Winthrop's time, when New England merchants reacted with amazement and resentment to charges that they were making too much money. The business community also resented the way the church controlled the politics of Massachusetts Bay. At every opportunity, the merchants sided with those who favored greater toleration rather than with the defenders of rigid Puritan orthodoxy. In the 1630s, this had meant supporting Anne Hutchinson; forty years later, it meant defending Charles II's Lords of Trade and that body's colonial agent, Edward Randolph, against the Puritan establishment. When the Massachusetts charter, which John Winthrop had defended so vigorously, was finally revoked in 1684, the reaction in the colony was mixed. Though the colonists were unhappy to lose a measure of their independence to England, many merchants welcomed anything that promised relief from the straitjacket of Puritanism. In the long run, economic freedom proved to be more potent in Massachusetts Bay than either spiritual purity or political autonomy.

As ship owners and shopkeepers, both sides of Benjamin Franklin's family had experienced the tension between the sacred and the secular. Benjamin's maternal grandfather, Peter Folger, had even written caustic verses attacking the magistrates of Massachusetts for their intolerance. Thus, the Franklins and Folgers were not unhappy about the prospect of colonial reorganization in the late 1680s. The Dominion of New England, as the revised plan came to be called, placed all colonies north of New Jersey under a royal governor. Representative assemblies were eliminated, but the prospect of escaping the Puritan oligarchy sweetened even this pill enough for merchant tastes. They could not, however, stomach Sir Edmund Andros, the Dominion's tactless governor. Miraculously, he managed to alienate all factions. In April 1689, Bostonians responded to news of the revolution against James II in England by imprisoning Edmund Andros. Two years later, Massachusetts Bay received a new charter that amounted to a compromise between the Puritan system of government and the Dominion. For people like the Franklins, the new arrangement was a signal improvement; property, rather than godliness, became the criterion for suffrage.

With the yoke of Puritanism partially lifted, Franklin's Boston surged ahead in pursuit of the main chance. By 1720 the population numbered more than 10,000 persons, and in terms of shipping the city was one of the busiest ports in the British Empire. Secular concerns seemed to carry all before them, but Puritanism had been too strong for too long to vanish overnight. James Franklin and his apprentice were made aware of this late in the spring of 1722, when their paper, the *New England Courant,* drew the fire of the conservative Boston clergy and the General Court. The leading spokesman of Puritan orthodoxy, Cotton Mather, cited the appearance of disrespectful articles, some of the most subversive of which appeared under the name of Mrs. Silence Dogood. For example, the disguised Benjamin Franklin had written: "It has been for some time a question with me whether a commonwealth suffers more by hypocritical pretenders to religion or by the openly profane. But some late thoughts of this nature have inclined me to think that the hypocrite is the more dangerous person of the two, especially if he sustains a post in the government."

Of course, the *Courant* took pains to accompany such statements with a defense of freedom of thought and speech. Nevertheless, James Franklin was arrested and imprisoned after his June 11 issue appeared on the streets. For a month he languished in jail while Benjamin carried on the paper. Unrepentant after his release, James continued his jibes at the establishment. Finally, in January 1723, an order from the General Court prohibited him from printing in the city of Boston. Not so easily defeated, the Franklins quickly arranged for Benjamin to assume ownership of the business. The subterfuge saved the *Courant* but fed the apprentice's already burgeoning ego to such an extent that coexistence with James was no longer possible. After repeated quarrels and some blows, Benjamin determined to find another master. The printers' guild closed ranks, however; when Benjamin applied for work, no Boston printer needed help.

At this low ebb in Franklin's life, the repulsive soap and candle business loomed ominously in his future. But Benjamin was nothing if not self-confident. A plan took shape in his mind. He would sell some of his precious books to raise a little money and, with nothing more than a rumor of a printing job in New York as enticement, would leave his native city for the first time. In the fall of 1723, he slipped quietly out of Boston to take on the world. Three days on a fast sloop brought him to New York. The city and colony had been in British hands since the ouster of the Dutch in 1664, but the pattern of large semifeudal landholding that persisted discouraged settlers. New York supported only a few printers, and Franklin found no openings. Undaunted, he pushed on to Philadelphia.

As a foil to his later achievements, Franklin's *Autobiography* takes pains to detail the lowly circumstances of his arrival in the Pennsylvania capital in October 1723. Dirty, disheveled, and dog-tired, the runaway apprentice, all of seventeen years old, staggered up Market Street. With the last of his money, he bought three large rolls. Franklin's appearance as he wandered aimlessly through the streets munching his rolls amused an attractive girl standing at the doorway of her father's house. Later she would become Mrs. Franklin, but for the moment he was too tired to notice her. As he went along, a crowd appeared in the streets, and Franklin followed it to the large Quaker meetinghouse. The service began with a period of quiet meditation that was too great a temptation for the exhausted apprentice. Sprawling on an empty bench, he fell sound asleep.

The Philadelphia into which Franklin had straggled so inauspiciously was the leading city of a colony that had made a comparatively late entry into North America. Yet Pennsylvania was already among the most vigorous settlements. The keys to success in this case were a favorable location and the genius of William Penn. The son of an admiral in the English Navy and a member of a radical Protestant sect called the Quakers, Penn wanted to found a colony based on the principles of religious freedom and popular sovereignty. In 1681 Charles II granted him a charter to a huge tract of exceptionally fertile land west of the Delaware River. It came to be known as Penn's woods, or "Pennsylvania." In stark contrast to most other American colonists, Penn negotiated treaties and land purchases with the Indians of the area. The colony's liberal and tolerant policies, so markedly different from those of early Massachusetts, attracted large numbers of immigrants. Speaking a dozen languages and worshiping in different ways, they spread into the hinterland and used some of the richest soil on the continent to raise wheat, corn, hemp, and flax, as well as livestock. Other, city-oriented people built a vigorous tradition of trade and craftsmanship in Philadelphia.

Two decades before Franklin arrived, Penn had taken the unusual step of responding to criticism by permitting his colonists to draft their own plan of government. They responded, as expected, with a proposal that elevated the representative assembly at the expense of the power of the governor and proprietor. Nonetheless, Penn approved this plan of government in 1701, and his colony prospered. Penn's administrative wisdom extended even to land policy: He stipulated that for every five acres of forest cleared, one acre must be left with trees. In his concern for conservation, Penn was at least two centuries ahead of his contemporaries. Penn himself had no interest in actually living in the colony, however, and spent only about five years of his life there.

In 1723, then, Benjamin Franklin entered a permissive, rapidly expanding, highly mobile, and commercially focused society that perfectly suited his ambitions and abilities. He lost no time in capitalizing on his good fortune. Upon awakening from his nap in the Quaker meetinghouse, Franklin proceeded to the printing shop of Samuel Keimer and immediately found employment. Quick, hardworking, and affable, Franklin made friends easily and moved ahead at a phenomenal pace. He became the New World's typical rags-to-riches success story, the creator of a legend that has shaped the aspirations of Americans ever since.

Arriving literally in rags at the age of seventeen, Franklin at twenty-four owned his own printing business and newspaper. At twenty-seven his name was known throughout the colonies as the creator of "Poor Richard," of almanac fame. Three years later, Franklin obtained the clerkship of the Pennsylvania Assembly, a post that proved a stepping-stone to elected membership. By the age of forty-two he had accumulated sufficient wealth to reach his goal of the "free and easy life." Turning the printing business over to a manager, Franklin began new careers as scientist, inventor, statesman, and diplomat.

Benjamin Franklin succeeded not only because he lived in a favorable time and place, but also because of his character and guiding principles. As early as 1726, three years after his arrival in

Philadelphia, Franklin referred in his journal to the necessity of fixing "a regular design in life . . . that, henceforth, I may live in all respects like a rational creature." In language as well as concept, such a statement places Franklin squarely in the Enlightenment. This movement in the history of ideas took recognizable shape in the 1690s with the work of Isaac Newton in the physical sciences and John Locke in the social sciences. Enlightenment thought rested on the assumption that all phenomena operated according to permanent designs or laws. The rational mind could discern these regularities and understand the cause-and-effect relationships that followed from them. According to the Enlightenment credo, everything had an explanation. All problems could be solved. Reason and the scientific method were the keys to knowledge.

Benjamin Franklin made a science of the conduct of his life. He began by fixing an ultimate goal: happiness. For Franklin, the chief components of the happy life were health, wealth, wisdom, and usefulness. He also included the principle of utility in his method for achieving the desired end. If a belief or course of action proved useful in securing happiness, it was good in Franklin's eyes; if not, it was bad. In this system of ethics, there were no other criteria. Vice and virtue, Franklin believed, had little meaning if divorced from the particular time, place, circumstance, and desired result. This was the essence of relativism. Franklin made his judgments according to how something worked; in this emphasis on results, he anticipated the philosophy of pragmatism. More exactly, the growing American tendency that Franklin personified—to judge by performance—was later given formal expression by the pragmatic philosophers. Franklin even extended this attitude to individuals: "Do not inquire concerning a Stranger," Franklin wrote in his *Autobiography,* "what is he? but, what can he do?" Imperfectly executed as this dictate was and is, it nonetheless constitutes one of America's most praiseworthy ideals.

Franklin's *Autobiography* records that in about 1728 he conceived the "bold and arduous project of arriving at moral perfection." The brash confidence of the Enlightenment permeated the plan. Franklin really wished "to live without committing any fault at any time." To carry out the idea, he systematized his beliefs into thirteen "virtues": temperance, silence, order, resolution, frugality, industry, sincerity, justice, moderation, cleanliness, tranquility, chastity, and humility. These were essential, he believed, to attaining happiness. For the purpose of measuring his progress in this direction, he devised a weekly chart on which he recorded his performance. He devoted a week to each of the thirteen virtues and repeated the course four times a year. The whole undertaking simply extended the campaign for self-improvement that Franklin had launched as a teenager in the Boston printing shop.

At first glance, it appears that no two Americans could be more dissimilar than John Winthrop and Benjamin Franklin. The printer's goals and conduct seem to represent the final collapse of Puritan ways. To some extent, this is true, of course. Success in this world, not salvation in the next, anchored Franklin's philosophy of life. And in sharp contrast to the Puritans, he believed that people could improve themselves—even approach perfection—by their own efforts. For Franklin, God's saving grace was the relic of an unenlightened age. Predestination made no sense to the self-made. Franklin also rejected the idea of divinely inspired Scripture as part of his rejection of all systems of fixed moral precepts. "Revelation," he declared, "had . . . no weight with me as such." So much for the Puritans' sacred Bible.

A closer examination of Franklin's philosophy, however, reveals some close parallels to Puritanism. Many of the virtues Franklin adopted on the basis of utility proved to be precisely those prescribed by revelation and stated in Scripture. Franklin saw that the Puritan virtues had utilitarian value, that they were often the means to ends he desired. The *Autobiography* presents Franklin's reasoning succinctly: "Vicious actions are not hurtful because they are forbidden, but forbidden because they are hurtful, the nature of man alone considered [and] . . . it was therefore in everyone's interest to be virtuous who wished to be happy even in this world." Starting from a secular perspective, Franklin arrived at a position much like that reached by Winthrop. Their missions differed, but they pursued them with common means and a common zeal.

Another trait that linked Franklin to the Puritans and partially redeemed him from a degree of self-esteem that bordered on the insufferable was his willingness in the long run to admit failure. After years of effort, Franklin abandoned his campaign for moral perfection. Characteristically, he made his point with an anecdote: A man with a rusty ax, Franklin began, desired to have the whole head as bright as the cutting edge. He took it to a blacksmith who agreed to polish the steel, provided the owner turned the grindstone. The process went on and on, but specks of rust persisted. At last the owner became exhausted and declared that he would take the ax in an unfinished condition. " 'No' says the smith, 'turn on, turn on; we shall have it bright by and by; as yet 'tis only speckled.' 'Yes' says the man, 'but I think I like a speckled ax best.' " So Benjamin Franklin gave up his idea of perfection and concluded he really liked himself best with a few bad habits. Rationalizing his decision on the familiar grounds of usefulness, Franklin pointed out that "a perfect character might be attended with the inconvenience of being envied and hated; and that a benevolent man should allow a few faults in himself, to keep his friends in countenance." While hardly an admission of original sin, Franklin's statement showed he had nonetheless come to terms with human frailty, just as John Winthrop had.

As for his formal religion, Franklin began to question many of the assumptions of traditional Christianity while still a Boston apprentice. He turned initially to deism, whose followers believed that the natural world was God's creation and that its design and function were all the evidence one needed of God's wisdom and power. Indeed, deists rejected all forms of revelation—along with creeds, mysteries, myths, and rituals—as unreasonable and unscientific. The organized church, as the embodiment of arbitrary authority, also suffered eclipse. Deists preferred their truth to be self-evident. They acknowledged a God, but He was a Creator or First Cause—a master mechanic who set the universe in motion and then withdrew to watch it work according to natural laws. Deism, in sum, was a scientific religion for rational people. It suited a young Benjamin Franklin perfectly.

With maturity, however, Franklin's dissatisfaction with deism increased. Observing the conduct of professed deists, he noticed a tendency to make virtue and vice "empty distinctions." The absence of an immediate God dispensing reward and punishment encouraged moral anarchy. "I began to suspect," Franklin commented, "that this doctrine, tho' it might be true, was not very useful." Again considerations of utility shaped Franklin's opinions.

What, then, was a useful religion in Franklin's terms? After considerable reflection, he decided it had to be based on the assumption that a deity or, as Franklin put it, "something" existed, that it governed the world, and that "all crime will be punished and virtue rewarded either here or hereafter." The last point ensured socially acceptable behavior. Perhaps some individuals could sustain their morality without a God, but Franklin believed most people needed Him. "If men are so wicked with religion," he observed, "what would they be if without it?" On another occasion, Franklin wrote to the atheist Thomas Paine that "talking against religion is unchaining the tiger . . . the beast let loose may worry his liberator." Whether real or not, God was useful. Franklin felt the same way about Jesus. Near the end of his life he remarked that, regardless of the truth, he saw no harm in believing Christ to be the Son of God, because it had the "good Consequence . . . of making His Doctrines more respected and better observed." As an afterthought, he added that at the age of eighty-four he was not overly concerned about Jesus and life after death, for "I expect soon an Opportunity of knowing the Truth with less Trouble." The comment struck to the core of Franklin's practical attitude toward religion.

As might be expected, Franklin had little interest in the colony-wide religious upsurge of the 1730s and 1740s known as the Great Awakening. The emotionalism of the revivals offended Franklin's reason, and the emphasis that revivalists like Jonathan Edwards placed on human help-lessness ran counter to his creed of self-help. Franklin did, however, admire and become a lifelong friend of the Reverend George Whitefield. What attracted him was not Whitefield's theology, but his prowess as a public speaker. As for doctrine, Franklin much preferred the position of the liberal opponents of the Awakening, who held that God was forgiving and predestination absurd.

Franklin adroitly shaped his faith to support his style of life. In 1728 he vowed "to be virtuous that I may be happy, that I may please Him, who is delighted to see me happy." The ultimate purpose of religion was not, in Franklin's view, the worship of God or even salvation, but humankind's well-being on earth. Like a warm coat, religion was useful in the here and now. Unwilling to renounce faith, Franklin tailored it to suit his purposes. He stands as a transitional figure between those for whom religion was an obsession and those for whom it was a bore.

During his Philadelphia years, which lasted into the 1750s, Franklin's philosophy was compressed into his most famous publication: *Poor Richard's Almanac.* First published in 1733, the annual quickly developed a colony-wide and even an international reputation. In a real sense, Franklin's almanacs were the first distinctively American literary productions, and they were certainly the best-known American books of their time. "As Poor Richard says" became a preface for maxims throughout the Western world.

To call Richard Saunders, the ostensible author of the almanac, "poor"—as Franklin did—was to camouflage the fact that from the perspective of success, he actually dispensed advice on how to get rich. In 1757 Franklin collected the best of Poor Richard under the title "The Way to Wealth." This how-to-do-it essay became a bible for the ambitious. It preached the gospel of getting ahead. "The sleeping Fox catches no Poultry," Franklin admonished, adding, "There will be sleeping enough in the Grave." Much of Poor Richard is based on the idea that "there are no Gains without Pains." But the almanacs also imply that, unless the effort is guided by intelligence, it will come to nothing. Franklin therefore urged his readers to live simply and frugally: "A fat Kitchen makes a lean will." He also provided advice on the management of money, marriage, and friendship to the end that one's pains may indeed produce gains.

On the basis of the almanacs, it is easy to brand Benjamin Franklin as hopelessly materialistic. After all, "nothing but money is sweeter than honey," as Poor Richard says. Yet there was more to Franklin than mere acquisitiveness. He was not entirely the "snuff-coloured little trap" that his critics (in this case, D. H. Lawrence in 1923) have alleged. Money *was* important for Franklin, but as a means, a tool for other tasks. Reflecting the old Protestant ethic, and revealing in the process another tie with Puritanism, Franklin believed that by being successful and socially useful, people pleased God.

In this sense, the most immediate influence on Franklin's thinking was the Reverend Cotton Mather. A pillar of the Puritan establishment in the late seventeenth and early eighteenth centuries, Mather published a tract in 1710 entitled *Essays to Do Good.* It elaborated on the idea that the Christian "may glorify God by doing of Good for others, and of Good for himself." Franklin encountered Mather's work as a Boston apprentice and took it to heart. His earliest religious creed declared "the most acceptable service of God was doing good to man." Years later, Franklin again acknowledged his intellectual debt to Mather in a letter to Mather's son, in which he said that the *Essays to Do Good* "gave me such a turn of thinking, as to have an influence on my conduct through life; for I have always set a greater value on the character of a doer of good, than on any other kind of reputation; and if I have been . . . a useful citizen, the public owes the

As a printer and a self-made man, Franklin must have been pleased with this handsome lithograph. In elevating moneymaking to the status of an art, it substituted a whole new set of images for those of Winthrop's generation. Such publications promoted the popular image of Franklin as a man obsessed by material concerns—and gave rise to the American reputation for materialism.

advantage of it to that book." As he would judge all things by their usefulness, so Franklin would have himself judged. As preparation, he launched a multifaceted campaign of public service. It became his major altruistic outlet and a primary ingredient in his growing reputation.

Franklin began his career as a "doer of good" in 1727, when he organized a "club for mutual improvement," called the Junto, among Philadelphia's younger artisans and intellectuals. This

The Morning Question, What Good shall I do this Day?	5 6 7	Rise, wash, and address Powerful Goodness; Contrive Day's Business and take the Resolution of the Day; prosecute the present Study: and breakfast?
	8 9 10 11 12	Work.
	12 1	Read, or overlook my Accounts, and dine
	2 3 4	Work.
	5 6 7 8	Put Things in their Places, Supper, Musick, or Diversion, or Conversation,
	9	Examination of the Day.
Evening Question, What Good have I done to Day?	10 11 12	
	1 2 3 4	Sleep

In the autobiography he wrote as an old man, Franklin included this breakdown of his typical day. The legend of Franklin as a person of superhuman discipline and organization has arisen from such evidence. Note this very secular man's way of referring to God, as well as the moralism of his morning and evening questions. Although worlds apart with respect to ends or goals, Franklin and John Winthrop had much in common with regard to means.

harbinger of the Junior Chamber of Commerce had as one of its "standing queries," which Franklin wrote, the problem: "Do you think of any thing at present, in which the Junto may be serviceable to mankind?" The initial project the Junto undertook was Franklin's plan for a circulating subscription library, the first of its kind in American history.

Thereafter, the club became a seedbed for most of Franklin's community improvement efforts. They included a fire-fighting organization, a night watch, and a street-lighting company. Not the least of his contributions was the spearheading of a movement to pave Philadelphia's dusty streets. In 1749 Franklin took the lead in drafting plans for the Pennsylvania Academy, which was opened two years later. Its course of study reflected some of Franklin's practicality and utilitarianism, although less than he would have preferred. In time, the academy evolved into the University of Pennsylvania. A city hospital and improved medical treatment occupied Franklin's abundant energy in the early 1750s. In every case, he contributed his money and his talent for raising money along with his ideas. "Avarice and happiness never saw each other," said Poor Richard, and Franklin did not forget his own maxim. After all, the three-part goal for which one went "early to bed and early to rise"—health, wealth, and wisdom—was only one-third material. And the almanacs just pointed the way to wealth; once arrived, Franklin expected, people should know how to apply their means to worthwhile ends.

The moneymaking talent that freed Franklin to serve his society also gave him the leisure to pursue scientific investigations. American interest in science, or *natural philosophy* as it was more commonly called, received its initial impetus from the newness of the New World. In an unknown land, mere observation was discovery. Botany and zoology, as a consequence, became the mainstays of early American science. Astronomy also ranked high, since the different perspective of North American observers resulted in data of great comparative interest to their English and Continental counterparts. The Puritans proved eager and talented natural philosophers. John Winthrop Jr., who corresponded frequently with Sir Isaac Newton himself, became a charter member of the world's leading scientific organization, the Royal Society, in 1663.

Puritans like the younger Winthrop had no difficulty squaring their science with their religion. Nature was God's handiwork; its processes showed the effect of His guidance. Consequently, to study natural phenomena was to observe the wisdom, power, and glory of God. Science for the Puritan mind was an act of worship. Benjamin Franklin's career as a scientist began with youthful curiosity. He wanted to know not only how things worked, but how such knowledge could be put to use. Young Franklin was an excellent swimmer, for example, but unlike the other boys who used the ponds around Boston, he studied the mechanics of propulsion in water. As a result of these observations, Franklin constructed "oval palettes" for his palms and "a kind of sandals" for his feet—the ancestors of swim fins. He also discovered that a flying kite would draw its holder across a body of water "in a very agreeable manner."

In 1724 Franklin made a trip to London. From the standpoint of his interest in science, the experience proved immensely stimulating. London in the 1720s was riding the crest of the Enlightenment, and English scientist Isaac Newton was the most celebrated figure of the age. As a young man he had developed a body of physical laws known as Newtonian mechanics, which explained gravitation, force, mass, and acceleration. And in addition to developing an ingenious system of mathematics known as the calculus, Newton had broken white light into colors through experiments in refraction. To a young scientist like Franklin, Newton stood alone as the master of Enlightenment thought. Franklin's hope to meet the eighty-two-year-old Newton did not materialize, but he did make contact with other members of the Royal Society. When he returned to Philadelphia in 1726, he brought with him the habits of careful observation and logical analysis. He began to apply them, as his journal shows, on the return voyage.

Back in Philadelphia, Franklin used the Junto as a forum for discussing scientific problems ranging from the nature of sound to the causes of earthquakes. Many of his experiments had practical consequences. His investigations of the circulation of air and the transference of heat led to his invention of the Franklin, or Pennsylvania, stove in the winter of 1739–1740. By 1743 Franklin thought it time that American scientists establish their identity and a means of communication, so he drafted "A Proposal for Promoting Useful Knowledge Among the British Plantations in America." Franklin prefaced the document with the accurate observation that "the first drudgery of settling new colonies, which confines the attention of people to mere necessaries, is now pretty well over." It was also apparent that "there are many in every province in circumstances that set them at ease, and afford leisure to cultivate the finer arts and improve the common stock of knowledge."

The American Philosophical Society, which emerged in 1744 from Franklin's "Proposal," was designed to bring these unoccupied, curious, and intelligent minds together through the medium of the mails. Franklin's utilitarianism was evident in the suggested list of subjects for discussion and correspondence. As deserving of particular attention, he mentioned the production of ciders and wines, the assaying of ores, the draining of meadows, and the clearing of land. More abstract questions had their place, too—particularly in the thought of such members as the botanist John

Bartram and the mathematician Thomas Godfrey, but for the most part the group directed itself to practical questions and applied science—"useful knowledge" in Franklin's terms.

In one notable instance, however, Franklin pursued the truth first; practical applications came later as a by-product. His fascination with electricity began in 1743, when he witnessed some demonstrations by a touring Scottish lecturer. The man could perform remarkable feats with his primitive generator, but he had no idea how it worked. Franklin determined to find out. He bought the Scot's apparatus and devoted his spare time to investigation. After his retirement from the printing business in 1748, he became a full-time scientist. The next four years were filled with electrical experiments. The field was new, and Franklin quickly moved beyond the existing knowledge. Rejecting the prevailing notion of two kinds of electricity, he proposed the idea of a single fluid with two forms, and he coined the terms *positive* and *negative* to describe them. To illustrate his point, he performed the first analysis of the principle of the Leyden jar, an electrical generator and condenser.

Franklin's discoveries, communicated to the European scientific community by Peter Collinson of the Royal Society, attracted immediate and widespread acclaim. Indeed, the slender volume Collinson had published for Franklin was the most widely hailed American publication of the eighteenth century—next to *Poor Richard's Almanac*. Yet on both the intellectual and the popular level, Franklin's reputation as a scientist rested chiefly on his investigation of lightning. As his knowledge of electrical phenomena grew, Franklin began to suspect that lightning was actually electricity. In 1751 he suggested a way of testing the hypothesis by erecting an iron rod on the steeple of a high building. A team of French investigators performed the "Philadelphia experiment" successfully in May 1752. Franklin did not know this, however, when on a sultry evening in June he went into the fields near Philadelphia with his famous kite and key. As a thunderhead approached, Franklin flew the kite, but the first clouds passed overhead with no apparent effect. The second batch of clouds did the job. An electrical charge surged down the string and leaped from the key into Franklin's hand. After rain had wet the string, electricity flowed abundantly into the collecting device. Franklin succeeded on two counts: The hypothesis was confirmed, and the investigator escaped the electrocution that later killed a Swedish scientist engaged in an identical experiment.

Only after several years of work with the theory of electricity did Franklin draw the practical application in the form of the lightning rod. Yet so widely known is this invention that it is commonly believed that Franklin was a tinkerer who experimented in order to produce lightning rods—for sale, of course. Nothing could be further from the truth. Franklin was a "pure" scientist and a good one; he was also a practical man. When the time came, he made the transition from theory to practice, and as in the case of his almanacs, his lightning rods soon appeared in almost every home. Franklin's own version was equipped with bells that clanged when electrically charged, much to the distress of his wife.

The honors Franklin received from his scientific avocation were legion. Harvard, which he had spurned as a critical apprentice, awarded him an honorary degree, as did Yale and the College of William and Mary. Oxford and St. Andrews topped these with advanced degrees, and Franklin quickly added Doctor to his name. The Royal Society conferred a medal and a membership. Yet probably his most cherished honor was his contemporary reputation as "the Newton of electricity." Success did not satiate Benjamin Franklin's inquiring mind, however. In later years, when time permitted, he investigated theoretical problems in astronomy, geology, and botany. He also kept the practical side of his nature alive; he invented a glass harmonica, bifocal eyeglasses, and a "long arm" for grasping books on high shelves.

Many of Franklin's inventions were eminently practical. His invention of bifocal glasses (cutting two pairs of spectacles in half and putting half of each lens in a single frame) enabled him to see long distances when looking forward and to read when looking down.

Franklin's decade of concentration on science, 1743 to 1753, brought many satisfactions, not the least of which was a buoyant feeling of contributing to human progress. Writing to fellow scientist Joseph Priestley, he regretted that he had been born so soon. "It is impossible to imagine," Franklin continued, "the height to which may be carried, in a thousand years, the power of man over matter." Musing on the theme, he forecast the airplane: "We may perhaps learn to deprive large masses of their gravity, and give them absolute levity, for the sake of easy transport." And there were other wonders: "Agriculture may diminish its labour and double its produce; all disease may . . . be prevented and cured . . . and our lives lengthened at pleasure even beyond the antediluvian standard."

The optimism of the Enlightenment bubbles over in such statements. But Franklin was too wise in the ways of men to pretend that science held all the answers. "O that moral science were in a fair way of improvement," he continued to Priestley, "that men would cease to be wolves to one another, and that human beings would at length learn what they now improperly call humanity." With the hope, we may believe, of lessening the wolfish tendency in men and in nations, Franklin turned the energies of his later years more and more to public affairs. Undoubtedly, he also foresaw in statesmanship new levels of success for himself.

In 1751 the voters of Philadelphia elected the best-known member of their community to the Pennsylvania Assembly. For Franklin, this election marked a major triumph. At a time when gentlemen-aristocrats dominated politics, he had climbed the ladder from an apprenticeship. More exactly, Franklin became a one-generation aristocrat, proving in the process the exceptional fluidity of the American social structure. His first important assignment in government came in 1754, when the assembly chose him to be its representative at the Albany Congress. The background of this strange gathering in the wilds of northern New York lay in the tangled world of international relations 3,000 miles away. Ever since the 1690s, France and England had been engaged in a series of wars and hostilities. At stake was the so-called European balance of power. Neither nation wanted the other to gain dominance. North America figured only marginally in the conflict as far as the Europeans were concerned, but for the American colonists, the struggle became vital, because both sides were endeavoring to enlist the assistance of the Indians. For communities on the outskirts of civilization, this brought the prospect of Indians swooping out of the forest for a massacre. Indeed, Indians held the key to power on the North American frontier during the period of European rivalry.

The immediate roots of the Albany Congress lay in France's determination to enhance its position with respect to England after the unsatisfactory Peace of Aix-la-Chapelle ended the War of the Austrian Succession. North America seemed a promising starting place for the French in their renewed quest for power. With the aid of Indian allies, perhaps the French could force

England out of the New World entirely. In the early 1750s, therefore, the French began pushing south from their Canadian stronghold into western New York and along the Appalachian Mountains, building forts and making Indian friends. The prospect of a French–Indian alliance on their unprotected western flank terrorized the British colonists. In a powder-keg atmosphere of rumor and fear, Britain called the Albany Congress in 1754 to counter the threat. Iroquois chiefs from the Six-Nation Confederacy attended, along with representatives from most of the colonies. The goal was to prevent collaboration between the Indians and the French.

For Benjamin Franklin, the Albany Congress provided an opportunity to broach a plan for intercolonial organization—with Great Britain at its center, of course. In those years, Franklin recognized the need for some unity, but only under Great Britain's guidelines. The extent of his devotion to British authority was revealed in a 1751 essay on population growth. Franklin predicted a doubling of the British population in America every twenty-five years and celebrated it as "a glorious market wholly in the power of Britain." That the American colonial population would soon outnumber Great Britain's meant, in Franklin's view, a second British empire centered in the New World. Significantly, Franklin viewed America as the new center of the British Empire. No notion of American independence had crossed his mind in 1751, while he served as joint deputy postmaster-general of North America beginning in 1753, or as he rode to Albany in 1754.

Franklin arrived in Albany with an ambitious idea for an intercolonial organization. His Albany Plan of Union called for the establishment of an intercolonial council with authority over defense, western expansion, and Indian relations. Representing the assemblies of the various colonies and headed by the king's representative, the council would maintain an army and navy, build frontier fortifications, execute Indian treaties, and buy western lands. Funds for these purposes would come from a tax levied by the colonists' representatives. Anticipating later developments in British–American relations, Franklin summarily rejected the idea of taxation without representation as inconsistent with the tradition of English liberty.

The gravity of the crisis in 1754 prompted the Albany delegates to adopt Franklin's plan. But when they carried it back to their respective assemblies, the reception was cool. An American national consciousness was in its infancy. The various colonies still eyed one another suspiciously, particularly with respect to western land claims. In reality, of course, the issue of intercolonial union was academic. Even if the assemblies had cooperated, Britain would certainly have vetoed the proposed organization. It held forth the prospect of too much colonial power and, although few admitted it at the time, of independence. Franklin took the rebuff philosophically. The assemblies, he pointed out, "all thought there was too much prerogative in it, and in England it was judged to have too much of the democratic." For Franklin, the plan was a sensible compromise; its failure revealed that there would be little room for conciliation between Britain and the colonies on questions of sovereignty.

In Pennsylvania the Indian problem of the 1750s sharpened the chronic tension between governor and assembly. William Penn's successors as proprietor lacked his facility for dealing with popular demands, and in a squabble over the tax exemption of his huge landholdings, the current governor refused to pass bills funding frontier defense. With the French and the Indians at the colony's western doorstep, this was a serious matter. Unable to resolve the differences in America, the Pennsylvania Assembly instructed Benjamin Franklin to go to England and plead its case directly with Parliament.

When Franklin sailed for England in 1757 to present the Pennsylvania Assembly's grievance against its governor, he became involved in long-standing problems in the British–colonial relationship. The difficulties centered on the gap between the theory and the practice of colonialism.

Theoretically, colonies were supposed to be the obedient and grateful servants of their mother country. The ideal received economic expression in the theory of mercantilism, according to which colonies were supposed to assist in the maintenance of the favorable balance of trade— a surplus of income over expenses—on which national power was thought to depend. The colonies would supply raw materials to the mother country and consume its manufactured goods. They would neither compete with the industries of the home country nor turn to other nations for supplies and markets. The outposts were to be subservient satellites.

Franklin was well aware of the history of mercantilism in British North America. As early as the 1620s, Parliament had passed laws limiting Virginia's lucrative tobacco trade to England and stipulating that tobacco be carried only on English ships. Beginning with the passage of the first laws in 1651, a body of legislation known collectively as the Navigation Acts spelled out the economic basis of the colonial relationship. Product after product was "enumerated"; that is, its sale or purchase was restricted. To some extent this policy proved advantageous to the American settlements. They enjoyed, after all, a guaranteed market and membership in the Western world's foremost commercial empire. Yet in the minds of the colonists it was security of the feudal variety—purchased at the expense of freedom—and they openly flouted the economic regulations.

Britain occasionally attempted to strengthen enforcement, but bribes and smuggling permitted the colonists to do much as they pleased. In practice, 3,000 miles from home, mercantilism failed. Virginia, for example, sent its tobacco where it could get the highest price, frequently the Netherlands. And the New England merchants who were engaged in a triangular trade involving rum, slaves, and West Indian molasses customarily obtained the latter from the French West Indies in preference to the British islands. The 1733 Molasses Act, designed to curtail this practice, failed completely. Even with the expense of bribing customs agents added to its cost, French molasses was still cheaper than British. Britain fumed but, before 1761, took little action. For the most part, the colonies went their own way, and when Franklin arrived in England in 1757, he became the target of British indignation at the uncooperative colonial members of the empire.

A gap between theory and practice also existed regarding Franklin's immediate mission as Pennsylvania's agent: government. Theoretically, a colony existed under a governor who either represented Parliament and the crown directly or, in the case of chartered or proprietary colonies, ruled at Parliament's pleasure. The governor was in control. He might appoint a few local leaders to a council, and most charters provided for an assembly representing the propertied citizens. Still, in theory, these groups had only advisory roles and were regarded by the British as liberal concessions. Authority resided in England.

Franklin had observed colonial politics long enough to know that, in reality, this theoretical political structure dissolved into more democratic forms. The colonists, in fact, regarded the assembly as their right and as a regularly constituted institution with the job of tempering the governor's will. This it did with a vengeance, using its power to introduce legislation, to tax, and to appropriate money to counter the governor's veto. As a result of this continual skirmishing with the assembly, the position of governor lost power steadily in the eighteenth century. Occasionally an exceptionally strong figure like Franklin's friend Thomas Hutchinson of Massachusetts would halt the trend temporarily. But the erosion of absolute authority in the colonies was irreversible.

Resistance to monarchical authority was not, of course, restricted to the American colonies. In his efforts to curb the power of the Pennsylvania proprietors, Franklin had the support of a tradition of English constitutionalism dating back to the thirteenth century. It had received a major boost in 1688, when the English Whigs, or liberals, deposed King James II on the grounds that he had disregarded the natural human rights of life, liberty, and the possession of

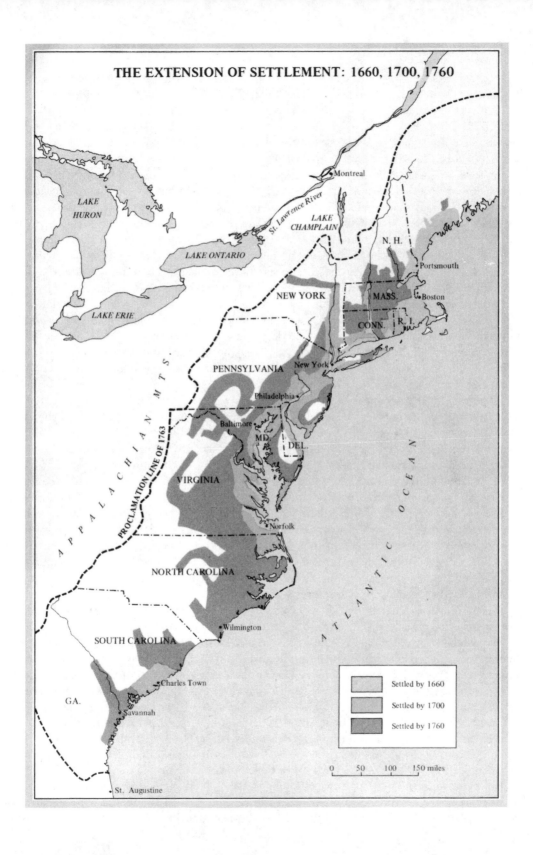

THE EXTENSION OF SETTLEMENT: 1660, 1700, 1760

LAKE
HURON

LAKE ONTARIO

LAKE ERIE

St. Lawrence River

Montreal

LAKE
CHAMPLAIN

N. H.

Portsmouth

NEW YORK

MASS.

Boston

CONN.

R. I.

PENNSYLVANIA

New York

Philadelphia

Baltimore

MD

DEL.

A P P A L A C H I A N   M T S.

PROCLAMATION LINE OF 1763

VIRGINIA

Norfolk

NORTH CAROLINA

A T L A N T I C   O C E A N

SOUTH CAROLINA

Wilmington

GA.

Charles Town

Savannah

St. Augustine

	Settled by 1660
	Settled by 1700
	Settled by 1760

0   50   100   150 miles

property. Immediately following the revolution, John Locke furthered the natural rights theory in his famous *Treatises.* In the eighteenth century, European journalists such as John Trenchard and Thomas Gordon publicized a variety of Lockean liberalism.

By 1760, when Franklin's case finally came to a head at court, a sizable number of Englishmen were jealously guarding their constitutional liberties and closely scrutinizing the conduct of the king. Franklin sensed the mood and took pains to phrase Pennsylvania's case against the governor in terms of "essential liberty" set against the vestiges of feudalism. After months of hearings and haggling, he succeeded in winning his point: The governor's lands would be subject to taxation like those of any man. Franklin's broader objective of eliminating the proprietary authority altogether proved premature. Still, he could declare the British Empire to be founded on "the greatest political structure human wisdom ever yet erected." Time would alter this opinion, but in 1760 Franklin was proud to be a subject of the king.

In 1762 Franklin returned to an America significantly changed from the one he had left five years before. The French and Indian War, which had begun inauspiciously for the British, was nearly over. At the very time Franklin was in Albany at the Congress, a young colonel of the Virginia militia named George Washington had surrendered ignominiously to a French force in western Pennsylvania. General Edward Braddock had repeated this act in 1755. With the advent of the William Pitt ministry two years later, however, England's fortunes had taken a turn for the better. In 1758 James Wolfe and Jeffrey Amherst had captured the French fortress of Louisbourg, and the following year Wolfe took Quebec. Montreal fell September 8, 1760, and with it the entire French empire in North America.

It was a great victory for an imperial-minded Britain, but there were unexpected consequences that boded ill for the future of British colonialism. In the first place, the war had been expensive, and Britain was determined to make the Americans, who had benefited directly from the victory, pay a substantial part of its costs. As a means of raising money, Britain decided to dust off and strictly enforce the old Navigation Acts. Especially after a century of indifference, the tough new policy harbored the seeds of conflict.

The second unpleasant result of Britain's victory became apparent after the Treaty of Paris (1763) eliminated French power from North America. With the enemy gone, the colonists were less dependent on British protection. They could afford to treat British authority less seriously. Instead of serving as their savior from the French and the Indians, Britain seemed more and more an expensive encumbrance. Finally, the French and Indian War created a basis for American unity and American pride. The colonists worked together and played a major role in the victory. Moreover, they saw the British redcoats utterly frustrated by backwoods warfare. If the occasion ever demanded, perhaps even Britain could be defeated.

The combination of Britain's need for revenue and the growth of colonial impatience with parliamentary control led to trouble even before Franklin's return in 1762. Beginning in 1759, Britain had actively attempted to control colonial elections and courts. On top of this, customs agents, using "writs of assistance" to search homes and warehouses, had cracked down on suspected smugglers. A colonial merchant accused of violating the Navigation Acts faced the prospect of being tried in a vice-admiralty court, without a jury, and in faraway Halifax, Nova Scotia. This was tantamount to conviction. Doubtless there were abuses on both sides. Merchants accustomed to being left alone bitterly resented the tightened regulations and redoubled their efforts to avoid them. Britain's officers retaliated with spies, frame-ups, and tight harbor patrols.

Emotions ran especially high over the Sugar Act of 1764, a revenue measure with which Treasury Minister George Grenville hoped to defray the cost of maintaining a standing army in the colonies. Americans liked neither the means nor the end involved. Another sore point of the early 1760s was the campaign of the Church of England to extend its influence in the colonies. With the exception of the first generation of Puritans, Americans distrusted state religions, and the prospect of enforced Anglicanism united all dissenters in opposition. The issue of westward expansion also contributed to the growth of animosity. Britain hoped to delay settlement of the trans-Appalachian region until such time as the Indians could be pacified and orderly procedures established. To this end, the Proclamation of 1763 forbade occupation of the West, and American frontiersmen boiled in anger.

Meanwhile, Pennsylvania was experiencing its own version of discontent in another dispute with its proprietors. Hoping to have the Penns' original charter revoked, the assembly once again dispatched Franklin to London. He arrived in the closing weeks of 1764 and was immediately caught up in the controversy swirling around Grenville's newest proposal, a stamp tax. Planned for enactment in the fall of 1765, it required the purchase of a stamp for every kind of legal document and for newspapers, pamphlets, and even almanacs. At first Franklin accepted the idea calmly, advising a friend that "we might as well have hindered the setting sun." He even recommended an acquaintance as Philadelphia's stamp agent and bought a supply of stamps for his own printing business. But Franklin was out of touch with the American temper on this issue. His fellow colonists regarded the Stamp Act as an outrage. It appeared to the colonists to violate a basic tenet of English constitutionalism and natural rights theory: the sanctity of property. Because Americans were not represented, it was argued, Parliament had no right to take their property through taxation. Again and again the colonists insisted that, if only they could levy their own taxes in their own representative assemblies, they would be willing to go a long way toward meeting Britain's fiscal demands. Otherwise, it was "No taxation without representation." Americans had found a unifying principle.

As the date for instituting the stamp tax approached, some Americans organized boycotts of the offending articles. Others supported an intercolonial Stamp Act Congress, which, after pledging "all due submission" to Parliament, resolved that this did not include acceptance of internal taxes or of juryless admiralty courts. The mood at the gathering was one of firm, united resolve. American nationalism had made considerable gains since Franklin's abortive efforts in Albany eleven years earlier. Still other colonists resorted to violence in that tense autumn of 1765. In Boston a mob destroyed the home of the local stamp agent and threatened his life. He resigned the following day. Observing such developments from England, Franklin also got the message. Repenting of his earlier support of the tax, he prepared to lobby for its repeal. An opportunity arose in February 1766. The House of Commons was holding hearings on the controversial tax, and Franklin appeared to testify. Questioned by several members of Parliament, Franklin made plain that his countrymen would not pay the tax unless compelled by armed force. He also used the occasion to review the events of the past decade. Before 1763, Franklin declared, the colonists had thought their government "the best in the world." They had submitted willingly to parliamentary authority and had been governed easily "at the expense only of a little pen, ink and paper." Not only "respect," but also "affection" had existed for the mother country. Then had come the end of the French and Indian War, the need for revenue, new taxes, and strict enforcement procedures. As a result, Franklin continued, the Americans' attitude was "very much altered." Parliament had betrayed their trust. Franklin concluded his testimony with his conviction that all the colonists desired were their rights as Englishmen, specifically the right of representation in taxing bodies.

At the February hearings many members of Parliament assured Franklin that there was no difference between tax laws and other kinds of legislation. If the colonists accepted the regulation of trade, for instance, they should not resent the Stamp Act. These Englishmen also made it

From Massachusetts to the Carolinas, the American colonists rebelled against the Stamp Act of 1765 as a classic example of taxation without representation. In this scene, sheaves of stamps, or possibly documents bearing them, are being burned on the cobblestones of a town square. The sticks, axes, and pitchforks in the background suggest that the mob was bent on a more violent expression of its displeasure, probably directed against the person and property of the local stamp agent.

clear to Franklin that, although Americans might not have "actual" representation in Parliament, as members of the empire they were "virtually" represented. The colonists' situation, they insisted, was analogous to that of people in England who had lost their personal representative to Parliament as a result of boundary changes but could still count on Parliament as a whole to defend their interests.

Franklin could not accept such reasoning. In his eyes and those of his compatriots, Americans were second-class citizens. They did not enjoy, Franklin insisted, "all the privileges and liberties of Englishmen," and they would rebel before conceding the point. First, however, they would refuse to purchase Britain's manufactured goods and, by means of this economic boycott, would put the power of the purse behind their cause. Franklin made the point neatly in examination form: "Q. What used to be the pride of Americans? A. To indulge in the fashions and manufactures of Great Britain. Q. What is now their pride? A. To wear old cloaths over again, till they can make new ones."

In retrospect, Franklin thought his testimony in Parliament on the Stamp Act "contributed much to its repeal." Actually, the replacement of Grenville by the Marquis of Rockingham, a man who had opposed the stamp tax idea from the beginning, combined with a widespread realization that the act would not work, sealed its fate. In March 1766 the Stamp Act was repealed, to the cheers of grateful Americans. But Franklin knew that the good feeling was premature. Parliament was not about to concede its principle. At the same time it withdrew the stamps, Parliament passed the Declaratory Act, which stated Britain's power to legislate for the colonies in "all cases whatsoever." "In my Opinion," Franklin wrote, "it will meet with the same Opposition, and be attended with the same Mischiefs that would have attended [the Stamp Act]." Again he misjudged public opinion. The Declaratory Act, unlike the Stamp Act, did not touch American pocketbooks. It engendered much less opposition in the colonies, a circumstance that suggests an intimate relationship between economic self-interest and constitutional principle in motivating American resistance to British government.

The situation changed radically, however, in 1767, when Britain's continuing search for revenue led Charles Townshend, Chancellor of the Exchequer, to secure the passage of duties on lead, paint, paper, glass, and tea imported by the colonists. Townshend also took steps to enforce the unpopular Quartering Act of 1765, under which Americans were required to feed and board British soldiers in public facilities. Finally, he expanded the customs service and the hated admiralty courts with the object of putting teeth in the new duties.

Again the colonies exploded. American merchants and consumers devised nonimportation agreements designed to choke off trade with Britain. The plan proved highly effective. Britain not only failed to collect the anticipated duties but also lost thousands of pounds worth of colonial business. In Boston, Samuel Adams's Sons of Liberty rode herd over local commerce, intimidating the royal tax collectors and whoever dared to trade with the British. In response, the British government sent in a regiment of troops in September 1768 to restore order to the city. Tensions grew rapidly between the British army and the rowdy Bostonians. The poorly paid British soldiers made themselves even more unpopular by taking on part-time work at lower wages than local dockworkers and sailors would accept. The poor economy in Boston, caused largely by the boycott on British goods, created a volatile situation between the local working classes and the British soldiers. Locals often gathered to jeer and harass the British army. On March 5, 1770, the first blood of the independence movement was drawn amid this animosity. When a group of local boys began pelting a British sentry with snowballs, an angry crowd gathered to join in the taunting. The other soldiers who answered the sentry's call for help were also showered with snowballs and other debris. After being felled by a piece of brick, one stunned soldier fired his musket into the crowd. The others followed suit. The five people killed by British gunfire on that evening were the victims of what colonists called the Boston Massacre.

For Franklin, who remained in London as agent for several colonies, the clash was deplorable. As a man who made a religion of reason and order, he preferred peace at any price. Yet it was becoming clear to him that "no middle ground can be well maintained. . . . [Either] Parliament has a power to make all laws for us, or . . . it has a power to make no laws for us." He added, "I think the arguments for the latter are more numerous and weighty, than those for the former." This conclusion supported independence, of course, but in company with most of his fellow colonists in the early 1770s, Franklin did not yet regard the prospect seriously. Surely those of goodwill on both sides would smooth out their differences. After all, the colonists were English. They wanted to remain loyal subjects of King George III, whom Franklin as late as 1768 termed "the best King . . . any nation was ever blessed with." If only George would protect their rights from an indifferent Parliament and a rapacious bureaucracy, the empire could enter a golden age.

As the 1770s progressed, however, such hopes became unrealistic. True, the Townshend taxes, except for that on tea, were repealed as the decade began. Yet the British government and society Franklin observed from his London vantage point seemed incapable of effective colonial administration. Bloated from a century of profit making and empire building, most of the English paid little attention to American grievances. Fewer still brought any consideration except profit to the colonial relationship. Again and again Franklin saw the protests and petitions of his compatriots brushed away like so many mosquitoes. Rare indeed were men like Edmund Burke and William Pitt, who with their keen sense of colonial realities could accept some limitation on British authority as the price for retaining any authority at all. As for George III, his empire was simply too large for more than cursory royal attention to American affairs. Franklin probably helped spread the story that the king persistently confused the Himalayas with the Appalachians and the Ganges with the Mississippi.

In the face of such ineptitude, Franklin lost patience and lashed out at what appeared to him to be Britain's mismanagement of the North American empire. The Tea Act of May 1773 was a particular sore point. The measure permitted the giant East India Company to sell tea directly to Americans at an extremely low price. Even with customs duty, the East India Company tea was cheaper than the untaxed product of non-British nations. As Franklin and his contemporaries saw it, the Tea Act was a deliberate attempt on the part of Parliament to make Americans buy taxed tea and thereby implicitly accept the principle of Parliament's taxing authority. Furious, Franklin wrote some tracts designed, in his words, to provide "a Looking-Glass in which some Ministers may see their ugly Faces, and the Nation its Injustice." The first essay was "Rules by Which a Great Empire May Be Reduced to a Small One." The second, "An Edict by the King of Prussia," used a transparent disguise to jab at Britain's edicts. It concluded with an expression of incredulity that a nation "so wise and liberal in its sentiments, so just and equitable towards its neighbors, should, from mean and injudicious views of petty immediate profit, treat its own children in a manner so arbitrary and tyrannical!"

Words came easily to Benjamin Franklin, but his compatriots frequently turned to deeds to express their opposition to British policy. The taxed tea met with a hostile reception as it arrived in America. In some ports citizen groups forced the ships to return to England without unloading their cargoes. Other communities locked the crates of tea in storehouses and defied anyone to remove them for distribution and sale. In Boston, where Samuel Adams and his Committee of Correspondence kept alive a tradition of radicalism, there were more serious consequences.

On December 16, 1773, a band of enraged colonists disguised as Indians boarded the tea ships, hacked open the boxes, and dumped them into Boston Harbor.

The "Boston Tea Party" elicited a mixed reaction. To radical colonial eyes it was a stroke of genius, a way of putting teeth in the American grievances. But for many Americans, and almost all the British, the destruction of the tea was an outright crime. Franklin, who sided with the shocked moderates, branded the tea party "an act of violent injustice" perpetrated on the owners of the tea and demanded "speedy reparation." In Franklin's opinion, the events of December 16 cost the American cause considerable sympathy throughout Europe. From oppressed disciples of natural rights, the Americans had descended to behaving like anarchists and thieves.

Britain's response to the tea party made Franklin change his mind, however. In quick succession early in 1774, Parliament closed the port of Boston, revised the Massachusetts charter to reduce popular sovereignty, curbed the authority of local juries, and appointed General Thomas Gage, the commander of British troops in North America, as governor of Massachusetts Bay.

The colonists labeled these measures the Intolerable Acts, and Franklin agreed that their severity shifted the burden of reconciliation from New World to Old. The Quebec Act added further fuel to the fire. Also passed in 1774, it finally settled the matter of governing the territory won from the French a decade earlier. The act made the governorship a permanent position, abolished representative assemblies of any kind, and encouraged the Roman Catholic Church. Although they were not directly affected, most Americans regarded the Quebec Act as a bad omen, particularly since it applied to all the land west of the Appalachians and north of the Ohio.

Massachusetts's misfortunes generated a wave of sympathy throughout the colonies. The Intolerable Acts created an atmosphere in which the kind of unified action Franklin had dreamed about at Albany twenty years before became feasible, and the First Continental Congress assembled at Philadelphia in September of 1774. Many viewpoints were represented, but the delegates shared a sense of fear, anger, and determination to prevent further loss of their rights as Englishmen and as men. Among the Congress's first actions was the institution of a tight boycott on all trade with Britain. The delegates also voted to support Boston in resisting the Intolerable Acts. Turning to long-range solutions, Joseph Galloway, an old political ally of Franklin's, tried to secure support for an intercolonial assembly to act in conjunction with Parliament as a kind of lower house. If it had been adopted on both sides of the ocean, Galloway's plan might well have averted the impending revolution. American radicals, however, resented its concessions to Parliamentary authority, and the idea failed by a single vote. Franklin was just as glad. He wrote to Galloway early in 1775, "When I consider the extream corruption prevalent among all orders of men in this old rotten state, and the glorious public virtue so predominant in our rising country, I cannot but apprehend more mischief than benefit from a closer union."

But independence for Franklin did not necessarily entail war. He consistently hoped that an adjustment of America's political status could be negotiated in the conference room by diplomats rather than contested on the battlefield by soldiers. Divorce, not murder, was the sensible alternative in his opinion, and during his final months in England he poured all his skill into this approach. The current ran the other way, however. Sentiment on both sides was hardening rapidly. Moreover, Franklin operated in 1775 under a cloud of suspicion cast by his recent involvement in the publication of some purloined letters of former Massachusetts governor Thomas Hutchinson. Sensing the futility of his compromise efforts and fearing imprisonment or worse if he remained in London, Franklin sailed for Philadelphia on March 20. While he was in midocean, full-scale war began in Massachusetts between Gage's troops and amateur colonial soldiers massed, thanks in part to Paul Revere's ride, at Lexington, Concord, and along the road to Boston.

Franklin landed in Philadelphia on May 5, 1775, and before he had unpacked, he was elected a delegate to the Second Continental Congress. This body found itself in charge of governing a group of rebellious colonies. Its first order of business was providing for the common defense. Franklin and his colleagues organized the Massachusetts militia into the Continental Army, appointed George Washington commander-in-chief, and issued paper money to finance the fighting.

Before Washington could take charge, however, Gage's force at Boston engaged the colonists in the Battle of Bunker (actually, Breed's) Hill on June 17. The Americans retreated, but not before engaging in a fierce resistance. Following reports of the action closely, Franklin concluded that the British must be "convinc'd by this time, that they have Men to deal with, tho' unexperienced, and not yet well arm'd." The Battle of Bunker Hill also pushed Franklin further toward a commitment to independence. Contemplating the ravages of the British in Charlestown, Massachusetts, following the colonial retreat, he remarked to a friend in July 1775, "I think I am not half so reconcileable now, as I was a Month ago." To an English correspondent, however, Franklin revealed a rare streak of emotional anger: "You have begun to burn our Towns, and murder our People.—Look upon your Hands! They are stained with the Blood of your Relations!" Yet Franklin and the Second Continental Congress only slowly abandoned the hope of reconciliation. In July the Congress addressed a petition to George III acknowledging its loyalty and begging for a restriction of Parliament's power over Americans to matters of trade only. If this were to happen, the petition made clear, Americans would gladly remain British.

Franklin supported the July petition and regarded it as a "Golden Opportunity" for Britain. Yet he was realistic. He knew the climate of opinion in that nation, and in his judgment, "She has neither Temper nor Wisdom enough to seize" the possibility of reunion. He was right. George III and his ministers were determined to put the unruly and ungrateful colonists in their place and insisted on Parliament's full power to make laws and assess taxes. Britain replied to the petition by adding 25,000 troops to its North American force.

By 1776 Franklin and many other American colonists were convinced that independence offered the only long-term solution to their problems with Britain. But untying the knot promised to be painful. Revolution was a serious matter in the late eighteenth century. The idea of the divine right of kings, of their absolute sovereignty, lingered on in the popular mind as a legacy from the Middle Ages. One did not defy a monarch casually. Moreover, the cultural background of most Americans was English. Mental as well as physical preparation for separation had to be made. Thomas Paine's *Common Sense,* published in January 1776, helped in this respect. Franklin contributed directly to the appearance of the tract, since his letters of introduction had smoothed Paine's move to the colonies from England two years earlier. Franklin also provided Paine with notes and documents for writing a summary of the British–American relationship. Indeed, when *Common Sense* appeared anonymously, many supposed that Franklin was the author, but the emotional tone of the piece should have dissuaded readers. Paine lambasted kings as the oppressive relics of an unenlightened age. Monarchy, he insisted, was inconsistent with liberty; Americans should pursue the republican way as more in keeping with their respect for the individual.

June of 1776 found Franklin enmeshed in the affairs of the Continental Congress. His tasks included membership on a committee charged with the preparation of a declaration of independence. Thomas Jefferson drafted a document that incorporated many of Franklin's suggestions—the most important involving an opening statement of principles with which the rebels hoped to justify their course of action to the rest of the world and to themselves.

Jefferson wrote, "We hold these truths to be sacred and undeniable, that all men are created equal, that they are endowed by their Creator with certain unalienable Rights, that among these,

The newly independent American colonies could not have chosen a better representative to send to France in 1776 than Benjamin Franklin. French society was dazzled by the unassuming wit and wisdom of the man who came from the "wilds" of America. At elegant receptions such as the one depicted here, Franklin gave his nation's appeal for support in its revolution a mighty assist.

are Life, Liberty, and the pursuit of Happiness." Franklin argued successfully for substituting "self-evident" for "sacred and undeniable." It was a significant and fortuitous change. Franklin used a term from science and based the rights on reason. Everyone, he implied, could investigate and prove the proposition that God-given rights are rational. Franklin made natural rights sacred because they were true, whereas in Jefferson's version they were true because they were sacred. It was a change consistent with both the character of Franklin and the experience of his compatriots.

On July 2, 1776, the Continental Congress adopted Richard Henry Lee's motion for independence. Two days later it approved the Declaration of Independence. At the signing ceremony, John Hancock supposedly warned, "We must be unanimous . . . we must all hang together." "Yes," Franklin replied, "we must, indeed, all hang together, or most assuredly we shall all hang separately." With the deed now done, the rebels set about the enormous task of justifying their action with success. Among the most pressing needs was a military and financial alliance with a foreign power. France, the chronic opponent of Britain in the eighteenth century, offered the best prospects, and late in 1776 Benjamin Franklin once again received his country's call for help: Would he, nearly seventy years old, join a delegation to Paris? "I am but a fag end," Franklin replied with characteristic understatement, but "you may have me for what you please." Franklin's record in France showed that he retained considerable vitality. Arriving in December of 1776, he was immediately swept up in a wave of popular adulation. The French, who knew Franklin from his almanac and his electrical papers, regarded him as a homespun disciple of the Enlightenment, a kind of noble savage, an American Socrates. The envious John Adams, who joined the American delegation when Franklin's popularity had peaked, observed, "His reputation was more universal than that of Leibnitz or Newton, Frederick or Voltaire. . . . His name was familiar . . . to such a degree that there was scarcely a peasant chambermaid or scullion in a kitchen who was not familiar with it, and who did not consider him as a friend to human kind. . . . They seemed to think he was to restore the Golden Age." Hardly one to let such a chance slip by, Franklin wore a little fur cap and played the role of backwoods sage to the hilt. He reaped dividends both romantic and diplomatic. The latter climaxed in a treaty of alliance with the French government, signed February 6, 1778, four months after the key American victory in the Saratoga campaign.

French aid sealed England's fate in the American war. A series of campaigns in the central and southern colonies led Charles Cornwallis's British force to a dead end on the Yorktown Peninsula in Virginia, with George Washington in pursuit and a French fleet offshore. Surrender came October 19, 1781.

With the fighting finally over, Franklin turned to the more congenial task of peacemaking. His frame of mind is revealed in a letter to an old English friend: "Let us now forgive and forget." Both countries, he believed, could help each other move on to great if separate futures. As one of the official negotiators of the peace, Franklin was instrumental in bringing about the agreement of September 3, 1783. It recognized the United States as a sovereign nation with a northern boundary along the Great Lakes–Saint Lawrence waterway and a western one at the Mississippi River. Spain remained on the south and the west, and Britain retained Canada, but the first nation independent of a European power had been carved from the New World. Franklin, for one, looked forward to a brilliant future. He participated in the Constitutional Convention of 1787, which restructured the federal government of the United States.° According to Thomas Jefferson, Franklin took a moment of the closing session to call the assembly's attention to the painting of a sun on the back of President George Washington's chair. "I have often and often," he declared, ". . . looked at [it] . . . without being able to tell whether it was rising or setting. But now, at last, I know that it is a rising . . . sun."

Later in 1787, Franklin focused his attention on the increasingly troubling issue of black slavery in the new nation. Accepting the presidency of Pennsylvania's antislavery society, Franklin, who in 1775 had participated in an organization to aid free blacks held illegally, now roundly condemned what Virginian George Mason dubbed as "the peculiar institution." Although in the 1780s the storm clouds of sectionalism were on the distant horizon, Franklin, like George Mason, feared that slavery would someday tear the United States apart.

America changed greatly during Benjamin Franklin's lifetime. He was born in 1706 into a society that still defined its purpose largely in spiritual terms, but the old Puritanism was losing its hold. Yet Americans were loath to lose the messianic role assumed by the Puritans; a mission that lent dignity and significance to their endeavor in the wilderness. As a people on the outskirts of civilization, they both wanted and needed the buoyant feeling of being singled out to lead humanity to a better world. As a result, Americans groped throughout the eighteenth century for a new mission. They found it in the Enlightenment concept of natural rights. Liberty, rather than salvation, became the new goal. Success, rather than salvation, motivated Franklin's society. He died in 1790 in a society that had turned from building a holy community to building a free and prosperous one. The good life had replaced the godly one.

°For a discussion of the Constitution of 1787, the Bill of Rights, the Articles of Confederation, and the government that preceded them, see pp. 118–119.

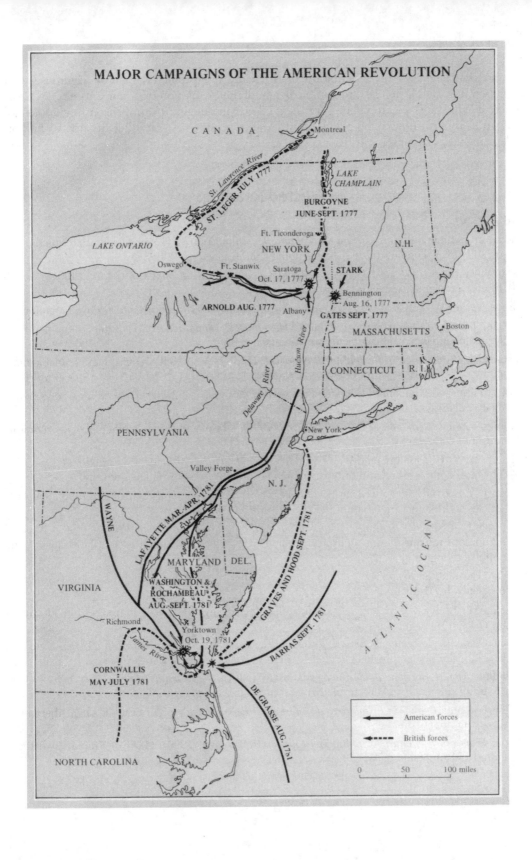

MAJOR CAMPAIGNS OF THE AMERICAN REVOLUTION

CANADA

Montreal

St. Lawrence River

ST. LEGER JULY 1777

LAKE CHAMPLAIN

BURGOYNE
JUNE-SEPT. 1777

Ft. Ticonderoga

LAKE ONTARIO

NEW YORK

N.H.

Oswego

Ft. Stanwix

Saratoga
Oct. 17, 1777

STARK

Bennington
Aug. 16, 1777

ARNOLD AUG. 1777

Albany

GATES SEPT. 1777

MASSACHUSETTS

Boston

Hudson River

Delaware River

CONNECTICUT

R.I.

PENNSYLVANIA

Valley Forge

New York

N.J.

WAYNE

LAFAYETTE MAR.-APR. 1781

MARYLAND

DEL.

GRAVES AND HOOD SEPT. 1781

ATLANTIC OCEAN

VIRGINIA

WASHINGTON &
ROCHAMBEAU
AUG.-SEPT. 1781

Richmond

James River

Yorktown
Oct. 19, 1781

BARRAS SEPT. 1781

CORNWALLIS
MAY-JULY 1781

DE GRASSE AUG. 1781

NORTH CAROLINA

	American forces
	British forces

0   50   100 miles

Nobody reflected this redefinition more clearly nor promoted it more vigorously than Benjamin Franklin. When he wrote at the height of the Revolution that "our Cause is the Cause of all Mankind, and we are fighting for their Liberty in defending our own. Tis a glorious task assign'd us by Providence," he echoed John Winthrop. America was still a city upon a hill, but with a new message for the world.

Selected Readings

The Person

Breitwieser, Mitchell Robert: *Cotton Mather and Benjamin Franklin* (1989). Concentrates on the idea of "self" to explain how these men exemplified different views of life.

Carr, William G.: *The Oldest Delegate: Franklin in the Constitutional Convention* (1991). Details Franklin's role in framing the Constitution.

°Crane, Verner W.: *Benjamin Franklin and a Rising People* (1954). A short, interpretive biography.

Durham, Jennifer L.: *Benjamin Franklin: A Biographical Companion* (1997). Subjects and people in Franklin's life listed alphabetically and discussed in brief.

Isaacson, Walter: *Benjamin Franklin: An American Life* (2003). A well-organized and readable biography.

Jacobs, Wilbur (ed.): *Benjamin Franklin: Statesman, Philosopher or Materialist* (1972). A collection of analytical essays.

Jennings, Francis: *Benjamin Franklin: Politician* (1996). A brief and readable biography incorporating recent historiography.

Labaree, L. W., W. J. Bell Jr., and W. B. Willcox (eds.): *The Papers of Benjamin Franklin* (1959–1978). The most complete and authoritative multivolume collection of Franklin's writing.

Lemay, J. A. Leo (ed.): *Reappraising Benjamin Franklin: A Bicentennial Perspective* (1993). Scholarly articles addressing various issues in Franklin's life and times.

°Lemisch, L. Jesse (ed.): *Benjamin Franklin: The Autobiography and Other Writings* (1961). A useful edition of Franklin's famous self-portrait, along with selections from his scientific, religious, and political thoughts.

Morgan, Edmund S.: *Benjamin Franklin* (2002). Another succinct and thoughtful colonial American biography by Morgan.

Randall, Willard: *A Little Revenge* (1984). Examines the stormy relationship between Franklin and his loyalist son William.

Seavey, Ormond: *Becoming Benjamin Franklin: The Autobiography and the Life* (1988). Examines Franklin's autobiography in light of eighteenth-century intellectual consciousness.

Tourtellot, Arthur Bernon: *Benjamin Franklin: The Shaping of Genius, The Boston Years* (1979). A careful study of Franklin's formative years in Boston and Philadelphia.

Wright, Esmond: *Benjamin Franklin and American Independence* (1966). Franklin's contributions to the revolutionary process.

Wright, Esmond: *Benjamin Franklin: His Life as He Wrote It* (1990). Many of Franklin's writings, edited and annotated by Wright.

°Available in paperback

The Period

Anderson, Douglas: *The Radical Enlightenments of Benjamin Franklin* (1997). Analysis of the Enlightment writings that influenced Franklin.

°Bailyn, Bernard: *Ideological Origins of the American Revolution* (1966). Traces the intellectual roots of independence.

°Bridenbaugh, Carl, and Jessica Bridenbaugh: *Rebels and Gentlemen: Philadelphia in the Age of Franklin* (1942). A social history that emphasizes the development of the American city.

Bushman, Richard L.: *From Puritan to Yankee: Character and Social Order in Connecticut, 1690–1765* (1967). A case study of a broad transformation in values and behavior.

Cohen, I. Bernard: *Science and the Founding Fathers: Science in the Political Thought of Jefferson, Franklin, Adams, and Madison* (1990). Analysis of the use of scientific thought and application in documents such as the Declaration of Independence and the Constitution.

Gipson, Lawrence H.: *The British Empire Before the American Revolution* (15 vols., 1939–1970). The standard source for colonial political history.

Greene, Jack P. (ed.): *The Reinterpretation of the American Revolution, 1763–1789* (1968). A collection of significant assessments of the revolutionary era.

°Hindle, Brooke: *The Pursuit of Science in Revolutionary America* (1956). A thorough examination of eighteenth-century American science.

Hofstadter, Richard: *America at 1750* (1971). Examines American civilization at the approximate midpoint of Franklin's life.

Kammen, Michael: *People of Paradox: An Inquiry Concerning the Origins of American Civilization* (1972). A social and intellectual history of Franklin's America.

Kelley, Robert: *The Cultural Pattern in American Politics: The First Century* (1979). A tracing of the rising ethnic and political tensions within the British colonies.

May, Henry F.: *The Enlightenment in America* (1976). Explores the philosophical and scientific impulses to which Franklin contributed significantly.

°Miller, John C.: *Origins of the American Revolution* (1957). A reliable general survey of the road to independence.

°Morgan, Edmund S.: *The Birth of the Republic* (1956). A clear and readable interpretation of the American Revolution.

For Consideration

1. What factors compelled young Benjamin Franklin to leave New England? How was his experience similar to that of many other colonists who made their way to the Middle Atlantic region in the early 1700s?

2. In what ways was Pennsylvania the ideal setting for a person of Franklin's initiative, work ethic, and intellect?

3. Franklin's views on religion underwent several transformations during the course of his life. How did those changing views reflect the intellectual and social movements of the era?

4. How did Franklin's scientific interest and writings draw strongly from the philosophy and practice of the Enlightenment?

5. In the 1750s Franklin was a loyalist to British rule. By the mid-1770s he was a willing revolutionary. Summarize the events that led to this transformation.

Chapter 4

Abigail Adams

Abigail Adams paused, the letter to her husband half completed. It was March 31, 1776, and the Revolutionary War was already under way. John Adams was in Philadelphia, working with the other delegates to the all-male Second Continental Congress to plan a new form of government for the loosely united colonies. It was this fact that gave Abigail pause. Thirty-two at the time, she had long been a vigorous advocate of American independence and the ideology of natural rights. Now she was obliged to face the meaning of those concepts in terms of American society. All men might be created equal, but women, quite plainly, were not. As Abigail saw it, women were to American men what the American colonies had been to Britain. And so, completing the letter, she implored John to "remember the Ladies, and be more generous and favourable to them than your ancestors." Indeed, she continued, if the new government did not temper the "unlimited power" men enjoyed, "the Laidies . . . are determined to foment a rebelion, and will not hold ourselves bound by any Laws in which we have no voice, no Representation." This was precisely the argument in use by revolutionary leaders such as John Adams to justify the end of colonialism. Concluding her letter, Abigail Adams urged that men stop calling themselves "Masters" and treating women as "vassals of your Sex."

These words were partly in jest, to be sure—a clever tease of her partner in a most successful marriage. Abigail Adams was too much a product of her time and place to plan a social revolution. For the most part, she worked contentedly within the limits prescribed for her sex by custom. This meant that the closest she would ever come to the weightiest issues of her time would be in thousands of letters. Of course, a large part of this correspondence was directed to America's second and sixth presidents, her husband and her son. Still, it remains a revealing commentary on this part of American history that one of its most able citizens is best known only for writing letters.

Weymouth, Massachusetts, exuded so much stability in 1744, the year of Abigail Smith's birth, that it would have been difficult to predict the changes that, within a lifetime, would transform the country and the woman. The town dated back to 1623. It had been one of the first "plantings" beyond the original settlement at Plymouth. The Pilgrims had simply fanned out along the shore of Massachusetts Bay, and Weymouth was on the way toward the good harbor at Boston. Abigail's father, William Smith, served the village as its minister. Like most of the leaders of eighteenth-century Massachusetts, Smith held a degree from Harvard. He answered the "call" to the Weymouth pulpit in 1734.

The next decade proved exciting for anyone involved in the ministry in New England. The religious revival known as the Great Awakening was gathering force. In 1733 in Northampton, Massachusetts, an intense young minister named Jonathan Edwards preached the first of his "hellfire" sermons. Edwards's theology revived the harsh doctrines of original Calvinism and brought to the fore transformations that had been developing in Christianity since the days of John Winthrop and Anne Hutchinson.

Edwards's emotional and evangelical oratory indeed harked back to Hutchinson's mystical message of receiving the Holy Spirit into the soul. Edwards was determined to use English philosopher John Locke's theory—that human beings were a blank slate at birth, ready for the input of data—as a starting point for his message. His sermons emphasized the utter depravity of humans and warned of the vast differences between the torturous existence in eternal hell and the everlasting joy of eternal heaven. By making his listeners feel the agony of God's absence, both in life and in the hereafter, Edwards pounded in the message that those who did not undergo emotional conversion and completely give themselves over to God could expect to burn in eternal hell. Edwards, a Congregational minister himself, attacked his own church for spreading Christian complacency through covenant faith and thus promoting human depravity. Covenants, by which the Puritan elect could expect to be rewarded for leading a moral life, were too convenient for Edwards. They gave Christianity a quiet, nonproselytizing complacency that he deplored.

The Reverend William Smith disagreed. In the tradition of orthodox Puritan ministers, he believed that religion was important for keeping people moral on earth as well as for saving them after death. Most Puritan ministers were not evangelistic, however, and, nearly a century after Winthrop's time, still resisted the overdemocratization that Edwards's religious fervor promoted. Moreover, many ministers, including Smith, were moving away from the stark Calvinism of Edwards and toward a more intellectual, less emotional, and more rational concept of God. Their true religion was marked by reason, not by the emotional outpourings characteristic of the Great Awakening. Abigail Smith grew up accepting the faith of her father. She never experienced the kind of violent conversion the revivalists prized, but she never doubted her eventual salvation. Religion, for Abigail, had utilitarian value. It provided the moral guidance essential to a happy life.

The Great Awakening brought conflict to many New England congregations. Some ministers lost their jobs, but Reverend Smith presided at Weymouth for forty-nine years. He avoided controversy by not publishing his sermons or engaging in theological hairsplitting. An easygoing, practical man, Smith tended to measure the success of his religious messages by how they influenced the day-to-day lives of his parishioners. But he never forgot, or let his children forget, that God presided over both their destiny and that of their country. The resulting tendency to justify personal and national decisions in terms of God's will was understandable.

Abigail's mother, Elizabeth Quincy, had married Reverend Smith in 1740. Her family roots went back to the Puritan founding fathers, including the Winthrops, and even to a signer of the Magna Carta (1215). Abigail was the second of four children. The Smith family had two black slaves, but "Nabby," as Abigail was nicknamed, grew up without the pretension that her status exempted her from household chores. In sharp contrast to the situation that was emerging on the southern plantation, upper-class New England families taught their daughters the virtues of usefulness. Idleness verged on being a sin.

Even as first lady, Abigail took pleasure in meeting domestic responsibilities. In Europe she mingled uncomfortably with the members of a leisure class to whom work seemed insulting. Puritanism might have paled as a theology by the end of the eighteenth century, but it remained a powerful influence on values and behavior. In this regard, Abigail had much in common with her contemporary, Benjamin Franklin.

Even for a well-to-do girl of the 1740s like Abigail, education was uncertain at best. A full 50 percent of American women of this era could not sign their names or read a sentence from the Bible. The public schools, mandated by law for every Massachusetts town, were for boys only. Occasionally, a woman might gather local girls in her home for informal instruction in basic reading and writing. Simple math might be taught to facilitate the keeping of accurate household records. But even this basic training generally ended at the age of eight or ten. A very wealthy family might engage a tutor to "polish" a girl beyond this point. The standard subjects were music, French, and possibly painting, intermixed with a bit of history and literature. The point of this education was to produce interesting wives rather than competent citizens. Latin and Greek, the languages that defined a well-educated person in the eighteenth century, were hardly ever taught to women. In later years, when Abigail Adams received letters with classical phrases, she was obliged to seek the help of her male children as translators.

The basis of this sexual discrimination in early American history was complex. Part of it was rooted in misconceptions about male and female physiology. It was assumed that the female intellect was inferior to the male. Prolonged mental effort was considered not only unnecessary for females but physically dangerous. In addition, there was the question of appropriateness. The role of women in Abigail Adams's society was almost exclusively defined—by women as well as men—as domestic. Wives and mothers, or unattached spinsters, did not need formal education. Since they could not vote or preach or hold public office, and since very few entered a business or profession, education was merely ornamental.

In the eighteenth and nineteenth centuries, these attitudes coalesced into what social historians subsequently labeled the "cult of domesticity." Its cornerstone was the conviction that a woman's place, or "sphere," was in the home. It is important to remember that in early American society, this idea lacked the insulting connotations it might arouse today. "Home" was sacred, a sanctuary from the world. It followed that "homemakers" were prized as the foundations of nothing less than civilization. The cult of domesticity accorded American women great importance. It did, however, keep them narrowly channeled.

The "cult of true womanhood," which also emerged during revolutionary times, helped stereotype sex roles and led to discrimination against women. According to this idea, the attractiveness of women varied to the degree that they were ladies. The ladylike ideal entailed extreme modesty, an emphasis on the emotions as opposed to the intellect, and a general helplessness in any relationship with any male. The only edge the cult conceded to women was in the matter of morality: Let men act and let women worry about the ethics of the deeds.

It was to Abigail Adams's credit, and that of her parents and husband, that she managed to transcend these concepts to become one of the most learned and spirited women of her day. The process began very early. As a minister's daughter, she grew up in a household that prized books and intelligent discourse. William Smith recognized his daughters' intelligence and made their education a serious personal responsibility. Along with her two sisters, Nabby was first taught to read and then encouraged to explore the library of the parsonage at Weymouth. There she met Shakespeare, Milton, Pope, and, in translation, the Greek and Latin classical writers. She read theology, history, and political theory (John Locke) and taught herself French. Abigail was a sickly child and spent much of the New England winter indoors with books. To her lifelong embarrassment, her penmanship, spelling, and "pointing" (punctuation) lagged behind formal standards, but her mind and intellectual interests blossomed. Indeed it was ironic, in view of the prevailing social ideas, that Abigail's only brother proved to be far less intelligent and ambitious. The fact that he did not gain church membership or attend Harvard was a constant source of disappointment to the family. Yet Abigail apparently never questioned the rules that kept her out of college regardless of her ability. She did, however, make the improvement of women's educational opportunities one of the major concerns of her later life.

In 1759, when she was fourteen, Abigail was admitted to membership in her father's church. At the time she was, by all reports, a curious and spirited, if not stubborn, teenager with piercing brown eyes made the more arresting by her clear, pale skin. Small in stature, she was barely five feet tall. Some family members and friends deprecated her fascination with books as unbecoming to a lady. Others mistook her forthrightness for a lack of "delicacy"—a quality regarded as a staple of "true womanhood." But her independence pleased her Grandmother Quincy, who, with an interesting metaphor, said "wild colts make the best horses."

Of course the teenage Abigail was hardly wild by contemporary standards. The biggest events in her life were trips to her aunt and uncle's home in Boston, a growing city that made Weymouth seem the quiet country village it in fact was. On these journeys, which might last for several weeks (there was, after all, no school to miss), Abigail met several young women with whom she became lifelong friends. They corresponded in an ornate prose designed to display their wit and wisdom. As for men, Abigail chose as her model Richard Cranch, a learned and fun-loving English immigrant who married her sister Mary in 1762. In retrospect, Abigail attributed to Cranch "my early taste for letters. . . . He it was who put proper Bookes into my hands." She meant the work of James Thomson, a contemporary English poet, who dealt with the joys and frustrations of the human condition and the importance, through faith in God, of acceptance. Abigail also devoured the novels of Samuel Richardson, such as *Pamela* and *Clarissa*. These books dealt quite frankly with topics of increasing importance to her: personal identity, sexuality, and marriage. In Richardson's *Sir Charles Grandison* she encountered a "man of true honour" and undoubtedly fantasized about being his wife. Someone like Grandison, it seemed, could protect a woman and still delight in the development and application of her intelligence. Marriage under other conditions appeared to be unpalatable in the extreme.

Abigail Smith was fifteen when John Adams, a twenty-four-year-old struggling lawyer, appeared in Weymouth, courting Abigail's cousin. It was a case of hate at first sight, of like initially repelling like. Adams's diary reports that the "S Girls" (Abigail and her sisters) lacked sufficient "tenderness" and "fondness." They seemed too intelligent to make good wives of the traditional mold. But Adams did judge them "Wits." For her part, Abigail saw John as short, chubby, opinionated, and overly talkative. But he was smart and a friend of Richard Cranch. Eventually John learned how to be irresistible: He brought Abigail books and discussed them with her. Here was a man, she began to think, prepared to accept her as an intellectual equal.

Adams's mind was changing too. By the end of 1761 he had stopped courting the cousin and become interested in the middle "S Girl." His diary noted that Abigail was "a constant feast . . . prudent, modest, delicate, soft, sensible, obliging and active." Seeking perhaps to force the lady into the appropriate stereotype for marriage, Adams may well have overstressed the first six qualities. But, covertly, he admired the "active" Abigail, particularly her "Habit of Reading, Writing and Thinking." By 1763 admiration had blossomed into love, and there was talk of marriage. According to family legend, Mrs. Smith had reservations about the parentage and prospects of the future president, but she eventually accepted the ambitious young lawyer.

The next year and a half was difficult for the young lovers. Adams worried about his financial competency and reluctantly put off the wedding day. Then a smallpox epidemic struck eastern Massachusetts. Because he traveled frequently on legal business, Adams decided to undergo the then risky procedure of inoculation. This amounted to deliberately infecting a patient with a theoretically mild case of the disease. Choosing inoculation represented a vote of confidence in medical science, but many New Englanders remained skeptical. Mrs. Smith, for example, would not allow Abigail to be inoculated with her fiancé, and his obligatory seclusion for six weeks elicited a flow of love letters. In an effort to kill germs, John smoked his letters before mailing them. Tom, the Smiths' slave, smoked them again before passing them to Abigail.

Physical attraction and passion constituted another problem for Abigail and John. The supervision of courting couples was less intense than it had been a century earlier, and the pair had ample time to be alone. Abigail even accompanied John on one of his business trips to the courts of western Massachusetts. She knew that hasty marriages and "seven-month pregnancies" were commonplace among her contemporaries and were socially acceptable. But she also knew the severe stigma attached to unwed mothers, some of whom killed themselves or their child out of shame. Moreover, birth control technology was primitive. Finally, Abigail was a minister's daughter with strong moral convictions. John apparently shared them, though not without diffi-culty. On one occasion when a snowstorm prevented him from visiting Weymouth, he thanked the weather "for keeping me at my Distance." His attraction to Abigail, he continued, was like that of "the steel and the Magnet." In the end, the lovers waited for sex—but, on the evidence of their firstborn child, only a matter of hours after their wedding.

The marriage of Abigail Smith and John Adams took place in Weymouth on October 25, 1764. Abigail was nineteen. Her willingness to opt for such an early union might seem inconsistent with her intelligence and her willfulness. But she was also a woman of her time. She knew that for a woman of her social and economic standing in the 1760s, marriage represented the only real option. Girls like Abigail Smith grew up assuming they would marry; not to do so was to fail as a woman and a person, as the standing jokes about "old maids" attested. There was simply no place in eighteenth-century America for single women. The whole economy and social order revolved around the household. If a woman did not find a husband, she had to remain under her father's roof or move in with a sister and brother-in-law. Honorable women just did not live alone. Neither did they take jobs. A few, to be sure, kept shops or offered services, but successful businesswomen were so exceptional as to be remarkable in colonial America. Eliza Lucas Pinckney, for example, achieved widespread notice when she introduced the cultivation of indigo (a blue dye) into South Carolina agriculture. At one point, Pinckney operated seven plantations—but she began her horticultural experiments on her father's farm and finished them on her husband's.

The legal and financial relationship of women and men was another social reality Abigail Smith had to confront at the time of her marriage. Under English common law, marriage took two persons and made them one: the husband. Sir William Blackstone, whose *Commentaries on English Law* appeared the year after Abigail's wedding, noted that "the very being or legal existence of the woman is suspended during the marriage." Under *coverture,* as this doctrine was called, a wife lost all her rights. She could not legally own property, not even her own clothing. She had no rights over her children. She could not sue in the courts, so that the institution of divorce proceedings by the woman was virtually impossible. Even the money she might make as an independent worker belonged to her husband.

This blatant inequality derived from the long-standing tradition, dating perhaps from the hunting mode of life, that the man "provided" and the woman "applied," or utilized, the provisions. Related was the equally hallowed concept, implicit in the "Adam's rib" theory of female genesis, that happiness in a marriage depended on absolute obedience of the wife to the husband. The advice of Dr. Benjamin Rush, a contemporary of John Adams, to a young woman contemplating marriage spoke clearly to the point: "From the day you marry, you must have no will of your own. The subordination of your sex to ours is enforced by nature, by reason, and by revelation." Rush realized that this situation "will often require unreasonable sacrifices," but he was convinced that "it must produce the most happiness to both parties." The assumption that subordination spelled happiness probably reconciled many women to tyrannical and loveless relationships. It was a rare eighteenth-century American woman who could say with the articulate, well-read, and wealthy New Englander, Eliza Southgate, "I am at liberty to refuse those [suitors] I don't like, and . . . I have firmness enough to brave the sneers of the world and live an old maid, if I never find one I can love."

Abigail Smith might well have agreed with Southgate, but she was fortunate to find a man she loved and one who regarded and respected her as an intellectual and economic equal. A sign of the success of their relationship is the fact that they could communicate freely on the sensitive subject of women's rights. One instance was Abigail's "Remember the Ladies" letter to John. In his reply, John acknowledged the existence of the "Masculine systems" but pointed out to his wife that "they are little more than Theory." He continued, "In Practice you know We are the subjects. We have only the Name of Masters." But of course John and Abigail were not involved in a legal struggle over property. Had they been, the harsh "Masculine system" guiding American law would have been readily apparent.

After their wedding the Adamses moved to a ten-acre farm in Braintree (now Quincy), Massachusetts, about two miles from the ocean. Although they had a servant girl, Abigail, like most New England wives, began a lifetime of heavy domestic and farm labor. She cooked over a big wood fireplace in the kitchen, made clothes and linens, scrubbed the wood floors, and tended to the animals and crops. The couple was largely self-sufficient. What manufactured goods they needed came the ten miles from Boston, since Braintree had no stores.

Abigail conceived a child as soon as she was married, and her pregnancy was time for somber reflection on the subject of life and death. She was well aware that many women died in childbirth. Statistics for the time show the loss of one mother in every thirty births. And since married women then averaged eight births per lifetime, the odds were not encouraging. One reason was the primitive state of obstetrics and gynecology. Midwives attended to almost all "female problems," including births, in the mother's home. Although often very skilled in their craft, these women learned by trial and error. Only as the new medical schools increased the number of trained doctors did midwifery come to be associated with the frontier and the poverty-stricken. Abigail Adams had a midwife and delivered a daughter quite successfully, if a little prematurely, on July 14, 1765. She was part of the process that doubled the population of the colonies almost every generation. It was common for a wife to have an uninterrupted series of pregnancies from marriage to menopause. It is interesting that the birthrate in America in the eighteenth century was as high as it is today anywhere in the world. But 200 years ago there was a frontier to the west, an abundance of resources, and enough work for many hands. Moreover, the death rate was also high. Illnesses ravaged the Adamses' world, and the treatments, ranging from bloodletting to submersion in ice water, frequently proved to be worse than the disease. A person past fifty was very old. In 1790, of 100 persons born in a given year in Philadelphia, only sixteen remained alive

As New England residences went, the home of the Adams family in Quincy, Massachusetts, was one of the most elaborate. This was the home in which Abigail dreamed of spending years with John, but in fact the couple were together there only a small fraction of their lives.

thirty-six years later. Of course, high infant mortality accounted for some of these statistics. It was a rare mother who did not bury several children. Abigail Adams was no exception. Her third child, Susanna, lived just a little more than a year.

A 1766 portrait of Abigail Adams at age twenty-two (see page 78) reveals a strong face, framed by tightly drawn-back dark hair. The nose is finely chiseled, and thin eyebrows set off wide-set, piercing eyes. The contrast to her husband's companion portrait (see page 86) is pronounced. John's face is round, almost flaccid, and devoid of the decisiveness so evident in his wife's. Yet in the next decade, John would emerge as a leading American statesman, while Abigail, in her own words, became a "Domestick Being."

Almost certainly Abigail pondered the disparity. As much as she loved John and supported his career, it was tempting to think where, but for the accident of gender, she might have gone. In a letter of the early 1770s to a friend departing for Europe, she observed, "had nature formed me of the other Sex, I should certainly have been a rover [that is, traveler]." She might have added "politician." It became important, therefore, for Abigail Adams to justify her existence as the one who remained behind.

One method was to manage her home, farm, and family as competently as possible. "I hope, in time," she wrote John in 1776, "to have the Reputation of being as good a Farmeress as my partner has of being a good Statesman." And, in company with many American women of the revolutionary years, Abigail became the effective head of the household. With John absent for months at a time, Abigail assumed the extensive responsibilities of single parent, business manager, accountant, and provider. She bought and sold land, made decisions about crops, hired

John Adams sat for this portrait in 1766 when he was thirty-one. His portly demeanor and dull eyes contrast sharply with the countenance of his wife, whose companion portrait opens this chapter.

and fired help, and conducted other traditionally male business. The evidence suggests, moreover, that she performed splendidly. In a time when the affairs of other statesmen fell into disarray, the Adamses' family fortune increased, providing John with the opportunity to pursue largely uncompensated tasks of importance to the emerging nation.

Abigail's other line of self-justification has been identified as "Republican Motherhood" by contemporary historian Linda Kerber. The logic ran that because the success of a republican form of government depended on the quality of its voters and leaders (all of whom were then male), and because mothers were the primary influence on their male children, women could be "Domestick" and still exert a profound effect on the political life of their country. Abigail was convinced that women had a special opportunity to influence their world by the proper nurturing of young male minds. Daughters, too, might be educated and their interest in national affairs encouraged, since they, in turn, would shape young men of the republic. This line of reasoning reassured Abigail regarding the significance of her own studies and interests: Any improvement in the quality of female education would pay dividends in the quality of national life.

The Adams family became caught up in the rising tide of revolution when they moved to Boston in April 1768. Although Boston contained only about 16,000 people, the size, pace, and noise of the city contrasted sharply with the pastoralism of Braintree and Weymouth. Shopping and visiting friends in Boston, Abigail became familiar with the relatively new social phenomenon called the "mob," a loosely organized group of propertyless sailors, young boys, servants, and slaves whose political muscle had first been flexed during the Stamp Act riots of 1765 (see pages 67–69). The actions of the Boston mob led to the decision to station two regiments of British troops in the city about the time the Adamses arrived. Their immediate purpose was enforcement of the Townshend Revenue Act of 1767, and it was obvious from the outset that trouble lay ahead. Indeed, in one of his first revolutionary acts, John Adams wrote the "Boston Instructions" (1768), protesting both the presence of the troops and the seizure of his friend John Hancock's boat, *Liberty.*

Then, on the evening of March 5, 1770, the mob threw snowballs and bricks at the red-coated "lobsterbacks," and the soldiers fired a volley into the crowd. Five Americans died in the "Boston Massacre." Abigail Adams heard the shots and worried until John, who was away discussing politics with male friends, rushed home. Subsequently, John was approached by a Tory (pro-British) leader with the proposition that he defend the soldiers and their commander, Thomas Preston. John worried about what the mob might do to him and Abigail, but after discussing it with her, he agreed to take the case. It was not that John Adams supported the presence of the troops in Boston; rather, he recognized the importance of upholding constitutional rights such as a fair trial. Mob rule could not be tolerated. In the trial, Adams succeeded in obtaining the acquittal of Preston. Two soldiers were convicted of manslaughter and, in the manner of the eighteenth century, branded on their thumbs and released.

John Adams's response to the Boston Massacre suggests that in 1770 he was far from ready to endorse rebellion and independence. And the fact that he was elected during the Preston trial to the Massachusetts legislature indicates that many of his peers shared his views. After all, they were still British subjects. But the decision to accept the election and join the legislature was momentous. John and Abigail both knew that such an action would probably mark him as a dangerous radical in the eyes of the British officials. After a long discussion during which, according to John, Abigail "burst into a flood of Tears" at the thought of the risks ahead, the couple reached the consensus they apparently needed for every major decision. John would serve in the legislature, and Abigail would "place her trust in Providence."

In the early 1770s, the sympathies of the Adamses for revolution deepened, Abigail's almost certainly more rapidly than John's. Several encounters influenced her thinking. One was conversation with John's distant cousin, Samuel Adams, whose radicalism was always several degrees warmer than that of her husband. More important, in the summer of 1773 she met Mercy Otis Warren. Sixteen years older than Abigail, Warren was the sister of James Otis, the firebrand orator who helped inspire the origins of American radicalism. Her husband, James, was a Plymouth businessman also sympathetic to the cause of independence. But, significantly for Abigail, Mercy Warren was an intellectual and a writer who, in 1772, had actually published a political satire in a radical newspaper, *The Massachusetts Spy.* Although Mercy Warren used a male pen name, Abigail was thrilled to find a woman actually influencing, rather than just discussing, the politics of her time.

As she talked and corresponded with Mercy Warren, Abigail shaped her own ideas about American independence. She began with the conviction, familiar from the philosophy of John Locke, that all of the English had traditional and inalienable or "natural" rights and that governments that violated them should be resisted if not replaced. As Abigail saw it, Britain was clearly violating the rights of the American colonists. Her feelings on this point ran strong, as her use of words like *slaves, chains,* and *tyranny* suggests. For instance, she applauded an event that took place a few blocks from her house on the night of December 16, 1773—the Boston Tea Party. Even Benjamin Franklin disapproved of this lawless destruction of property, and John Adams probably sided with Franklin. But for Abigail, the dumping of the taxed tea was an appropriate response to Britain's disregard of American liberties. She thereafter called imported tea "the weed of slavery."

Searching for a deeper explanation of the growing difficulty with the mother country, Abigail Adams turned to the most familiar axiom of constitutional political theory: Power corrupts. People, she reasoned, were selfish and ambitious by nature. Unchecked power would certainly be abused. As she wrote Mercy Warren in 1774, "The passions and interests of Men" would, given exploitable opportunities, "pervert to very base purposes." The same view of human nature appeared in her 1776 letter to her husband regarding the relationship of men and women. "Remember," she wrote, "all Men would be tyrants if they could." Later in the same letter she used the phrase "Naturally Tyrannical." The idea of government, as Abigail understood it, was to encourage such innately depraved people to virtue by keeping the corrupting influence of power out of their hands.

Using this philosophy, Abigail Adams could make sense of the deteriorating relationship between Britain and the colonies. The British, as she saw it, exercised a dangerous degree of power over the colonies and had consequently become corrupt. "Artful and designing men," she explained to Mercy Warren, set colonial policy. So Britain had ceased being a "parent State" and had become a "tyrant State." In a 1774 letter to another woman she admired, the English historian of liberty Catharine Macaulay, Abigail ticked off a list of alleged abuses that anticipated Thomas Jefferson's catalog in the Declaration of Independence: "We are invaded with fleets and Armies, our commerce not only obstructed, but totally ruined, the courts of Justice shut, many driven out of the Metropolis, thousands reduced to want . . . and the chains of Slavery ready forged for us."

If Britain was the slave master, Abigail believed, then America was as virtuous as it was powerless. Surely, God was on the American side. Revolution was the inevitable conclusion. "Let us renounce [the British]," she declared in 1775, and "beseech the Almighty to blast their counsels and bring to nought all their devices." She concluded, in rhetoric familiar to the time, "The only alternative which every American thinks of is Liberty or Death." From such a perspective, violence could be only a step away. Abigail Adams was convinced that a revolutionary war not only would release the colonies from the "chains of slavery" but would ensure the continuation of constitutional liberty everywhere on earth. In the manner of her ancestor, John Winthrop, she would cut the ties with Britain to advance the work of God on earth. America had a new mission, one for which Abigail was prepared to sacrifice comfort and even safety.

In August 1774, John Adams left home to represent Massachusetts at the Continental Congress in Philadelphia. It was the first colony-wide political assembly since the brief Stamp Act Congress nine years earlier. It was the beginning of almost a decade of loneliness for Abigail, as her husband served the emerging nation first in Philadelphia and then as a diplomat in Europe. For a couple as close as the Adamses, this was a major sacrifice. That they could undertake it at all is a testimony to their degree of enthusiasm for the American Revolution. A thirst for fame drove the ambitious John, but there is no reason to suspect that he was insincere in telling Abigail he would renounce statesmanship permanently if she desired. At any rate, she never put him to the test, perhaps deriving satisfaction from her contributions to the career of a major architect of independence. In fact, Abigail's letters to John constituted an important source of information for the Philadelphia delegates about the progress of the hostilities in Massachusetts, the early focus of the war. Some were quoted in the formal assemblies. It is important to remember that, in the absence of radio, telephone, television, and regular, unbiased newspaper publication, personal letters were a major way of exchanging news. Abigail Adams's diligence and skill with her pen gave special meaning to the still-current phrase "foreign corre-spondent." But from Abigail's point of view, letters could never replace her husband. Once, in 1776, with the ever-present prospect of her world's falling apart in the chaos of war, she told John that she had entertained herself for three days with the idea of "a joyfull and happy meeting." "I have," she continued, "held you to my Bosom till my whole Soul had dissolved in Tenderness and my pen fallen from my Hand." Of course, it was all the more disquieting for Abigail to realize that by then her husband was a marked man. She knew he would be one of the "Early Victimes" should Great Britain regain control of its American colonies.

Meanwhile history swirled around Abigail Adams. In the winter of 1774–1775, the British commander in Boston, General Gage, turned the city into an armed camp, and Abigail led her family back to the Braintree farm. On April 19, 1775, British soldiers marched on Concord to seize a stockpile of ammunition the colonists had gathered. Seventy "Redcoats" died in the ensu-ing clash with the "Minutemen," who were warned, as widely celebrated, by Paul Revere. This initial action in the Revolution occurred about thirty miles from the Adams farm. Indeed, Abigail had reason to recall John's advice to "fly to the Woods with our Children" in the event of British attack. Then, on June 17, Abigail woke up to the booming of cannon. From a hill not far from her home she and her son, John Quincy, watched the Americans attempt to defend Bunker Hill. The British won, but at a heavy cost. Refugees began pouring south toward Braintree. Abigail tried to accommodate them for a few days, and she allowed a company of American militiamen to drill on her property. Johnny, aged eight, marched along with the revolutionaries. It was one of the first things the future president recalled about his childhood. When George Washington arrived in Massachusetts in the summer of 1775 to take charge of the American war effort, Abi-gail, as the wife of one of the congressmen who employed him, had the chance to visit his camp. Washington impressed her as possessing "Dignity with ease . . . the gentleman and the Soldier look agreably blended in him." About the same time she also met Benjamin Franklin, judging him a "true patriot."

Even the coming of the war did not settle the question of whether America should declare independence or seek to reform its status in the British Empire. In 1775 Abigail could still attend dinner parties where patriots clashed verbally with those who favored patching up relations with the crown. For her part, however, there were no doubts. She had devoured Thomas Paine's *Common Sense* after John sent her a copy in February 1776 and cheered his strong arguments for independence. In March she wrote to John at the Second Continental Congress, declaring "I long to hear that you have declared an independancy." John responded that it was hard to get a large fleet (the colonies) sailing in a single direction. But finally, in mid-July, ten days after the fact, Abigail learned from John of the historic vote of July 2, 1776, and of the signing of the Declaration of Independence two days later. Proud of her association with a principal in the proceedings, she relished the thought of "the future happiness and glory of our Country."

But there was one cloud on the horizon. Abigail knew full well that when her husband signed a declaration stating that all "men" were created equal, he and his colleagues meant white males only. "I can not say that I think you are very generous to the Ladies," she reminded him, "for whilst you are proclaiming peace and good will to Men, Emancipating all Nations, you insist upon retaining an absolute power over Wives." Abigail went on to observe that like all hard things, "Arbitrary power" was subject to breakage. Men would be aware that women "have it in our power not only to free ourselves but to subdue our Masters, and without violence throw both your natural and legal authority at our feet." Exactly how she planned to implement this threat was unclear, but Abigail did discuss with Mercy Warren the idea of petitioning the Continental Congress on behalf of women's rights. She dropped the plan, however—perhaps because she knew that deep down, John felt that women should keep their places. Trying to link that subordination to republican principles, he observed that his study of history indicated that nations lost their "republican principles . . . and forms of government, when they lost the modesty and domestic virtues of their women." Thomas Jefferson put it more bluntly when he said "the tender breasts of ladies were not formed for political convulsion." Such reasoning effectively excluded women from federal politics until 1920.

The way Americans would govern themselves after independence fascinated Abigail, who, in her son's words, relished an occasional "dish of politics." There was much to savor. Long before they won independence on the battlefield, Americans began thinking about the structure of the system they would substitute for the hated colonial regime. Abigail favored a republic, in which ultimate power rested with the people, rather than a constitutional monarchy such as the colonists had just rejected. But republics were rare in history and existed only in Switzerland and the Netherlands in eighteenth-century Europe. Abigail was familiar with classical history and had to look all the way back to Greece and Rome to find examples of functioning republics. But these, she knew, were on a small scale compared to the sprawling North American civilization. Moreover, there were troubling inconsistencies in the republican ideal her compatriots held. Abigail's "Remember the Ladies" letter to John underscored one major loophole in republican theory.

Slavery was another. Abigail had grown up with slaves in the house, but her family's relationship to them was far different from that which existed on southern plantations. Slaves in New England at that time were comparable in many respects to servants—but not quite, and it was that discrepancy that tormented Abigail Adams. "I wish most sincerely," she wrote to John on the eve of independence, "there was not a Slave in the province. It always appeared a most iniquitous Scheme to me—fight for what we are daily robbing and plundering from those who have as good a right to freedom as we have." Later Abigail put her principles into practice, sending a young slave boy to an evening school to learn mathematics. When a neighbor, who had two sons in the same school, objected, Abigail responded, "Merely because his Face is Black, is he to be denied instruction? How is he to be qualified to procure a livelihood?" And she added, "I have not thought it any disgrace to my self to take him into my parlour and teach him to both read and write."

The life of Phillis Wheatley was significant to Abigail Adams in this respect. Born in Africa about 1750, Wheatley had been enslaved as a child and brought to Boston. She was completely illiterate in English, but her master, John Wheatley, had noted her intelligence and begun a program of education for her that even extended to the language Abigail was never permitted to acquire—Latin. In the late 1760s and 1770s, Phillis wrote a number of creditable poems, some of which were published and widely acclaimed. New Englanders such as Abigail Adams could point to her as proof that only unequal opportunities kept blacks and women from the same intellectual accomplishments as white males. Phillis was freed after John Wheatley's death, but only to face hard times. The free black man she had married impoverished and deserted her. She was reduced from writing poetry to working as a cleaning woman in a boardinghouse. She died in 1784 in her early thirties. As Abigail Adams saw it, Phillis Wheatley had overcome one obstacle—race—but not the inequities of sex.

Many in the North agreed with Abigail's feelings about blacks, and slavery was abolished in most northern states shortly after the end of the Revolutionary War. In Abigail's case, her lifelong concern for women's rights certainly figured in her opposition to slavery. Still, it was disquieting to realize that part of the society proposing to organize itself under republican principles endorsed the institution as a positive good. Thinking of southerners, she noted in 1776, "the passion for Liberty cannot be Eaquelly Strong in the Breasts of those who have been accustomed to deprive their fellow Creatures of theirs." In this idea lay the dynamite that would, in less than a century, blow the young republic apart.

Officially, the Revolutionary War was for men only, but Abigail Adams was pleased to note how women were contributing to the success of the American cause. Organizations calling themselves "daughters of liberty" not only sewed for the troops but led boycotts and sometimes resorted to physical violence against those who remained loyal to the British. The largest of these organizations, The Association, headed by Esther D. Reed, operated in six states. Other women served in the field, cooking for the soldiers, nursing the sick and wounded, doing laundry, and mending uniforms. Prostitution was not common, although many of the "camp followers" were destitute and homeless. American officers were strict about prohibiting adultery, sharing Abigail Adams's view that it was vital to maintain the link between the American cause and virtue.

Occasionally, women actually fought. Cannon crews needed the barrels swabbed after each firing, and women frequently carried the pitchers of water for that purpose. Long after the Revolution, the name "Molly Pitcher" became associated with this activity. Apparently it was generic, referring to no one in particular, but a good candidate would have been Mary Hays, who took a regular place on a cannon crew after one of its male members was injured during the Battle of Monmouth (1778). Margaret Corbin also fired cannons, was wounded during battle, and became the first woman to collect a federal pension as a veteran. She is buried in the military cemetery at West Point. Several women disguised themselves as men and fought as regular soldiers. Deborah Sampson Gannet of Massachusetts fought alongside male soldiers who believed that she, too, was a man. A leg wound revealed her gender to a doctor, who kept her secret. After recovery she returned to the fighting and later made a postwar career of lecturing about her experience. Many women engaged British soldiers in hand-to-hand combat in the course of defending their homes. They used conventional muskets, hatchets, farm tools, and even pots of boiling lye. Nancy Hart of Georgia held five British soldiers at gunpoint until help arrived.

In view of the abundance of real heroines in the Revolution, it is surprising to find Betsy Ross's name best remembered. A Philadelphia seamstress, Ross did make a few flags for Pennsylvania's troops during the war. But research has exposed the story of her 1776 charge from George Washington to make the first "Stars and Stripes" as largely the stuff of her grandson's imagination. The most famous early American flagmaker should, in fact, be Mary Young Pickersgill, who produced a huge flag, forty-two by thirty feet. It flew over Fort McHenry in the nation's next conflict: the War of 1812. This was the star-spangled banner that Francis Scott Key caught sight of in the dawn's early light before writing the national anthem.

Although he had done much to bring it about, John Adams experienced very little of the Revolutionary War firsthand. On February 13, 1778, Abigail and the children bid him a tearful farewell as he left Boston for Paris. His charge from Congress was to join Benjamin Franklin as an American representative in the negotiation of a treaty of alliance with France. This was not a difficult task. After fighting them for decades in North America, the French relished the prospect of the British losing their colonial empire. When the rebels won the Saratoga campaign in October 1777, France decided they had a chance of winning the entire war and recognized

American independence in December. Setting aside her lifelong aversion to the Catholic monarchy that ruled France, Abigail wrote that "Americans are now bound to transfer their affections" to the new champion of freedom. She had a chance to put her new enthusiasm into practice in August 1778 when a French fleet anchored off Boston. As the wife of the American commissioner in Paris, Abigail received an invitation to dine with the Comte d'Estaing on board his flagship. She described the event as "entertainment fit for a princess," but it is doubtful that the French came away similarly impressed from an evening at the Adamses' humble Braintree cottage. As an example of republican simplicity, however, Abigail's lifestyle was perfect. Subsequently, the French declared war on England and provided vital support in the campaign that led to the surrender of Cornwallis at Yorktown in 1781 and the end of the war.

Meanwhile, as John's infrequent letters home revealed, all was not going smoothly in Paris. He did not get along with Franklin. The Philadelphian's enormous popularity with the French wounded the ambitious New Englander's fragile ego. Adams also disapproved of Franklin's obvious delight in French ladies. To make matters worse, in early 1779, Congress advanced Franklin into the dominant role in the Paris negotiations. Missing Abigail intensely, John yearned to return to Massachusetts, but transatlantic passages being what they were in the eighteenth century, he did not make the trip until August. Even then, Abigail had no notice that he was on his way until he walked in the front door. But the happiness of the couple was short-lived. On November 3, 1779, Congress called on John Adams once more, this time to be the primary negotiator of peace with Great Britain. As it turned out, accepting the appointment would mean four more years of separation, but John was consistent in allowing his passion for fame and his desire to serve his country to win out over domestic bliss. On November 13 he sailed away once more, in the company of his sons, John Quincy and Charles.

The next few years were the most difficult in Abigail Adams's life. The treason of Benedict Arnold, a trusted American officer who in 1780 conspired unsuccessfully to turn the garrison at West Point over to the British, outraged her. She decided that Arnold must be one of those "Unprincipled wretches" who lacked religious principles and therefore could not discern right from wrong. Then there was her relationship with James Lovell, a Massachusetts delegate to Congress who, without much indirection, offered himself to Abigail as a lover. She resisted, but not before accepting a substantial amount of flattery. Abigail was desperately lonely and struck by the feeling that the best years of her life were slipping away thousands of miles from her husband. To make matters worse, the peace agreement dragged on two years after the end of hostilities. Not until September 3, 1783, did John and his colleagues succeed in obtaining the Peace of Paris. Even then he lingered in Europe, hoping to be named the first ambassador to the former mother country.

Finally, Abigail determined to join him, and on June 20, 1784, the lady who had never left Massachusetts sailed for Europe with her daughter Nabby, two servants, and a milk cow. The passage was a trial. The cramped ship was filthy, the food deplorable, and seasickness common. But characteristically, Abigail rose above the circumstances and organized a massive cleanup of the entire ship. She even entered the galley to show the cook how to "dress his victuals." Impressed, the captain taught Abigail the rudiments of sailing and navigation. Landing at last in England, Abigail proceeded to Paris, where John was arranging commercial treaties for his new government. The Adamses moved into a thirty-room mansion complete with an army of servants, but New Englander to the core, Abigail was not impressed. She found the house dirty and the servants lazy. French culture was also troublesome. It might be superficially elegant, but underneath Abigail detected hedonism and immorality. At one dinner party, she noted, shocked, how one lady openly held hands with Benjamin Franklin and even threw her arm "carelessly upon the

Abigail Adams is forty-one in this portrait. She had recently joined John in Paris, and her expression reflects some of her displeasure in what she perceived to be a decadent French culture.

Doctor's neck." When the lady sat in a chair, Abigail observed that she "shew more than her feet." To cap the evening off, the lady's lap dog wet the floor, whereupon she wiped up the mess with the hem of her gown. "I own I was highly disgusted," Abigail concluded.

On the other hand, Europe was striking to the woman from the provinces. Abigail delighted in the theater, the opera, and, in spite of the "indelicacy" of the dancers' short skirts, the ballet. She agreed with John that the French queen was "an object too sublime and beautiful for my dull pen to describe." It was a difficult admission for the recent rebel against monarchy to make, but Europe clearly surpassed the colonies, as Abigail put it, "in the cultivation of the arts and the improvement in manufactures." Still, the patriot in her did resurface, as when she noted that her country had "native genius, capacity, and ingenuity, equal to all their improvements, and much more general knowledge diffused among us." This was the standard American response: Europe might have impressive social and cultural heights, but these rested on a degree of inequality and exploitation unknown in the New World republic. Europe might have palaces, huge cathedrals, and great universities, but America was building its own magnificent institutions and had a boundless frontier only scarcely settled. Europe was old, America new.

After May 1785 the Adamses lived in London, where John, his wish fulfilled, served as the American ambassador. Although Abigail liked England better than France, her perception of European immorality and "dissipation" did not decrease. On one occasion she met Catharine Macaulay, the woman whose success in the "man's sphere," political writing, had so greatly impressed her in the 1770s. To Abigail's relief, she found that Catharine had not sacrificed femininity to intellectual achievement, but the fact that she had recently married a man half her age scandalized Abigail. Despite the couple's obvious happiness, she concluded that the union revealed the "frailty in humane characters."

From the standpoint of the official reasons for their presence in Europe, the Adamses also experienced disappointments. As John discovered anew almost every day, the United States was something of a joke abroad. He reported the "dry decency" and cold civility with which he was received. His efforts to obtain concessions from the British fell flat. Thomas Jefferson, whom the Adamses had enjoyed visiting in Paris, wrote that "all respect for our government is annihilated on this side of the water from an idea of its want of energy." This was not just an idea. The Articles of Confederation, under which both Adams and Jefferson were serving, had deliberately created a very weak central government. There was no chief executive. Congress could not tax citizens, regulate commerce, or raise an army. The states could deal directly with foreign governments. Moreover, the federal government was nearly bankrupt. No wonder Europeans expected the American attempt at nation building to veer off in thirteen directions. John and Abigail could not help wondering if the end result was worth the sacrifices of the last two decades.

The winter of 1786–1787 brought further cause for concern. In the western part of the Adamses' home state, poor people forcibly stopped the operation of courts seeking to enforce tax laws. Arming themselves under Daniel Shays, 1,500 men threatened to bring down the state government. But a group of rich Bostonians contributed enough money to permit the governor to organize a militia and, in January 1787, quash the rebels. Had they been at home, John and Abigail Adams would have unquestionably backed the governor. In their eyes this lawlessness had been unprovoked and was intolerable, an unpleasant throwback to the mob rule of the Stamp Act riots and the events preceding the Boston Massacre. Shays's Rebellion caused Abigail to wonder, "Have we been contending against the tyranny of Britain to become the sacrifice of a lawless Banditti?" Forgetting her own recent rebelliousness against Britain on similar grounds of unpopular taxation, Abigail branded the Shaysites "Ignorant, wrestless desperadoes, without conscience or principals, . . . mobish insurgents [who] are for sapping the foundation" of the new government. This blast occurred in a letter to the Adamses' close friend Thomas Jefferson, then in Paris, who responded with praise for the Shaysites (see page 118). Abigail was aghast and broke off correspondence with Jefferson for months. It seemed to her that the Virginian had lost sight of the meaning of the American Revolution, but in fact it was Abigail who was becoming increasingly conservative. Along with John, she assumed that only men of property and talent should govern. Once chosen by the people, they should rule without pressure from the mob. Class distinctions must be maintained. "A *levelling* principal," Abigail stated, was "very unfavourable to the existance of civil Liberty." The American Revolution, as she saw it, represented the substitution of a virtuous ruling class for a corrupt one. The broader significances of the American rebellion were either unknown to her or, if known, feared.

When pressure to reconstruct the national government led to the calling of the Constitutional Convention in May 1787, the Adamses, still in England, hoped for a much stronger central authority. Early in the year, John wrote a treatise entitled "Defense of the State Constitution," which was so enthusiastic about a strong chief executive that Abigail correctly predicted he would be accused of favoring a monarchy. As they learned piecemeal about the Constitution, John and Abigail were generally pleased. The new arrangement greatly strengthened the federal government; the states, at least, were clearly subordinate and the "people" even further removed from power.

Abigail Adams returned to Massachusetts with John in 1788, relishing the resumption of "Domestick happiness" and "Rural felicity." The three years abroad, she decided, had made her "only more attached to America." But Europe had changed Abigail Adams. She had tasted luxury and now she set about embellishing her life in Braintree. The house was doubled in size, and fine furniture appeared, imported from Europe, of course. After John was elected vice president under George Washington in February 1789, Abigail looked forward to living in Philadelphia and enjoying the social rewards of his office. She participated with enthusiasm in the elaborate receptions hosted by the first administration and, by all reports, outshone Martha Washington. Indeed, her strong opinions, interest in politics, and forthrightness gave rise to the rumor that, in effect, *she* was vice president of the United States. Abigail liked her carriage with six horses and four servants, and, hoping to give the new government dignity, she supported grandiose titles for its officers. John proposed "His Excellency" for Washington and was vigorously criticized in the press for monarchical leanings. One writer even suggested "His Rotundity" for the plump vice president. It was said that the Adamses had been too long in the courts of Europe and had lost their republican instincts. To some extent this was true. John and Abigail had been impressed by the ceremony, tradition, and sense of hierarchy and "place" they had encountered in the Old World. It was not that they wanted a king for the United States. But now that the "right" government existed in America, the Adamses wanted it to have the same degree of permanency.

The Philadelphia to which Abigail Adams moved as the wife of the vice president in 1789 was one of the nation's most active cities. Abigail, or more likely her servants, could have purchased chickens in the same location as the group in the left foreground. Imposing receptions, or "levees," held in the adjacent buildings attempted to give the new American government a measure of dignity.

For a man who had helped write the Declaration of Independence and had made the peace with Great Britain, John Adams found his two terms (1789–1797) as second in command to George Washington boring and frustrating. "The Vice Presidency," he wrote to Abigail in words that would be echoed repeatedly by subsequent holders of that office, was the most "insignificant office . . . ever . . . contrived." Abigail must have agreed, because she chose to remain at home in Quincy (formerly Braintree) during John's second term. She retained her interest in politics, however, and the most hotly discussed subject of the time was the revolution under way in France.

Beginning in 1789, and partially inspired by the American example, the French Revolution escalated through a series of increasingly violent phases that climaxed in the execution of the king and widespread use of the guillotine to silence opposition permanently. Particularly in its early stages, many Americans followed Thomas Jefferson in applauding the French people's advancement of the cause of freedom. But Abigail Adams remained unconvinced. She had deep misgivings about the French tendency to use the words *liberty* and *equality* interchangeably, as in the slogan that ended with *fraternity*. She believed that political and social equality could actually threaten liberty just as surely as a corrupt monarch. At the root of this belief was her view of human nature: Most people were shortsighted and selfish and inclined to stray from the paths of virtue unless constrained. For that reason, she wrote in 1794, they were "unfit for freedom." The behavior of the Boston mobs, the Shays rebels, and now the French revolutionaries, or "Jacobins," were cases in point. It was also clear to Abigail from her study of the history of "all Ages and Nations from Adam to the present day" that "some [people] were made for Rule [and] others for submission." Abigail meant that the people were legitimately the source of power, but their passions had to be filtered through an "enlightened" minority—the governing class. If this class was hereditary and artificial, as it was in the case of Europe's clergy and nobility, tyranny might result. But in America, Abigail reasoned, the ruling minority emerged naturally on the basis of intelligence, ability, and virtue. The French had gone much too far in their revolution, at any rate, throwing out the baby along with the dirty bathwater as it were. The chaotic Reign of Terror proved to her satisfaction the liabilities of "equality" as a social and political philosophy.

Abigail happily found many Americans coming around to her point of view as news of the guillotine's bloody work reached the New World. By the time of the U.S. election of 1796, the nation had signed against France in its new war with England and, through the Jay Treaty (1795), had settled outstanding economic and territorial differences with the former mother country.

By the 1790s, Abigail's thinking about women's rights had lost some of the radicalism implicit in her 1776 threat to "foment a revolution" on behalf of American "Laidies." She read with great interest the 1792 work of the English feminist Mary Wollstonecraft entitled *A Vindication of the Rights of Woman,* noting especially the argument that females' intellectual capacities were fully equal to males'. But Abigail did not agree with Wollstonecraft's attack on domesticity or her criticism of women "immured in their families, groping in the dark." What ultimately appealed to Abigail Adams were women's rights within the existing social structure. She had always regarded the domestic sphere as being of primary importance as a foundation for social order. As she grew older and more conservative, her feelings about place, role, and duty became stronger. Consequently, she could argue that the sexes were equal but still assert that men should govern and women remain at home, supporting husbands and educating their children. It was the same logic that allowed her to affirm the natural rights of all humans and then advocate division into those who ruled and those who submitted. Social order, she believed, depended on this sense of appropriate place. And she could never condone the liberties that extreme feminists took.

She was shocked, for example, when it became public knowledge in the late 1790s that Mary Wollstonecraft had lived for a time with a man other than her husband.

The year 1796 was a pivotal one for Abigail Adams and her husband. John was one of the first Americans aware of George Washington's determination to retire after two terms in office. On January 5, 1796, he wrote to Abigail about the "Consequences" of that decision: "Either we must enter upon ardours more trying than any ever yet experienced; or retire to Quincy Farmers for Life." Abigail did not need further explanation. She knew John longed for the ultimate reward in American politics, and she had long since abandoned the hope that he would follow through on his often-stated intent to retire. Although she pleaded once more for retirement, she told him, "I dare not influence you."

In September 1796, Washington announced his decision and bade the country farewell, with a warning to avoid the "spirit of party." His compatriots were moved—"All America is in mourning," Abigail wrote—but went right ahead with party politics. Indeed, with Washington's fatherly and restraining presence removed, factionalism became more pronounced than ever. To be sure, eighteenth-century politicians on the national level were not expected to campaign on their own behalf. Adams, Jefferson, and Thomas Pinckney, the front-runners for the presidency, withdrew to a gentlemanly distance while party leaders and "electors" determined their fate. Jefferson's opposition to Adams, particularly on the question of France, was well known, but Abigail Adams focused her fear on the challenge within the Federalist Party that Pinckney posed. She thought that Alexander Hamilton, the architect of the nation's fiscal policy, wanted Pinckney to prevail over her husband. "H——n," she wrote John late in 1796, "is a man ambitious as Julius Caesar, a subtle intriguer. His abilities would make him dangerous if he was to espouse a wrong side, his thirst for fame is insatiable. I ever kept my Eye on him." But by Christmas Abigail knew that John had won the election and that Jefferson, because of the prevailing election laws, would be vice president. She also knew the social responsibilities that would soon be hers and worried that her bold and sharp tongue might embarrass John.

Abigail's tasks, first at Philadelphia and then at Washington (the seat of government moved in November 1800), included staging receptions and dinners and managing the presidential household on John's relatively small salary ($25,000)—and without the assistance of an administrative staff. Abigail hired, fired, and directed the servants herself and also continued her management of the family's Massachusetts interests. Meanwhile, John narrowly averted a war with France that many Americans, Abigail included, thought desirable in the wake of a diplomatic insult known as the XYZ affair (1797–1798). Still, there were many in the nation who sided with France and opposed Adams's allegedly pro-British policy. The attacks on his administration became increasingly bitter in 1798. Benjamin Franklin Bache, a Republican, referred, in print, to the "old, querulous, bald, blind, crippled, toothless Adams." A Vermont congressman, Matthew Lyon, spat in the eye of a Federalist colleague and wrestled him to the floor of the House of Representatives.

Abigail was enraged by what she called "the vile incendiaries." She equated political opposition with disloyalty to the nation, even with treason. Consequently, Abigail applauded a series of federal laws known collectively as the Alien and Sedition Acts, designed to curb the influence of foreigners and to suppress the voices and, if necessary, the constitutional rights of critics of the administration. The Sedition Act of July 14, 1798, made possible the fining and imprisonment of Matthew Lyon after he published a criticism of John Adams. Abigail was delighted but told her son the act was far too weak. Unquestionably the one-time revolutionary was now an arch-conservative. Abigail even questioned the desirability of popular elections.

When Abigail Adams moved to Washington, D.C., in the winter of 1800, she found a raw frontier community. This sketch of 1799 features the Executive Mansion, where Abigail lived with the president. Her letters noted the necessity of keeping its many fireplaces burning around the clock to dispel the cold dampness of the riverside location.

The circumstances surrounding the Adamses' move in 1800 to the new capital called "Washington" were not happy. Another of Abigail's children, Charles, aged thirty-one, died at this time. And Washington, newly hacked out of a swampy forest on the edge of the Potomac River, lacked the environmental and social charms of Philadelphia. Indeed, Abigail and her companions became quite lost on their first attempt to find Washington and would have spent the night in their coach had not a plantation owner accommodated them. The next day she found the capital a city in name only. Only a few hundred people lived there, scattered among "trees and stumps in plenty." There were no paved streets; mud was a constant fact of life. Abigail and her servants had to keep all thirteen fireplaces in the presidential residence burning constantly to dispel the darkness. Also, Abigail was deeply disturbed by the slave labor system that was largely building Washington, which, after all, was a southern city. She noted how the lack of incentive made the slaves inefficient, but she reserved special contempt for the whites, who considered idleness a sign of social status. "The lower class of whites," she remarked, "are a grade below the negroes in point of intelligence, and ten below them in point of civility."

To make matters worse, it was clear to Abigail in the fall of 1800 that John would not be reelected. Widespread anger at the Alien and Sedition Acts, along with unpopular taxes, sealed the Federalists' fate. But characteristically loyal and narrow-minded about such things, Abigail accused the nation of ingratitude and predicted chaos under the Republicans and Thomas Jefferson. The nation survived the change in leadership, however, and Abigail was pleased to see her son John Quincy elected senator from Massachusetts in 1803. By this time Abigail had finally settled down in the town of Peacefield to enjoy the family life denied her by John's decades of public service. There were grandchildren to care for, in-laws to criticize, and, as always, the farm and home to maintain. In 1808 John Quincy shifted his political affiliations from the fading Federalists to the Republicans, and the next year he became the first American ambassador to Russia. Abigail was changing, too. The Federalists, she had come to understand, were just as partisan as the Republicans. In the election of 1808 she actually favored Jefferson's hand-picked successor, James Madison—although, of course, she could not vote.

The passage of time helped mend political fences. The Adamses repaired their old Parisian friendship with Thomas Jefferson, breaking a silence of twelve years to begin a brilliant correspondence. Abigail came to understand that Jefferson's "natural aristocracy" provided the same safeguard against the tyranny of the majority as did her concept of an enlightened governing class. Democracy, they agreed, was dangerous unless controlled. Abigail also came to side with the Republicans in their attacks on pro-British Federalist foreign policy. When war with England came in 1812, Abigail, unlike many in New England, supported it enthusiastically. At this time she also resumed her friendship with Mercy Warren, whose 1805 book, *History of the Rise,*

Progress and Termination of the American Revolution, had so strongly criticized John Adams as to rupture the relationship. "History," John had written, "is not the Province of Ladies." But by 1812 Abigail was wearing a pin featuring a lock of Mercy's hair enclosed in glass and surrounded with pearls, while John and Mercy settled their differences in a lengthy correspondence.

James Monroe's lopsided victory in the election of 1816 pleased Abigail, especially when John Quincy became Monroe's secretary of state. It amused Abigail that the Republicans held "entertainments" even more lavish than those for which she had been criticized. Had she done as much, she wrote in 1818, "the cry of Monarchy, Monarchy would have resounded from Georgia to Maine."

In the fall of 1818, Abigail contracted typhoid fever, a bacterial infection usually caused by contaminated water or milk. On October 28, after a bout of high fever and dehydration, she died. Sharp and witty to the end, she could take satisfaction in fifty-four years of happy marriage and in the fruits of "Republican Motherhood," as evidenced in the rising political star of John Quincy Adams. His subsequent defense of women's rights and his advocacy of the abolition of slavery owed much to his mother's ideals. John Adams lived on eight more years, dying, remarkably, on July 4, 1826, the fiftieth anniversary of American independence and the same day that Thomas Jefferson died.

Abigail Adams championed ideals of women's rights when they were emerging for the first time in human history. She was an incomplete revolutionary, however. Realistically, she accepted the constraints of time, place, and circumstance. Near the end of her life she wrote, "If we live in the world and mean to serve ourselves and it, we must conform to its customs." Eventually, to be sure, the customs changed, as the careers of future American women would attest, and Abigail Adams would come to be recognized as a harbinger of those social transformations.

Selected Readings

The Person

Adams, Abigail: *Letters of Mrs. Adams, the Wife of John Adams* (1940). The classic edition, with an introduction by her grandson, Charles Francis Adams, that enjoyed several expansions and reprintings.

Akers, Charles W.: *Abigail Adams: An American Woman* (2000). A short and undocumented but readable addition to the *Library of American Biography* series (second edition).

Butterfield, Lyman H. (ed.): *Adams Family Correspondence* (4 vols., 1963, 1973). Part of *The Adams Papers,* these volumes collect most of Abigail Adams's letters before 1782.

Butterfield, Lyman H. (ed.): *The Book of Abigail and John* (1975). A convenient selection of the most revealing letters from the 1760s to the 1780s.

Gelles, Edith B.: *Portia: The World of Abigail Adams* (1993). A topically arranged biography removing Abigail's world from John's.

Gelles, Edith B.: *First Thoughts: Life and Letters of Abigail Adams* (1998). Selected letters analyzed by the author.

Hecht, Marie B.: *John Quincy Adams* (1972). Treats Abigail Adams's influence on the most famous of her children.

Levin, Phyllis Lee: *Abigail Adams: A Biography* (1987). A thorough and intimate biography, focusing on the partnership of Abigail and John and employing extensive correspondence.

Nagel, Paul C.: *The Adams Women: Abigail and Louisa Adams, Their Sisters and Daughters* (1987). Biographies of the second and sixth first ladies, as well as other familial histories.

Russell, Francis: *Adams: An American Dynasty* (1976). An illustrated history of the Adams family from the second president to historian Henry and beyond.

Smith, Page: *John Adams* (2 vols., 1962). A thorough biography that gives considerable attention to Abigail Adams.

Withey, Lynne: *Dearest Friend: A Life of Abigail Adams* (1981). The definitive biography.

The Period

Berkin, Carol R.: *Within the Conjurers Circle: Women in Colonial America* (1974). Discusses the position of women in everyday life.

Berkin, Carol R., and Mary Beth Norton (eds.): *Women of America: A History* (1979). Collective scholarship on the social and intellectual history of women in the United States from the revolutionary period to the 1970s.

Cott, Nancy F.: *The Bonds of Womanhood: "Women's Sphere" in New England, 1780–1835* (1977). Treats the ordinary woman and her relationship to work, domesticity, education, religion, and other women.

Diamant, Lincoln (ed.): *Revolutionary Women in the War for American Independence: A One-Volume Revised Edition of Elizabeth Ellet's 1848 Landmark Series* (1998). Elizabeth Ellet's 1848 book updated and annotated; includes Adams.

Depauw, Linda Grant: *Founding Mothers: Women of America in the Revolutionary Era* (1975). A more scholarly and detailed companion volume to the DePauw and Hunt book.

Depauw, Linda Grant, and Conover Hunt: *Remember the Ladies: Women in America, 1750–1815* (1976). An excellent social history plus an outstanding collection of illustrations.

Evans, Elizabeth: *Weathering the Storm: Women of the American Revolution* (1975). A collection of the unpublished diaries and journals of eleven women.

George, Carol V. R. (ed.): *"Remember the Ladies": New Perspectives on Women in American History* (1975). Useful essays, including one concerning the relationship of Abigail Adams and Thomas Jefferson.

Gerlach, Larry R. (ed.): *Legacies of the American Revolution* (1978). A variety of essays, including one on the philosophy of Abigail Adams.

Kerber, Linda K.: *Women of the Republic: Intellect and Ideology in Revolutionary America* (1980). Solid intellectual history.

Norton, Mary Beth: *Liberty's Daughters: The Revolutionary Experience of American Women, 1750–1800* (1980). A detailed exploration of change and continuity in the lives of American women who experienced the Revolution.

Smith, Page: *Daughters of the Promised Land: Women in American History* (1970). A good general history, although completed before important recent scholarly works.

Young, Alfred F. (ed.): *The American Revolution: Essays in the History of American Radicalism* (1976). A collection of interpretative essays emphasizing the meaning of revolution to American society.

For Consideration

1. What were some of the unusual aspects of Abigail Adams's childhood regarding her intellectual skills?

2. Evaluate the state of medicine and childbirthing in Adams's day.

3. Discuss the cult of domesticity and "Republican Motherhood" in the context of John and Abigail Adams's marriage.

4. Abigail Adams wrote passionately of the injustices of British rule well before her husband took up the cause. What were some of her justifications for breaking away from England? How do some of those justifications harken back to John Winthrop and the Puritans during the Great Migration?

5. How did Abigail Adams change her views of revolution and republicanism when troubles, such as Shays's Rebellion, challenged the new nation? How did she view the French Revolution?

6. What were some of the political and social challenges presented to the Adamses during John's presidency (1797–1801)?

Chapter 5

Thomas Jefferson

The crowd that had gathered for breakfast at Conrad and McMun's boardinghouse arose as one as the lanky, broad-shouldered Virginian descended the stairs. Nervously, the hostess gestured to a chair left vacant at the head of the table. Thomas Jefferson dismissed the offer and chose instead a seat along the side with the other diners. After the meal he strolled outside, squinting into the March sunlight at the collection of half-finished buildings, swamp, and forest that for less than a year had served as the capital of the United States. Elaborately uniformed soldiers paraded in the muddy streets, doing their best to dignify the occasion. George Washington and John Adams, the two previous presidents, had coveted such trappings, with their connotation of Old World aristocracy. Four years earlier, Adams had ridden to his inauguration in a luxurious coach drawn by six horses. But the election of 1800 had defeated the Federalists and had brought a different temper to American life. Jefferson reflected it as he left Conrad and McMun's for the day's business. Spurning the suggestion of a coach and ignoring the armed guard, the president-elect walked to his inauguration.

On a clear day you can see a long way from Thomas Jefferson's beloved hilltop home, Monticello. Immediately below, the town of Charlottesville, Virginia, nestles in the soft-forested folds of the Southwest Mountains. To the west, dominating the horizon, lies the Blue Ridge, backbone of the southern Appalachians. When Jefferson was a boy in the 1740s, those hazy mountains marked the edge of settlement. Few even knew what lay beyond: Some decades earlier, Virginia's Governor Alexander Spotswood and his expedition had topped the Blue Ridge in full expectation of seeing the Pacific Ocean. The creeks and streams south and east of Monticello joined to form the James River, then flowed onward to the Atlantic. A seedbed of American settlement, the James was also a key artery for subsequent development. Great planters like William Byrd and Robert Carter, whose holdings included hundreds of thousands of acres of rich bottomland, located their mansions on its shores. Ocean-going ships served these plantations, carrying hogsheads of tobacco to eager Old World markets. Tidewater and navigation ended where the James plunged over the edge of the Piedmont Plateau in a series of waterfalls and rapids. Richmond, located at this transition point, became the nerve center for the tidal lowlands and the interior.

With visions of tobacco profits luring them on, planters pushed up the James so quickly that by the 1730s, when Thomas Jefferson's father, Peter, sought land, he had to journey some 100 river miles above Richmond to a tributary called the Rivanna. Peter Jefferson exemplified the one-generation aristocrat so often encountered early in the history of the developing nation. Starting as a surveyor, Peter acquired land, cleared it, built houses, bought slaves, and eventually gained political and military office and the status of squire. The country was new, and he grew up with it almost exactly as did another surveyor-soldier-squire in the adjacent Shenandoah Valley—George Washington.

A man of prodigious physical strength, Peter Jefferson could simultaneously push several 2,000-pound hogsheads of tobacco from a prone to an upright position. On the frontier, where performance determined reputation, news of such feats spread rapidly. But Peter also used marriage as an avenue of advancement. Jane Randolph, who became his wife in 1739, belonged to the upper crust of eighteenth-century southern society—the First Families of Virginia. The Randolph pedigree extended far back in Great Britain as well as Virginia, "to which," Thomas Jefferson later advised, "let everyone ascribe the faith and merit he chooses." His own preference inclined him toward the self-made man, a natural aristocrat in his father's mold. But later kinship ties such as that between the Jefferson and Randolph families did provide the basis for Virginia's domination of the political life of the new nation, as well as for the structure of southern elitism.

Peter and Jane Randolph Jefferson celebrated the birth of their first son, Thomas, on April 13, 1743, at Shadwell, the estate they had carved from the wilderness of the upper James River. The boy grew up with all the advantages of a gentleman at Shadwell and at Tuckahoe, the sprawling Randolph holding downstream. Private tutoring began at the age of five, intensive instruction in Greek and Latin when he was nine. A smattering of French, some contact with the English classics, and the customary heavy dose of religion completed Thomas's early formal education.

But he had other teachers. His father, whom he revered, was a living example of the rewards of resolution, diligence, and organization in the manner of Benjamin Franklin. And there were the red-earth hills of Albemarle County and the Blue Ridge country of Virginia. Because Jefferson's perspective on this environment was that of the gentleman rather than the frontiersman, he found delight, not challenge, in nature. Living comfortably amid cleared fields in the aftermath of the first wave of settlement, he could love the frontier in a way quite foreign to those who did the clearing. The freedom and simplicity of the American wilderness permeated Jefferson's life, while its mysteries sparked a lifelong interest in science and exploration and its beauty inspired an intense patriotism.

In 1760, at the age of seventeen, Thomas Jefferson left the quiet foothills of the Blue Ridge for two years of instruction at the College of William and Mary in Williamsburg. Founded in 1693, William and Mary was the pride of the South and, next to Harvard, the oldest collegiate institution in North America. Jefferson made the perfect student. Intensely serious and capable of sustained study, he became enthralled by the world of scholarship and refinement. To be sure, there were parties, girls, and drinking, but hangovers seemed only to drive a contrite Jefferson to greater concentration on his courses. His intelligence impressed all his associates, particularly George Wythe, a professor of law.

Wythe also enjoyed good living and high thinking, and he introduced his students to the circle that gathered from time to time at the home of Francis Fauquier, royal governor of Virginia. Jefferson took special delight in these occasions, brilliant by eighteenth-century provincial standards. He contributed to the musical entertainment, partook of the fine food, and participated enthusiastically in the spirited discussions. Jefferson's life and the history of his country were caught for a moment in a quiet eddy. As the music and laughter drifted from the governor's palace into the velvet of a Chesapeake evening, revolution seemed inconceivable. And George Wythe could hardly have imagined that in a dozen years he would sign a declaration of independence written by his red-haired student from the backwoods academies of Albemarle County.

Jefferson's college idyll ended in 1762, but he continued to study, reading law with George Wythe. Two years later he assumed title, under the terms of his father's will, to an estate of several thousand acres and several hundred slaves—and he became one of the colony's most eligible bachelors. But this windfall did not bring Jefferson luck in love. After months of agony, his passion for sixteen-year-old Rebecca Burwell produced, he ruefully admitted, only "a few broken sentences, uttered in great disorder" as the couple danced at a Williamsburg ball. Reconciled to being single, Jefferson continued his legal studies with even fiercer determination. When he finally took the bar examination in 1767, he probably knew more than his examiners.

The ineptness Jefferson demonstrated in the presence of Rebecca Burwell undoubtedly led him to admire masters of the spoken word. One of the best in Jefferson's time was another backcountry boy named Patrick Henry. Jefferson first encountered this firebrand, seven years his senior, at a Christmas party in the late 1750s. He at first felt Henry to be somewhat coarse and crude—but then Henry passed his bar examination after only five weeks of study. In 1763 Henry further impressed Jefferson, Virginia, and the colonies with a brilliant performance in a case known as the Parsons' Cause. The parsons were the Anglican clergymen in Virginia; their cause was to secure a higher salary from hostile local taxpayers. Americans distrusted any hint of an established religion and readily associated the Anglican Church with British government. At the climax of the dispute, Patrick Henry addressed a jury sitting to decide the amount of back pay to award a disgruntled parson. In an emotional flood of eloquence, Henry accused King George III of having "degenerated into a tyrant" by overruling a Virginia law respecting the pay of clergy. The jury responded by awarding the beleaguered clergyman the grand total of one penny. Americans chortled gleefully, and Henry became a hero overnight.

He did not rest on his laurels for long. In 1765 the House of Burgesses in Virginia took up the question of Parliament's right to impose a stamp tax on the unrepresented colonists, and Henry assumed leadership of the radicals. On May 30 Jefferson was standing in the doorway of the Burgesses' chamber as a spectator when Henry arose to defend a set of seven resolutions repudiating the Stamp Act. "Caesar had his Brutus," he allegedly thundered, "Charles the First his Cromwell, and George the Third . . ." Jefferson was aghast, and cries of "Treason!" rang through the assembly, but Henry continued, " . . . and George the Third may profit by their example." Then, turning to his hecklers, Henry shouted, "If this be treason, make the most of it." After more heated exchanges the sharply divided Burgesses passed four of Henry's resolutions and thereby helped define the ideological grounds for the American Revolution. Jefferson was moved. Henry, he confessed, "appeared to me to speak as Homer wrote." And soon after hearing Henry's tirade before the Burgesses, Jefferson adopted as his personal motto: "Rebellion to tyrants is obedience to God."

The friction between Patrick Henry and the more conservative Virginia politicians that surfaced during the debate on the Stamp Act Resolutions was part of a pattern in many colonies in the decade before independence. As historian Carl Becker has put it, Americans were concerned at this time not only about the question of "home rule," but also about "who should rule at home." In other words, there was an internal or domestic aspect to the Revolution paralleling the external conflict with Great Britain. At stake at home were political leadership and the power, privilege, and prestige that accompanied it. Before 1760 royal officers, sometimes in collaboration with important colonists, had held the keys to such power. In many colonies, a single man or family controlled the political machine. John Robinson, treasurer and speaker of the House of Burgesses, for instance, ran Jefferson's Virginia. Few went far in Virginia politics without his blessing. Although younger, ambitious men were frustrated, the Robinson-led gentry held tight rein.

About 1763, however, the issue that was to upset the traditional power structure—American independence—appeared. The young insurgents recognized its potential as an avenue of political advancement: if they could associate the colonial establishment with Great Britain, patriotism could be used to engineer its downfall. Natural rights might cut a wide swath and level the colonial oligarchy as well as Parliament and George III. Indeed, some old-line American leaders came to regret their championing of John Locke and the entire independence movement. Better to suffer British rule, they concluded, than to risk losing their favored position in a reshuffling of the American deck.

Before the Revolution, Patrick Henry led the forces of internal insurgency in Virginia. It is significant that he came from the western up-country and had the backing of small farmers and traders. The tension between this geographic and economic group and the tidewater aristocracy of great planters had long been a fact of political life in Virginia and other southern colonies. A century before Henry, for instance, Nathaniel Bacon had led frontier forces in an abortive revolt against the coastal elite that was no minor squabble. In the aftermath of Bacon's Rebellion, twenty-three men were executed.

The "young hotheads," as Governor Fauquier termed them, did not precipitate such a direct confrontation in the 1760s and 1770s, but Virginians looked worriedly at neighboring North Carolina, where an association of western farmers known as the Regulators fought a pitched battle with tidewater planters. Patrick Henry preferred more subtle means, however. Associating the oligarchy with British authority, he succeeded in swinging the balance of power in the House of Burgesses to the "hotheads." The Stamp Act debates of 1765 proved that John Robinson's system of government was on the wane. The next year, the old elite received a further jolt when an examination of Robinson's accounts revealed considerable corruption. The tidewater gentry never fully recovered. By the mid-1770s, when vital questions about the imperial relationship had to be decided, the House of Burgesses was in the hands of radical newcomers: Patrick Henry, Richard Henry Lee, Francis L. Lee, George Mason, George Washington, and Thomas Jefferson. Without the loosening effect of the American Revolution on the internal power structure of the colonies, it is possible that none of these men would have achieved political leadership.

Thomas Jefferson first assumed political office in 1769, when Albemarle County elected him a member of the House of Burgesses. Only twenty-six at the time, he won the approval of both gentry and plain people. Such double backing was common in the eighteenth-century South and proved effective in identifying political talent. The necessity of pleasing both camps discouraged both the haughty aristocrat and the popular rabble-rouser. The final products of the system were leaders who, like Jefferson, combined democracy and aristocracy.

As Jefferson gained experience and confidence as a burgess, he gave increasing attention to the protest against Britain. In 1773 he joined Patrick Henry and Richard Henry Lee in calling for a Committee of Correspondence to solidify the colonial cause. Samuel Adams had begun this practice in Massachusetts the previous year but had confined the communications to towns within the colony. The Virginians had an intercolonial organization in mind, and Jefferson personally helped get it under way with his facile pen. In the process, he began to acquire a reputation outside Virginia.

The first months of 1774 brought the disquieting news of the Boston Tea Party and Parliament's punitive response. Jefferson was among those who strongly sympathized with the people of Massachusetts, and he represented their plight as an American problem rather than a local one. He also sponsored a measure in the House of Burgesses calling for twenty-four hours of fasting in Virginia on June 1, 1774, the day the Boston Port Act went into effect. An enraged Governor John Dunmore dissolved the assembly, but its members defied him and regrouped in the Raleigh Tavern next door. There they proposed an intercolonial congress and resolved "an attack on any one colony should be considered as an attack on the whole." Although few realized its implications, this breakdown of the royal governor's authority was Virginia's revolution.

Later in the summer of 1774, representatives of the various Virginia counties convened in Williamsburg to choose delegates to the Continental Congress. In preparation for the meeting, Jefferson wrote *A Summary View of the Rights of British America*. The tract was intended as a handbook for Virginia's members at the congress, but in pamphlet form it quickly reached a much wider audience on both sides of the Atlantic. In *A Summary View,* Jefferson stood squarely on natural rights philosophy as he had learned it from John Locke and other English constitutional theorists. He began by pointing out that the English settlers who had immigrated to the New World had not thereby relinquished their liberties as English citizens and as human beings. Specifically, they had not agreed to be governed by an assembly—Parliament—in which they were not represented. As for George III, Jefferson made it clear that in his view, "kings are the servants not the proprietors of the people." Submission to monarchs was voluntary and could be voluntarily abandoned if the relationship threatened natural rights. Clinching his argument, Jefferson asked, "Can his majesty . . . put down all law under his feet? Can he erect a power superior to that which erected himself? He has done it indeed by force, but let him remember that force cannot give right."

These were strong words, but Jefferson stopped short of actually proposing revolution. He referred to the colonies as "British America" and called for the end of Parliament's power to tax and regulate trade rather than for outright independence. Yet even this seemed too much for the majority of the Williamsburg gathering, which adopted resolutions that in Jefferson's opinion were mild as a "sucking dove." In a candid moment, however, Jefferson admitted that the leap he proposed in *A Summary View* was "too long as yet for the mass of our citizens." In 1774 all but a radical fringe of colonists regarded themselves as loyal British subjects and stood by the distinction conceding Parliament the right to regulate trade but not the right to tax colonists in order to raise revenue. A conception of American nationality was growing steadily, however. Thomas Paine expressed it in *Common Sense*. In no instance, he wrote, "hath nature made the satellite larger than its primary planet; and as England and America, with respect to each other, reverse the common order of nature, it is evident that they belong in different systems. England to Europe: America to itself."

Jefferson soon had an opportunity to take the leading role in implementing this idea of independence. He arrived in Philadelphia in June 1775 to sit as one of Virginia's delegates to the Second Continental Congress. Although he was the second youngest member of the assembly, necks craned as Jefferson entered the hall. His reputation for logical thought and, in John Adams's words, a "masterly pen" had preceded him. Shortly thereafter, Congress entrusted

Jefferson with the drafting of several important papers, including the rejection of a proposal of conciliation from Britain's prime minister, Frederick, Lord North.

On June 7, 1776, the congress passed Richard Henry Lee's motion that "these United Colonies are and of right ought to be free and independent states." A five-man committee, including Jefferson, John Adams, and Benjamin Franklin, was instructed to draft a formal declaration of the congress's intent. Franklin, whom Jefferson revered, might well have done the writing, but he declined. Jefferson then proposed that Adams undertake the task, after which, according to Adams's recollection, the following dialogue ensued:

ADAMS: Oh! no.

JEFFERSON: Why will you not? You ought to do it.

ADAMS: I will not.

JEFFERSON: Why?

ADAMS: Reasons enough.

JEFFERSON: What can be your reasons?

ADAMS: Reason first—You are a Virginian, and a Virginian ought to appear at the head of this business. Reason second—I am obnoxious, suspected, and unpopular. You are very much otherwise. Reason third—You can write ten times better than I can.

JEFFERSON: Well, if you are decided I will do as well as I can.

So it was that on June 11 the thirty-three-year-old Thomas Jefferson retired to the tiny parlor of his lodgings at Seventh and Market and began to write his way to immortality.

For over two weeks, Jefferson's quill pen scratched out draft after draft of a declaration. Eighteen hundred highly polished words finally emerged. Franklin, Adams, and the rest of the committee looked at them and made several suggestions. On June 28 the congress scrutinized Jefferson's work. He must have cringed inwardly as his painstaking efforts were criticized, revised, and abridged. Yet the version signed on July 4, 1776, was a monument to one man.

Jefferson was modest, to be sure. He never pretended that the Declaration of Independence was anything but a compilation of the ideas of others, a summary of the spirit of the time and place. Years afterward he wrote of the Declaration, "Neither aiming at originality of principle or sentiment, nor yet copied from any particular and previous writing, it was intended to be an expression of the American mind." Jefferson's most obvious intellectual debt was to John Locke and the other Enlightenment philosophers of natural rights. But the Virginian did alter the usual trio of life, liberty, and property to read "life, liberty, and the pursuit of Happiness." George Mason had made the same substitution in his Virginia Bill of Rights of June 12, 1776, and Jefferson clearly used his friend's manifesto as inspiration and guide. Still, the flowing, compelling style of the Declaration of Independence was Jefferson's alone. Although the word was yet to be coined, he had produced a masterpiece of *propaganda*—a justification as well as a declaration.

That Jefferson was well aware of his function as a propagandist is evident in his opening lines. "A decent respect to the opinions of mankind" is stated as the reason for the declaration. Jefferson knew that "a candid world," as well as reluctant revolutionaries at home, would look at the document as an explanation of the legitimacy of the Revolution.

Indeed, many colonists were frankly pro-British and loyal to George III. These Tories had no desire for independence and actively discouraged the movement. Their opposition made it imperative that the revolt be made respectable—a matter of duty rather than choice. The action

This is a portion of Jefferson's original four-page draft of the Declaration of Independence, which he began composing June 11, 1776, in Philadelphia.

of the colonies had therefore to be defended on the highest grounds of universal principle. British taxation, for example, was disliked because it flattened the colonists' purses, but economic self-interest was an unacceptable reason for a revolution. Good revolutionary technique required the expression of grievances in terms of violations of "the laws of nature and of nature's God." Using Lockean theory, Jefferson sublimated self-interest (that is, taxes and the loss of property) to principle (that is, the natural right of the sanctity of property and liberty). Using Enlightenment ideas, he made George III appear to be not merely an inconvenience in certain ways but a threat to a widely held ideal of human freedom. Indeed, George emerged from Jefferson's scathing pen a tyrannical ogre. Much could have been said for the British side, of course, but in writing the Declaration, Jefferson's purpose was persuasion, not scholarship.

With independence declared, Jefferson, like other newly minted Americans, faced the sobering task of justifying the Revolution with success. Not only did the proclaimed state of independence have to be confirmed on the battlefield, but the new nation suddenly had a host of awesome responsibilities thrust upon it. These ranged from creating a viable economy to establishing a workable system of government based on republican principles. Thomas Paine had written ecstatically in *Common Sense* about the glorious opportunity that an independent America had to "begin the world over again." Doing it, however, was another matter. Americans were now alone, without Great Britain to provide government, defense, and economic stability.

John Trumbull's painting *Declaration of Independence* was executed in the 1780s, partly while Trumbull was in Paris as Thomas Jefferson's guest. A perfectionist, Trumbull painted thirty-six of the figures from life. Facing John Hancock (standing, right) are, from the left, John Adams, Roger Sherman, Roger Livingston, Thomas Jefferson, and Benjamin Franklin.

Matters were even more daunting when one recognizes that Britain, with its long experience in government and its immense resources, had been unable to solve many of the problems inherent in the American situation. Mercantilism had proved unworkable; the economy was in chaos, and thirteen separate and self-seeking entities were each going their own way. The same internal discord had doomed any permanent effort at unified government of all the American colonies. Britain, moreover, had failed to discover ways of raising revenue for defense and administration. And there was the western land issue, which had simply been swept under the rug with the Proclamation of 1763. Inexperienced Americans were now confronted with all these same problems. Moreover, the wealth and leadership ability of 80,000 Tories, or Loyalists, who fled the country during and after the Revolution were no longer available to help build a nation.

Amid the doubt and uncertainty, Jefferson's America could count a few assets in facing the formidable task of creating a nation. One was a determination to establish the legitimacy of the Revolution, to prove the scoffers and critics wrong, to erase self-doubts. In addition, Jefferson and his contemporaries clung to the old idea that they were God's chosen people, destined to lead humankind in the paths of righteousness. From this perspective, the entire world had a stake in what happened on the edge of the North American wilderness. "The cause of America," as Paine put it, "is in great measure the cause of all mankind." And Philip Freneau, whose newspaper Jefferson later sponsored, solemnly proclaimed American independence an event commensurate in importance with the birth of Christ. True or not, the belief of many Americans in this rejuvenated conception of mission was one of their chief advantages in meeting the responsibilities of nationhood.

Despite all the talk about America, the united colonies, and the Continental Congress, when Thomas Jefferson thought of his country in the late 1770s, he had Virginia in mind. Most of his contemporaries shared this geopolitical orientation. Their loyalty to their respective colonies was, after all, of much longer standing than that to the larger united body. Indeed, there were serious doubts about whether there would be unification after the fighting ended. Perhaps the various colonies would go their separate ways in the manner of the smaller European nations. Understandably, then, Jefferson's thoughts turned to Virginia immediately after publication of the Declaration of Independence. In his view, the reshaping of Virginia's laws and policy "is the whole object of the present controversy; for should a bad government be instituted for us . . . it had been as well to have accepted . . . the bad one offered to us from beyond the water." Jefferson also knew that the end of British rule meant a rare opportunity to translate political and social ideals into reality. He grew restless in Philadelphia throughout the spring and summer of 1776. Even as he wrote the Declaration of Independence, he yearned to be in Williamsburg, and at the first convenient moment after its adoption, he resigned his seat in the congress.

Happily returned to Virginia, Jefferson at once launched a comprehensive effort to bring the new state's laws and institutions into conformity with republican principles and natural rights. His first target was the Virginia aristocracy. Although part of it himself, Jefferson realized that true liberty could not exist in a society dominated by an entrenched oligarchy. It was not the concept of an elite to which Jefferson objected but the fact that the elite had been established and perpetuated by artificial means. Instead of earning a silver spoon, its members had been born with one in their mouths. What Jefferson hoped to do was "to annul this privilege, and instead of an aristocracy of wealth . . . to make an opening for the aristocracy of virtue and talent." The result should be a "natural aristocrat"—a happy blend of Jefferson's contact with both Enlightenment philosophy and the American frontier.

The foundation of Virginia's pre-Revolutionary aristocracy was land: Huge holdings passed from generation to generation according to the rules of entail and primogeniture. In this arrangement, which dated from feudal times, estates passed intact from the owner to his firstborn son. They could not be subdivided nor sold outside the family.

In Jefferson's words, primogeniture and entail operated to create "a distinct set of families who, being privileged by law in the perpetuation of their wealth, were thus formed into a patrician order, distinguished by the splendor and luxury of their establishments." Such a situation not being consistent with the right of everyone to life, liberty, and the pursuit of happiness, Jefferson proposed the abolition of both entail and primogeniture. The oligarchy was suspicious, of course; only his popularity and political tact eventually pushed the bills through.

Religion also attracted Jefferson's reforming energies. For more than a century, the Church of England had enjoyed a favored position in Virginia. Anglicanism was, in fact, the established religion, virtually a branch of the government. Jefferson deplored this situation. A disciple of the Enlightenment doctrine of freedom of thought, he believed that truth needed no enforcement other than its own inherent logic and reasonableness: "It is error alone which needs the support of government. Truth can stand by itself." This was the sense of the term *self-evident* that Jefferson, at Franklin's suggestion, used in the Declaration of Independence.

Jefferson was therefore bitterly opposed to any government effort to enforce or even assist a particular creed, not only as a violation of individual liberties but also as a poor way of making converts. Illustrating his point from the history of science, Jefferson pointed out that "the

Newtonian principle of gravitation is now more firmly established on the basis of reason than it would be were the government to step in and to make it an article of necessary faith." Throughout history, Jefferson concluded, force in matters of belief only made "one half the world fools, and the other half hypocrites. . . . Reason and free inquiry are the only effectual agents against error." He held that one's religion did not fall under the jurisdiction of civil authority. "The legitimate powers of government," he explained, "extend to such acts only as are injurious to others. But it does me no injury for my neighbor to say there are twenty gods, or no God. It neither picks my pocket nor breaks my leg."

To implement his ideas, Jefferson drafted a bill for establishing religious freedom in Virginia. After a ringing preamble, it declared in part that "all men shall be free to profess, and by argument to maintain, their opinions in matters of religion." Here was a guarantee of freedom of conscience for every citizen, whether Hindu, Christian, or atheist. Even more, Jefferson's arguments and his sweeping definition of free thought supported the principle that the opinions of any person on any subject were not the concern of civil government.

The final enactment of Jefferson's bill in 1786 was a major milestone. The young nation had lived up to the promises of Roger Williams and William Penn. To the delight of Jefferson and his compatriots, the Virginia Statute for Religious Freedom was translated into several languages and circulated widely in Europe. Several publishers reprinted the document as an expression of Enlightenment philosophy. Jefferson believed that this particular law put Americans a thousand years ahead of Europeans with respect to human freedom. "It is comfortable," he wrote to James Madison in 1786, "to see the standard of reason at length erected, after so many ages, during which the human mind has been held in vassalage by kings, priests, and nobles." And with an eye to the American obsession with justifying the Revolution successfully, he added, "It is honorable for us to have produced the first legislature who had the courage to declare that the reason of man may be trusted with the formation of his own opinions."

Jefferson regarded education as another key to the transition from a monarchic to a democratic society. He was convinced that a people could not be both ignorant and free. Indeed, he wrote to Wythe, the most important part of the whole revision of Virginia's code of laws concerned "the diffusion of knowledge among the people." There was much to support his view. Democracy meant popular sovereignty—that is, government by the people. Yet if the people were uninformed and incapable of making judgments about their own lives, unscrupulous opportunists could lead them into tyranny. History, he knew, offered many examples of the enslavement of an uneducated citizenry. And Virginia society, like that of the rest of the new states, was composed of a few islands of refinement in an ocean of ignorance. Such gross inequality created ripe soil for oppression.

As a remedy, Jefferson proposed three years of free education for every citizen in the state, male and female. The basic skills of reading, writing, and arithmetic would be emphasized, and so would the study of the past, for Jefferson believed that "history, by apprizing [children] of the past, will enable them to judge of the future . . . it will qualify them as judges of the actions and designs of men; it will enable them to know ambition under every guise it may assume; and knowing it, to defeat its views." Though only three years of free elementary schooling were provided, the educational ladder would have more steps. Jefferson felt students on the intermediate level would come from families "in easy circumstances" who could afford to pay tuition and board, but he stipulated that up to seventy of the best impoverished students in Virginia be given full scholarships. After a year, the state-supported scholars would be pared to the twenty "best geniuses." They would study for five more years. Finally, a select group of ten scholarship students would receive a free education at the College of William and Mary.

It was a brilliant and farsighted plan, "adapted," as Jefferson declared, "to the capacity, and the condition of every one and directed to their freedom and happiness." Unfortunately, Virginia adopted only portions of the plan, and those only gradually. Not until 1825 did an aging Jefferson have the satisfaction of seeing the University of Virginia, an institution he created almost single-handedly, open in Charlottesville as the capstone of the state's educational pyramid.

In 1779 the Virginia legislature called Thomas Jefferson to succeed Patrick Henry as governor. He assumed the office in an atmosphere of fear and gloom. The war with Britain was not going well. Supplies and money had run short. Even General George Washington's repeated and personal pleas for aid found Governor Jefferson helpless. His own plantations were stripped on behalf of the Revolution, and he had many companions in poverty. Fewer than half of Virginia's counties paid taxes in 1780. The state militia could be equipped with only one musket for each five men. In addition, the British decided to shift the focus of their military efforts to the South. Charleston, South Carolina, fell on May 12, 1780, to a naval strike under generals Henry Clinton and Charles Cornwallis. On December 30 a fleet of twenty-seven British ships appeared at the mouth of Chesapeake Bay. Virginia could offer no resistance, and the force, under the American deserter Benedict Arnold, sailed up the James toward the new capital city of Richmond. Jefferson supervised the removal of the state papers, transferred his family to a safe location upriver, and then returned to watch despondently from across the James as Arnold's men burned the city.

In the dark months of early 1781, it must have seemed to the harassed Jefferson that America's hopes of winning its independence were also going up in smoke. No sooner did he move the seat of government to Charlottesville than Cornwallis was at its door. On June 4 Jefferson slipped away from Monticello only minutes before a British force arrived to capture him. Seven legislators were taken. But even as the remainder fled across the Blue Ridge, the tide was turning in the southern theater of war. Tough American mountaineers under generals Nathaniel Green and Daniel Morgan had already decisively defeated British regulars at King's Mountain, Cowpens, and Guilford Courthouse in the Carolina backcountry. The Charlottesville raid was, in fact, the last offensive move Cornwallis made. Less than four months later he stood defeated at Yorktown.

With the fighting and his term as governor both at an end, Jefferson retired to Monticello, his family, his library, his horses, his music, and his science. In 1772, he married a young, attractive Martha Wayles, who was a widow at the age of 23. Deeply devoted to her and to his work at home, Jefferson vowed he would never leave his hilltop oasis for the hurly-burly of public service. With enthusiasm he turned to writing *Notes on the State of Virginia,* a proud answer to a European's inquiry about the ideals and circumstances of the new society. The book was printed privately in Paris in 1785. He entertained another European, the traveling Chevalier de Chastellux, at Monticello. After four days of companionship, the visitor wrote, "Let me describe to you a man, not yet forty, tall, and with a mild and pleasing countenance . . . an American, who without ever having quitted his own country, is at once a musician, skilled in drawing, a geometrician, an astronomer, a natural philosopher, legislator, and statesman . . . in voluntary retirement from the world."

A classic portrait, but Jefferson was unable to play this idyllic role for long. The first crack came late in 1782 when Martha succumbed to a long illness. Not long afterward, another opportunity for public service, this time in the national arena as a congressman, came Jefferson's way. At first he refused, claiming both personal grief and pique over criticism of his governorship as

Among the many skills the versatile Jefferson perfected were architecture and horticulture. His own home, Monticello, overlooking Charlottesville in western Virginia, is a monument to its owner's sense of grace and proportion.

reasons for his aloofness. But interesting developments were taking place on the federal level, and just as in the case of Virginia's government, he realized that the success of the whole revolutionary effort hinged on whether satisfactory political forms could be devised. Here was a challenge calculated to stir Jefferson to action. He knew that republics were rare in the history of civilization. People had usually relied more on authority from above (monarchy, oligarchy, or theocracy) for government. In fact, the Greek city-states were among the few examples of true republics in history; these had been small units of several thousand citizens in which popular sovereignty had had great meaning. The United States, however, proposed to govern three million people in a republican framework. There were no precedents for such an undertaking, and many felt a republic on this scale would degenerate inevitably into either anarchy or tyranny.

The Continental Congress began to experiment in national government immediately after proclaiming independence. John Dickinson of Pennsylvania proposed a strong central government in which the states had little power. Some of his colleagues, however, thought such a government too similar to the one they had just overthrown. They countered with the Articles of Confederation, which deliberately created a weak national government. Under the Articles, the central government had no courts, no executive leadership, no power to regulate trade and commerce, and no independent source of revenue apart from requisitions from the states. Moreover, on most important issues, the approval of all the member states was required. This plan for a spineless central government was submitted to the states in November 1777 and, with unanimous approval finally obtained, was instituted on March 1, 1781. For Americans who thought in terms of the nation rather than the states, the approval of the plan was no cause for celebration. In their estimation, Americans had overreacted, had rushed headlong from one undesirable extremity of the political spectrum to the other.

Thomas Jefferson reentered the national political arena in December 1783, when he rode to Annapolis, Maryland, to take his seat in Congress as a delegate from Virginia. Widely respected throughout the country, he immediately assumed a major role. One of his first assignments was to arrange for the visit of General George Washington. Already a demigod in American eyes, Washington came to Annapolis to relinquish his sword to Congress. The ceremony of December 23 was charged with emotion. Many wept openly in gratitude. To Jefferson, however, Washington's appearance had a deeper significance. By turning over his sword, the general in effect rejected the idea that he had become a military dictator. In the 1780s, with an insecure nation yearning for leadership, this was not a farfetched possibility. In the winter of 1782–1783, a group of army officers, joined by proponents of strong central government, had approached Washington with the idea of seizing power. The general had made his disapproval very clear. Now, at Annapolis, the one American who had the popularity to undermine republicanism formally and publicly made his commitment to a republic. Like Jefferson, Washington had rebelled in the name of republican principles, and he meant to give them a fair trial. Had he been otherwise inclined, American history could well have been totally different.

While adamantly opposed to monarchical substitutes, Jefferson remained critical of the central government established under the Articles of Confederation. As a congressman he had ample opportunity to study its weaknesses. Some problems, he believed, were related to the time and circumstance. Congress had no money, for instance, but only because the war-ravaged state economies were temporarily in disorder. The financial position of the central government would improve with that of the country in general. A more serious difficulty was the contemptuous attitude of many of the states. Some did not even bother to send representatives to Congress. Jefferson was present, however, and he was determined to make the best of the Articles. His service to the new government was, typically, brilliant. One of his reports made order out of the chaotic coinage system of the time by proposing the adoption of the basic unit of the "dollar," divided into tenths and hundredths.

Of still greater consequence was Jefferson's influence on western land policy. Congress inherited this thorny problem from Great Britain when several states, led by New York and Virginia, ceded their western land claims to the central government. The cession itself was a triumph for federalism, but it obliged the United States to become an imperial power with all the attendant responsibilities. The western territories, in other words, bore the same relation to the United States as the thirteen colonies had once had to Great Britain. There was the same perplexing question of management, the same danger of rebellion should Congress become as unsatisfactory as Parliament.

The colonial policy that emerged owed a great deal to Thomas Jefferson. On March 22, 1784, he submitted a plan of government for the territories. Its genius was embodied in the provision that the western lands would be organized into states, which, when they had a sufficient number of settlers, would be welcomed into the union on an equal basis with the original thirteen—no virtual representation, no taxation without representation, no second-class citizenship, but rather an invitation to join the union. Had Britain granted as much in the early 1770s, the professed need for the American Revolution would have been eliminated, and war, in all probability, would have been averted. Jefferson's plan had the further advantage of encouraging

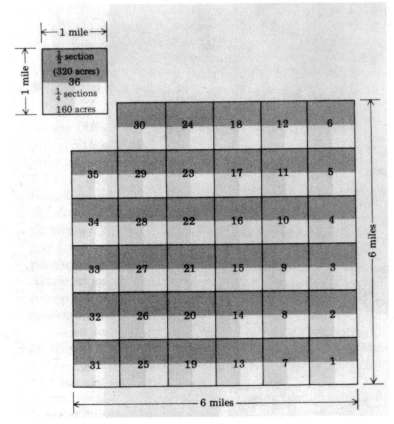

The influence of the Enlightenment and science in general on Thomas Jefferson is evident in his plan for surveying the unoccupied territory of the West. Adopted by Congress as the Land Ordinance of 1785, the plan's geometric regularity shaped the landscape of an expanding nation. The entire six-mile square was called a township, and it consisted of thirty-six sections, each one mile square. These, in turn, could be divided according to the detail shown in Section 36. One disadvantage of Jefferson's system was that its rigid structure did not take the natural features of the environment into account. The lines ran straight, regardless of rivers, mountains, or lakes.

settlement of the West by assuring those who migrated that they would suffer no loss of rights or liberties. It even guaranteed manhood suffrage in the territories, a step toward democracy that none of the original states had yet taken. A slave owner himself, Jefferson proposed that slavery be prohibited in the western territories after 1800. Finally, as a disciple of order, he suggested a rectangular survey system for the unsettled land.

The essentials of Jefferson's western plan were incorporated in the Land Ordinance of 1785 and the Northwest Ordinance of 1787. These great laws, the high point of government under the Articles of Confederation, made possible one of the most successful colonizing efforts in history. The United States expanded from the Appalachians to the Pacific without losing a single acre to an independence movement. Every territory ultimately entered the union in preference to forming a separate nation. As students of Great Britain's imperial misadventures, Jefferson and his colleagues had learned their lessons well.

Valuable as Jefferson was at home, Congress needed able representatives abroad. On July 5, 1784, he sailed for France. After assisting John Adams and Benjamin Franklin for a year in negotiating commercial treaties, Jefferson took Franklin's place as American ambassador to France. It was a happy choice. Although he lacked Franklin's enormous popularity, Jefferson's reputation as an architect of American independence endeared him to French liberals. As the French Revolution gathered momentum, Jefferson's counsel was increasingly sought. He personally believed that "the American war seems first to have awakened the thinking part of the nation . . . from the sleep of despotism in which they were sunk." Young French officers, Jefferson explained, had returned from service in the New World enthusiastic about the republican regime they had seen in operation. When they joined other republicans in launching a revolt against their king, Jefferson was understandably delighted. Even as the course of the French Revolution turned toward the guillotine, he never lost faith that its basic energies had sprung from the same concepts of human dignity and freedom that had motivated Americans.

Jefferson remained abroad five years. His characteristic response to what he termed "the vaunted scene of Europe" was awe. Patriotic as he tried to be, he could not help but be reminded of his provincialism by the brilliance of European cultural and intellectual life. "Were I . . . to tell you how much I enjoy their architecture, sculpture, painting, music," Jefferson wrote in 1785, "I should want words." He also coveted European books and returned from Paris with enough to fill 250 feet of shelves at Monticello. And then there were the charms of sophisticated European women—notably Maria Cosway, the wife of an English painter, with whom Jefferson traveled through France in the summer of 1786.

But at the same time, Jefferson almost desperately resisted European attempts to turn his attention from his own country. Groping for ways to maintain pride in the United States, he pointed out that Americans enjoyed greater civil and economic equality than in the Old World, where everyone "must be either the hammer or the anvil." Americans were also more moral, Jefferson generalized, and in their natural environment they possessed a resource of matchless beauty. If not culture, then nature would distinguish the young nation on the edge of the wilderness. Still "the vaunted scene" was compelling to the self-styled "savage of the mountains of America." Not for many decades would Americans acquire the cultural confidence to trust their own judgment and taste.

Critics of democracy, especially in Europe, predicted that mob rule would soon break out in the United States. The winter of 1786–1787 reinforced that prediction when, in Massachusetts, a pitched battle between impoverished western farmers, organized under Daniel Shays, and the state militia began. Actually, Shays's Rebellion was simply a continuation of the internal contest over who should rule at home, which had accompanied the larger struggle with Great Britain. Both the Shaysites and the Boston establishment understood their cause to be sanctified by natural rights and thus in keeping with the principles of the American Revolution. The problem was that this doctrine made no distinction between human rights and property rights. Both were sacred, and if the two came into conflict (as they did, for example, in debtor–creditor relationships), there was no easy solution. Those responsible for the Declaration of Independence and the Articles of Confederation assumed that those of goodwill could work together in interpreting and institutionalizing natural rights. But Shays's Rebellion, and the prospect of similar mass uprisings elsewhere, suggested that the spirit of 1776 had not erased old social and economic inequities.

The fundamental tension juxtaposed those traditional antagonists, the haves and the have-nots. Shays, representing the latter, preferred a weak central government with its assurance of a maximum of local control by the people. He had the support of people like Jefferson, who leaned toward a human rights interpretation of Locke and who trusted democracy. Commenting on Shays's Rebellion while in Paris, Jefferson even went so far as to declare "the spirit of resistance to government is so valuable on certain occasions, that I wish it to be always kept alive. It will often be exercised when wrong, but better so than not . . . at all. I like a little rebellion now and then. It is like a storm in the Atmosphere." Continuing in an even more radical vein, Jefferson wrote, "What signify a few lives lost in a century or two? The tree of liberty must be refreshed from time to time with the blood of patriots and tyrants. It is its natural manure."

Dissatisfaction with the weak central government under the Articles of Confederation continued to grow during the 1780s. No matter how well it functioned, Congress simply did not possess the power to coordinate state economic policies or protect the nation's commercial interests abroad. If the critics of the Articles of Confederation had a low opinion of human nature, they had a high one of human reason. With it, they believed, man could build a system of government capable of curbing his passion, greed, and selfishness. Armed with this conviction, twenty-nine men (later joined by twenty-six others) had gathered in Philadelphia in May 1787 to reconstruct the government of the United States. Fortunately for the outcome of their efforts, they were in agreement in certain crucial areas. All were advocates of a strong central government. Most also agreed that the Articles of Confederation were so deficient in this respect as to be totally useless. It was better to start from scratch than to revise and repair. In this reconstruction, the members of the convention believed, two principles must be incorporated. First, the new constitution must be the supreme law of the land, its power unquestionably greater than that of the various states. Second, the constitution must be a combination of monarchy, aristocracy, and democracy so arranged as to prevent the dominance of any one of these political options.

Nobody in Philadelphia seriously doubted that the people should be the basis of sovereignty in the new government. The question was how to check and balance popular opinion in the interest of the nation's well-being. Here was where reason came into play. Rather than trusting men to know and work for the good, the Founding Fathers assumed, with Lord Acton, that "power corrupts." They also took pains to remove direct elective power from the people—three stages in the case of the president, four in the case of judges. Like engineers, the constitution makers of 1787 built a series of automatic cutoffs into their power system. The result, approved on September 17, was a masterpiece. In a single summer and without precedents or guides, the Constitutional Convention created a framework of government that has lasted for more than two centuries.

Jefferson, following the Constitutional Convention from Paris, had mixed reactions. He liked the tripartite division of power among the executive, legislative, and judicial branches. He approved of giving the new legislature the power to levy taxes, and he was "captivated" by the compromise that established a bicameral legislature, with the states represented on the basis of population in one house and equally in the other. But other aspects of the Philadelphia convention disturbed him deeply. In the first place, he did not agree with most of the delegates that the country was teetering on the brink of anarchy in 1787. The Articles of Confederation, in Jefferson's opinion, had not been all that bad. "I would rather be exposed to the inconveniences attending too much liberty," he tartly observed, "than those attending too small a degree of it."

He felt that the convention would have done better to patch up the Articles of Confederation. As for the new system, Jefferson disliked the executive position created in Philadelphia. "Their President," he wrote to John Adams in November, "seems a bad edition of a Polish king." One man might be elected to the office every four years for life. Jefferson's major complaint, however, was the failure to specify the rights and liberties retained by individuals. "A bill of rights" he told James Madison, one of the prime movers at Philadelphia, "is what the people are entitled to against every government on earth . . . and what no just government should refuse, or rest on inferences." Civil liberties, in Jefferson's mind, were the reason for the American Revolution. If a strong central government destroyed them, there was no point in independence.

Jefferson therefore followed the controversy over ratification of the Constitution closely and anxiously. He noted with approval that in Virginia, such patriots as Richard Henry Lee and Patrick Henry spoke emotionally against ratification. Lee referred to the proponents of the Constitution as "a coalition of monarchy men, military men, aristocrats and drones whose noise, impudence and zeal exceeds all belief." This was extreme. Of all the so-called Federalists, probably only Alexander Hamilton considered monarchy a serious possibility. But as historian Charles A. Beard pointed out in 1913, most of those who designed and favored the Constitution were men of means, who stood to benefit economically from the stability and protection of a strong central government. Some even held for speculation on Congress's paper money, the value of which was directly proportional to the vigor and power of the United States.

This is not to say that economics alone explains the new Constitution; rather, economic self-interest was evident along with idealistic principle in the summer of 1787. No contemporary of Jefferson would have found this point far-fetched; only those who insist on sanctifying America's beginnings with totally idealistic explanations profess shock at an economic interpretation of the Constitution. The variety of economic interests that were represented at the convention, and that therefore contributed to the document, served as a type of filtration system that denied excessive power to any specific group. The desires of tidewater plantation owners had to be addressed as well as those of the Middle Atlantic merchants, and those diverse interests would never have permitted the creation of a monolithic document. While the Constitution clearly protected property rights, the Framers provided for greater popular input by enabling future Americans to amend the document. If the Framers were concerned about their own economic self-interest, they also considered the national stability provided by a supreme federal government to be crucial to the country's security. The resulting document therefore reflected a balance of democracy, federalism, and republicanism, which recognized the supremacy of the national government.

Opponents of ratification ultimately lost their struggle. Although its margin of approval was narrow (89 to 79 in the Virginia ratifying convention, 187 to 168 in Massachusetts), the new government went into operation in 1789. Americans were not long in amending the Constitution. James Madison, who had opposed a listing of individual rights as unnecessary, noted the widespread national displeasure caused by its omission and decided to correct the matter himself. He wrote a declaration of rights and sent a copy to Paris for Jefferson's comments. The reply, full of praise, contained a few suggestions for improvement. Madison took them and, in June 1789, introduced the Bill of Rights in Congress. Two years later, after approval by the states, the Bill of Rights became the first ten amendments to the Constitution.

Positive action on the Bill of Rights greatly encouraged Jefferson, and the selection of George Washington as the first president in 1789 further reduced his anxieties about the new government. Washington, he felt confident, had no ambition to become a king. Indeed, the more Jefferson thought about how the Constitution of 1787 had smoothed out the institutional wrinkles in America's republican experiment, the more enthusiastic he became. The Constitution, he declared, was "unquestionably the wisest ever yet presented to men." How it would work in practice, of course, no one yet knew.

George Washington was determined that Jefferson should take a leading role in establishing the new central government. He invited Jefferson to become secretary of state on his return from France in 1789. Given his interest in the success of the American experiment, Jefferson could not resist. After a brief stay at Monticello, he made his way north to New York, then the federal capital. There was a dramatic meeting en route at Philadelphia between Jefferson and an aged Benjamin Franklin. The two friends talked largely of mutual acquaintances and politics in France. Franklin was particularly excited about the burgeoning French Revolution. "They served their apprenticeship in America," he observed, "and now they mean to set up for themselves."

Pushing on through a snowstorm, Jefferson arrived in New York in March 1790 to take charge of a State Department consisting of five clerks. The government was already well under way. In Jefferson's opinion, however, it manifested some disturbing tendencies. Most of them stemmed from the activities of Alexander Hamilton, once Washington's aide during the war and now his secretary of the treasury. Jefferson hardly knew the ambitious and talented Hamilton when he joined the administration, but soon the two of them were "daily pitted in the cabinet like two cocks." The conflict was predictable. In direct contrast to Jefferson, Hamilton made no secret of the fact that he despised the common masses, distrusted democracy, and preferred an aristocratic or, better yet, a monarchical regime. Saddled with the Constitution, Hamilton determined to make the most of an imperfect situation. This meant maximizing the strength of the central government and encouraging the development of a wealthy elite.

To these ends, Hamilton pushed through Congress a program for funding the debt of the United States at its full face value. He also successfully advocated federal assumption of all state debts incurred in the War of Independence and the creation of a government-dominated national bank. Expensive as these measures were, they established the national credit, asserted federal superiority over the states, and encouraged those of wealth, chiefly northern businessmen, to support the United States. In 1791 Hamilton's "Report on Manufactures" proposed a protective tariff and a system of bounties, both to encourage domestic manufacturing. Jefferson was able to help block this plan, but he could not prevent Hamilton from obtaining in the same year a 25 percent excise tax on the domestic production of whiskey. This levy struck particularly hard at small farmers, who were accustomed to converting their grain into alcohol. When a group of several hundred farmers in western Pennsylvania refused to pay these taxes, Hamilton personally led a force of 13,000 militiamen to crush the Whiskey Rebellion.

Jefferson looked askance at these developments. From his perspective, it appeared that Hamilton was creating a far stronger central government than necessary—one, in fact, that posed a threat to individual liberties and republican principles. Moreover, Hamilton's advocacy of manufacturing, cities, and high finance ran directly counter to the Virginia planter's precept that "those who labor in the earth are the chosen people of God." Agriculture, Jefferson insisted, had to be the backbone of any happy society. "Let our workshops remain in Europe," he declared. America could trade for needed manufactured goods. Jefferson grew to have a well-honed contempt for Hamilton himself. In as strong language as he ever used, Jefferson labeled the secretary of the treasury "not only a monarchist, but for a monarchy bottomed on corruption." With far more regret, Jefferson said almost as much of his old revolutionary colleague John Adams, whose doubts about democracy had increased substantially. Even Washington's head sometimes seemed to have been turned by a vision of grandiose living in the ceremonial manner of the Old World courts. Inescapable in the growing rift between Hamilton and Jefferson was the former's vision of a nation based on industry, manufacturing, and commerce and the latter's vision of a nation of yeoman farmers.

With the tide thus running against republicanism, Jefferson struggled desperately. He had a few allies. Friends of his ideals in the Senate, who refused to be pressured by a president eager for certain decisions, established a precedent for legislative autonomy. These senators also resisted attempts to make Washington's official title "His Elective Majesty" or "His Most Gracious Highness," in the manner of European kings. The designation *highness,* one skeptical legislator dryly remarked, should be reserved for the tallest man in a company. This viewpoint ultimately prevailed, and the accepted form of addressing the president became, to Jefferson's delight, simply "Mr. President."

After 1791 Jefferson also had the support of Philip Freneau and his newspaper, the *National Gazette.* In fact, Jefferson gave Freneau a position in the State Department and helped him start the paper as a challenge to John Fenno's *Gazette of the United States,* which Hamilton patronized. In the hallowed tradition of eighteenth-century journalism, the papers abused each other unmercifully and in vituperative language. Washington, for one, was shocked and disappointed. He had expected, somewhat naively, that political parties would not develop in the United States. Yet by 1792 it was clear that the Federalists, grouped around Hamilton and Adams, and the Jefferson-led Democratic-Republicans were determining the course of national politics. This realization led a reluctant Washington to agree to a second term as president. He knew he was the only American capable of holding back the partisan deluge.

Questions of foreign policy added fuel to the political fires of the 1790s. Once again, Hamilton and Jefferson squared off. The secretary of the treasury tended to admire and favor Britain both as a commercial power and as a monarchy. Jefferson, on the other hand, supported France and its revolution on both philosophical and personal grounds. Even after the execution of Louis XVI in 1793 and the massacres by the Jacobins, Jefferson's loyalty held firm. But in Federalist circles around the capital and among the upper classes generally, Jefferson was a marked man. People crossed streets to avoid encountering the "Jacobin," and Hamilton exploited his advantage to the hilt. As a result, when war broke out between France and Britain, Jefferson was at a severe disadvantage. He attempted to obtain sympathy for France by reminding Washington of the 1778 Treaty of Alliance that had been so helpful to the American revolutionary cause. Hamilton countered with the argument that the old treaty had been made with the now-dethroned French monarchy and was, consequently, void. When Washington supported this interpretation, Jefferson had little choice but to resign as secretary of state, a step he took at the end of 1793. By this time, the brazen behavior of the French emissary, Citizen Edmond Genet, in commissioning American privateers to prey on English shipping had alienated even Jefferson.

In 1794 a pro-British foreign policy seemed likely, but Britain did little to cultivate American support. In fact, Britain harassed the United States both on the high seas, where American ships were seized, and on the northwest frontier, where Indians were encouraged to take the warpath. War with Britain seemed imminent in 1794, but John Jay warded off hostilities by negotiating a controversial treaty. It succeeded in removing the British from frontier forts in the Ohio Valley, establishing formal commercial relations, and settling boundary and war debt questions remaining from the Revolution. On the burning issue of maritime rights, however, the Jay Treaty said nothing. It also ignored the fact that Canadian fur traders had unrestricted access to American soil and freely sold arms and ammunition to the Indians.

Leading the Democratic-Republican opposition, Jefferson branded the Jay Treaty neocolonial. The Senate barely approved the agreement in June 1795. Washington, too, was torn but finally yielded to Hamilton's arguments and signed the document, in the face of widespread national criticism. His decision almost certainly postponed a second war with Great Britain, the major objective of Federalist foreign policy. Washington's diplomacy was further distinguished in the 1790s by the favorable Treaty of San Lorenzo (the Pinckney Treaty) of 1796. According to its terms, the United States received important concessions from Spain regarding rights and boundaries in the West. The final movement in the diplomatic minuet of the 1790s involved the United States in an undeclared war with France. An insult to America's foreign ministers by Talleyrand (the XYZ affair) led to a state of open maritime conflict for several years.

John Adams and the Federalists won the presidential election of 1796, but under the awkward electoral college system, Thomas Jefferson, the Democratic-Republican nominee for president, became Adams's vice president. From this vantage point of honored obscurity, Jefferson had ample opportunity to observe Federalist dominance playing itself out.

Using the threat of war with France as an excuse, the Federalists pushed through the Alien and Sedition Acts in the summer of 1798. The Alien Act was designed to weaken the political influence of immigrants, who were generally Democratic-Republicans, by giving the president the power to imprison and deport dangerous noncitizens. The Alien Act also lengthened the residence requirement for citizenship from five to fourteen years. Far more sinister, in Jefferson's eyes, was the Sedition Act, for under its terms the federal government could suppress American citizens. The Sedition Act provided for fines and imprisonment for persons composing, printing, or uttering "any false, scandalous, and malicious writing or writings against the government of the United States, or the President . . . with intent to defame . . . or bring them . . . into contempt or disrepute." In other words, the law sought to end criticism of the government.

Jefferson was enraged—the more so when Matthew Lyon, a Democratic-Republican congressman from Vermont, was actually jailed for verbal attacks on his Federalist opponent. In Jefferson's eyes, the Alien and Sedition Acts made a mockery of those cherished principles of the American Revolution embodied in the Bill of Rights. Freedom of speech, press, and even thought were being denied for purely partisan purposes. In November 1798 Jefferson channeled his wrath into a set of resolutions he introduced in the Kentucky legislature. Taking the position that the federal government had assumed undelegated powers in passing the acts, the Kentucky Resolution set forth the doctrine of nullification. The illegal measures, Jefferson wrote, are "altogether void and of no effect," at least as far as Kentucky was concerned. Meanwhile, writing for Virginia, James Madison promulgated a similar doctrine. The other states did not follow suit in 1798, but the controversy raised questions about the nature and purposes of the union that would not be settled conclusively until the Civil War.

The Alien and Sedition Acts prompted some Democratic-Republicans, chiefly in the South, to give serious consideration to leaving the union. Jefferson, however, believed that the Federalists had dug their own grave. The great majority of Americans, he felt, would not accept such curtailment of their hard-won liberties. "A little patience," he advised his more radical colleagues, "and we shall see the reign of the witches . . . pass over and the people . . . restoring the government to its true principles." Events proved him correct, for during the closing years of the 1790s, the Federalists committed one political blunder after another. They levied heavy taxes on personal property, then used the revenue to support a large standing army. In 1799 that army marched against a group of protesting Pennsylvanians under John Fries, and cries of tyranny rose on all sides.

Federalism also suffered from divisions in its own camp. After a brief trial, President Adams found he could not abide Alexander Hamilton. Adams also wanted to extricate his administration from the undeclared war with France. The "High Federalists" resisted the idea, but Adams finally repudiated his advisers and concluded a satisfactory peace. Meanwhile, the

Democratic-Republicans were preparing for the election of 1800 by developing an effective party organization. There were local and statewide committees, some of them holdovers from the Democratic Clubs that had appeared earlier in the decade in support of Jefferson, republicanism, and the French Revolution. Several influential Democratic-Republican newspapers sprang to life and, in defiance of the Sedition Act, attacked the Adams administration for monarchical ambitions. The Federalists replied in kind and organized their own party. The stage was set for a showdown political battle.

The election of 1800 was unprecedented in several respects. It was the first to take place outside the shadow cast by George Washington, for with him, in December 1799, died the last gentlemanly reservations about the propriety of partisan politics. Previously, neither Democratic-Republicans nor Federalists had quite dared bring their animosities into the open. Now it was bare knuckles. In addition, the 1800 election was the first in which the contesting parties took their campaigns to the people. It was to be more of a national election and less an agreement among political insiders. With Adams put forward for reelection by the Federalists and Jefferson the natural choice of the Democratic-Republicans, the start of the new century promised to be exciting.

The Federalists understandably chose to base their campaign on their opponents' shortcomings rather than on their own record. The charges against Jefferson were predictable. For one, he had spent too much time in close association with the radical democracy of France. If Jefferson were elected, charged the Federalists, guillotines would appear in the squares of the major cities, and the privileged classes could expect the worst. Another favorite Federalist smear involved Jefferson's alleged atheism. Actually, he was a deist, who demanded that his religion, like his other beliefs, be supportable by reason and evidence. In Federalist eyes, however, it was a question of "God—and a religious president; or . . . Jefferson—and no God!!!" One hysterical Adams partisan went further, forecasting that, if Jefferson were elected, "murder, robbery, rape, adultery, and incest will all be openly taught and practiced, the air will be rent with the cries of distress, and the soil will be soaked with blood."

Perhaps the most credible Federalist charge concerned Jefferson's philosophical nature and agricultural orientation. The Virginian, it was contended, would be too impractical for the presidency, and his rural bias would spell hardship for America's struggling commercial and industrial enterprises. Giving no quarter in their struggle for political survival, the Federalists also attacked Jefferson's personal morality. It was alleged that the master of Monticello had defrauded a poor widow of her inheritance and had fathered several children by one of his slaves. The first charge could be dismissed quickly, for Jefferson kept himself in chronic poverty as a result of honoring financial promises made to unlucky acquaintances. As for the illegitimate children, historical and recent scientific evidence seems to confirm that as a widower in the 1790s, Jefferson was intimate with a teenage slave named Sally Hemings, who had been with him for part of his stay in France. Hemings was actually the half-sister of Martha Wayles; both had the same father.

The Democratic-Republican campaign of 1800 was based on the simple promise to return the nation to the path of freedom from which it had strayed under Federalist guidance. Hamilton, Adams, and even Washington were accused of undermining the intent of the American Revolution. The strategy proved successful. Not even the forest fires the Federalists lit on election day to preoccupy the country people, who were largely Democratic-Republican, could prevent Jefferson and his Democratic-Republican running mate, Aaron Burr, from sweeping to victory with seventy-three electoral votes each. The unanticipated tie threw the election into the House of Representatives, which had to decide which of the two was to be president and which vice president. The embittered Federalists tried every means to block Jefferson's bid, but after more than thirty inconclusive ballots, he emerged as president (and Burr as vice president).° In the end, the Federalists, at the urging of Hamilton, threw their support to Jefferson, fearing that Burr would be worse.

In later years, Jefferson spoke of the outcome of the election as the "revolution of 1800," adding that it was "as real a revolution in the principles of our government as that of 1776 was in form." In one sense, of course, this was incorrect. The election of Thomas Jefferson took place under procedures established by the Constitution. There was no overthrow of the government's principles. No secession or civil war followed the counting of the votes. Neither did the new president revolutionize economic or legal procedures. Jefferson himself interpreted the national mood quite accurately in his conciliatory inaugural address, when he declared "every difference of opinion is not a difference of principle. . . . We are all Republicans, we are all Federalists."

Still, in some respects, a sweeping social and intellectual revolution did occur in 1800. The Federalists were an avowed aristocracy. Openly distrusting the masses of common people, they took as their model the privileged upper classes of the Old World. In a nation of new land and new opportunity, such ideas had become anachronisms. The Jeffersonians, on the other hand, drew their inspiration from the New World. They had confidence in the reasonableness of people and advocated an open, fluid social order. Their elite would be a natural one, the product of talent and diligence. Every man, they believed, should enjoy equality of opportunity and the freedom to exploit his potential to the fullest. Under Federalism, in sum, the nation had drifted away from democracy. After 1800 the cause of the people was in the ascendancy, at least as an ideal. While Jeffersonian democracy opened new vistas of opportunity, the bounds of its egalitarianism stretched only to white men, however. As an enlightened libertarian, Jefferson struggled intellectually with equality for other groups—including women, black slaves, and Indians. As a practical politician, however, he was willing to support new rights for none of them. Believing women too tender for politics, blacks incapable of handling their own affairs, and Indians an impediment to westward expansion, Jefferson, as president, limited his message of opportunity to white males.

President Jefferson surrounded himself with a distinguished group of associates headed by James Madison as secretary of state and Albert Gallatin as secretary of the treasury. Among the first problems facing their administration was one created by a Federalist-dominated national judicial system. John Adams, tired and bitter at the close of his administration, had deliberately filled the national courts with Federalist judges. These "midnight" appointments were designed to give the Federalists a measure of influence in Jefferson's administration. Already suspicious of the judiciary because of its protection from popular control (judges had life tenure), the Democratic-Republicans attacked. At one stroke, Congress abolished sixteen circuit courts and their sixteen Federalist judges. The House of Representatives moved to impeach the highly partisan Supreme Court Justice Samuel Chase, but after a sensational trial, the Senate wisely refused to supply the necessary confirmation.

The real center of judicial power, however, was John Marshall, chief justice of the Supreme Court. Marshall was a Virginian and a distant relative of Jefferson, but there was no love lost

°In 1804, the Twelfth Amendment changed this system to have the electoral college cast separate ballots for president and vice president.

between the two. A leading Federalist and Adams's secretary of state, Marshall had been appointed in the closing weeks of the Adams administration. For the outgoing president's purposes, the choice was brilliant. Marshall, who dominated the Supreme Court for thirty-four years, handed down a series of decisions that institutionalized the Federalist interpretation of the Constitution. His first important ruling, and the foundation of many of the rest, concerned the power to determine the constitutionality of laws passed by Congress. Jefferson believed that the authors of the Constitution had intended that all three branches of the federal government work together, checking and balancing, to determine the meaning of that document. Marshall took the position that the Constitution was "superior paramount law," unalterable by legislative act or executive order. Hence only the judicial branch could pronounce on the question of constitutionality.

In 1803 Marshall found an opportunity to create a precedent. The case of *Marbury v. Madison* involved William Marbury, a Federalist who had received one of Adams's controversial appointments, and the secretary of state, James Madison, who refused to honor his appointment. Marbury went straight to the Supreme Court with the intention of using a section of the Judiciary Act of 1789 to force the executive branch to honor the commitment. Marshall agreed that the law was on Marbury's side but ruled against him on the grounds that the Judiciary Act gave the Supreme Court an unconstitutional power. The chief justice thus decided against both his party and the power of his court, but he established a far more important principle: the right of the judicial branch to decide if an act of Congress was in conformity with the Constitution.

After *Marbury v. Madison,* Jefferson and his Democratic-Republican successors to the presidency could only chafe in frustration as the "crafty chief judge," in Jefferson's words, handed down a series of major decisions. *Martin v. Hunter's Lessee* (1816) and *Cohens v. Virginia* (1821) resulted in the establishment of the right of the Supreme Court to review, and if necessary to reverse, the decisions of state courts respecting the Constitution. The ruling confirmed the principle of federal supremacy. In *Fletcher v. Peck* (1810) and *Dartmouth College v. Woodward* (1819), the Marshall Court protected the structure of American business by affirming the obligation of contracts in the face of popular criticism. Hamilton would have been delighted. *McCulloch v. Maryland* (1819) set forth the broad or "loose" interpretation of the powers of the federal government under the Constitution. If the purpose was legitimate and constitutional, Marshall ruled, then Congress had the power to take any constitutional action necessary to achieve that purpose. The decision was a direct slap at the Jeffersonians' narrow, or "strict," interpretation of constitutional authority.

The Jeffersonians were, in theory, proponents of weak central government. But relative positions had much to do with this preference. When the Federalists held the national reins, the Jeffersonians opposed a strong central government. Once they were in control themselves, a powerful nation acquired much greater appeal. In fact, the deposed Federalists soon became the new critics of strong national authority.

The course of events substantiated this reversal of roles. In contrast to what many had hoped—or feared—the Democratic-Republicans did not use their control of Congress and the presidency to undo major Federalist policies and institutions. Although he let the charter of the Bank of the United States run out, Jefferson created a second Bank of the United States. In 1816 Jefferson's successor, James Madison, created a central bank more than three times the size of Hamilton's prototype. Neither did Jefferson change the Federalist objectives of upholding the national credit, assuming state debts incurred in the Revolutionary War, and encouraging shipping and commerce. In time, the Democratic-Republicans even instituted and improved on a Hamiltonian ideal: a protective tariff to encourage manufacturing. The new president did reduce the size of the army as part of his plan for federal economy, yet he took a leading role in establishing the U.S. Military Academy at West Point, New York. Jefferson also started a sixteen-year plan to abolish the national debt, which the Federalists had deliberately created for the purpose of securing loyalty to the central government. Secretary of the Treasury Albert Gallatin worked brilliantly on the reduction plan and, for a time, succeeded. But a final accounting showed that Jefferson and Madison had been as skillful spenders as the Federalists. After the allotted sixteen years, the indebtedness of the United States had never been higher.

Jefferson's foreign policy also changed with his acquisition of power. Previously sympathetic toward France, he turned hostile when Spain's retrocession of Louisiana to France became public. After France's defeat in the Seven Years' War, that nation awarded the Louisiana Territory to Spain, which had supported France in the losing effort. In 1800, the aggressive emperor Napoleon insisted that Spain return Louisiana, intending to reestablish a North American empire west of the United States. Jefferson contemplated an alliance with his old nemesis, Great Britain, to prevent the French takeover on the western U.S. border, but a French military blunder solved the problem. On their way to occupy Louisiana in 1802, 27,000 French troops stopped in the French colony of Haiti to put down an insurrection led by Toussant L'Overture. At least 20,000 died there of yellow fever, and Napoleon, needing troops for European campaigns, recalled the remainder. In 1803 France gave up plans for a New World empire and offered to sell all of Louisiana to the United States for $15 million.

The proposal stunned Jefferson's representatives in France. Although the offer violated Jefferson's ideals of frugality and constitutionality, it was nonetheless an incredible and irresistible bargain. When they learned of the purchase, the Federalists, of all people, accused Jefferson of going beyond the limits of his authority in buying land. In truth, there was nothing in the Constitution sanctioning such an action. Jefferson wrestled with the problem for several months, finally rationalized the Louisiana Purchase as an extension of the "empire of liberty," and pushed the required treaty through the Senate as quietly as possible. Even he realized that theory had to give way occasionally to practical considerations.

Planning for the exploration and settlement of the West was considerably more enjoyable for Jefferson. In 1804 he fulfilled a dream by sending an expedition under his private secretary, Meriwether Lewis, and William Clark to the headwaters of the Missouri and thence down the Columbia to the Pacific Ocean. Two years and more than 7,000 miles later, Lewis and Clark returned from the wilderness with a wealth of information. Zebulon Pike brought back additional data from his expeditions to the source of the Mississippi and to the Colorado Rockies. The blank map of the American West was gradually being filled in, and Jefferson was delighted both as a citizen and as a scientist. He also took pleasure in the thought that the virgin land to the west would soon support a population of hardy yeoman farmers, those mainstays of the republic. To help them, the Jefferson administration altered the land laws to make possible the purchase of small farms at attractive prices. Under the Land Act of 1804, individuals could obtain title to 160 acres for as little as $80 (one-fourth the purchase price) down.

As the pressures and conflicts of national politics swirled around him, there were times when Jefferson thought wistfully of Monticello—if not of Lewis and Clark's lonely camps. The strange case of Aaron Burr caused him special pain. A suicidally ambitious man, Vice President Burr became disenchanted with the Democratic-Republicans midway through Jefferson's first term. Seeking a fresh ladder, he turned to a group of embittered Federalists who were exploring the possibility of persuading New York and the New England states to secede from the union. In the

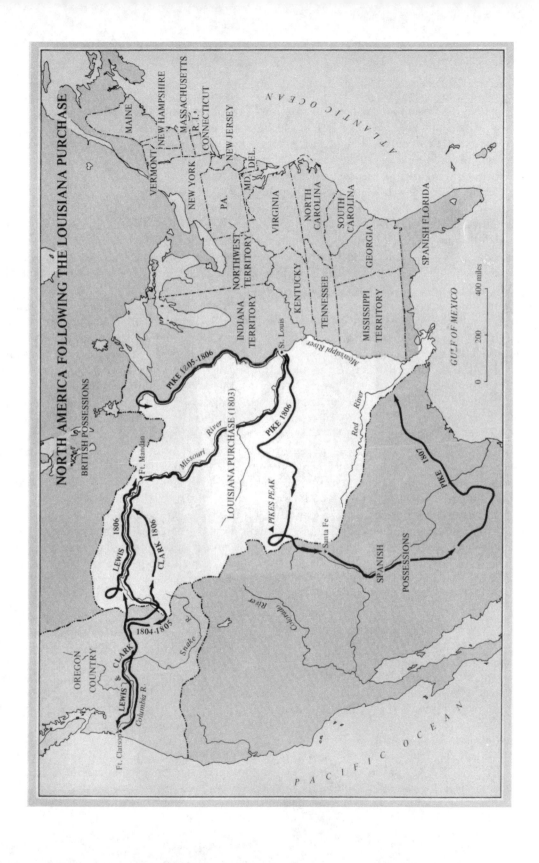

NORTH AMERICA FOLLOWING THE LOUISIANA PURCHASE

course of this plot, Burr's enormous ego ran afoul of Hamilton's, and a feud quickly developed. The climax was a duel on July 11, 1804, on the western bank of the Hudson River. Hamilton reputedly fired first and missed, whereupon Burr coolly delivered a fatal shot. He next appeared in the Mississippi Valley, again investigating the chances for leading a revolt from Jefferson's government. The complex deal, involving both Spain and England, eventually collapsed, and Jefferson ordered Burr arrested on charges of treason. But Chief Justice Marshall, before whom the case was tried, defined treason so narrowly as to ensure Burr's acquittal.

Jefferson was deeply embarrassed, but the bulk of the American people, those who had swept him to a decisive victory in his reelection in 1804 (with a new vice president, George Clinton), stood behind their president. Burr was nearly lynched and eventually was obliged to leave the country. Jefferson and his party stood unchallenged. The citizenry had become fond of the president's understated, effective, and unmistakably American style. They liked his abolition of the weekly "levee," a lavish reception that was a Federalist holdover from the fashionable world of European courts. They chuckled at his insistence on a round table for state dinners so that no guest would have precedence over another. And they roared with glee when the new British ambassador, dress sword and all, was received by Jefferson in bedroom slippers!

It was one thing to slight Britain at a diplomatic reception, something else again on the high seas. In 1805 Lord Horatio Nelson reconfirmed British mastery of the oceans with a smashing victory over the French navy in the Battle of Trafalgar. But Napoleonic France remained the master of continental Europe, and war between the powers continued. One result was that American ships engaged in international trade were subject to seizure by one or the other of the belligerents. It was not a trifling matter for President Jefferson. Between 1804 and 1807, more than 1,500 American vessels were seized and searched. The British went further, "impressing" American seamen. Under this ancient practice, the captain of a warship could, in time of emergency, compel service from any of his countrymen. Theoretically, then, only Englishmen could be impressed, but on the high seas such niceties were often ignored. Many American citizens found themselves working for the British navy under circumstances that amounted to slavery.

In June 1807 Jefferson received word that the British frigate *Leopard* had dared to fire on and search America's *Chesapeake* within sight of the Virginia coast. Three Americans died in the encounter, and four men were impressed. The people were furious. Jefferson noted, "never since the battle of Lexington have I seen this country in such a state of exasperation." There was more than enough support to declare war on England, but Jefferson stood by his opposition to America's "entangling" itself in the affairs of Europe. Instead of taking sides in the Anglo–French conflict, he proposed an embargo on all American trade with Europe. Jefferson hoped that the boycott would force respect for the rights of neutral nations.

The embargo, instituted December 22, 1807, proved a failure. In the midst of blockades of British ports by Napoleon and French ports by the British, an embargo was impossible to enforce. Moreover, the United States was not united behind the policy. Shippers and merchants, especially those in New England, regarded the whole idea as a Jeffersonian plot to destroy commerce and punish the Federalists. Many merchants simply resorted to smuggling to move their goods. Still, American exports dropped by 80 percent and bankruptcies rose by an equal amount. Jefferson received a torrent of abuse. "You Infernal Villain," one New Englander wrote, "how much longer are you going to keep this damned Embargo on to starve us poor people."

The election of 1808 reflected this criticism. Jefferson declined renomination, feeling that Washington had set an admirable precedent in limiting his service to two terms. Instead, he advanced the candidacy of his secretary of state. Madison won, but New England was solid in its opposition. It appeared to Jefferson that continuation of the embargo would only further divide the country, so he repealed it on March 1, 1809, three days before leaving office. Now an observer rather than a participant, Jefferson watched as the final acts of the diplomatic drama were played out to a sad conclusion. Madison tried several modified trade boycotts without success. Impressments continued. Finally, Napoleon maneuvered Madison into believing that France would cooperate in respecting neutral rights. Madison thereupon sided with France and severed diplomatic relations with Britain. In good time, Britain also repealed its offensive maritime policies, but too late. Before news of the repeal reached America, Madison asked Congress for a declaration of war. In June 1812, for the second time in less than forty years, the United States was at war with Great Britain.

Both Jefferson and Madison were well aware that the explanation for the War of 1812 was more complicated than violation of maritime rights. Many westerners were anxious to remove the British from Canada. There was the danger of British-inspired Indian attacks from this quarter; moreover, there was the prospect of annexing Canada. Henry Clay and the other "War Hawks" in Congress effectively marshaled this sentiment into an argument for war. Another motive was a vague but potent sense of national honor. Regardless of where they lived or how they made their living, Americans resented being treated as if they were still colonists. Perhaps, they reasoned, a second war of independence was needed to convince the world that the new republic meant to be taken seriously.

Gratefully retired to Monticello after four decades of continuous public service, Jefferson eagerly turned to his library, his gardens, his inventions, his science, the founding of the University of Virginia, and a correspondence that amounted to more than a thousand handwritten letters a year. There was also a steady stream of visitors, paying homage to the Sage of Monticello.

As a participant in the beginnings of the controversy, Jefferson took a keen interest in the War of 1812. Its formal outcome, embodied in the Treaty of Ghent, December 24, 1814, was inconclusive and unsatisfying. But Americans proved adept at finding, or perhaps creating, glory. Oliver Hazard Perry was elevated to the rank of a national hero after his September 1813 victory over the British fleet on Lake Erie. A year later the invasion of Baltimore was repelled, and Francis Scott Key created a song that later became the national anthem. But from the standpoint of the national ego, nothing compared to the Battle of New Orleans. Jefferson shared the thrill that rippled through the nation when news arrived that on January 8, 1815, Andrew Jackson and an untrained force of frontier riflemen had crushed the cream of the British army. Two thousand Englishmen died in the encounter and only six Americans—one of the most lopsided victories in military history. Newspapers headlined their accounts of the battle "Almost Incredible Victory!!" and "Rising Glory of the American Republic."

Few could doubt it, and in the aftermath of the War of 1812, a feeling of national unity and well-being prevailed. President Madison and Henry Clay advanced an "American System," under which domestic manufacturing and consumption were encouraged by protective tariffs and improvements in internal transportation. The last vestiges of the Federalists as a national political party withered in the sun of the new nationalism. One indication was the collapse of the plan for revising the Constitution that a group of New England Federalists formulated at Hartford, Connecticut, late in 1814. Representatives of the gathering arrived in Washington at the same time as the news from New Orleans, and the Federalists attracted only jeers. This is not to say, however, that the United States entered a political "era of good feeling" after 1814. Jefferson, for one, knew better. Factionalism was inherent in politics. Beneath the veneer of national solidarity were ambitious men eager to crack the hold of Virginia (of the first five

As the high point of their efforts in the War of 1812, the British captured Washington, D.C., on August 24, 1814, and burned the public buildings, as shown here. President James Madison and other officials fled in disgrace. But three weeks later, Americans regained some measure of pride when they successfully defended the city of Baltimore against a British attack. At the conclusion of the battle, Francis Scott Key observed the American flag still flying over Baltimore's Fort McHenry and composed the words for "The Star-Spangled Banner." Set to the tune of an old drinking song, it later became the national anthem.

presidents, only John Adams had come from a different state) and the Democratic-Republicans on the central government.

Sectionalism offered one means of shaking up this political status quo. In his declining years, Jefferson observed a sharp rise in sectional consciousness. The financial panic of 1819 and the subsequent depression set hard-pressed westerners and laborers everywhere against eastern financial interests. Far more serious, in Jefferson's estimation, was the crisis of 1819 and 1820 occasioned by the Missouri Territory's application for admission to the union. At issue was the geographical extension of slavery.

As a young man, Jefferson, along with most national leaders, had entertained the vague hope that slavery would gradually disappear. To this end, Jefferson had written a passage for the Declaration of Independence attacking the international slave trade as a violation of the "sacred rights . . . of a distant people." Although the passage was deleted from the final version of the document, Jefferson continued his campaign. In 1784 he called for the exclusion of slavery from the western territories, and he applauded the action of the Constitutional Convention of 1787, which did provide for cessation of the slave trade after twenty years. But all the while, Jefferson struggled with massive uncertainties. If the slave trade and the extension of slavery were wrong, what about slavery itself? Jefferson the philosopher of liberty and natural rights answered this question one way; Jefferson the southerner and owner of some 200 slaves answered it another. The latter viewpoint prevailed, but only because Jefferson carefully created and maintained, in the face of increasing evidence to the contrary, the myth of innate black inferiority. All men were created equal, in other words, but blacks were not fully men. This shabby reasoning was the only way Thomas Jefferson could reconcile his conflicting beliefs.

Contrary to Jefferson's expectations, the passage of time did not bring the weakening of slavery. The advent of large-scale cotton production in the early nineteenth century led to a dramatic rise in the value of slaves. Moreover, the abolition of the slave trade in 1808 was more than offset by rising birthrates among the black population and by smuggling. By 1820 most southern slave owners had accepted black bondage as an unpleasant necessity, and some had come to see it as a positive good. Fear, as well as economic considerations, shaped their point of view. Jefferson and his fellow slaveholders disliked and feared blacks. Even if they had wished to do so, they could not have abolished slavery in the South without creating a large population of free blacks who would, southern whites believed, run rampant over every civilized value and institution. The colonization of freed blacks in Africa had long been considered a solution to this dilemma, but it had never materialized. White America, it appeared, was stuck with blacks and, because of the supposed need to control them, with the institution of slavery. "We have the wolf by the ears," Jefferson lamented in 1820, "and we can neither hold him, nor safely let go." Then, in a comment that penetrated to the heart of his personal dilemma, he added, "Justice is in one scale, self-preservation in the other."

With Jefferson one might have hoped that the former would take precedence, but the plain fact is that it did not. During the Missouri controversy, he joined the most closed-minded southerners in regarding the whole issue as a Federalist plot and resisting any limitation of slavery. Henry Clay eventually bailed the nation out temporarily with a compromise proposal that accepted slavery in Missouri, balanced that state's admission to the union with the inclusion of Maine, and set the latitude 36°30′ as henceforth the northern limit of slave labor in territory acquired in the Louisiana Purchase. Jefferson doubted that the compromise would work. He knew that an arbitrary line could not settle a difference of moral principle. The Missouri debates, "like a fire bell in the night," filled Jefferson with terror. "In the gloomiest moments of the Revolutionary War," he wrote in 1820, "I never had any apprehensions equal to what I feel from this source." Upon the shoals of the slavery issue, he predicted, the union would founder.

In October 1823 Jefferson, now eighty years old, was flattered to receive a communication from President Monroe soliciting his advice on a delicate question of foreign policy. Britain, it appeared, was concerned that Spain, with assistance from France, Austria, and Russia, might try to recover the rebellious colonies in South America. The British foreign minister had approached the United States with the idea of issuing a joint declaration opposing any further changes in the political geography of the New World. Jefferson thought the proposal had much merit and advised Monroe to abandon, for once, the policy of nonentanglement. An alliance with powerful England would help to keep the New World independent.

The president tended to Jefferson's position, but Secretary of State John Quincy Adams opposed it on the grounds that the United States should not preclude its own territorial expansion

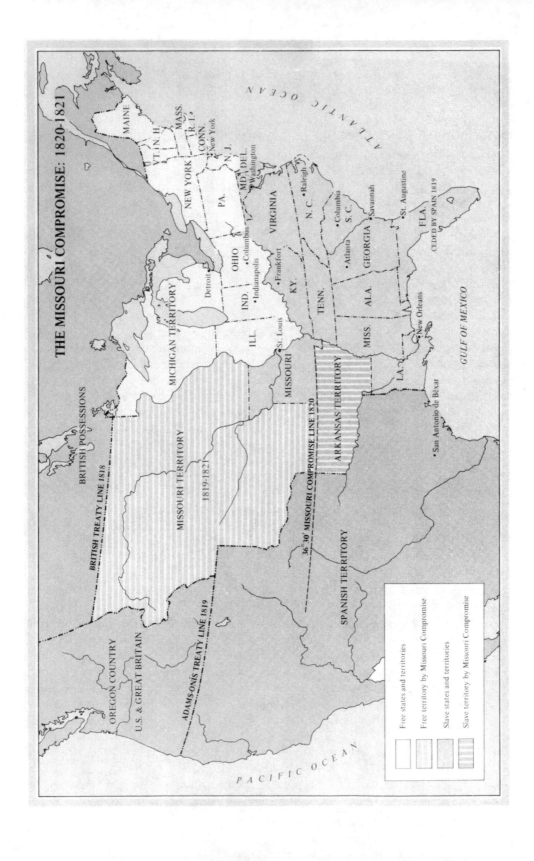

THE MISSOURI COMPROMISE: 1820-1821

ATLANTIC OCEAN

MAINE

VT. N.H. MASS.
R.I.
CONN.
NEW YORK • New York
N.J.
PA. MD. DEL.
• Washington
OHIO VIRGINIA
• Columbus • Raleigh
IND. KY. N.C.
• Indianapolis • Frankfort Columbia
ILL. • St. Louis TENN. S.C.
• Atlanta • Savannah
MISSOURI GEORGIA
MISS. ALA.
• St. Augustine
FLA.
CEDED BY SPAIN 1819
LA. • New Orleans

Detroit

MICHIGAN TERRITORY

BRITISH POSSESSIONS

BRITISH TREATY LINE 1818

MISSOURI TERRITORY
1819-1821

ARKANSAS TERRITORY

36° 30' MISSOURI COMPROMISE LINE 1820

SPANISH TERRITORY

• San Antonio de Béxar

GULF OF MEXICO

OREGON COUNTRY

U.S. & GREAT BRITAIN

ADAMS-ONIS TREATY LINE 1819

PACIFIC OCEAN

Free states and territories

Free territory by Missouri Compromise

Slave states and territories

Slave territory by Missouri Compromise

by agreeing to preserve the current arrangement. Florida, he argued, had been acquired from Spain in 1821, and there was reason to believe that Cuba, Texas, and perhaps all of South America would one day join the union. Moreover, Adams did not favor riding Britain's coattails in this matter. Why not, he asked, make a separate statement that the Western Hemisphere was not open to further colonization by any European power? In the end, Adams prevailed. The Monroe Doctrine of December 2, 1823, rejected Britain's proposition, affirmed the principle of New World autonomy, and kept the door open for American expansion.

Late in June 1826, Thomas Jefferson marked the approach of the fiftieth anniversary of U.S. independence by writing a brief statement for the celebration of the Fourth of July. The American Revolution, he reflected, had been a "signal" for oppressed people everywhere to burst their chains and "assume the blessings and security of self-government." Reason and the free exchange of opinion had replaced ignorance, superstition, and fear. Because of July 4, 1776, Jefferson continued, "All eyes are opened, or opening, to the rights of man." Finally, Jefferson's own eyes closed, for the last time, on that very day.

Selected Readings

The Person

°Bedini, Silvio A: *Thomas Jefferson: Statesman of Science* (1990). Focuses on Jefferson's scientific accomplishments and highlights his many inventions.

Berstein, Andrew: *The Inner Jefferson: Portrait of a Grieving Optimist* (1995). A close examination of Jefferson's personal struggles.

°Boorstin, Daniel J.: *The Lost World of Thomas Jefferson* (1948). Places Jefferson in the context of the American Enlightenment.

Boyd, Julian (ed.): *The Papers of Thomas Jefferson (1950–).* The authoritative collection, expected to reach fifty volumes.

Brodie, Fawn: *Thomas Jefferson: An Intimate History* (1974). An essentially critical interpretation of Jefferson and his relationship with Sally Hemings.

Brown, David S.: *Thomas Jefferson: A Biographical Companion* (1998). Subjects and people in Jefferson's life, arranged alphabetically.

Cunningham, Noble E.: *In Pursuit of Reason: The Life of Thomas Jefferson* (1987). A biography integrating changes in recent scholarship on the period with the life of Jefferson.

Dewey, Frank L.: *Thomas Jefferson: Lawyer* (1987). Traces Jefferson's career as a practicing lawyer from 1767 to 1774.

°Koch, Adrienne: *The Philosophy of Thomas Jefferson* (1943). An analysis of the many facets of Jefferson's thought.

Koch, Adrienne (ed.): *Jefferson* (1971). A well-organized collection of past and present impressions of Jefferson, including those of the Adams family.

Koch, Adrienne, and William Penn: *The Life and Selected Writings of Thomas Jefferson* (1944). A thorough one-volume treatment.

Malone, Dumas: *Jefferson and His Time* (1948–1977). A definitive six-volume biography.

°Available in paperback.

Matthews, Richard K.: *The Radical Politics of Thomas Jefferson* (1984). A brief but suggestive exploration of Jefferson's political thought.

Peterson, Merrill D.: *Jefferson and the New Nation* (1970). A thorough biography of Jefferson and nation-building.

Randall, Willard Sterne: *Thomas Jefferson: A Life* (1993). An exhaustive biography that refutes Jefferson's alleged affair with Sally Hemings.

The Period

°Adams, Henry: *History of the United States During the Administrations of Thomas Jefferson and James Madison* (9 vols., 1889–1891). One of the classics of American historical writing. Adams treats social and intellectual as well as political and economic history in an elegant literary style.

Aptheker, Herbert: *Early Years of the Republic: From the End of the Revolution to the First Administration of Washington, 1783–1793* (1976). Political history of the Confederation period and the framing of the Constitution.

Banning, Lance: *The Jeffersonian Persuasion: Evolution of a Party Ideology* (1978). Insights into the ideas of the first Democratic-Republicans.

Banning, Lance: *Jefferson and Madison: Three Conversations for the Founding Fathers* (1995). Analysis of documents and conversations.

°Cunningham, Noble: *The Jeffersonian Republicans* (2 vols., 1957–1963). The rise to power of a political party.

°Dangerfield, George: *The Era of Good Feelings* (1952). National political developments in Jefferson's declining years.

Davis, David Brion: *The Problem of Slavery in the Age of Revolution, 1770–1823* (1975). An exploration of the intellectual dilemmas that slavery created for revolutionaries like Jefferson.

Gilreath, James (ed.): *Thomas Jefferson and the Education of a Citizen* (1999). Scholarly essays on issues of Jefferson's day.

Horsman, Reginald: *The Causes of the War of 1812* (1962). One interpretation of a much-discussed war.

°Jensen, Merrill: *The New Nation* (1950). The achievements of Americans in constructing their first federal organization.

°Jordan, Winthrop: *White over Black* (1974). Broad treatment of the difficulties that slaveholding posed for Jefferson as a natural rights philosopher.

Nettels, Curtis P.: *The Emergence of a National Economy* (1962). A reliable survey of the nation's early economic history.

°Nye, Russel B.: *The Cultural Life of the New Nation* (1960). Intellectual and social history.

Rhonda, James P. (ed.): *Thomas Jefferson and the Changing West: From Conquest to Conservation* (1997). Essays on Jefferson's westward thinking and other figures in westward expansion.

°Wood, Gordon: *Creation of the American Republic 1776–1787* (1969). Political theory and political institutions.

Wright, Louis B.: *The First Gentlemen of Virginia* (1940). Social history of the milieu from which Jefferson emerged.

°Young, Alfred F. (ed.): *The American Revolution: Explorations in the History of American Radicalism* (1976). Essays on class conflict, radical ideology, and the roles of women and minorities before, during, and after the Revolution.

For Consideration

1. Identify some of the philosophical arguments young Thomas Jefferson applied to his composition of the Declaration of Independence in 1776.

2. What were some of the reservations Thomas Jefferson had regarding the Constitution of 1787? What was his opinion of the Articles of Confederation? How did the Bill of Rights ease some of his misgivings about the Constitution?

3. Identify some of the basic philosophical differences between Jefferson and Alexander Hamilton.

4. As president, Jefferson drew back from his weak central government philosophy to engage in some actions that outraged even the Federalists. Discuss some of those actions and the Jeffersonian rationale behind them.

5. Jefferson's egalitarianism ran counter to his position as a slaveholder. Evaluate this dichotomy.

Chapter 6

Tecumseh

The attack plan had been disrupted, but there was no turning back now for the Shawnee warriors. From the Indians' standpoint, this assault on the troops of British colonial commander Andrew Lewis, on the banks of the Ohio River in the western Virginia frontier, was entirely justified. Leading up to this Battle of Point Pleasant in October 1774, British frontiersmen had repeatedly violated treaties made by their government, trespassing on the Indian hunting grounds, initiating skirmishes, and indiscriminately killing people. For this they would pay. The Shawnee chief, Cornstalk, had developed what seemed to be a good battle plan for his 300 warriors. Unfortunately for the Shawnees, two men from Lewis's army stumbled onto the advancing Indians while hunting game in the early morning hours. The hunters' warning to their encampment foiled the Shawnee surprise attack.

For a while the skillful Shawnee warriors besieged the colonists' camp, inflicting casualties far greater than their own. Puckeshinwa, one of Cornstalk's best war chiefs, led the assault on the Virginians. His fourteen-year-old son, Chiksika, fought at Puckeshinwa's side. But soon the ammunition ran low, and the Shawnees had no choice but to retreat across the Ohio. British gunfire struck Puckeshinwa before he reached the river, and a group of warriors carried the mortally wounded chief to the west bank. With his dying breath, he told Chiksika never to trust nor make peace with the whites. The tearful Chiksika vowed to Puckeshinwa to raise his younger brothers to be great warriors and to avenge his death.

True to his word, Chiksika oversaw his brothers' training. And one of them, Tecumseh, would become one of the great leaders of his time and would attempt to build a great confederation of Indian tribes strong enough to defeat the "Long Knives." The name Tecumseh would come to create awe among the tribes of the Old Northwest; it would also create fear and respect among his white enemies during the early nineteenth century. But Chiksika also helped his widowed mother, Methoataska, raise his seven other siblings. Another brother, yet unborn at his father's death, would become the legendary mystic known as the Prophet. His vision of American Indian unity and a return to traditional ways inspired Tecumseh, whose skill as a warrior and an orator gave hope to the besieged Indians and spread fear among white American settlers throughout the Ohio River Valley.

Before Tecumseh was born in 1768, hundreds of centuries of his people's history in the New World had unfolded. The precise time and circumstances of the real beginning of American history swirl imprecisely in the mists of long ago. But there is general support for the following hypotheses: (1) *Homo sapiens* did not evolve in the Western Hemisphere, so every American has been an immigrant; (2) human beings first reached the New World in Alaska and came from Asia; and (3) the date of the first arrival was between 10,000 and 40,000 years ago.

The vast ice fields and glaciers of the Pleistocene were the most important factors influencing the timing and direction of prehistoric migrations. With massive quantities of frozen water on the land, the sea level dropped by as much as 300 feet. For Tecumseh's distant ancestors, the greatest consequence was the transformation of the sixty-mile-wide Bering Strait between Siberia and Alaska into a grass-covered land bridge. Like the Isthmus of Panama, the exposed land provided a highway between continents.

The same glaciation that lowered the sea also determined the pattern of life on land. There is evidence that expanding Siberian glaciers pushed animals and those who hunted them against the east coast of Asia and eventually funneled them across the Bering bridge. North America had glaciers, too. They spread outward over the Canadian Shield from the area of Hudson Bay. But for thousands of years in the Pleistocene, much of lower-elevation Alaska was free of ice. Given prehistory's long time span, it was possible for successive generations of hunters to filter up the Yukon River along the base of the Brooks Range, down the Mackenzie River Valley, and then south along the unglaciated corridor east of the Rocky Mountains. At the height of Pleistocene glaciation, it is true, the ice probably cut off this route. By this time, the first Americans could have been south of the snow, spreading through the temperate and tropical latitudes.

This image of the first generations of humans exploding into a territory where there was no human competition has inspired some anthropologists to postulate the theory of a very rapid occupancy of the Western Hemisphere. Perhaps in only a thousand years the skilled hunters of the north raced from Alaska to the tip of South America. Physically, this was possible. In the course of his missions to outlying tribes, Tecumseh regularly traveled 2,000 miles a year. But the pace of the geographical expansion of his racial stock need not have been so hurried. Hunting-and-gathering people were not explorers by choice. They certainly were not tourists. They vacated a territory only when forced to do so as a result of a diminishing food supply or when challenged by superior tribes. More determined, fiercer, and better-armed groups pushed weaker ones out of the way. The Navajos and Apaches, for instance, arrived in the American Southwest only a century or two before the Spaniards. A powerful people, they annihilated prior occupants of the area or drove them away. So Siberian hunting people moved down the mountainous continental spine to stand at land's end. Beyond Tierra del Fuego was only the Antarctic. Humans now lived from one ice cap to the other. Thus, the European colonization of North America was only the most recent act in a drama of human competition in the New World.

Tecumseh's distant ancestors had had many geographical options along the way. There were ecological niches in which a hunter with limited agricultural skills could fit. Wave after wave of migrants crossed the Bering bridge, penetrating to the far corners of the continent. Some braved the Southwest, not yet a desert in the Pleistocene, to reach the California coast. This route eventually helped to inhabit the Pacific Northwest, forming a great arc, again pointing northward. Others followed the slope of the land down the rivers of the Great Plains and into the eastern woodlands. Tecumseh's people were among them.

Shawnee means "southerner," but the itinerant language group that went by this name ranged widely in the eastern forests. The constantly shifting stream of time and people that produced Tecumseh ran back some 4,000 years to a sophisticated Indian culture that existed in the Ohio Valley and southeast along the Appalachian Mountains to the Gulf of Mexico.

It was one of the supremely arrogant ideas of American history to regard these people as a handful of ragged savages living precariously on the brink of starvation. Although less sophisticated than the Mayas and Aztecs of Mexico (whose civilizations rivaled Europe's and even surpassed them in some areas), many woodland Indians of North America lived in well-organized towns. They constructed elaborate burial mounds and ceremonial centers. Buildings such as the longhouse of the Iroquois reached a length of 300 feet. Their Six Nations confederation was an effective form of decentralized government that worked well in the absence of American agrarian intrusions on the Indian hunting grounds. The eastern Indians farmed expertly, a fact the first English settlers appreciated, and they practiced an effective medicine based on the use of plants and herbs. Mining for the purpose of fashioning art objects was well developed, and the Native Americans traded in a loose confederation extending from New York to Kansas. Relying on the tradition of such contact among the dozens of tribes and subtribes, Tecumseh later attempted to build unified resistance to the white presence.

The number of Indians in the New World at the time of first contact with Europeans is significant when one judges the legitimacy of European dispossession. To suppose that the precontact Indian population of the hemisphere totaled about 10 million, of which fewer than 1 million lived in North America, is—at least in European and American eyes—to justify dispossession. More recent scholarship, however, suggests much higher figures: perhaps as many as 15 million for North America and up to 120 million for the Western Hemisphere. The total is more than the combined population of the western European nations at the time of Christopher Columbus. From this perspective, the European occupation of the New World was clearly a conquest. The land was hardly "vacant." European acquisition of the Americas was less discovery and exploration than it was invasion. The white newcomers did not settle a wilderness so much as they stole someone else's home. This knowledge fired the determination of patriot chiefs like Tecumseh.

Tecumseh is a Europeanized spelling of a term Shawnees would have understood as "panther lying in wait." Events proved the aptness of the name. Tecumseh's birthplace (in March 1768) and the home of his youth was Old Piqua, a village on the Mad River in western Ohio, not far from its confluence with the Miami and the present-day city of Dayton. The Shawnees were wanderers. Puckeshinwa, father of both Tecumseh and the Prophet, was born in Florida. The pressure of advancing white settlement had pushed Puckeshinwa's band out of Pennsylvania and into a nomadic existence that led far south. Around 1740 his people entered the Creek country in eastern Alabama. There he married Tecumseh's mother, Methoataska. Tecumseh was their fifth child and the first born at Old Piqua.

Shawnees like Tecumseh's family were already refugees when they moved to Ohio, and the problem of resisting white expansion dominated the first discussion the boy remembered. In 1774, when he was six, Methoataska told him that his father and his oldest brother had left Old Piqua to contest the hunting grounds called Kentucky, south of the Ohio River. Tension had been building in the region for several decades. As early as 1750, Dr. Thomas Walker and a small party prospecting for land had discovered the Cumberland Gap, a natural pass through the Appalachian Mountains into "Kaintuck." John Finley, a Pennsylvania trader, brought back additional reports after a 1752 adventure. Captured by Shawnee warriors as he floated down the Ohio River in a canoe, Finley had been taken to their village in the heart of the bluegrass country. After being released, he returned glowing with news about a lush land abounding in deer, wild turkey, and buffalo, which at that time still existed in the eastern woodlands. Reports like Finley's fueled the fires of westward expansion, but the French and Indian, or Seven Years', War temporarily halted colonial contact with Kentucky. Pontiac's Rebellion, which occurred late in the war, further discouraged immigration westward. In 1763 Pontiac, chief of the Ottawas, formed an alliance with other tribes that wreaked havoc on British settlements in western Pennsylvania, Maryland, and Virginia for the next three years.

Then, in the late 1760s, came the backwoodsmen, preeminent among them a man named Daniel Boone. Living in the remote Yadkin Valley of North Carolina, Boone spent the winter of 1768 with John Finley. In the spring, the men secured financial backing and supplies from Judge Richard Henderson, a part-time land speculator, and headed through the Cumberland Gap. For two years Boone roamed Kentucky. He was alone for months at a time, living off the land in the manner of the Indians, whose skills he imitated and perfected. In December 1769, when Tecumseh was a year old, a band of Shawnees captured Boone and Finley and took most of their supplies. The men escaped by diving into a canebrake and eluding the Indians in the dense thirty-foot-high vegetation. Continuing to trap and hunt, Boone began his return to the frontier settlements in the spring of 1771. He had a modest fortune in furs. But near the western entrance to the Cumberland Gap, Indians stole his furs, horses, and remaining supplies. A disappointed Boone walked back to his cabin empty-handed after two years.

The reports of white faces in Kentucky that filtered back to Tecumseh's village were profoundly disturbing. The Shawnees were aware that the British had proclaimed, in 1763, that no settlement could take place west of a line drawn down the crest of the Appalachians. But here were the "long hunters," so-called because, like Boone, they made extended hunting trips into the backcountry, in the forbidden territory. In 1773 the first group of land speculators entered what came to be called the Dark and Bloody Ground. Equipped with land bounties issued to Virginia soldiers during the Seven Years' War, the speculators contended that they were not bound by the Proclamation of 1763. Rejecting this reasoning, the Shawnees organized to resist. They were unable to secure the aid of either the Iroquois Six Nations or the Cherokees, who were kept on the British side by skilled Indian agents, but the Ottawa and Mingo tribes became allies.

War became inevitable in 1774, when Virginia claimed Kentucky under its 1609 charter and sent Dr. John Connolly to Pittsburgh to enforce its title. Connolly, who had an eye for rich land holdings, aroused frontiersmen against the "savages." The Shawnees, under their chief, Cornstalk, called for peace and rational discussion. But the whites had little to gain in this land dispute by reasoning with a society that had preceded them in the area by several thousand years. From their perspective, the best policy was simply to drive the Indians off the contested land. So the Shawnees' effort to work with the Pennsylvania Quakers—the only colonial group that consistently recognized Indian rights—and to send peace messengers to Connolly at Pittsburgh proved futile. On June 10, 1774, after Shawnees killed thirteen whites to avenge the death of an equal number of their own tribesmen, Lord Dunmore, governor of Virginia, declared a state of war. Daniel Boone traveled 800 miles in sixty days to warn the outlying settlements.

In July 1774 Governor Dunmore began his war of territorial conquest by sending 1,500 frontiersmen against the Shawnees. Chief Cornstalk responded by gathering several hundred warriors, including Tecumseh's father and brother, crossing the Ohio River, and moving toward their foiled surprise attack on the Virginia army at the mouth of the Great Kanawha River. When the Battle of Point Pleasant began on October 9, 1774, it was a behind-the-trees frontier fight, with no clear gains by either side. With ammunition running low, however, and acting on misinformation regarding colonial reinforcements, the Shawnees withdrew across the Ohio, where Puckeshinwa was killed. Seizing the advantage, Dunmore marched on Indian villages in

Kentucky, with the avowed purpose of slaughtering every man, woman, and child. Terrified, the Shawnee leaders agreed to peace; it was, understandably, on terms dictated by the Virginians. The Treaty of Camp Charlotte obliged the Shawnees to acquiesce to white occupation of Kentucky, to stop hunting in that region, and to refrain from attacking boats on the Ohio River. For their part, the Virginians agreed not to disturb Old Piqua, where Tecumseh was a boy of six, and the other Shawnee villages north of the Ohio. The betrayal of this assurance was evident when the Shawnees saw invaders near Old Piqua shortly after the treaty.

Even though Cornstalk emerged the loser from Lord Dunmore's War, Tecumseh idolized the dignified Shawnee chief. In his youthful innocence he may have believed that, at the price of Kentucky, Cornstalk had bought peace and territorial security for the Ohio Shawnees. Events belied this assumption, however. The settlements south of the Ohio grew rapidly in size and confidence. After a brief fling with Richard Henderson's semifeudal plans for a separate colony of Transylvania, Kentucky was annexed to Virginia in 1777. At about the same time, Cornstalk paid a friendly visit to the U.S. fort at Point Pleasant, scene of his retreat three years earlier. Unfortunately, a Kentuckian had recently been killed along the Ohio River. Assuming the murderer to be an Indian, and applying the principles of Old Testament justice so common on the frontier, enraged soldiers broke into Cornstalk's cabin and gunned down the defenseless Shawnee chief.

By the late 1770s, the fortunes of Tecumseh's Shawnees and other tribes had been caught up in the American Revolution. From the very beginning of hostilities in 1775, it was clear that the Indians would play a vital role in the conflict. Both the British and the rebellious American colonists attempted to secure Indian allies. The British were more persuasive in this endeavor. Their Indian superintendents, John Stuart in the South and John Johnson in the North, were widely respected. The British also had strong frontier posts—notably, Detroit and Niagara—a well-organized fur trade, and superior trading goods. The American rebels could offer the Indians little more than rhetoric about liberty and natural rights, which, in view of the frontier disregard of Indian claims to ancestral lands, were hardly compelling. In fact, many Ohio Valley tribes, such as the Shawnee, the Delaware, and the Miami, regarded the hostilities surrounding America's attempt at independence as an opportune moment to remove the settlers from their hunting grounds. In general, the Indians and British fought together in the War of American Independence.

The Shawnees used the murder of Cornstalk as justification to initiate raids against Kentucky settlements. Chief Blackfish, Tecumseh's adopted father, and 300 warriors so terrorized the frontier that by 1777 the pioneers had been forced to take refuge in "Kentucky Stations." These rectangular forts, with blockhouses located at each corner, proved effective in withstanding Indian attack. But the besieged Americans quickly found their supplies dangerously low, as Blackfish continued to rampage through their abandoned cabins and fields. In January 1778, Daniel Boone led an expedition from one of the Kentucky forts to obtain a supply of salt from a spring on the Licking River. On February 7, while hunting alone, Boone was surprised and captured by four Shawnees. The ten-year-old Tecumseh was on hand when the warriors returned in triumph to Blackfish's village, Chillicothe. Boone lived with the Shawnees for five months and proved so impressive a woodsman that Blackfish adopted him into the tribe as his foster son. Through this tie, Boone became foster brother to Tecumseh.

Despite the honor of adoption, Boone's assumptions and ambitions remained worlds apart from the Shawnees'. In the late spring of 1778, he learned of Blackfish's intended attack on Boonesborough, in Kentucky. Realizing that he must warn the settlers, Boone lagged behind a group of Shawnees walking on a trail and just "melted away" into the forest. Four days and 160 miles later the legendary frontiersman pounded on the gates of the fort at Boonesborough.

By the time a furious Blackfish arrived on the scene, the fort had been secured against attack. Before his abortive siege, the Shawnee chief tried to persuade Boone to return as his son, but the white man refused.

Despite resistance to Blackfish at Boonesborough, the American war effort on the western frontier was not impressive in the early years of the Revolution. In the Ohio Valley, Americans cowered in the available forts. In western New York, the powerful leader of the confederated Iroquois, Joseph Brant, ravaged outlying settlements almost at will. The British appreciated, and in some instances paid bounties for, scalps and prisoners brought to their posts. American fortunes began to improve in June 1778, when a young Kentucky woodsman, George Rogers Clark, took the offensive. Together with a company of veteran Indian-fighters, Clark marched on the British posts in the Illinois country, capturing Kaskaskia, Cahokia, and Vincennes. French inhabitants of the area were won over to the American side by Clark's announcement of the alliance that the Continental Congress had concluded with France on February 6, 1778. Even the Indians were impressed by Clark's toughness and fighting skills. But the warriors were disillusioned, because the undermanned and poorly equipped armies failed to mount an attack on the key British post at Detroit. Clark agreed that a golden chance had been missed, blaming the unwillingness of frontiersmen to fight outside their immediate neighborhoods as the fundamental cause. By the end of 1780, the Indians were solidly pro-British, and the Americans had lost almost everything Clark had gained in Illinois.

But if Americans lost the war in the West, they won the peace. Taking advantage of animosity between Great Britain, France, and Spain, John Adams and his colleagues at the Paris peace talks secured the Mississippi rather than the Ohio River as the western boundary of the new nation. The preliminary accord of November 1782 (ratified September 3, 1783) opened the entire Old Northwest to American expansion. The fact that thousands of Indians also had claims to this territory never occurred to the negotiators in Paris.

Young Tecumseh saw a considerable portion of the Revolutionary War in the West in and around his home in central Ohio. Old Piqua, his birthplace, was burned by the Americans and rebuilt—inevitably, farther west—on the Miami River. Chillicothe, where Tecumseh lived with Blackfish, was burned to the ground three times between 1779 and 1782. George Rogers Clark directed the last two raids. In the summer of 1782, Tecumseh furthered his training as a warrior by watching his tribesmen and a British force from Detroit lead overeager Kentuckians into an ambush on the Licking River and thrash them soundly. Later that same summer, fourteen-year-old Tecumseh participated in his first battle against white men. It was not an auspicious beginning. When his older brother was wounded, Tecumseh ran in panic from the battlefield. Overcome by personal shame and filled with rage against the invaders of his homeland, he vowed that this moment of cowardice would be the last time he would ever show fear.

The vow may have influenced Tecumseh's decision not to follow the large group of Shawnees, including his mother, who had wearied of the strife in Ohio. Hoping to find peace and security, they headed for what in the 1780s was the far west—Missouri. Tecumseh knew better. He was already forming the belief that guided his life: The Indians' only real and permanent security would come from resisting the white invasion and forcing a recognition of Indian territorial rights. It was necessary to take a stand; with the newly independent American nation gaining westward momentum every year, the time for effective action was running out.

The end of the American Revolution saw Tecumseh's people living north of the Ohio River, without an ally, in the face of a territorially ambitious United States. The territorial settlement of 1783 (Peace of Paris), which conferred the Northwest Territory on the United States, was synonymous, in most American minds, with possession of the land itself. The Indians had a different idea. The 1780s witnessed increasing hostility on the part of the Shawnees toward the advancing Americans. Tecumseh, by now well over his early qualms about battle, joined with and soon led one of the bands attacking boats on the Ohio. By 1786 the new nation, rather than the individual states, was injured in such hostilities. Maryland's 1778 refusal to ratify the Articles of Confederation unless the states claiming western lands ceded them to the central government was the first in a series of rejections of all state claims to the politically unorganized West.

So it was that a commission appointed by Congress and representing the nation as a whole began, in the winter of 1784–1785, to negotiate with Indians regarding the Ohio country. From the Shawnees' perspective, the resulting treaties of Fort Stanwix, Fort McIntosh, and Fort Finney were insults. Valuable land concessions were wrung out of the Indians in exchange for trifling gifts. Even more infuriating was the fact that the U.S. commissioners cajoled the Iroquois into signing away other tribes' interests in lands north of the Ohio. From the American point of view, *any* Indian's agreement sufficed to validate a land treaty. The Shawnees found this view incomprehensible and outrageous. By 1788 they had repudiated the treaties and taken steps, with covert British encouragement, to organize a multitribe Indian nation that could resist American acquisition of the Ohio country. Two factors worked against this plan. One was the chronic difficulty of the various tribes in acting concertedly. The other was the fact that, authorized or not, Americans were already dividing the land spoils of the Old Northwest. The Land Ordinance of 1785 created a legal apparatus within which they could operate (see pages 115–116). Two years later, the Ohio Company organized to promote the settlement of a huge plot of rich land in the Muskingum Valley. Conniving with members of the central government who wanted a piece of the action without publicity, the Ohio Company arranged the sale of 1.5 million acres at about eight cents an acre. An additional five million acres went to the Scioto Company. From the whites' standpoint, these deals ranked among the best in the history of real-estate transactions.

While the land promoters opened the doors in the East, Tecumseh and his forest guerrillas were more directly concerned about the unorganized squatters and frontier ruffians who swarmed across the Ohio into lands still claimed and occupied by Indians at the conclusion of the Revolution. The national government attempted to check this premature and unauthorized surge. Calling the white intruders "banditti whose actions are a disgrace to human nature," Colonel Josiah Harmar tried unsuccessfully to bully them into leaving. Democracy was in vogue following the Revolution, however, and the pioneers assumed it was their "right" as citizens to settle on the newly acquired public domain.

Unable to intimidate his own compatriots, Colonel Harmar tried his luck with the Indians. In 1790, commanding 1,400 troops, he marched on the Shawnees and the Miamis. Chief Little Turtle of the Miami issued a call for warriors. Tecumseh was now twenty-two, strikingly handsome, and gifted both physically and intellectually. Burning with indignation at the cumulative personal and tribal losses that had begun with his father's death, Tecumseh responded at once to Little Turtle's appeal. He played a major role in the ambush that cost Harmar 183 men, then turned, in the fall of 1791, to the 3,000-man army of Arthur St. Clair. Little Turtle, Blue Jacket of the Shawnee, and Buckongahelos of the Delaware were the commanding chiefs who planned the surprise attack on the inept Americans the night of November 3. At dawn the next day, the Indians struck. Tecumseh was in the thick of the action. St. Clair finally managed to break through the encircling warriors, but he left over 900 men behind, 630 dead and the rest wounded. It was one of the worst American defeats in the history of Indian warfare in North America.

Emerging from the encounter with St. Clair as a leading warrior of his tribe, Tecumseh led effective raids against settlements in both Ohio and Kentucky. In 1792 he responded to a call from his eldest brother, traveled to Tennessee to help the Cherokees resist white expansion, and

This 1790 lithograph shows how Fort Harmar (foreground) and the Ohio Company's village of Marietta looked when Tecumseh was twenty-two years old. It was at about this time that he adopted the warrior's stance against the expansion of white civilization into the Ohio Valley.

after a particularly fierce encounter, buried his adored brother. Now Tecumseh was recognized as war leader of the Shawnees in the South. Several months of raiding, from Tennessee to Florida, added to his growing reputation. In the summer of 1793, war messages circulated through the eastern woodlands. They told Tecumseh that the U.S. Army, this time under the command of General Anthony Wayne, was again on the move in the Ohio country. Hurrying north, Tecumseh learned that British spokesmen at Detroit had assured the Indians full support in their campaign against Wayne. To an eager Tecumseh it seemed the opportune moment to drive the Americans back across the Ohio and to proclaim an Indian nation. Supported by 2,000 warriors, Tecumseh took up a position near Britain's Fort Miami, just west of Lake Erie and within the borders of the United States. Deploying themselves among an extensive tangle of wind-felled trees, the Indians waited for the climactic encounter. But when it came to forest fighting, Wayne was no St. Clair. He knew that Indians customarily fasted before battle. Announcing his day of attack as August 17, 1794, Wayne instead waited until August 20, when many Indians, weak from hunger, sought food at Fort Miami. Then he struck frontally and on the Indians' left flank. Tecumseh raged among the downed logs, inspiring his warriors to battle. But seeing that the promised aid from the British garrison was not forthcoming, the Indians fled. The Battle of Fallen Timbers, a year in preparation, was over in less than two hours. Only fifty Indians died, including another of Tecumseh's brothers, but their cause in the Ohio country had received a severe check.

Pressing his advantage, Wayne called the defeated chiefs together in 1795 at Fort Greenville, located in the western Ohio region near Tecumseh's birthplace. The Treaty of

Greenville (August 3, 1795) fueled the fires of hatred between Indians and white Americans in the Old Northwest for the next two decades. The agreement was essentially of Wayne's dictation. The Indians who were present agreed, for a small monetary payment, to surrender most of Ohio, including the Shawnee homeland, to the United States. The Indians also gave up the sites of cities later to be called Chicago, Detroit, Toledo, and Peoria.

Tecumseh did not attend Wayne's council at Greenville. After the council's damaging results became known, he denounced the treaty and the Shawnee negotiator, Blue Jacket. Tecumseh declared that Blue Jacket had not spoken for him. He did not regard the fight at Fallen Timbers as decisive, and he would not give up his homeland. Behind Tecumseh's adamant refusal, which won him widespread respect among several tribes and an extensive following in the late 1790s, was a deeply rooted attitude toward land and its significance in Indian culture.

Tecumseh conceived of land in a way entirely different from the view of Europeans and white Americans. In the first place, land could not be bought and sold. The earth, created by the Great Spirit, was the basis of a life community to which the Indians belonged. They used the land, but it was not "theirs" in the same sense that a buckskin garment or a knife was property. True, a tribe like the Shawnee occupied a region, and families had responsibility for fields of crops and hunting territories. But such occupancy and use did not, in Indian culture, confer the right to sell what had initially been a gift from the Great Spirit. "Sell a country?" Tecumseh incredulously asked William Henry Harrison in 1810. "Why not sell the air, the clouds, and the great sea?"

It is fair to say that many North American Indians misconstrued the whole treaty-making process. The Americans understood a treaty like the one executed at Greenville in 1795 as a sale of land by the Indians. The Indians, with no conception of selling land in their culture, interpreted the treaty as a gift to the whites in the same sense that the Great Spirit had initially given the land to them. In many instances the Indians clearly did not feel that "transferring title" to the land meant anything more than a willingness to share the area with the newcomers. So when the whites appeared, treaty in hand, and told the Indians to leave the land that now "belonged" to them, there was disbelief, confusion, and, finally, anger and resistance.

Even if Blue Jacket and the other chiefs at Greenville understood that they were "selling" Ohio, Tecumseh had reason to protest. The use of land, he believed, was an inherent right of the Indian race as a whole. Every member had a right to use the earth. It consequently followed that no single member could surrender the rights of those who did not agree with the transaction. This was the philosophical basis of Tecumseh's conviction that no portion of the Ohio Valley could be sold or ceded to the Americans without the consent of *all* Indians everywhere.

There was also the question in Tecumseh's mind of appropriate ways of using the earth. He shared the Shawnee belief that the land was sacred—literally Mother Earth—and that various life forms had a rightful share in its bounty. Cutting away the forests, "clearing" the land, was wrong, as was the use of metal tools to plow the soil. According to Shawnee tradition, only a pointed stick or a bone hoe should be sunk into the body of Mother Earth. From this viewpoint, the white passion to transform the environment with the most sophisticated technology available was—treaty or no treaty—morally wrong.

Whereas Wayne saw the 1795 Treaty of Greenville as the end of "the Indian problem" in the Ohio country, Tecumseh knew it was only the beginning. After Greenville, Tecumseh became the dominant Indian leader in the Old Northwest. Handsome and powerful, Tecumseh struck an impressive figure. A British officer described his eyes as "clear, transparent hazel, with a mild, pleasant expression when in repose . . . but when excited in his orations, or by the enthusiasm of conflict, or when in anger, they appeared like balls of fire." He stood erect, elegantly dressed in tanned buckskin and, according to the Englishman, was "one of the finest looking men I have ever seen." Among his own people, Tecumseh was stern and fiery. When challenged, he would say, "I am Tecumseh" and simply touch the handle of his tomahawk.

Around the charismatic Shawnee, who had moved west to Indiana following Greenville, there gathered independent and disgruntled warriors from several woodland tribes. They watched in despair as the traders' liquor ravaged those Indians who remained close to the expanding line of settlements. The once-proud Miamis became, in the words of one American observer, "a poor, miserable drunken set, diminishing every year." Many became beggars or thieves. Tecumseh refused to drink and unsuccessfully opposed the traders who created and then fed the Indians' habit. He had no more luck resisting the succession of land cessions that Governor William Henry Harrison, of the Indiana Territory, engineered after 1802. Statehood in 1803 brought tens of thousands of white settlers to Ohio, many of whom soon pushed into Indiana and Illinois territories. With President Thomas Jefferson committed to advancing white settlement, Harrison was instructed to "purchase" lands from the Indian tribes. Carrying out the president's Indian policy usually involved defrauding the Indians of their land in one way or another. Harrison was the instrument of policies that often denied Indian land claims altogether. But it was Jefferson, the architect, who informed Harrison on February 27, 1803, that "our strength and their weakness is now so visible that they must see we have only to shut our hand to crush them." The tribes, Jefferson declared, had only two options—incorporation into the United States as citizens or removal beyond the Mississippi: "Should any tribe be foolhardy enough to take up the hatchet at any time . . . seizing the whole country of that tribe . . . would be an example to others and a furtherance of our final consolidation." It was a matter, then, of taking what Harrison offered or risking getting nothing at all. Bribes to key chiefs and an ample supply of whiskey were also standard tools of Harrison's trade. By 1805 Indian claims had been "extinguished" in most of Michigan, Indiana, Illinois, and part of Wisconsin.

It was a low point in Tecumseh's life. He must have wondered if resistance could be anything but temporary and symbolic. Then, in 1805, he caught fire. Crucial to the revival of Tecumseh's determination was a remarkable transformation in the life of one of his remaining brothers, the slovenly Lalawethika. A twin to another of Tecumseh's siblings—and thus, according to Shawnee culture, endowed with magical abilities—Lalawethika displayed no special talents for some years. Much to his brother Tecumseh's disgust, he became a heavy drinker. A handkerchief covered the eye he had lost in a self-inflicted accident with an arrow. Lalawethika devoted his life to loafing and bragging in the reflected glory of his famous brother. Even his name was appropriate: it meant "the loud mouth."

Never much of a warrior, Lalawethika nonetheless would have a great impact on Tecumseh and all the Shawnees. Ridiculed for his inability to hunt or fight, Lalawethika slipped into a deep depression accompanied by heavy drinking. Between binges, however, he sought the advice of the village medicine man, who taught him many of his herbal secrets and incantations. When the old medicine man died in 1804, Lalawethika claimed to know all of his secrets. But when an epidemic hit the village and Lalawethika could do nothing to stop his fellow villagers from dying, his credibility as a shaman vanished. He shrank back into his wigwam and fell into a drug-induced trance so deep that most villagers—including his wife—believed he was dead. Upon his miraculous emergence, he reported meeting the Master of Life, an Indian deity, who had shown him the evils of drink. Lalawethika may have been influenced by the Christian revivals sweeping frontier settlements during those days. He may have heard of the great camp meeting at Cane Ridge, Bourbon County, Kentucky, in 1801, where 20,000 people gathered in the hope of conversion and salvation. Lalawethika had come into contact with a Shaker colony that had been established between

This 1836 George Catlin painting shows Tenskwatawa, the Prophet, in full dress. He died the same year.

Cincinnati and Dayton and was certainly familiar with the work of itinerant Shaker preachers and their strange jerking dances. Lalawethika also may have known of a Delaware prophet who practiced revivalism in the 1760s. It was a curious grafting of American onto Indian religion that led him to change his name, in 1805, to Tenskwatawa, which means "the open door"—a reference to Jesus' saying, "I am the door." Within two years, Tecumseh's brother was known widely on the frontier to Indians and whites alike by his famous nickname, the Prophet.

The message of the Prophet included abstinence from alcohol, "the white man's poison." He claimed this to be a part of the Master of Life's message, but Tecumseh undoubtedly influenced it as well. The Prophet also advocated the end of intertribal bickering and the adoption of a united Indian front against white civilization. An Indian confederacy, the Prophet believed, could resist the piecemeal erosion of Indian land holdings. Finally, the Shawnee Prophet invoked Indian pride, dignity, and self-respect. He urged his people to cease imitating the ways and using the materials of the whites. Only by being true to their own cultural traditions could Indians maintain the strength and the will to resist dispossession.

Tecumseh was overjoyed by the transformation in his brother. Indeed, many of the Prophet's ideas were simply those of the Shawnee war chief stated in a more emotional and mystical manner. The brothers made a formidable team: the prophet who could envisage better times and the warrior who could fulfill the prophecy with the force of arms. In 1806 Tecumseh and the Prophet moved from Indiana back east to Greenville, Ohio, where they built a village at the exact site where Anthony Wayne had wrung land cessions from the tribes a decade earlier. Their following grew daily, swelled by dissatisfied Indians from various woodland tribes. Although few Indians shared the Prophet's mystical vision, his message made good sense amid the white siege of their lands. Unity, abstinence from white ways, and tradition spoke strongly to those who had witnessed the degradation and corruption of disunity and emulation. Moreover, the Prophet's remarkable recovery from alcoholism reinforced his claim of contact with the Master of Life.

At this point, in April 1806, Indiana territorial governor William Henry Harrison inadvertently aided the cause of the two Shawnees. In a speech to the Delaware tribe, Harrison issued warnings about following a "pretended prophet" into renewed resistance. Demand proof of this prophet's powers, said Harrison: "If he is really a prophet, ask of him to cause the sun to stand still—the moon to alter its course—the rivers to cease to flow or the dead to rise from their graves." When news of Harrison's challenge reached Tecumseh and the Prophet they were delighted; they knew from white informants that a total eclipse of the sun would occur on June 16, 1806. Calling a huge assembly of Indians together at Greenville, the Prophet waited for the right moment. At 11:32 A.M. the moon began to move between the sun and the earth. The Prophet commanded night to fall. It did. Then he commanded the sun to reappear, which, of course, it did. The performance astounded the assembled Indians. Reports of the Prophet's miracle and his message were carried far up the Missouri to the Sioux, Blackfeet, and Arikaras—tribes hardly aware, in 1806, of the enemy presence to the east.

While Tenskwatawa's leadership strengths were in accord with Native American culture, Tecumseh's were derived partly from his knowledge of the white people. And he gained a good deal of that knowledge at the home of a white family that had settled in the Ohio village of Chillicothe. John Galloway had been a participant in the 1782 expedition of George Rogers Clark against British-supported Indians at Chillicothe and had returned to the beautiful spot on the Little Miami River to make his home. Tecumseh spoke excellent English, although as part of his antiwhite philosophy he refused to use it in formal situations involving U.S. leaders. But Galloway was just a pioneer farmer, traveling with his family into land opened for settlement by the Treaty of Greenville, and Tecumseh liked his manner. When they parted, Galloway extended an open invitation for the Shawnee to be his guest.

A continuous traveler, Tecumseh had several contacts with the Galloway family over the next decade. He delighted in Galloway's library, which, at 300 volumes, was probably one of the best in the territory at that time. The many hours that Tecumseh spent with his host opened a whole new dimension to him. He learned that the white culture did not mean just rifles, hatred of Indians, and land hunger, but also Homer, Shakespeare, the Bible, and the Declaration of Independence. Although there was speculation of a romantic interlude between Tecumseh and Galloway's daughter, Rebecca, recent scholarship has dismissed this as myth.

The new Prophet's Town rose in 1808 at the confluence of the Wabash and Tippecanoe Rivers, on Wea and Miami land in Indiana. From this safer base west of Ohio, Tecumseh began his crusade to make the Prophet's dream of a great Indian confederacy of interior tribes a reality. Over the next three years, he traveled through the Great Lakes region to make the Prophet's message known. In 1811 Tecumseh traveled south to deliver a similar message to the Choctaw, Chickasaw, and Creek tribes that then occupied parts of Tennessee, Alabama, and Mississippi.

At the hundreds of council fires he attended, Tecumseh adopted a standard role. The pacifism and intertribal rivalries of the older chiefs had to be discredited in favor of the fiercer spirit of the younger braves, who realized that the only rivalry that really mattered was that between native and Anglo-Americans. From the reports of Americans who occasionally observed Tecumseh in action, we know something of his manner and his message. After the requisite number of ceremonial pipes had been passed, Tecumseh began by offering his audience a history lesson. "Where today is the Pequod?" he asked. "Where the Narragansetts, the Mohawks, Pocanokets, and many other once powerful tribes of our race?" Because of the tendency of some of their leaders to believe the promises of the newcomers from Europe, these people had "vanished before the avarice and oppression of the white man as snow before a summer sun."

As a widely traveled intertribal diplomat and a keen observer of the injustices suffered by his race, Tecumseh knew a great deal about the history of Indian–white relations in North America, and he used this historical knowledge effectively in his orations. His reference to the Pequod (or Pequot) Indians was particularly effective. In 1637 the desire of Massachusetts settlers for land west of Narragansett Bay had launched the Pequot War (see pages 44–45). In one ruthless campaign the entire tribe—every man, woman, and child—had been killed or captured. The Narragansett had been next in line along the route of whites in Connecticut, Rhode Island, and Massachusetts. But under the leadership of a Wampanoag chief the colonists called King Philip, they had struck back. Anticipating Tecumseh in his advocacy of an all-Indian alliance against the settlers, Philip succeeded, in 1675 and 1676, in actually pushing back the New England frontier. The Deerfield Massacre was his work. In all, one-sixth of the colonial male population of New England had been killed in King Philip's war.

But systematic destruction of Indian grain fields in the Connecticut Valley had changed the momentum. The white settlers began the task, as one colonist put it, of "exterminating the rabid animals." Even Roger Williams, who was almost unique in his questioning of the ethics involved in dispossessing Indians, turned against the Wampanoags and their allies. It was an all-out racial war; barbarism characterized the behavior of both sides, but the New Englanders prevailed. Aware that he was at the end of his ability to resist, Philip returned to his homeland, where, on August 12, 1676, he was betrayed by an Indian, cornered in a Massachusetts swamp, and shot. The overjoyed frontiersmen brought Philip's head to Plymouth, where it remained on display for a quarter of a century, stuck on the end of a pole. His severed hand was pickled in a pail of rum and displayed by the Indian betrayer "to such gentlemen as would bestow gratuities upon him."

As an advocate of Indian unity, Tecumseh prized past examples of concerted Indian action. The most notable achievement in this field in North America was the confederacy or "League" of the Iroquois. Its origins antedated the coming of Europeans, and its purpose appears to have been directed at establishing a "Great Peace" among the constantly warring tribes of the eastern woodlands. The legendary Hiawatha was the architect of a federal government remarkable for its constitution of laws and its democratic principles. A tireless traveler, Hiawatha visited tribes as distant from his New York home as the Sauk in Wisconsin. Only five eastern "Nations" joined the Iroquois League in the sixteenth century; a sixth entered about 1715. But the government was strong enough to last for two centuries and to make the Iroquois the foremost Indian power before the American Revolution. The political theory and concepts of social morality that underlay the strength of the Six Nations were the object of extensive, if rather embarrassing, colonial admiration. Even as they were breaking the Iroquois' power, Benjamin Franklin and other architects of colonial and (later) state unity found the Indians' confederation instructive and inspiring. Joseph Brant, a talented Iroquois leader of the 1770s and 1780s, had a direct influence on the maturation of Tecumseh's vision of power through unity.

The Ottawa war of Chief Pontiac offered Tecumseh the best recent example of aggressive Indian leadership. The conclusion in 1763 of the French and Indian, or Seven Years', War had

A pipe, a tomahawk, and a spear rolled into one. During the eighteenth century, these objects were traded by the English and the French to Indians throughout the eastern woodlands.

eliminated French holdings on the mainland of North America. It was a major setback for the Indians, because French colonial aims centered on fur rather than farms. Hence, France had no reason to dispossess Indians of their hunting grounds. On the contrary, Indian hunters were needed in the first steps of the lucrative fur trade. Moreover, with Britain as the sole dominant force, Indians could no longer play one nation off against another. Without competition, fur traders and land speculators could be even more unscrupulous in their dealings with Indians. But westward expansion remained the dominant problem. Great Britain did nothing to solve it in issuing the Proclamation of 1763, which, in theory, prevented settlement west of the crest of the Appalachians. In practice, it was rather different. Acquiring land was essential to the colonization of North America, and the colonists were not about to be restrained by such considerations as parliamentary authority and Indians' rights. There were, to be sure, a few colonists who cared. Sir William Johnson, his assistant George Croghan, and Colonel John Stuart were Indian superintendents, and they took seriously their job of establishing fair trade relations with the tribes. This was difficult, however, when Lord Jeffrey Amherst, their superior, openly advocated distributing blankets loaded with smallpox germs to the Indians during Pontiac's rebellion in 1763.

Driven to the breaking point, in the summer of 1763 Pontiac struck back. His skills as a warrior had been honed against the British in the recently concluded French and Indian War. He was also, in the pattern Tecumseh would follow, a compelling orator, a charismatic leader, and a crusader for unified Indian action. The attacks he led in 1763 featured Shawnee warriors. They staggered Great Britain in the West: Eight out of twelve British forts in Indian country were captured, and hundreds of settlers were killed. For a moment Pontiac must have believed that his temporary alliance of eighteen tribes would drive the British away. But Pontiac did not understand the terms on which the French and Indian War ended. France was through with North America. The assistance he had counted on in his war against Great Britain did not materialize, and in 1764 the English launched an effective counterstrike against the Shawnees and the Delawares. Pontiac's "conspiracy"—as nineteenth-century historian Francis Parkman curiously dubbed this war for native self-determination—had failed. British supremacy in the trans-Appalachian West continued. But Pontiac's example inspired the Shawnee chief Cornstalk, who, in turn, fired Tecumseh's youthful enthusiasm. The cause of Indian resistance would also continue.

Drawing on these and other examples, Tecumseh invariably directed many of his speeches to a consideration of the future. "Will we not soon be driven from our respective countries and the graves of our ancestors?" he asked his audiences, his superb voice rising with emotion. There was even a worse fate in store for those who did not resist encroachments on Indian liberty. Tecumseh was fully aware of the institution of slavery, and he asked his listeners to consider how long it would be before the Americans "tie us to a post and whip us, and make us work for them in their cornfields as they do . . . their blackfaces." The only way to prevent such a catastrophe, Tecumseh continued, was to "form one body, one heart, and defend to the last warrior our country, our liberty, and the graves of our fathers." This was not an easy point for the Native Americans to grasp. The Indians were not all one tribe. Thousands of years of competition for territory had left a legacy of diversity and enmity. Indians had rarely acted together as Tecumseh now called on them to do.

Building to a climax at the conclusion of his talk, Tecumseh would demand all-out war: "Back, whence they came, upon a trail of blood, they must be driven. . . . Burn their dwellings! Destroy their stock! Slay their wives and children! . . . Dig their very corpses from the grave." Tecumseh's hatred of whites, a tribesman once observed, "was the most bitter of any Indian I ever knew." Tecumseh himself admitted that he "could not look upon the face of a white man without feeling the flesh crawl on his bones."

At times, hundreds of Indians gathered to hear Tecumseh deliver such speeches. He frequently spoke bare-chested, in breechcloth and moccasins. He held a tomahawk. Red war paint lined his eyes. Those who heard him and reported their impressions were astonished at his oratorical abilities. His words, said General Sam Dale, a white military officer, "fell in avalanches from his lips. . . . His eyes burned with supernatural lustre, and his whole frame trembled with emotion. His voice resounded over the multitude—now sinking in low and musical whispers, now rising to the highest key, hurling out his words like a succession of thunderbolts." The general concluded his report with the observation that he had heard many great orators, "but I never saw one with the vocal powers of Tecumseh."

Tecumseh frequently made effective use of the Prophet's alleged connections with the Great Spirit, enlisting that potent Indian deity on the side of his program. As a representative of the Great Spirit, Tecumseh could do wondrous things. In 1811 he told the Creek tribe, on several occasions, that when he returned to Tippecanoe (Prophet's Town), he would stamp his foot and the ground a thousand miles to the south would tremble and houses would collapse. Then, in December 1811, came the great New Madrid earthquake, which altered the course of the Mississippi River and thoroughly shook the trans-Appalachian West. As their houses fell, Indians remembered Tecumseh's words and flocked to his cause. Prizing the red-painted sticks he had given them as a symbol of his wrath, the Creeks launched a major war against the United States in the Old Southwest.

Tecumseh's success in converting Indian tribes to his thinking was more illusory than real. The implication of unity and leadership, however, aroused fears among whites. Although Governor William Henry Harrison worried about the Prophet's message, he was even more concerned about Tecumseh, whom he called "the Moses of the family." Respecting Tecumseh as a revolutionary of great potential, Harrison arranged a meeting to size up the Indian chief. In the summer of 1810, they met at Harrison's headquarters in Vincennes, Indiana. It was one of the most dramatic confrontations in the history of Indian–white relations in North America. Harrison had recently concluded another of his land-grabbing treaties with a handful of older and weaker chiefs. In return for $7,000 and some liquor, they had ceded three million acres of land, much of it not even under their control, to the United States. Determined to confront him with the injustice of this 1809 Treaty of Fort Wayne, Tecumseh and about seventy-five brightly painted warriors accepted Harrison's invitation to come to Vincennes. They traveled down the Wabash River, sweeping up to a landing a few miles above Harrison's headquarters in gaudily decorated war canoes. An American soldier at the scene observed that Tecumseh "is one of the finest looking men I ever saw—about six feet high, straight, with fine features, and altogether a daring, bold-looking fellow." On August 12, 1810, the two men, representing such different cultural perspectives, met for the first time.

Speaking Shawnee as he always did on such formal occasions, Tecumseh denounced the Fort Wayne agreement. The land, he said, had been ceded by a few powerless chiefs, whom Tecumseh would kill if the agreement was not invalidated. Harrison must recognize that, according to the Indian concept of property, no individual or small group could sell land. There were no "owners" of Indian land; it belonged equally to the natives. In accepting the cession from the discredited chiefs, the white people had proved once again that they could not be trusted. Harrison replied in the only way he could, upholding his principal objectives: The treaties were valid. The land in question would be occupied by force if necessary. The United States had always been fair in its dealings with Indians. An enraged Tecumseh leaped to his feet and, in Shawnee, denounced the startled Harrison as a liar. One soldier standing by who knew the language ordered more soldiers to approach. For a few tense moments, guns were cocked and tomahawks were drawn. Harrison rose and drew his sword, but then ordered his men to lower their weapons. Tecumseh waved his warriors back to their camp and later sent apologies to Harrison for losing his temper.

In the morning, Harrison came to the Shawnees' camp for more talks. Tecumseh used humor to make his point. When the men took seats on a bench, Tecumseh took a position very near Harrison and continually edged him toward one end of the board. The governor readjusted his position several times and, finally, as he was about to be pushed off completely, protested. Tecumseh capitalized at once on the opportunity to draw a moral about American treatment of Indians. If present trends continued, he remarked, the United States would drive the red people "into the Great Lake, where they can't either stand or walk." But Tecumseh made clear that his followers were determined to retreat no longer. Harrison was also adamant, although he wisely withheld his remarks until a few weeks following the conference with Tecumseh. Concerning the remaining Indian land in the Northwest, Harrison asked, "Is one of the fairest portions of the globe to remain in a state of nature, the haunt of a few wretched savages, when it seems destined, by the creator, to give support to a large population, and to be the seat of civilization, of science, and true religion?" It was a sentiment typical of the frontier mind, and, set against Tecumseh's philosophy, it could only mean renewed war.

Tecumseh and Harrison met again at Vincennes, Indiana, in the summer of 1811. This time the immediate problem was the death of several settlers at the hands of Indians whom Harrison had accused of being followers of the Prophet and Tecumseh. They probably were, but Tecumseh refused to give them up to Harrison. Instead, he left Prophet's Town for another long southern journey aimed at recruiting tribes to his cause. Harrison, the crafty soldier, seized on Tecumseh's absence to march on Prophet's Town. At the Battle of Tippecanoe, on November 7, 1811, Harrison scattered the Indians and burned their town and their stored corn. In terms of losses, the engagement was a draw, but it established Harrison's reputation as an Indian-fighter and paved his way to the presidency of the United States in 1840.

Returning from the southern tribes early in 1812, Tecumseh seethed with anger on hearing what had happened. First, he turned against his brother, the Prophet, berating him for his ineptitude in the Battle of Tippecanoe and driving him from the rebuilt Prophet's Town. Indeed, Tenskwatawa, on whom the residents of Prophet's Town depended for leadership, had failed to do anything but remain in his tent and pray for intervention by the Master of Life. That he took no part in the fighting enraged not only Tecumseh, but others who had earlier considered him the leader of the pan-Indian movement. His medicine gone, the Prophet made his way in disgrace to Canada to live under British protection.

After Tippecanoe, Tecumseh launched raids against American outposts throughout the Northwest. Even in the now heavily populated region of Kentucky and Ohio, white settlers banded together, united in their efforts to repel the Shawnee attacks. Meanwhile, Tecumseh still had to deal regularly with the problem of warrior bands acting independently of one another and without the clear sense of unity that the whites displayed. Their failure to act in unity, Tecumseh knew, would soon prove to be disastrous.

On June 18, 1812, a new factor entered the already stormy seas of Western affairs: war with Great Britain. The Indian hostilities that Tecumseh had inspired played an important role in causing the War of 1812. Western settlers blamed the British for arousing the Indians against the Americans. In a typical overstatement, William Henry Harrison said, "The whole of the Indians on this frontier have been completely armed and equipped from the British King's stores." To settlers in the West, it seemed that the only answer to the problem was conquest of Canada. The economic pressures that Thomas Jefferson's and James Madison's administrations had attempted to use against Great Britain as early as 1807 had not been signally successful. It was imperative, insisted war hawks like Henry Clay of Kentucky, to break the British–Indian alliance by eliminating British territorial holdings in North America.

While frontier statesmen like Clay and Harrison tended to see Tecumseh as a puppet of the British, the Shawnee leader had a different perspective. The British were invaders and consequently no better than the Americans, but they could be used. If the whites were divided and at war, Indians might emerge the biggest winners. Tecumseh saw in the War of 1812 a golden opportunity to drive the Americans out of the West—and perhaps even off the continent. At an 1812 council at Fort Wayne, called by the Americans to win Indian support—or at least neutrality—in the war, Tecumseh made his position clear. "Here is a chance," he told the assembly, " . . . yes,

In 1813, Margaret Reynolds, the daughter of a British officer stationed at Fort Malden, painted this watercolor entitled "View of Amherstburg." The figure in the foreground wearing the Shawnee headdress and British military trousers may be Tecumseh.

a chance such as will never occur again—for us Indians of North America to form ourselves into one great combination and cast our lot with the British in this war." If the British won, Tecumseh reasoned, the woodland tribes could reestablish their claim to the Northwest. The king would welcome a buffer nation confining the recently rebelled colonists. An American victory, on the other hand, would confront the Indians with a monolithic power. Then, he continued, "It will not be many years before our last place of abode and our last hunting ground will be taken from us, and the remnants of the different tribes . . . will all be driven toward the setting sun." It was a prophetic observation. The War of 1812 was indeed the Indians' last real chance to resist the American invasion. For a moment, a free Indian nation hung in the balance. By the time the tribes of the Great Plains waged the last campaigns of Indian resistance, the "chance" Tecumseh spoke of was gone.

At the conclusion of the Fort Wayne council, Tecumseh broke the peace pipe offered him by an American representative. Then, at the head of about 1,000 warriors, he marched north to the British garrison at Fort Malden. In late July and early August 1812, Tecumseh and his warriors succeeded in bewildering and defeating the inept U.S. forces under Detroit-based General William Hull. By this time the Shawnee's name was legendary; the very rumor that Tecumseh was in the forest across from the line of battle was enough to panic American troops. On August 13, with Tecumseh holding Hull at bay in Detroit, General Isaac Brock arrived at Fort Malden with

British reinforcements. His relationship with Tecumseh was one of mutual admiration; together they almost realized the Indian's dreams. At the time of their initial meeting, the dignified, talented Brock clearly acknowledged Tecumseh's skills by expressing his desire to "take lessons from you and your warriors, that we may learn how to make war in these great forests." Brock then assured Tecumseh that "their great father beyond the great salt lake" would protect the interest of "his red children" against the Americans. Sizing up Brock, who was well over six feet tall and powerfully built, Tecumseh simply turned to his followers, stretched out his hand, and exclaimed, "Hoo-e: This is a man!"

Immediately thereafter, Brock and Tecumseh planned the capture of Detroit. Overruling the opinion of his own staff, Brock took the advice of the Indian and launched an immediate attack. He also allowed one of his couriers to be captured by the Americans. The courier carried false news that 5,000 Chippewa were on their way from the north to join Tecumseh. For his part, Tecumseh carried out the ruse by marching 1,000 warriors in single file through a clearing three times. Thoroughly shaken, Hull raised the white flag of surrender on August 16, 1812. The most important border post in the West had fallen. Tecumseh's humane treatment of the captured Americans added to his growing legend. Brock noted that as soon as an enemy surrendered, his life was sacred in the eyes of Tecumseh.

The fall of Detroit fired Tecumseh with hope for his independent, all-Indian nation, and he left in the winter of 1812 for another round of recruiting councils among the southern tribes. The content of his message was the same, only more impassioned: "Let the white race perish. They seize your land, they corrupt your women, they trample on the ashes of your dead! Back whence they came, upon a trail of blood, they must be driven." Then Tecumseh added his standard plea: "Unless every tribe unanimously combines to give a check to the ambition and avarice of the whites, they will soon conquer us apart and disunited, and we will be driven away from our native country and scattered as autumnal leaves before the wind." He returned north in April 1813 and was greeted with the news that his friend Brock had been killed in action against the Americans near Fort Niagara.

The chief must have sensed trouble when he met Brock's replacement as the military leader in the West. Colonel Henry Procter was a weak, unimaginative man who despised "savages," whether they fought on his side or not. Although Procter and an Indian force had scored a major victory on January 22, 1813, against Americans at the River Raisin, near Detroit, in the aftermath of the battle, Procter exercised no control over the Indians. Without a Tecumseh to provide leadership, butchery of the defenseless American captives took place. Such behavior had no place in Tecumseh's code of conduct as a warrior. In April 1813, after leading a brilliant victory (480 Americans killed, 150 captured) against William Henry Harrison's reinforcements near Fort Meigs, Tecumseh learned that Procter was once again permitting the murder of captives on their way to the British camp. Riding full speed into the midst of the slaughter, Tecumseh screamed, "Are there no men here?" The killing and scalping stopped abruptly. Next Tecumseh confronted Procter, demanding to know why he permitted such behavior. The Englishman had no answer. To the delight of the other Indian warriors, Tecumseh hurled insult after insult at Procter, finally comparing him to "a fat animal, that carries its tail on its back, but when affrightened, he drops it between his legs and runs off."

In the ensuing months, British–Indian relations deteriorated rapidly. Over Tecumseh's heated objections, the vacillating Procter abandoned the siege of Harrison and Fort Meigs. The time for decisive action against the Americans in the West was running out. The balance of power was shifting. Then, in the early fall of 1813, the end came with stunning suddenness. The first

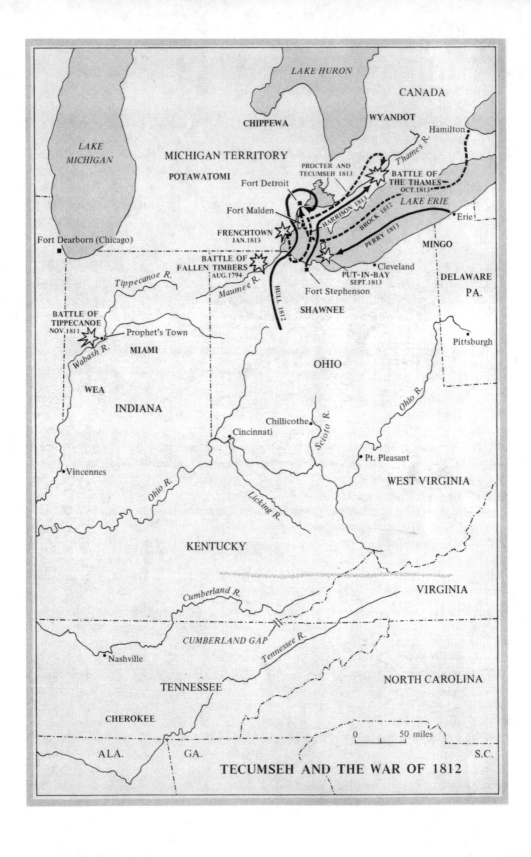

TECUMSEH AND THE WAR OF 1812

setback for the British and the Indian cause was signaled by U.S. Commodore Oliver Hazard Perry's victory at Put-in-Bay, in Lake Erie. Aggressive British policy, such as Brock would have favored, could have destroyed Perry's ships while they were still under construction on the lakeshore at Erie, Pennsylvania. But Procter delayed repeatedly. Finally, in a single day, September 10, 1813, Perry's newly built vessels completely destroyed British naval power and supply routes on the Great Lakes. His famous message to William Henry Harrison was written on the back of an old envelope the following day: "We have met the enemy and they are ours." So, it turned out, was the Indian.

With his source of supply cut off, the timid Procter began preparations for a British retreat along the north shore of Lake Erie. Harrison moved his forces against the British. Tecumseh pleaded with Procter to stand firm, and when his pleas failed, he shouted, "Listen, Father! You have the arms and ammunition which our great father sent for his red children. If you have an idea of going away, give them to us, and you may go and welcome. Our lives are in the hands of the Great Spirit. He gave to our ancestors the lands which we possess. We are determined to defend them, and if it is His will, our bones shall whiten on them, but we will never give them up." Failing to persuade the badly frightened Englishman, Tecumseh ended by calling him "a miserable old squaw" to his face.

Knowledgeable in military strategy, Tecumseh understood the British retreat was the beginning of the end. "We are going to follow the British," he notified his warriors, "and I feel certain that we shall never return." On the night of October 4, his pessimism was directed more at himself. "Brother warriors," Tecumseh told the men who had followed his cause for a decade, "we are about to enter an engagement from which I shall not return."

The Battle of the Thames began on October 5, 1813. Procter's spirit was totally broken; he fled eastward in a special carriage after the first clash with Harrison's advancing soldiers. Tecumseh became the de facto leader of the combined British and Indian forces. Raging through the forest like one possessed, he urged the men to hold firm, at the same time throwing his own formidable strength into the heaviest fighting. Toward dusk, Tecumseh was shot and killed at close range by Harrison's troops. The fact that his body was not recovered, or at least not clearly identified, gave rise to years of wild speculation that the great Shawnee still lived. Even the memory of Tecumseh was enough to make the nocturnal forests of the Northwest Territory a terrifying place for the new American owners.

The western campaign of the War of 1812 not only marked the demise of the idea of an Indian confederation but also signaled the end of white–Indian cooperation in warfare. Never again would interior tribes be able to play one power off against another, as Indians had done for the past two centuries with the French, British, and Americans. By the end of the War of 1812, Indians had to face the unified power of an American nation hell-bent on settling the continent from the Atlantic to the Pacific. It was only a matter of time before all North American Indian tribes would be removed from their traditional homelands and placed on reservations scattered across the continent. From the forced march of the Cherokees on the "Trail of Tears" during the 1830s to the subjugation of the Apaches in the 1880s, no tribe escaped the removal policies of the U.S. government. The Prophet himself, whose vision had sparked the idea of Indian unity, died quietly on a Kansas reservation in 1836. Tecumseh's grand effort, bolstered by Tenskwatawa's early vision, had been a noble, yet futile, attempt to protect the heritage of American Indians in the face of inexorable white incursions into their land. As exponents of a hopeless but worthy cause, Tecumseh and the Prophet nonetheless stand tall as legends of their time and defenders of their own American dream.

Selected Readings

The Person

Drake, Benjamin: *The Life of Tecumseh and His Brother the Prophet* (1841). The first biography.

Eckert, Allan W.: *The Frontiersmen: A Narrative* (1967). Although fictionalized, the book is based on fact and features Tecumseh.

Eckert, Allan W.: *A Sorrow in Our Heart: The Life of Tecumseh* (1992). A thorough account of Tecumseh and the Shawnees, including maps and correspondence.

Edmunds, David R.: *The Shawnee Prophet* (1983). The story of Tecumseh's brother Tenskwatawa and the impact of his vision on the unity movement.

Edmunds, David R.: *Tecumseh and the Quest for Indian Leadership* (1984). Places the Prophet alongside Tecumseh in importance and dispels much mythology of earlier biographies.

Josephy, Alvin M., Jr.: "Tecumseh, The Greatest Indian," in Alvin M. Josephy Jr., *The Patriot Chiefs: A Chronicle of American Indian Resistance* (1958), pp. 131–173. The best short biography, with a sensitive understanding of the historical forces that shaped Tecumseh's life.

Klinck, Carl F. (ed.): *Tecumseh: Fact and Fiction in Early Records* (1961). Edited documents about and by Tecumseh, including his important speeches.

Sugden, John: *Tecumseh's Last Stand* (1985). An account leading up to and including the Battle of the Thames.

Tucker, Glenn: *Tecumseh: Vision of Glory* (1956). A good, complete biography.

The Period

Arnow, Harriette S.: *Seedtime on the Cumberland* (1960). A history of the trans-Appalachian white frontier.

Bakeless, John: *Daniel Boone* (1938). A biography of a man Tecumseh opposed but also admired.

Billington, Ray Allen: *Westward Expansion: A History of the American Frontier* (2d ed., 1960). The best single volume on a subject that involves Indians at almost every juncture.

Brandon, William: *The Last Americans: The Indian in American Culture* (1974). A monumental cultural history of the whole Indian experience.

Carter, Samuel, III: *Cherokee Sunset: A Nation Betrayed* (1976). The expulsion of the Cherokees was even more brutal than that of the Shawnees.

Cleaves, Freeman: *Old Tippecanoe: William Henry Harrison and His Time* (1939). The white perspective on the Indian wars of the Old Northwest.

Dowd, Gregory Evans: *A Spirited Resistance: The North American Indian Struggle for Unity, 1745–1815* (1992). An examination of Tecumseh in the context of the pan-Indian movement among woodland tribes.

Hagen, William T.: *American Indians* (1961). A brief, fast-paced history of the entire Indian experience.

Jacobs, Wilbur R.: *Dispossessing the American Indian: Indians and Whites on the Colonial Frontier* (1972). Valuable interpretations of the woodland Indians and the effect of their contact with white civilization.

Jennings, Francis: *The Invasion of America: Indians, Colonialism, and the Century of Conquest* (1975). A revisionist interpretation of the settlement of North America, particularly the Northeast, that stresses the injustices of the white dispossession of the Indian.

Josephy, Alvin M., Jr.: *The Patriot Chiefs: A Chronicle of American Indian Resistance* (1958). Essays on Indian leaders, from Hiawatha to Chief Joseph, that illuminate the entire course of Indian–white relations.

Sheehan, Bernard: *Seeds of Extinction* (1973). Shows how the Jeffersonians devised a policy of Indian removal long before Jackson's.

Underhill, Ruth Murray: *Red Man's America* (rev. ed., 1971). An ethnologist's interpretation of Indian history.

Washburn, Wilcomb E. (ed.): *The Indian and the White Man* (1964). A collection of documents.

°Washburn, Wilcomb E.: *The Indian in America* (1975). Inclusive chapters dealing with Indian personality, social structure, and religion are blended with a chronological history.

For Consideration

1. During the American Revolution, tribes of the Ohio Valley, including Tecumseh's Shawnees, sided with the British. What were some of the reasons for such alliances?

2. Describe some turning points in Tecumseh's emergence as the acknowledged military leader of the Shawnees.

3. Tecumseh's concept of land stood in stark contrast to the views of the people of the United States. Analyze the significance of those differences with regard to the treaties of the late 1700s.

4. What were some of the historical arguments used by Tecumseh in attempting to persuade other tribes to join his confederation during the early 1800s?

5. How did the outcome of the War of 1812 spell an end to Tecumseh's Indian confederation and resistance to white incursions into the Ohio Valley?

°Available in paperback.

Kit Carson

The stocky man with the pale blue eyes and the sandy blonde hair rode ahead on the final miles of the trail to Taos, a Pueblo Indian village now in United States territory. The year was 1848. Kit Carson was coming home after living on the vast western frontier for nearly five years. His journeys had taken him over many horizons to the upper Missouri River basin, to Oregon Country, and to California. As a member of the first three expeditions of U.S. Army Captain John C. Frémont, Carson had participated in mapping, surveying, Indian-fighting, and negotiations—as well as in a war with Mexico that resulted in the American occupation of the Southwest by the United States. The relatively young American nation needed heroes, and Carson stood larger than life, lionized in pulp fiction stories of the Wild West. Uneasy with such hyperbole, Carson now only wanted to return to his wife, Josefa, his ranch, and a more normal life. His horse's pace quickened as he neared his home. Kit Carson would be home for a short time, but a whirlwind of events in the American West would again and again sweep this mountain man turned scout and rancher away from his desire for a normal life and back to the military and Indian affairs inevitably associated with expanding national boundaries.

Traditional American heroes invariably came from log cabins, and Christopher Houston Carson was no exception. His birth took place on Christmas Eve, 1809, in a three-room log cabin in Madison County, Kentucky. Less than two years later, Lindsay and Rebecca Carson sold their Kentucky farm and moved west to Boone's Lick, in Howard County of what would become the state of Missouri. The family's move to Missouri culminated more than one hundred years of steady migration by the Carsons, from Scotland to northern Ireland to the wilds of Pennsylvania, South Carolina, and Kentucky. On the road to the new home in central Missouri, Christopher (Kit, as he was called) rode in the front of his mother's saddle and later claimed that this early horseback riding led to his bowleggedness as an adult. The fifth of eleven children, Kit was the last born in Kentucky. Carrying on a Carson family tradition of mobility, Kit would make his life in the West, following the sun to the Pacific and figuring prominently in the process of discovery, exploration, settlement, and development. Like Christopher Columbus 350 years earlier, Kit Carson had the good fortune of living in an age of expanding horizons.

The Carson family's move to Missouri Country was motivated by economics and the lure of the West. It also coincided with the actions of trailblazer and surveyor Daniel Boone. Having lost his land in Kentucky through legal disputes, the angry frontiersman lit out for the west in 1799, acquiring a Spanish land grant west of the Mississippi and north of the Missouri and establishing the settlement of Boone's Lick. Travelers making their way back to Kentucky and passing through Madison County told of new, fertile land, good hunting, and friendly Indians around Boone's Lick. The Carson farm, with its crowded cabin and marginal land, had never paid off the way it should have. A bright spot in this dark picture was the West. People like the Carsons talked about it as a dreamland of opportunity. As the New World had once attracted Europe's dissatisfied, so the land of the trans-Mississippi West beckoned failures in the eastern states. The urge to move was a compound of pushing and pulling forces. Adversity pushed pioneers westward, while visions of success in new lands drew them like a magnet. In 1811 the Carson family succumbed to the dual force, packed its belongings, and followed Daniel Boone to find a new start in the West.

As they left Kentucky, families such as the Carsons took advantage of several policies of the United States. Two of these were the systems of land sale and territorial government established in the 1780s and now functioning with great success. Low minimum acreage requirements, cheap prices, and liberal credit allowances permitted people of modest means to get a start on the public domain. Because extreme poverty, such as that of some immigrants and factory laborers, precluded pioneer farming, it was possible for people like the Carsons, who sold their property in Kentucky, to raise the requisite capital. As for government, stories such as that of the growth of Ohio to independent statehood impressed everyone. A wilderness in 1790, the territory had claimed 60,000 settlers in 1803, enough for statehood under the terms of the Northwest Ordinance. By 1810 the population of Ohio stood at 231,000.

A major factor in this growth was the improvement of overland transportation to the Ohio Valley and Midwest. Graded all-weather roads facilitated the movement of people and produce. Many of these were privately built turnpikes that required tolls, but the condition of the traillike alternatives made the private roads cheap at almost any price. In 1806 Congress authorized government financing for a road from western Maryland across the Appalachians to Wheeling on the Ohio River. Although delayed by the War of 1812, the National Road soon became the primary artery of east–west travel. The Carsons traveled graded roads from eastern Kentucky to Louisville, where they paid for ferry transit across the Ohio River. Then they followed what became the westernmost leg of the National Road to Saint Louis and took another ferry across the mighty Mississippi. Finally, they traveled a barely cleared wilderness road to Boone's Lick, north of the Missouri River.

The gradual establishment of the authority of the United States in trans-Appalachia was another precondition of migrations such as that of the Carsons. French intrigue in the West had ended in the mid-1790s, when George Washington and Thomas Jefferson blocked the efforts of Citizen Edmund Genet to recruit a private army in support of the French Revolution. Spanish claims had been weakened in 1796 with the approval of the Treaty of San Lorenzo (the Pinckney Treaty). The new states of Kentucky (1792) and Tennessee (1796) were now safe from Spanish intrigue and the possibility of secession. Also, by the same treaty, the United States obtained a promise of free navigation on the Mississippi River and the right to deposit goods for transshipment at New Orleans, a port essential to the western economy. Spain's retrocession of Louisiana to France in 1800 and its sale to the United States three years later substantially ended the claims of both foreign powers to trans-Appalachia. Spain did retain possession of East Florida, however, and also claimed a strip of land along the Gulf of Mexico (West Florida), until an invasion by General Andrew Jackson in 1818 and the negotiation of the Adams-Onís Treaty the following year. Great Britain was slow to evacuate western frontier posts following the American Revolution and, with a foothold in Canada, retained an active interest in the Ohio Valley. The land the

Carsons came to in 1811 was officially Missouri Country, soon to be Missouri Territory and part of the United States.

As they passed through Saint Louis, the Carsons were impressed by its size. Located at the strategic junction of the Missouri and the Mississippi rivers, this city founded by the French in 1762 already claimed several thousand inhabitants and a settled hinterland extending up and down the Mississippi for forty miles. The Carsons moved about 100 miles west of the city, in land barely settled. Before Lindsay and Rebecca could build a cabin on the land they chose, hostilities began between Great Britain and the United States in the War of 1812. Because the British were skillful at gaining Indian allies, new settlers like the Carsons were compelled to seek protection. For the duration of the war, the family was "forted" at Fort Kinkead, several miles away from Carson's homestead. Kit's earliest memories were of these tense times when his father and older brothers served in the local militia. On one patrol, Lindsay Carson had two fingers of his left hand shot off in a battle with Indians allied to the British.

Completion of the Carson cabin after the war's conclusion marked the next phases of Kit's early life. Boone's Lick was far from any other settlement, and in this frontier setting, he learned the skills that served him well throughout his life. Vigilance and self-sufficiency were the products of living in the frontier, where on occasion the Carsons would still need to seek the security of the nearby fort when the threat of Indian attack was high. The settlers had developed strong bonds while being forted; now they helped one another build a community. There was much hard work and little or no formal education for the children. Log felling, barn raisings, quilting bees, and hunting were among the many activities that made men of boys and women of girls. The work was onerous and often hazardous. In September 1818, Lindsay Carson died when a flaming limb from a burning tree he was working near fell and crushed him. One week later, Lindsay Carson Jr. was born. Now Rebecca had eight children at home and no husband.

Running the farm fell to Kit and his brothers. When Rebecca remarried a widower with children four years later, Kit and his brothers resented the orders they now received after being their own bosses. At the age of fifteen, Kit, ready for new challenges, became an apprentice to David Workman, a saddle-maker in nearby Franklin. As Kit learned the art of saddle-making, there was constant talk of the West among Workman, his brother, and customers. Much was said about the mountain men and the fur trade. After the return of Lewis and Clark, numerous expeditions had pushed northwest on the trail of the beaver. Trappers had already depleted beaver populations from the Atlantic to the Mississippi in satisfying the beaver hat craze in urban Europe, Asia, and America. Now trappers looked to the Missouri Valley and beyond. Every spring they left the city, poling and pulling keelboats laden with trade goods and traps. One of the first to organize the business had been Manuel Lisa, a man whose Spanish heritage did not preclude a Yankee eye for the dollar. In 1807, just a year after the return of Lewis and Clark, Lisa followed the Missouri and the Yellowstone to the mouth of the Bighorn River in present-day Montana. There he built a fort, which he eventually named Fort Raymond.

From Fort Raymond, Lisa sent John Colter, a veteran of the Lewis and Clark expedition, into the Yellowstone country. Traveling alone in midwinter with only a thirty-pound pack, Colter covered 500 miles and returned with stories of geysers and boiling springs that everyone found hard to believe. But the unbelievable was always part of the New World's fascination, and when Colter's report reached Missouri, it only increased the determination of the adventurous to go west.

Young men like Carson's contemporary Jim Bridger, born in Virginia in 1804 and orphaned at twelve in Saint Louis, took up the call of the Northwest. His opportunity came in 1822, when an advertisement appeared in the *Missouri Republican*. William H. Ashley, the lieutenant governor of the new state of Missouri, was seeking "one hundred young men to ascend the Missouri River to its source, to be employed for one, two or three years." Excitedly, Bridger sought out Ashley's associate in the trapping venture, Major Andrew Henry, and signed on. Ashley had acquired two sixty-five-foot keelboats with a loading capacity of twenty-five tons, equivalent to an entire wagon train. Bridger was assigned to help maneuver the heavy boats upstream against the power of the Missouri. As one man kept the boat in the water with the use of a sweep rudder, the others trudged along on shore pulling long ropes attached to its bow. It was an exhausting business, requiring that the men stumble over rocks and fallen logs, wade wide streams, and climb steep embankments. Occasionally, an upriver wind and a crude sail would offer some relief, but otherwise the entire trip was blisters and sweat.

On May 1, 1822, the Henry-Ashley party reached Fort Atkinson near Council Bluffs and the Platte River. The garrison at the fort had had warnings of Indian hostility, and some of the men in the party chose to return to Saint Louis. With the remainder of the Henry-Ashley group, Bridger continued up the Missouri and into the Dakotas, where the Mandan Indians made their home. Among these friendly tribes, Bridger began to gain the knowledge of native tongues and customs that played a major role in his later success as a scout and guide. Pushing on to the mouth of the Yellowstone, the Henry-Ashley men constructed shelters and ran trap lines. By early 1823, there was a rich harvest of pelts to send back to Saint Louis. There were also Indian problems. Outraged by the white men's invasion of their traditional hunting grounds, the Arikaras and Blackfeet struck back. In one surprise attack the Indians killed fourteen Ashley trappers. Bridger managed to survive, and he joined a force of trappers, Sioux Indians, and federal soldiers under Colonel Henry Leavenworth in the destruction of the Arikara village. Still, Ashley and Henry decided to move their operations farther south in the Rocky Mountains, where Indian opposition was less intense. In the winter of 1823–1824, Henry dispatched Bridger, Thomas Fitzpatrick, Jedediah Smith, and several others to probe the country west of Wyoming's Wind River Mountains, and seek out the friendly Crow Indians to trade for supplies and horses.

Hiking along the eastern face of the towering Wind River range and up the Sweetwater River, Bridger and his companions discovered South Pass, a low and level route across the Continental Divide and the key to the opening of the West. Its significance was not lost on the trappers. Here, they realized, was a route by which loaded wagons could reach the Columbia River watershed and the Pacific Northwest. South Pass led to the headwaters of the Green River and to beaver country of a richness beyond any trapper's wildest dreams. Reluctant to build Indian-provoking forts, Ashley hit on an ingenious plan for exploiting the fur resources.

Under the rendezvous system, trappers were dispatched in small groups to work widely scattered waterways. In the early summer, they gathered at a prearranged spot in the mountains for several weeks of trading, gambling, boasting, and drinking. The pack trains that had brought trade goods from Saint Louis were ready to return loaded with beaver pelts. The first rendezvous, held in July 1825 at Henry's Fork on the Green River, attracted over a hundred trappers and Indians. Bridger was there and became a center of attention with his tale of Great Salt Lake. In subsequent years, the annual rendezvous grew larger and more profitable. After the 1826 season, Ashley retired, a wealthy man, to Saint Louis and a political career. Four years later, Jedediah Smith, David Jackson, and William Sublette assumed direction of his Rocky Mountain Fur Company.

For settlers living west of Saint Louis, the siren song also beckoned from the Southwest. As he dutifully pulled heavy leather straps through the saddle holes, Kit Carson overheard romantic talk of Santa Fe and the land of the Pueblos. Settled at least one thousand years before by Native American groups the Spaniards named the Pueblos, the lands of northern New Mexico provided a cornucopia of foods and plenty of irrigation water for crops. Spanish conquistador

In 1837, a young Scottish-born painter, Alfred J. Miller, accompanied the Scottish nobleman William Drummond Stewart to the fur traders' annual rendezvous. Among the participants that year was Kit Carson's mentor Jim Bridger (left foreground), dressed, in Miller's sketch, in the suit of armor Stewart had presented to him.

Francisco Coronado's wild goose chase through the American West in 1542 and 1543 included a lengthy and sometimes violent encounter with the Pueblos. For much of the 1600s, Spanish attempts to advance the frontier of New Spain northward meant war and retreat from the Pueblo country. By the 1700s, the Spaniards and Pueblos shared the upper Rio Grande River Valley. Santa Fe, for example, was a Spanish settlement; Taos was a Pueblo town.

Because the hostile nomadic Apaches and Comanches constantly threatened and attacked travelers on the Chihuahua Trail from Mexico City to Santa Fe, supplies and trade were limited. When the Republic of Mexico displaced New Spain in the 1820s, the situation with the Apaches and Comanches remained the same. Underserved, the prosperous New Mexico country looked elsewhere for trade, and enterprising Americans from Missouri stepped in. After trailblazers surveyed the route, the first wagon train of what would become the lucrative Santa Fe Trade made its way along the Arkansas River and then southwestward to New Mexico in 1824. By the 1830s, the Santa Fe Trail had two routes (the other through Colorado and Bent's Fort), and wagon trains were miles long and protected by as many as one hundred armed guards.

In 1826, after nearly two years of apprenticeship, Kit Carson succumbed to the lure of the West. Running away from the stability of a steady trade skill, and over the objections of his mother, who wanted him to finish his apprenticeship, he made his way to Fort Osage, Missouri. In August, he signed on to join a wagon train bound for Santa Fe. Kit's job on the trail was to keep the livestock from wandering too far from the wagon train. The vast prairie had thick, tall grass, a temptation to the grazing livestock and a hindrance to locating smaller animals. The well-guarded caravan had an uneventful trip to Santa Fe, but this had not been a certainty. Jedediah Smith, the first American trailblazer to venture overland to California, was killed by Comanches at a watering hole on the trail in 1831.

Not particularly interested in trade or in getting rich, Carson departed from Santa Fe as soon as his job was done. He made his way north with some of the traders to the Pueblo village of Taos. From then on he would call Taos his home, and he always returned there when possible. Enchanted with the Pueblo and Mexican people—the men in their white shirts and colored serapes, the women with gray rebozos draping their heads and shoulders—Kit was also taken with the scenery. Nestled in the front range of the southern Rocky Mountains, Taos was a tapestry of geological hues and deep blue skies. Aqueducts, which the Spanish called *acequias*, brought water from the mountains to irrigate the valley below, not only watering the blue corn, squash, and tomatoes, but also providing running water to the community. At the center of the town was the community square. The kiva, the seat of government of the Pueblos, was in a large building surrounding the square. The third largest town in New Mexico, Taos had a population of about 3,600 in 1827.

Kit Carson soon learned that Matthew Kinkead, from Boone's Lick, had settled in Taos and was in the process of establishing a distillery making *aguardiente de Taos*—the "mountain dew" of New Mexico. Matthew's father had built Fort Kinkead, one of the refuges taken by the Carsons when they first moved to Missouri. Happy to see a fellow Missourian, Kinkead invited Carson to spend the winter with him in Taos. During that winter of 1826–1827, the seventeen-year-old Carson hunted for game and did the cooking while Kinkead and his partner, William Workman, son of David Workman, built the distillery. Kit discovered during this winter that he had an aptitude for learning other languages. He quickly picked up the rudiments of Spanish and Pueblo dialects in only a few months.

In spring, a combination of a guilty conscience for leaving his mother without saying goodbye and homesickness compelled Carson to join a caravan headed for Missouri. Somewhere along the Arkansas River, the group met a caravan going to Santa Fe. A member of the caravan was David Workman, his old employer, who was now moving to New Mexico. When the two caravans parted, Kit Carson was a member of the westbound one. Once in Santa Fe, Carson got a job driving wagons to and from El Paso. After making the 250-mile journey to the West Texas border town, Carson resigned and returned to Taos on his own. One more attempt to return to Missouri ended the same way as the first, with Carson returning again to New Mexico. He then signed on with a trader, headed for the Mexican town of Chihuahua, who needed a teamster and an interpreter. After making the 500-mile journey from Santa Fe, Carson worked briefly in a copper mine near Chihuahua before returning to Taos in late 1828.

Over the next few months, Kit Carson forged the bonds that would define the next fifteen years of his life. He became acquainted with Ewing Young, another Missourian in New Mexico. Young had come west with William Becknell, the mountain man who had blazed the Santa Fe Trade in 1821. Branching out, the enterprising Young trapped in the Pecos River country of eastern New Mexico. In the following years, Young led trapping expeditions into the Gila River country, up the Colorado River, and into the Great Basin. In 1829 Young was back in Taos, setting up a store to buy and sell pelts. After sending an expedition southwest that was attacked by Apaches, Young decided to organize a larger force, and he enlisted forty seasoned American, Canadian, and French trappers. Young believed there was safety in numbers and security in experience. And like other mountain men, Young learned from his colleagues. The 1829–1830 Young expedition to California drew information from the 1826–1827 adventures of Jedediah Smith. Smith had left the 1826 rendezvous in Cache Valley, Utah, with "fifteen men, a Bible, and plenty of rifles to explore the Southwest." Skirting west of the Wasatch Range and the high plateaus of central Utah, Smith reached the Virgin River and then the Colorado. The next leg of the journey carried him across the Mojave Desert, through Cajon Pass, and into the Los Angeles basin, making this the first overland crossing to California by Americans.

The California that Smith entered was by then part of a new nation—Mexico. Spain had withdrawn from central and northern America in 1821, following ten years of rebellion fomented by priests of mixed ancestry. Thereafter, Mexico attempted to weaken the power of the mission system established during the 1770s by the Spaniards. Mexican officials in California were surprised, to say the least, by the appearance of the first Americans in this land isolated so long by distance and geography. Upon realizing that Smith had come to California over land, they demanded that he leave *pronto* by the same route by which he had entered their territory.

Determined to explore, Smith was not inclined to backtrack across the deserts. The solution was to define Mexico's "Alta California" as only the coastal region. He led his men up California's Central Valley past the sites of such present-day cities as Bakersfield and Modesto. Leaving part of the group behind to trap, Smith and two others, in an incredible feat, traversed the main crest of the Sierra Nevada at 8,700-foot Ebbets Pass, made their way across Nevada's arid Great Basin, where they nearly died of thirst, and at last arrived at the 1827 rendezvous at Bear Lake in northern Utah.

After a few days of swapping adventures with trappers at the rendezvous, Smith and eighteen other men were on their way back to California to explore and rejoin the men left behind. This time they were not so lucky. As they crossed the Colorado River, the Mojave Indians attacked, and the Smith party was reduced to nine. The remainder made their way to San Jose, where they were promptly arrested by the Mexican government for illegal entry into California. Mexican officials, not knowing what to do with Smith and his men, released them on the condition that they leave California. Heading north at the beginning of 1828, Smith's party was attacked by Klamath Indians in Oregon Territory. A short time later, Smith and two companions straggled to Fort Vancouver in Hudson's Bay Company territory.

Included in Ewing Young's forty men was Kit Carson, now an apprentice mountain man. The party departed in August 1829 and traveled southwest to the Zuni Pueblo in western New Mexico, then trapped in Arizona before heading west. Returning to the place where the Apaches had attacked the earlier party along the Salt River, Young plotted retaliation. Telling most of his men to hide under blankets in their camp, Young then sent a few men out to entice the Apaches to raid the seemingly undermanned camp. The Indians entered the camp, and were suddenly ambushed by the hiding trappers. Fifteen to twenty Apaches were killed before the rest fled in retreat. Then, Young sent twenty of his men back to Taos loaded with furs and with orders to return with more traps to replace those stolen by another group of Apaches.

The remainder of the trappers, including Carson, headed west for California. Crossing the vast, desolate Mojave Desert proved near deadly. Friendly Indians told them that excellent beaver hunting lay ahead, but there would be no game and little water for a long way. The men killed three deer and found no more. They dressed the meat and filled the skins with water. Two weeks later, the bedraggled group struggled one by one to the Colorado River east of the Grand Canyon, nearly dead from starvation and thirst. A group of Mojave Indians found them camped at the river and sold them a mare, which they slaughtered, butchered, and devoured. After three days, they set out across more desert, finding the Mojave River and Cajon Pass before being welcomed at two Franciscan missions: San Gabriel and San Fernando. From San Fernando Mission, they marched north to trap beaver in the San Joaquin and Sacramento valleys. As summer 1830 waned, they moved southwest to Los Angeles. Enroute they helped Father Narciso Duran of the San Jose Mission recapture some escaped mission Indians. From Los Angeles, it was back to the Colorado River, the Gila River, and finally to Taos. By all accounts, the expedition was a success. Young singled out Carson for performing admirably and heroically. He was now accepted as a mountain man.

Kit Carson's first ten years in the West coincided with the high point of the fur trade and the mountain man. Carson rose with the tide. He grew fearless, tough, and wise in the ways of a wilderness that usually permitted a man only one mistake. Like other successful trappers, Carson had a knack for geography and an innate sense for avoiding trouble. Hostile Indians were part of the life of the trapper. Often, the skirmishes merely entailed chases, scattering or confiscating the enemy's horses, or raiding supply stores. But mountain men were no strangers to violent conflict. Every rendezvous produced stories of trappers whose hair had been "lifted." Indeed, Kit Carson was an exception among his contemporaries in that he died of natural causes. Yet in the final analysis, the mountain man had much in common with the Indian. African-American backwoodsman Jim Beckwourth actually joined the Crow tribe. Jim Bridger married the daughter of the chief of the Flathead tribe during the 1830s. Outliving her, Bridger married Indian women two more times and was devoted to all of his children. Kit Carson, too, would marry two Indian women in the 1830s. His first wife died, and the second divorced him. (See page 170.)

It is easy and has long been the custom to style mountain men like Kit Carson as carefree primitivists and the fur trade as a romantic adventure. The western trapper seemingly had cut the ties with civilization and, by virtue of his leap into the wilderness of the Far West, stood apart from the mainstream of American life. While this is generally accurate, the mountain men and the residents of the eastern states actually had a great deal in common. The trapper was a highly skilled professional, motivated by monetary gain. And the fur trade was a sophisticated industry, in the forefront of the evolution of American economic life toward patterns at once larger and more integrated. Fur was among the first American businesses to function on a nationwide scale in a time of greatly expanding economic and entrepreneurial horizons.

Typifying the era that bears his name was Andrew Jackson. The Tennessee Indian-fighter and hero of the Battle of New Orleans was elected president of the United States in 1832 and 1836. Especially in comparison to the previous occupant of that office, the staid New Englander John Quincy Adams, Jackson appeared to be a man of the people, a champion of democracy. What Jackson really championed was equality of economic and social opportunity. He and his followers believed in loosening the hold of an entrenched, privileged, and usually wealthy elite on American political and economic life. When he attacked the most glaring special interest of the time—the Bank of the United States—in 1832, Jackson himself declared that he opposed those "artificial distinctions" whereby the "rich and powerful" had come to dominate and suppress the ambitions of the "humble members of society." Jacksonians did not mean to imply by this that they opposed all privilege or that they rejected the concept of failure. Rather, they felt that privilege and prosperity should be the result of ability and ability alone. Failure should result from inability.

The Jacksonian philosophy was an extension of the Jeffersonian concept of a natural aristocracy, and it was therefore essential that everyone (and Jackson defined *everyone* more liberally than Jefferson) have a chance at success. Its pursuit, furthermore, was to be regulated by rules that would ensure the triumph of the talented. Jacksonianism did not pit the poor against the rich; it was the attempt of the poor to *become* rich. The liberation, not the destruction, of capitalism and its rewards was the objective of the Jacksonian democrats. Typically, they were ambitious entrepreneurs. Hardly revolutionaries or anarchists, they wanted to tear down privilege and interfere with private property only when they believed these blocked their own pursuit of these goals. Jacksonianism, in sum, defined human rights as the free opportunity to get rich. It was the perfect philosophy for an acquisitive society such as that of the mountain man.

To examine the evolution of the fur trade and the lives of the mountain men is to see excellent examples of Jacksonianism in practice. The West in the early nineteenth century meant equal opportunity. Special interests, family, and background counted for little. Performance—what an individual could *do*—is what mattered. The wilderness played no favorites, and only the talented succeeded and survived. It was the ideal Jacksonian situation. Consider Kit Carson. Adventure was important to him, but again and again he responded when traders and trappers were looking for enterprising young men who were economically motivated. Contrary to romantic legend, they went west not to escape from civilization but to extend it and rise within it. Beaver pelts were not an excuse for a wilderness outing to Carson but, in his jargon, "hairy bank notes"—cold cash. The risks were great, but so were the returns. A few boatloads or wagonloads of pelts in Saint Louis or Santa Fe meant affluence.

In this environment, the capitalistic entrepreneur, so crucial a part of the age of Jackson, flourished. Manuel Lisa is an example. He was among the first traders to recognize that only large, well-organized, and well-heeled companies would succeed in exploiting the fur potential of the Rockies. Another economic visionary was John Jacob Astor, who in 1808 organized the American Fur Company. Astor planned to construct a chain of forts from the Great Lakes to the Pacific Northwest and to compete with Great Britain's Hudson's Bay Company. He sent a land and sea expedition to the Columbia River and founded Astoria at its mouth. But the War of 1812 ruined Astor's plans, and Indian hostility frustrated Lisa. Still, these entrepreneurs were portents of the new economic order that began to flower during Jackson's presidency.

After returning to Taos with Young in early 1831, Kit Carson joined another in a series of trapping ventures. Tom Fitzpatrick, a partner in the Rocky Mountain Fur Company, led this one. Other partners included Jim Bridger, Jean Baptiste Gervais, Milton Sublette, and Henry Fraeb. Fitzpatrick, whom the Indians had named "Bad-Hand" due to a firearm injury, was so impressed with the young Carson that he allowed him to join the group as a free trapper. This meant that Carson was an independent contractor of sorts in the expedition. Not being paid a wage by the Rocky Mountain Fur Company, Carson instead collected a percentage on the pelts he took. It was a testament to his trapping skills. The small group made its way north in the fall of 1831 and quickly moved through the front range of the Rockies, to the Platte, Missouri, and into the rendezvous country. After wintering with Bridger's main force of trappers on the Salmon River, Fitzpatrick's party fanned out into the Snake River valley. Moving southwest from there, they trapped along the Green River, the North Park country of Colorado, and then wintered in 1832–1833 on the Arkansas River. The next season was spent in the Colorado mountains, with a return to Taos in October to sell pelts and resupply. Before the end of the year, Carson and the Taos Trappers were back on the trail, heading northwest for wintering quarters at Fort Uinta in Utah.

In 1834 Kit Carson became involved with the principal partner in the Rocky Mountain Fur Company, Jim Bridger. Bridger retained Carson as a free trapper, and from then on the two were fast friends. Carson was one of some 600 trappers working for the Rocky Mountain company who now combed over the last untouched beaver country. But the Rocky Mountain trappers soon learned an axiom of capitalism: Where there are profits, there will be competition. It came first in the form of smaller companies, whose agents began to appear at the annual rendezvous and bid for the trappers' harvests. Meanwhile, the giant Hudson's Bay Company dominated Oregon Country, and after 1832 the American Fur Company offered stiffer competition. With the large and diversified Astor assets behind it, American Fur was in a position to outbid and outlast Bridger and Rocky Mountain Fur. Its advantage increased when its steamboat, *Yellowstone,* reached the confluence of that river and the Missouri in June 1832. Not the smallest dividend of the unprecedented voyage was the awe that the "Fire Boat That Walked on the Waters" produced among the Indians, who now confined their trade to American Fur agents. Such competition had increased steadily since 1830. By the end of 1834, the Rocky Mountain Fur trappers had lost too much ground, and they sold out to and became employees of the American Fur Company.

Unlike Bridger, Fitzpatrick, and the other partners, Kit Carson's stake in the Rocky Mountain Fur Company was minimal. As the one company collapsed, he was welcomed into the other. Carson also spent time working for Hudson's Bay Company during the late 1830s. From the time he joined Bridger in 1834 until 1842, when he quit the fur business, Carson trapped throughout a rectangle from Oregon Country in the northwest to Dakota Country in the northeast to New Mexico in the southeast and California in the southwest. Success was measured in the fact that he survived and financially prospered through the waning years of beaver hunting. This is not to say, however, that there were not hardships. In 1835, for example, Carson and fifty other trappers were wintering along the Snake River when a group of Blackfeet warriors stole eighteen horses. The trappers pursued the Blackfeet through the snow, and when negotiations for the return of the horses failed, a fight ensued. In the gun battle, Carson was hit in the shoulder by a musket ball. The ball tore through the shoulder and shattered a bone before exiting the other side. Carson fell back, unable to fight. His comrades treated the heavily bleeding wound with snow, but dared not light a fire that night for fear of giving away their position. The next day they returned to camp and properly cleaned and dressed Carson's wound. The Blackfeet raiders were never found.

At the 1835 rendezvous along the Green River, a recovered Kit Carson fought a duel with a bragging Frenchman that sealed his fate as a frontier hero. The trapper's name was Shunar, and he worked for the American Fur Company. After beating up on two men in one day, Shunar boasted that he could defeat any man in the camp. Although small in stature, at five and a half feet, compared to the large Frenchman, Kit Carson took up the challenge. In a duel fought in mountain man style, with guns and horses, Shunar's shot was a near miss, while Carson's musket ball pierced his opponent's arm. Carson later remembered: "During our stay in camp we had no more trouble with this bully Frenchman."

Two additional events made the 1835 rendezvous exceptional. First, Dr. Marcus Whitman, who later set up a Presbyterian mission in Oregon Country with his wife Narcissa, successfully removed a three-inch Blackfoot arrowhead from the back of Jim Bridger in an operation deemed extremely risky even by modern standards. Bridger later sent one of his half-Indian daughters to the Whitman mission. The second event was when Kit Carson met Waanibe, a young Arapaho woman who was with her people trading at the rendezvous. Deciding it was time for him to have a wife, Carson initiated the traditional process with the Arapahoes, and he and Waanibe were soon married. Carson and Waanibe remained together until her death in 1839 or 1840. They had two daughters. After Waanibe's death, Carson married a Cheyenne woman, Making Out Road, in 1841, probably in hopes of having a mother for his daughters. A few months later, however, she divorced him in the traditional Indian way—putting all his belongings outside their tepee. Carson took his two children with him to New Mexico, where other family members temporarily cared for them.

As the 1830s closed, the end was near for the fur trade. The climax of the economic war over fur came with the entrance of Hudson's Bay Company into the Rocky Mountain arena. Beaver were disappearing in the Pacific Northwest, and the Hudson's Bay men moved farther and farther up the Snake River. A race began. Frantically, the trappers pursued the remaining beaver, to the detriment and near destruction of the resource on which they depended. By the late 1830s, the end was in sight for those who could bring themselves to look. The 1840 rendezvous was the last. Not only were pelts scarce, but the beaver hat craze had eclipsed. The trappers became disgruntled, and, with easy profits gone, few elected to live the free wilderness life that legend has them loving for its own sake. Instead, these Jacksonians pursued opportunities in ranching, farming, shopkeeping, politics, banking, and even opera house management. They developed the West.

While Jacksonianism was influencing the frontier, the frontier style was shaping national politics. Jackson was the first president from outside the original thirteen colonies, and he was the first to step out of the gentlemanly tradition of the Virginia dynasty (Washington, Jefferson, Madison, and Monroe) and the Harvard line (John Adams and John Quincy Adams). Hardly embarrassed by this fact, Jackson had based his 1828 campaign on his experience as a man of action, a warrior-hero, and a supreme individualist, who blended nature and civilization into a new, allegedly superior and distinctively American, character. The fact that in the winter of 1814–1815 he had defeated both the powerful Creek tribe (at the Battle of Horseshoe Bend) and the best of England's army (at the Battle of New Orleans) lent substance to this claim. In the person of Jackson, the frontiersman acquired the status of a superman.

Next to Old Hickory, as Jackson was called, the hero of the 1830s was unquestionably Davy Crockett of Tennessee, king of the wild frontier. The well-known frontiersman deliberately turned down an honorary degree from Harvard and cultivated a demagogic, bombastic, and often fraudulent political style in his campaigning for political office. But at a time when the spread of universal white male suffrage was transforming the guiding values of politics from gentlemanly idealism to win-at-any-price, Crockett succeeded in spectacular fashion. Uneducated white men turned out in droves to vote for Crockett, who was said to have "grinned" a bear to death and "kilt a bear when he was only three" and to be "half-snapping turtle and half-alligator." Voters elected Crockett to Congress three times between 1826 and 1835.

Andrew Jackson's momentum carried his vice president, Martin Van Buren, to the presidency in 1836. By this time, opponents of Jackson and the Democrats had organized the Whig party around Henry Clay, Daniel Webster, and John C. Calhoun, none of whom gained the highest office in the nation. That was reserved, in 1840, for the old Indian-fighter and hero of the Battle of Tippecanoe—William Henry Harrison. Discarding gentlemanly politics, the Whigs elected Harrison with a grassroots, frontier-style approach. Their campaign of 1840 featured log cabins (Harrison was falsely portrayed as having been born in one) and the frontier wine—hard cider. Harrison's running mate, John Tyler, also adopted a frontier persona, although he was raised on a plantation in eastern Virginia. Four years later, the Jacksonian faction regained the White House with James K. Polk of Tennessee, an enthusiastic exponent of the expanding American frontier.

After a disappointing spring hunt in Colorado and Utah during 1841, Kit Carson reluctantly acknowledged it was time to begin a new livelihood. Returning to Bent's Fort, he signed on as a hunter responsible for providing the guards and workers with meat. It was here he married Making Out Road and here that she divorced him. Soon thereafter, his younger daughter was killed in a scalding accident in New Mexico. Carson decided to take his older daughter, Adaline, to be raised in Missouri. Joining a Bent wagon train headed east, Carson returned home for the first time since he had run away in 1826. Missouri was a state now, and his childhood home was hardly recognizable to the mountaineer. Saint Louis to the east now had 40,000 people, and its influence had reached into the countryside. Carson left Adaline with one of his sisters, and after some deliberating about where to go next, caught a steamer headed up the Missouri River. It was there and then that the next phase of his life was determined; another passenger on the steamer was none other than John C. Fremont, soon to be known nationwide as "the Pathfinder."

One of the most enigmatic and mercurial figures of the antebellum American West, John C. Fremont had great impact on California, the West, and Kit Carson. The son of a French émigré and a debutant from Georgia, Fremont had a wayward childhood following his father's death (when John was five years old). He was expelled from the College of Charleston, and bounced from career to career until landing a surveyor's position with the U.S. Army in 1837. Because of his recent practical studies with a renowned surveyor, Fremont not only was awarded a bachelor's degree from the College of Charleston, he also was commissioned by the Army as a lieutenant, even though he had no prior military experience. In 1841 he married seventeen-year-old Jesse Benton, daughter of Missouri senator Thomas Hart Benton. This gave Fremont access to a talented writer—Jesse—and to the most powerful and exuberant westward expansionist in Congress—her father.

Senator Benton's enthusiasm for westward expansion led him to seek congressional approval for Army surveys of the West. J. J. Abert, Chief of the Corps of Topographical Engineers, gave final approval for John C. Fremont to command a group of surveyors west to the Platte River country in early 1842. It was on the steamer taking the expedition members up the Missouri River that Fremont met Kit Carson. Carson, needing work, approached Fremont and said he had "been some time in the mountains and thought [he] could guide him to any point he wished to go." Fremont was not long in deliberating before hiring Carson.

The first of three Fremont expeditions in the 1840s followed the Platte River west through Nebraska country and into the Rocky Mountains. Carson served as guide and hunter, shooting several buffalo and elk along the way. Near the forks of the North and South Platte rivers, the Fremont group met Jim Bridger, who was leading a fur caravan back to Missouri. Carson was overjoyed to see his old mentor, and Bridger had important news. First, Bridger said he had recently constructed a fort on the Green River, in 1841, and another one on Black's Fork, in 1842. Although he had built these posts for fur-trading purposes, more than a thousand emigrants had passed by while he was away trapping, and now he was thinking about expanding the forts to service these emigrants. Bridger's other news was an ominous warning that the Indians ahead on the trail were becoming hostile. With Carson's knowledge and Fremont's

John C. Fremont enlisted Kit Carson's services three times in the 1840s. Each of Fremont's congressionally funded expeditions served to make the West known to the United States. Fremont later served as one of the first two U.S. senators from the state of California and was the Republican party's presidential candidate in 1856.

bravado in dealing with Indians, however, the expedition achieved its westward goal of finding the source of the Sweetwater River and returning to Missouri.

The first Fremont expedition mapped and surveyed the eastern half of the increasingly traveled Overland Trail. But it was up to entrepreneurs like Jim Bridger to find profit in the emigrants. In the summer of 1842, Bridger met another old fur-trading companion, Louis Vasquez, in Saint Louis after leading the fur caravan. Vasquez, a Missourian of Mexican descent, had gone into the trading post business during the 1830s. Having recently sold a post on the South Platte River, Vasquez was ready to move farther west. Convinced that they would strike it rich, Vasquez talked Bridger into forming a partnership. Traveling west as soon as possible after the winter of 1843 waned, they surveyed the area and chose a new site along Black's Fork. Fort Bridger, a permanent establishment, with a store and a blacksmith shop that catered to the needs of travelers on the Overland Trail, was open for business by August 1843.

Fort Bridger was the first outpost in the West to be built solely for the purposes of serving emigrants and trading with Indians. Bridger and Vasquez used their knowledge of the territory to select the best-watered site for hundreds of miles, with ample grass for livestock to feed on. With arid desolation all around them, emigrants who arrived at Fort Bridger were happy to find an oasis of trees, water, and grass. To promote the post, Bridger dictated a letter to be sent back east: "The fort is a beautiful location on Black's Fork of the Green River, receiving fine, fresh water from the snow of the Uintah range. The streams are alive with mountain trout. It passes the fort in several channels, each lined with trees, kept alive by the moisture of the soil."

Buoyed by the agrarian myth of plentiful and rich agricultural land, the wave of migrants grew in the 1840s. The roots of this complex of emotions, values, and hopes lay in the mystique surrounding the New World and drew sustenance from both the Spanish mirage of El Dorado and the romantic notion of the noble savage. But the major sources of the agrarian myth were the dreams of everyday Americans and the promises of those who wished to lure them west. The myth held that the American West was a pastoral paradise in which self-sufficient yeoman farmers lived wholesome, happy lives in a beautiful environment, close to nature. It was a rose-colored view of the frontier, laced with Jeffersonian agrarianism, that ignored the realities both of the West and of human nature. Still, around the kitchen table or living-room fireplace of dissatisfied easterners or Europeans, the myth was hard to resist. Even if they did not move west themselves, people liked to think that the idyllic life really existed in the direction of the setting sun. For Americans, it was a basis of national pride.

Obviously, land speculators and western developers benefited from promoting the agrarian myth. The innumerable emigrant guidebooks that appeared in the nineteenth century sounded a chorus of praise for life on the frontier. In most of the descriptions, Eden itself paled by comparison. Of course, there was the counterimage of a Great American Desert first espoused by Stephen Long, a U.S. Army officer who explored the front range of the Rocky Mountains in 1820. Although his report discussed the Rockies, more important, it incorrectly identified the Great Plains as a desert that could only be inhabited by nomadic Indians. Long's description of searing droughts, fierce storms, and bloodthirsty Indians caused the migrants of the early 1800s to shun the nearer plains for faraway Oregon and California.

Believing in both their ability to get there and the bounty of the land once they arrived, the migrants left Illinois, Indiana, and Missouri. Following the Panic of 1837, which slashed agricultural prices, many farmers in those states had little to lose by leaving. After purchasing a covered, or Conestoga, wagon, they had to wait for a nucleus of other emigrants to gather—and then wait for a guide. Once organized—and weather permitting—the wagon trains left as early in the spring as possible from western Missouri and Iowa. Traveling first to Fort Kearny in eastern Nebraska

Territory, the emigrant trains then followed the Platte and North Platte rivers through Fort Laramie and Casper, the Sweetwater River through Devil's Gate, across the Continental Divide at South Pass, and then to Fort Bridger. Any number of "elephants" (problems such as disease, equipment failure, inadequate provisions, tornadoes, floods, or droughts) could and often did disrupt their advance to Fort Bridger. Many groups had "seen the elephant" too many times and turned back, but the ablest and luckiest made it to Bridger's outpost. Having made it that far, they often listened skeptically to warnings at Fort Bridger of what lay ahead. Cheap, arable farmland, reportedly in abundance in Oregon Country and Mexican California, was the irresistible lure.

Most migrant families passing through Bridger's fort were ill equipped for the journey ahead. Fort Bridger thus served as a vital way station. No matter what the cost of the fort's services, it was usually worth it to those who had reached the point of no return on the trail. Journal accounts generally suggest that Bridger and Vasquez were fair dealers. But many scoffed at the extra provisions the proprietors tried to sell them for the thousand-mile trip ahead, believing that it could be no more difficult than the thousand miles they had already come.

They were wrong. After leaving Fort Bridger in midsummer (if all had gone well thus far), the pioneers made their way through the arid Wasatch Mountains north of the Great Salt Lake to the Hudson's Bay Company's Fort Hall on the Snake River. Parting company with the California-bound settlers a few days west of Fort Hall, they followed the Snake River through a multitude of geographic conditions—including narrow cliffs and passes, rugged deserts, and roaring river rapids—and through climatic conditions ranging from searing desert heat to hard freezes, rain, sleet, and snow. The lucky ones arrived in Oregon's Willamette Valley sometime in October, after eight months and 2,000 miles of travel. It still remained for the settlers to find and claim a good piece of land, build some kind of dwelling, and gather provisions before the wet, cold Oregon winter set in.

Farming the new land often proved as difficult as the journey itself. And while hardships fell on all family members, women handled the most diverse burdens. On the trail, women often kept diaries detailing the daily rigors of the trek. They told stories of maintaining a mobile household with all the attendant chores of cooking, cleaning, mending, and mothering, while also driving and pushing, pulling, or levering the wagon on treacherous parts of the road. Once established on a farm, the woman's slate of duties expanded further, as the isolated agrarian setting required even greater self-sufficiency. In no place was the old axiom that a woman's work was never done truer than on the frontier farm of the West, as women usually added gardening, food preserving, dairying, and raising small livestock to their other household duties.

Life on the farm was hard for everyone, however. Men and male children labored outdoors in the elements all day long—plowing, fencing, clearing, building, or working the large livestock. Such backbreaking labor served to sharpen the divisions of labor between men and women, for by sundown the men were usually too exhausted to do more work, while the women still had hours of chores left to do. Farm life taxed the physical and emotional spirits of both sexes. But farm men and women formed a partnership of hard work, and to those who moved west for agrarian reasons, new land on which to grow crops and raise a family was generally worth the hardships.

Beyond the lure of farmland, a second complex of ideas that moved the nation west was Manifest Destiny. The term was coined, two years after the founding of Fort Bridger, by John L. O'Sullivan, a Jacksonian journalist. It drew heavily on the old idea of the American mission and the belief that the nation had a right—indeed, a duty and a God-appointed destiny—to expand across the continent to the Pacific Ocean. Proponents of Manifest Destiny argued that, because America had a mission to lead humanity to a better way of life, the expansion of American civilization was unquestionably good. Freedom and democracy, as well as heavenly

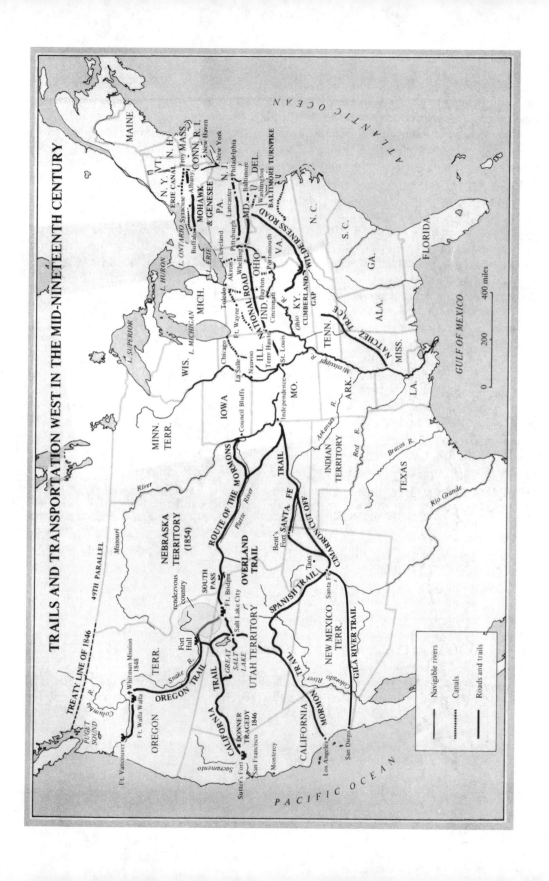

TRAILS AND TRANSPORTATION WEST IN THE MID-NINETEENTH CENTURY

purposes, would be served. There was, to be sure, the problem caused by previous occupants of the land. But expansionists using the Manifest Destiny doctrine blithely dismissed the claims of the Indians, the Mexicans, and the English, with the argument that, although American civilization might not be immediately appreciated, it would eventually benefit those to whom it was given. Skeptics contended that Manifest Destiny was merely a rationale for American land hunger—intellectual oil to smooth guilty consciences and the way west—but most of Kit Carson's contemporaries did not question the legitimacy of such a convenient idea.

The expansion of the United States, which opened new careers for people like Kit Carson, inevitably pressed at the borders of Mexico, its neighbor to the south and west. After having won its independence from Spain in 1821, Mexico at first welcomed American settlers to the northeastern part of the state of Coahuila, which was called Tejas. In the early 1820s, Moses Austin and his son Stephen took advantage of the opportunity and led the first Americans into Mexico. By 1825 about 2,000 Americans, a quarter of whom were slaves, lived south of the border. Cotton production flourished, but predictably, the settlers chafed under Mexican rule and compared their situation to that of the American colonists before 1776. After 1830 the Mexican government, aware of a problem, tried to discourage American immigration, but it was too late. More than 22,000 Americans now lived in Texas, the Anglicanized name of Tejas.

The combination of an authoritarian Mexican ruler—Antonio López de Santa Anna—and the inclination toward autonomy characteristic of frontiersmen soon proved too much for the tenuous relationship. On March 2, 1836, the American-Mexicans declared their independence. In the ensuing war, Santa Anna killed every one of the 182 Texans defending the Alamo mission, including frontier heroes Davy Crockett and Jim Bowie. After being defeated in a bid for reelection to Congress, Crockett had angrily declared that he was going to Texas. That unfortunate decision resulted in his death, but the siege of the mission also cost 1,544 Mexican lives. The cry "Remember the Alamo!" aroused Americans organized under Sam Houston, and on April 21, 1836, they crushed Santa Anna at the Battle of San Jacinto. Mexico still did not officially recognize Texas independence, but on the frontier, possession and strength counted heavily. The Americans had both, and in the fall of 1836, the Texians, as they called themselves, created the Republic of Texas, with Houston as president.

The Texians enjoyed the private support of President Jackson before and after the Alamo. Jackson, like John C. Calhoun and other southern Democrats, wanted the Republic of Texas to enter the union as a slave state. The Texas boosters, many of whom were slave owners and already growing cotton on the fertile plains, agreed. However, Jackson's successor, Democrat Martin Van Buren of New York, was less enthusiastic about bringing Texas into the union. Although he shared Jackson's views on such issues as fiscal conservatism, hard currency, and a strict interpretation of the Constitution, as a northern Democrat, Van Buren focused his expansionary interest on Oregon Country.

"Make way, I say, for the young American Buffalo," an eastern politician shouted during the heyday of Manifest Destiny, "he has not yet got land enough." Ironic as the remark sounds in the light of the near extermination of the buffalo by westward expansionists, it is true that the annexation of Texas seemed only to whet the nation's appetite for expansion. One logical outlet for these energies was the Southwest. Santa Fe, New Mexico, and the lucrative Santa Fe Trade, so familiar to Carson, also came under the American sphere of economic influence. The other object of American interest in Mexican territory was California. Ecstatic reports of this lotus land beyond the mountains had filtered back east as a result of early commercial contacts involving sea otters, whales, and cattle. A few gentleman-adventurers added embellishments; most notably, Richard Henry Dana, in *Two Years Before the Mast*, described an 1835–1836 journey. "In the hands of an enterprising people," Dana exulted, "what a country this might be!" The Mexicans, in his estimation, were charming, but ill equipped to spearhead progress. After the pathbreaking overland journeys of Jedediah Smith (1826), James Ohio Pattie (1828), Ewing Young and Kit Carson (1829–1830), and Joseph Reddeford Walker (1833), the number of Americans living in California gradually increased. Remembering Texas, the Mexican government exhibited a marked coolness toward them, but the immigration persisted. In 1841 John Bidwell led the first emigrant party over the Sierra and into the promised land. Luck, rather than geographic knowledge or wilderness skill, explained Bidwell's successful migration, but after 1843, California emigrants had the benefit of Jim Bridger's fort and advice to help them over the last thousand-mile leg of the journey.

On their 1842 expedition of the Rocky Mountains, John C. Fremont, Kit Carson, and company encountered westbound emigrant trains. The day of the fur trapper was passing, but Carson's acquired skills now served him as a guide for the government surveyors. After guiding the 1842 Fremont expedition back to Fort Laramie, Kit Carson returned alone to Bent's Fort and then to Taos. His reasons for returning this time included marriage to fourteen-year-old Josefa Jamarilla, daughter of one of Taos's most prominent citizens. Carson had asked for her hand in marriage before leaving for Missouri. When he returned, the family gave its consent for Josefa's marriage to a white mountain man twice her age; the wedding took place in February 1843. Carson was taken by Josefa's beauty, but he also hoped to gain a mother for his half-Cheyenne daughter. His intent was to bring Adaline back from Missouri to live with him and Josefa.

Events of 1843 kept Kit Carson from settling into his home in New Mexico. In spring, he helped quell an invasion of Santa Fe threatened by the Republic of Texas, which claimed all land to the east bank of the Rio Grande. While at Fort Saint Vrain in northern Colorado, Carson reconnected with Fremont, who was now leading an expedition of forty men to Oregon Country. Although Fremont had already hired Tom Fitzpatrick as his main guide, he eagerly offered Carson a position as hunter at a higher rate of pay than the first expedition. Carson was learning that his best-rewarded skills required extensive travel. After returning to Taos to say goodbye to Josefa, Carson rejoined Fremont at Fort Saint Vrain in July 1843.

On the basis of Fremont's first expedition report, Congress now sent the Pathfinder to probe deep into the Pacific Northwest and California. From July 1843 to July 1844, the expedition made a huge loop of the West, crossing the Oregon Trail, down the Columbia River to The Dalles, south along the eastern slope of the Cascades and Sierra, crossing the Sierra to winter at Sutter's Fort on the Sacramento River, then across the Sierra, south to the Mojave River, and northeast to Fort Uinta in Utah, to Colorado's North Park, Middle Park, and South Park, and finally back to Bent's Fort. The journey included numerous encounters with Indians—some peaceful, some violent. Along the Mojave River, Carson and another mountain man, Alex Godey, rode off to avenge a deadly attack on a caravan of eastward-bound New Mexicans. Days later they returned to camp with two Indian scalps hoisted above Godey's saddle. Charles Preuss, a German-born scientist on the expedition, was generally disgusted with Fremont and the American mountain men. Of the scalping event, he later lamented: "Are these whites not much worse than the Indians?" For mountain men like Godey and Carson, however, avenging one depredation with another was a necessary response in Indian country.

The expedition returned with a wealth of information, which soon appeared in *Report of the Exploring Expedition to the Rocky Mountains in the Year 1843, and Oregon and North California in the Years 1843–44*. Authored officially by Brevet Captain John C. Fremont, the report was probably more the wordsmithing of Jesse Benton Fremont. Lavish in detail, the report, of which the government made 10,000 copies, lavished praise on the heroism and frontier skills of Kit Carson. Calling Carson "the finest horseman I have ever seen," Fremont recounted events in which the frontiersman saved individuals and indeed the entire expedition. The widely read report made an instant frontier hero of Carson. Soon pulp and dime novels appeared lionizing Kit Carson to a level before known only to Daniel Boone and Davy Crockett.

Upon completing the expedition, the unassuming Carson returned to Taos and Josefa. With $1,200 in his pocket from payment for the expedition, he was a man of means in the West. Ready to settle down, Kit and Josefa moved fifty miles east of Taos to Rayado, built a home, and started farming. The farming idea was shared in partnership with Dick Owens, a fellow fur trapper who also saw that times were changing. They farmed on the Little Cimarron River and spent the coming months settled and happy. But this was not to last long.

Before parting Fremont's company, Carson had promised the Pathfinder he would join him on another westward expedition if there were one. When word came in the summer of 1845 that Fremont was back in the West and organizing a journey to California, Carson and Owens sold their farming interest and traveled to Bent's Fort. This time the group of regular army sharpshooters and mountain men numbered about sixty (plus twelve Delaware Indians)—a force to be reckoned with on the frontier. Fremont's orders were to map and survey potential routes to California and Oregon, but the real purpose of the third expedition has always been shrouded in espionage and intrigue. James K. Polk's election to the presidency in 1844 was pivotal. The proslavery Democrat from Tennessee was also an enthusiastic expansionist. For Polk, the only question in his mind was *how* to get New Mexico and California. First he tried negotiation; John Slidell was sent to Mexico City in 1845 with a cash offer and other concessions. But the Mexicans, already incensed by recent events regarding Texas, were not about to cooperate. In 1844, the United States annexed the Republic of Texas, and in 1845 it became the twenty-eighth state. Enraged by the Mexicans' rejection of Slidell's offer, Polk began to make ready for war. Polk and expansionists in Congress sent Fremont west again amid this strife. What, if any, the unofficial orders were regarding California has remained speculative.

The experienced party made a fast crossing of the intermountain West in late 1845 and early 1846. In January, they arrived at Monterey, the principal town of northern Mexican California. With his men encamped nearby, Fremont met first with American citizen Thomas O. Larkin, the United States ambassador in California, and then with Don José Castro, the commandante general of the Mexican government in Monterey. The speculation is that Fremont brought word to Larkin from President Polk that he should welcome California into the United States if any hostilities began. Larkin had openly worried that British ships were lurking nearby ready to take over California if the Mexican government collapsed. Fremont's meeting with Castro was less pleasant. When Fremont asked permission to remain in California and complete their surveying, Castro ordered him to take his men and leave the way they came in. With such a well-armed force, Fremont could have openly defied Castro's order, but instead, he raised the American flag on a mountaintop (today, Fremont Peak) east of Monterey before marching his army north toward Oregon Country.

As Kit Carson and the others guided the army through the Sacramento Valley, a series of events led to the overthrow of Mexican control of California. In spring 1846, Fremont's company was overtaken by Achibald Gillespie, a U.S. Marine Corps captain and spy for President Polk, posing as an American merchant in California. Gillespie had landed in Monterey, talked to Larkin, and then taken a fast horse to catch up with Fremont. The secret message he bore

Kit Carson's reputation for heroics is illustrated by this dime novel cover from 1874. In the wake of John C. Fremont's glowing praise in his congressional reports of the 1840s, sensationalist writers made Kit Carson a household name.

from the president probably allowed the military officers to do what was necessary to gain California. Fremont's group turned around abruptly. Shortly thereafter, rumors began spreading through the American settlements between Sutter's Fort and Sonoma that the Mexican government was organizing an army to expel all Americans from California. There was no truth to such rumors, and it is unclear who started them, but Fremont has been named. Although there were fewer than 1,000 Americans in California in 1846, they dominated the area east and north of San Francisco Bay. Now, like the Texians, they had received a call to arms.

On June 14, a group of about thirty Americans descended on the village of Sonoma. Organized out of the American villages and farmsteads of the area, the militia planned to preempt the rumored expulsion and take control themselves. The Bear Flag Revolt began when the militia took over the headquarters of Mariano Vallejo, commander of the northern military district of California. Vallejo put up no resistance, since he had long ago let go of his soldiers. The Mexican government rarely sent money to pay the troops. In fact, Vallejo believed an American takeover would be good for California. Arresting Vallejo, the militia leaders proclaimed the establishment of the Bear Flag Republic, and designed a flag to reflect the new nation. A few days later, Fremont's army marched into Sonoma, and the American flag replaced the Bear Flag.

By this time, the United States was officially at war with Mexico, although the participants in the Bear Flag Revolt did not know it. A skirmish between American and Mexican troops on disputed land in southern Texas gave Polk the reason he needed to ask Congress for a declaration of war. On May 13, 1846, a deeply divided Congress declared war on Mexico.

Although this was the height of Manifest Destiny, many Americans believed that the bullying tactics and the undisguised land greed of the Polk administration was despicable and was designed to expand slave territory. The Massachusetts legislature, for instance, solemnly proclaimed the war "hateful in its objects . . . wanton, unjust, and unconstitutional," and New England refused to provide dollars and troops for what it regarded as a fight to extend slavery. Henry David Thoreau, the principled transcendentalist, went to jail rather than pay taxes in support of the Mexican War. But the South and the West were generally in favor of the war, and their support enabled the Polk administration to act. The U.S. Army quickly won the upper hand in Mexico and in disputed parts of Texas. Generals Winfield Scott and Zachary Taylor routed the Mexican army, by then under the direction of Antonio López de Santa Anna. Taylor's men expelled the Mexicans from north of the Rio Grande in Texas, while Scott, after landing at Vera Cruz, made a steady trek toward Mexico City. Meanwhile, Polk's Army of the West, under Stephen W. Kearny, proceeded along the Santa Fe Trail, captured New Mexico without firing a shot, and then marched on to California.

Shortly after the Bear Flag Revolt, Kit Carson and John C. Fremont were involved in an incident that darkened both of their images. In retaliation for the brutal murder of two Americans at the beginning of hostilities, Fremont's men, including Carson, captured three Mexican Californians. Although accounts vary, as do responsibilities, Fremont either ordered the execution of the three captives or approved of the action after the fact. Kit Carson, acting either on his own or under orders from Fremont, was among those who carried out the executions. In a mostly peaceful *coup d'état*, this incident engendered great hostility among the Mexican people of northern California. In Carson's autobiography, written a few years later, there is no mention of this incident. Later, those who wanted to promote Fremont's political career absolved him and placed the blame for the executions on Carson.

Having secured the San Francisco Bay area eastward, Fremont organized a group of 350 regulars and volunteers into the California Battalion. Moving south and west to take San Francisco and Monterey, they found the American flag already flying at both ports. When official word of hostilities arrived, the commander of the U.S. Naval Squadron stationed at Mazatlan, Mexico, sent two warships to California. In early July, naval commanders John Sloat and Robert Stockton led amphibious invasions and met no resistance in taking the two Mexican ports. Although there was disagreement among the military officers over who was in charge, they all agreed it was time to move the fighting forces to Mexican strongholds in southern California. Kit Carson and other landlubbing members of the California Battalion spent several seasick days aboard Navy ships plying the Pacific toward San Diego. Upon landing Carson swore he would never travel that way again. After arriving at San Diego, the U.S. forces steadily—and mostly bloodlessly—took control of southern California. At the end of the summer of 1846, Stockton declared martial law throughout the area and became its self-appointed governor.

At about the same time, Kit Carson found himself leaving Los Angeles in command of fifteen men and bound for Washington, D.C. Fremont and Stockton intended to inform federal authorities of the successful California campaign, and they believed that Carson, with a few mountain men and a few Delaware Indians, could deliver the dispatches more quickly and more reliably than if they were sent via ship on the six-month voyage around the tip of South America. Carson believed he could do it in about sixty days and still stop by and see his wife in New Mexico. Setting out on September 5, 1846, Carson's men were already in central New Mexico when they met General Stephen Kearny's advancing army on October 6. After the bloodless takeover of Santa Fe, Kearny ordered most of his 2,700-man army south to El Paso and Chihuahua. He left a small detachment in Santa Fe and divided the remainder of the troops into two parts bound for California. Informed of the pacification of California, Kearny sent more troops back to Santa Fe and demanded that Carson guide the remaining men to California. After Kearny arranged for the dispatches to be delivered by Kit's old friend Tom Fitzpatrick, Carson reluctantly obeyed the general's order.

After two months of hard marching, Kearny's army reached southern California. They soon learned that the area was no longer pacified and that the Californios were organizing under the leadership of brothers Pio and Andres Pico. On December 6, Kearny's men stopped to rest, after a long march through a hard winter rain, near the Indian village of San Pasqual. Before they could rest, however, a group of Californio horsemen under the command of Andres Pico attacked. Wielding mostly lances, the Californios killed as many as twenty-two of Kearny's men, with no casualties of their own. Carson may have been partly responsible for this defeat, since he had not believed that the Californios would put up a fight. After the battle, the Californios surrounded the Americans. Kearny sent Carson and two others to get a message to Stockton. Stealing through the enemy lines, they found Stockton and his men already advancing on the Californios, who then scattered ahead of the superior numbers. In early January 1847, the combined forces of Stockton and Kearny defeated Pico's men at the Battle of Los Angeles. On the thirteenth, Andres Pico agreed to sign a letter of capitulation at Cahuenga, west of Los Angeles. For all intents and purposes, California was now in American hands.

The war raged on in Mexico, however, until the fall of Mexico City to General Winfield Scott on September 14, 1847. Next came the signing of the Treaty of Guadalupe Hidalgo on February 2, 1848. According to the agreement, the United States, for $15 million, received California, the sprawling New Mexico territory, and the Rio Grande as the southwest border to Texas. All of Mexico might have been annexed had not Polk's repudiated agent, Nicholas Trist, defied recall and negotiated the treaty without proper authorization. Trist worried that the Mexican government would collapse before a treaty could be signed and therefore acted on his own. Enraged, Polk still offered the treaty to Congress. The United States now owned the territories of Texas, New Mexico, and California at a cost of $15 million—amazingly, the same price paid in 1803 for a piece of land comparable in size: the Louisiana Territory. From the territory of the Mexican cession came all or parts of Texas, Oklahoma, Kansas, New Mexico, Colorado, Wyoming, Utah, Nevada, Arizona, and

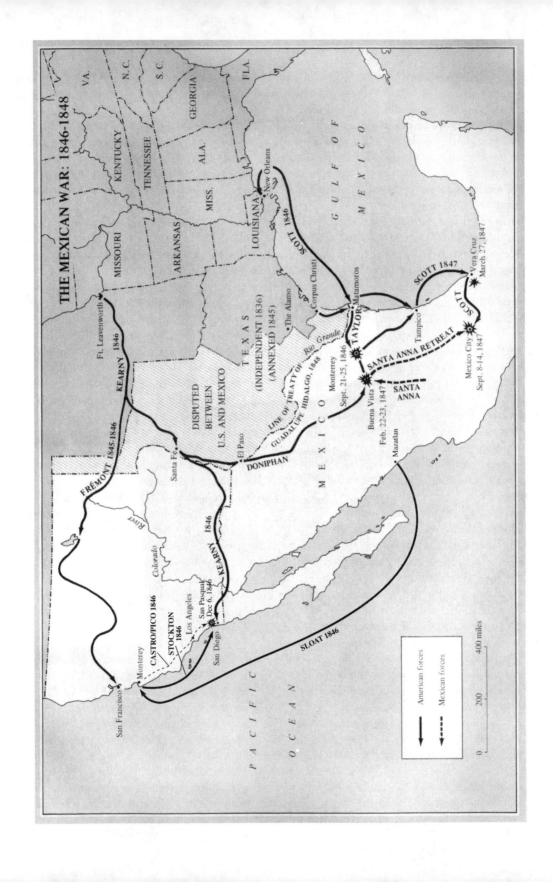

California. Casualties in the Mexican War included 15,000 American troops, however—almost half of whom died after contracting tropical diseases—and 50,000 Mexicans—many of them civilians killed in the siege of Mexico City.

Shortly after the hostilities ended in California, Kit Carson was back on the trail for Washington, D.C., with dispatches from Fremont. In April 1847, he returned to Josefa in New Mexico and learned of the recent Taos Rebellion. A group of Taos Indians and other locals had rebelled against American rule, killing and scalping several Americans, including the Kearny-appointed governor and Carson's good friend, Charles Bent. By the time Kit arrived, the rebels had been arrested and were being tried for treason and murder. After staying ten days in New Mexico with Josefa, Carson continued east, eventually arriving in the nation's capital. Jesse Benton Fremont met him at the train station, and while he was in Washington, Carson stayed mostly at Senator Benton's home. In his short visit, Carson attended social functions, learned about great literature from Jesse, and met with the president. Washington society got a firsthand look at the famous mountain man and scout, and Carson's reputation grew. October 1847 found Carson back in Los Angeles, with dispatches from President Polk.

After another dispatch journey to Washington to report the discovery of gold near Sutter's Fort in 1848, Kit Carson returned home to New Mexico with the idea of at last putting down roots. He and Josefa unsuccessfully tried their hand at farming again at Rayado. Kit then tried to make himself employable in short-haul trading ventures. He also found short-term work as a detective looking for missing children and apprehending robbers on the Santa Fe Trail. Although he was famous, Carson reaped no monetary benefits from the dime and pulp novels about him. He needed money for his family, and it seemed that the best place for him to accomplish that was, as usual, far from home. In 1851, he guarded a wagon train eastward-bound for Kansas City, and the next year he organized a group of eighteen trappers who traveled north and west to spend the season in the Colorado Rockies. In 1853, Carson drove a herd of sheep to California's Russian River Valley.

The two trips west clearly demonstrated to Carson how rapidly things were changing. There was a new force in the Great Basin west of Fort Bridger. The Church of Jesus Christ of Latter-Day Saints had begun in the "burned-over" district of western New York, a region frequently marked by the "fire" of reformers and religious zealots who bore the intellectual legacy of New England Calvinism. In 1827 church founder Joseph Smith claimed to have been visited by the angel Moroni, who told him of gold plates containing an account of an ancient people in the New World who had received the gospel. The angel also presented Smith with two magic stones with which he could translate the plates. The story was of two lost tribes of Israel that somehow made their way to North America. Around 400 A.D. there was a war between the two tribes in New York, where Smith found the plates. All but two people were killed from one tribe—Mormon and his son Moroni. These "latter-day saints" subsequently buried the plates. In 1830 Smith published *The Book of Mormon* from the translated plates. In New York, Smith attracted 15,000 followers and moved them successively to Ohio, Missouri, and Illinois. But Smith's advocacy of polygamy and his acceptance of dictatorial authority—to the extent of defying federal law—subjected the Mormons, as outsiders termed them, to fierce criticism and, ultimately, violence.

In 1844 a mob in Illinois murdered Smith and sent the Mormons, in the manner of the Puritans, searching for a sanctuary where they could live according to their beliefs. The trans-Mississippi West was an obvious candidate, and in Brigham Young the Mormons had a leader with the brilliance and tenacity to direct the migration. Like John Winthrop over two centuries before, Young was prepared to stake everything on the American wilderness. Midsummer 1847 found him and a well-organized pioneer band at Fort Bridger, conversing with the proprietor about the prospects of settling thousands of people in the Salt Lake Valley. Bridger scoffed at the idea. The country was too arid, its discoverer explained, and to dramatize his point he allegedly said he would give $500 for proof corn could be grown in the valley. Bridger suggested that the Mormons try Oregon's rich Willamette Valley, but the saints were not easily swayed. Their primary requirement was isolation, and Salt Lake had that in abundance.

The Mormons struggled through the Emigrant Canyon to their haven. Once installed in Salt Lake Valley, the Mormons made few mistakes. Hard work, a genius for irrigation, and the assistance of a timely invasion of insect-devouring sea gulls solved the agricultural problem, and the relieved settlers joked about Bridger's $500 ear of corn. In 1848 the main body of migrating Mormons filed past Fort Bridger in a caravan that one observer described as being "600 miles and forty days long." Having established their own way stations along the trail, the Mormons usually did not require Bridger's, or any other trading post proprietor's, services—thus saving themselves time and money.

Brigham Young proved a skillful administrator—able to subordinate individual desires to the welfare of the community. The result was rapid and efficient Mormon colonization of the Great Basin, from Idaho to southern California. When the United States acquired this territory at the end of the Mexican War, the worried Mormons proposed the creation of a gigantic State of Deseret, which would include all of present-day Utah, all of Arizona, most of Nevada, and parts

Salt Lake City, Utah, shown here in 1853, was something of a miracle. Less than a decade before, only lizards and jackrabbits had occupied the arid sagebrush benchland between Great Salt Lake and the Wasatch Mountains. The growth of the town was a tribute to the perseverance of the Mormons—one of the most effective groups of pioneers in American history.

of Idaho, Wyoming, Colorado, and California, with an ocean port at San Diego. Congress disapproved, but in 1850 President Millard Fillmore did make Brigham Young governor of the more modest Territory of Utah.

On his second trip west, Carson observed the advance of Americans into Oregon and California. Carson had much firsthand knowledge of events leading to the American takeover of Oregon. He knew personally of the Cambridge, Massachusetts, merchant Nathaniel J. Wyeth, who rode into the 1832 rendezvous with a few dozen followers. Wyeth's expedition was a response to the promotional efforts of Congressman John Floyd of Virginia and Hall J. Kelley, a Massachusetts schoolteacher obsessed by the idea of transplanting an entire New England town to the Pacific Northwest. Both Floyd and Kelley, along with Wyeth, were convinced that if Americans did not settle this region, Great Britain would. They also knew that the flag followed the fireplace. Dissent racked the party at the rendezvous and more than half of them turned back. In October 1832, Wyeth and ten companions reached Fort Vancouver on the Columbia, only to learn that the ship that was carrying their heavy goods had been lost attempting to round South America.

Frustrated, Wyeth returned overland to the trading camp of Milton Sublette, chief representative of the Rocky Mountain Fur Trading Company. Wyeth persuaded Sublette to support a new venture, wherein Wyeth would return to Boston and bring back a shipment of trading goods for Sublette's post. Wyeth hurried to Boston, purchased goods, sent part of them by ship to restore his Oregon venture, and returned by land to Sublette's post with the remainder. When he arrived, however, Wyeth found that Sublette had moved his operation and gone into business with a rival supplier. With no trading post or market, Wyeth built Fort Hall on the Snake River to protect his goods and then rushed to the mouth of the Columbia River to meet the ship he had sent from Boston. But this ship, too, was lost at sea. Wyeth then traveled south to establish a colony along the Willamette River. With this venture and Fort Hall teetering on bankruptcy, Wyeth was forced to sell his trading post to Hudson's Bay Company in 1836.

Spiritual rather than economic considerations motivated the next wave of American interest in Oregon. In the early 1830s, bogus pleas by allegedly religion-starved Flathead Indians elicited contributions of thousands of dollars to Christianize the heathen. Jason and Daniel Lee responded in 1834 with a Methodist mission, school, and temperance society on the Willamette River, a tributary of the Columbia. The following year, the Reverend Samuel Parker and Dr. Marcus Whitman took the trail for Oregon with the support of the American Board of Commissioners for Foreign Missions. Carson was at the rendezvous of that year, when Whitman removed the arrowhead from Jim Bridger's back. The following spring, Whitman, who had returned east for additional support, again met Bridger and Carson in the mountains. With him was Mrs. Narcissa Whitman and Mrs. Eliza Spaulding, the first white women to cross the Continental Divide. The Whitman group established a successful settlement in Oregon, with the Whitmans themselves opening a school. But in 1848, the Whitmans and eleven others were killed in a raid by Cayuse Indians.

Before this unhappy ending, Whitman had done his best to promote the settlement of the Pacific Northwest. In 1843 he personally guided a long emigrant train over the Oregon Trail. Its 1,000 members paused gratefully at Fort Bridger, which was 1,070 miles from the jumping-off place—Independence, Missouri—and almost exactly as far from their destination—Fort Vancouver and the Willamette. In the next two years, about 4,000 more emigrants came over the trail and, in terms of residents in the Northwest, gave the United States an approximate parity with Great Britain. The growth also increased the urgency of solving "the Oregon question." Because Great Britain and the United States jointly claimed Oregon, the key was to determine what parallel of latitude would be established as the boundary between the United States and

Canada. President Polk and other expansionists wanted to secure all of the Oregon country up to the southern boundary of Russian-held Alaska—latitude 54°40′. England favored the opposite extreme—the northern boundary of California, which was at latitude 42°. The settlement of 1846, designating latitude 49°, was a reasonable compromise, because it extended the eastern Canadian–American boundary to the Pacific. From this agreement came all or part of the states of Oregon, Washington, Idaho, and Montana. The huge Canadian province of British Columbia comprised Oregon Country north of the 49th parallel. Instead of insisting on the 54°40′ line, Polk chose not to risk another war with the British.

From the standpoint of the Oregon pioneers, the boundary settlement did not rank in importance with the details of local government. The farming families that had migrated to Oregon Territory had, merely by their presence, established the framework for law and order. For every outlaw with a smoking six-shooter, there were a dozen families and businessmen determined to put local affairs on an orderly basis. The extreme individualism of the early generation of mountain men typified only the first wave of pioneers—men who lived a nomadic, wilderness existence and, because they were few, could literally be a law unto themselves. But when settlers arrived, they quickly erected a legal framework and enforced it, when necessary, with informal but effective vigilante justice—posses and hangmen's nooses. In Oregon the need to dispose of the estate of a man who died without leaving a will occasioned the first steps toward political organization. In true social-compact tradition, the neighbors of the deceased convened to decide the issue. Someone vaguely recalled the New York law dealing with unbequeathed property, so that statute became the Oregon guideline. In 1843 a First Organic Law was pieced together from the fragmentary legal knowledge of the community. Two years later, a more complete set of laws regularized such matters as marriage, landholding, and criminal procedures. Taxation was voluntary, but with the understanding that those who did not pay had no vote and no recourse to the law for any purpose. Under such conditions, few refused. The machinery of government was therefore well established by 1848, when Oregon became a territory of the United States.

Having even more firsthand experience in California, Kit Carson was stunned to see the changes there in the time since he had been there with John C. Fremont. The trail through the Sierra to Sacramento now bustled with wagon trains and riders, whereas it had been arduous for all and disastrous for some before. Just months before, in 1846, Carson and Fremont had crossed the Sierra Nevada at the site of what soon became known as the Donner Party tragedy. Victimized in many ways by their own arrogance, members of the Donner Party of 1846–1847 also were the victims of bad luck and bad advice. The advice came from one Lansford W. Hastings. Hastings had made the overland journey to California in 1843, after which he wrote *The Emigrant's Guide to Oregon and California* and set himself up as the resident expert at Fort Bridger, dispensing advice at ten dollars per person. Hastings was obsessed with taking California from Mexico, and to do this he needed to attract emigrants to the area. For this purpose, he extolled the wonders of California to those considering going to Oregon. He also enticed them to save 250 miles by abandoning the accepted California Trail, which ran north from Fort Bridger to the Hudson's Bay Company's Fort Hall and then followed the Humboldt and Truckee rivers to the Sierra Nevada. Hastings instead advocated a cutoff through the rugged Wasatch Mountains, south of the Great Salt Lake, and across the most arid part of the Great Basin. This was the route that had almost killed Jedediah Smith on his return from California in 1827, and it certainly could be suicidal for slow-moving emigrant parties. Still, the promise of cutting hundreds of miles off the California trip appealed to trail-weary travelers.

Lansford Hastings ventured out on the Oregon Trail during 1846 to advise emigrants. Among those who took his advice was a group from Illinois under the leadership of George and

Jacob Donner. Hastings had promised to lead the Donner party west from Fort Bridger but was nowhere to be found when they arrived there. Leaving Fort Bridger very late in the summer of 1846, the Donners wasted precious time struggling through the Wasatch range, only to spend six waterless days on the desert west of the Great Salt Lake. The ordeal broke the emigrants' spirit and discipline. They quarreled incessantly and refused to share precious supplies. By now fall was well advanced and the Sierra still blocked the way to California. Tragedy was in the making. A heavy snow trapped the Donner party in the mountains, and the death toll mounted. Of the eighty-nine who started from Fort Bridger, only forty-five survived, and some of these only by eating the roasted flesh of those who had died.

Less than one year after the remnants of the Donner party straggled down from the snowy mountains, a group of workers digging a diversion in the American River for a sawmill 50 miles east of Sutter's Fort discovered gold in the new riverbed. By May 1848, thousands vacated the towns of California to feverishly dig for gold. These "forty-eighters," mostly people already in California, had the best of the easily obtained placer gold; but others were on their way as news of the California gold rush reached around the world. Some 100,000 Americans streamed overland in quest of gold in 1849 alone. An additional 25,000 arrived by sea from New York, England, and France. Mexican territory until 1848, California skipped the territorial phase with its huge population and became the thirty-first state in 1850. Kit Carson was bewildered as he traveled through the gold country in 1853. The sleepy province of northwestern Mexico was alive with prospectors, outlaws, prostitutes, vigilantes, entrepreneurs, and government. The West he knew was but a memory.

Returning again to New Mexico following his successful sheep drive, Carson began the next phase of his life—as an Indian agent. Although on the surface it seems ironic that Carson—a man who had fought and killed Indians, had been wounded by Indians, and had engaged in innumerable Indian battles—would be offered and would accept a position as an Indian agent. But it must also be remembered that Carson married two Indian women, had a half-Indian daughter, and had rescued several Indian children from capture or death in his years as a trapper. Moreover, in New Mexico, Carson was known as a man who treated all people fairly. The federal government had offered him the position of Indian agent in March 1853, while he was driving the sheep herd to California. Government officials left the position open until he returned, reflecting both their faith in Carson and the low priority given to Indian affairs in New Mexico. Upon his return, Carson readily accepted this position of stability. He and Josefa now had a son, William, born in 1852. A daughter, Teresina, would be born in 1855, and Kit Jr. in 1858. They also brought Adaline back from a seminary in Missouri to live with them during the 1850s.

Kit's assignment was to be agent for the Taos Pueblos, the Muache Utes, and the Jicarilla Apaches. Throughout his tenure as Indian agent, Carson ran the agency from his home, because the government never paid for a public office. Carson had the misfortune of conducting Indian policy in a time of great transition in the American West. In the days of the mountain man, favorable dealings with Indians were crucial. Trappers needed the Indians for information, food, trade, and alliances, and trappers were as much a part of the frontier as Indians. By the time Carson became an Indian agent, however, gone was the notion of a vast western frontier where tribes could be sent to live in isolation from non-Indians. The "Indian problem" defied solution more than ever before as the West became crowded. Expansive American capitalists had no need for Native Americans and wanted them relegated to small reservations or exterminated. Since the Southwest was among the last regions to be pacified, Carson spent considerable time quelling rebellions, cooling hostilities, and trying to keep the word of the government. He regularly led federal troops to areas of tension erupting between Indians and non-Indians. Because

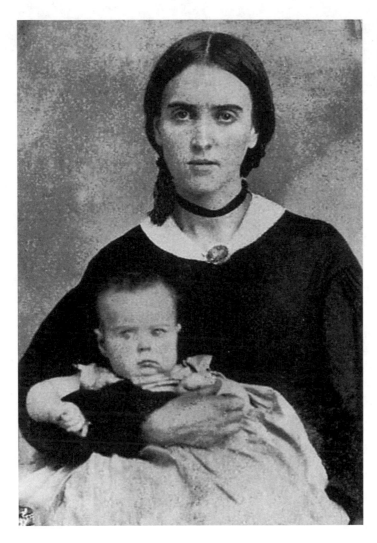

This photograph, probably taken about 1850, is believed to be Josefa Jamarillo Carson with one of her and Kit's children.

New Mexico and Arizona were territories, however, they did not garner the resources of the more populous states of the West. With one assistant to do the paperwork, the barely literate Carson performed the duties of an Indian agent. He was nonetheless well served by his rudimentary Spanish, sign language, and knowledge of several Indian dialects.

Despite the difficulties of laboring with such scant resources, Carson's position gave him time with his family and time to dictate his memoirs. In 1856 he told the story of his life to a clerk, who penned the manuscript. Whether the clerk was one person or more who worked for him in the office, or whether it was Jesse B. Turley—a local resident to whom Carson transferred the completed document "for our joint benefit"—is unknown. Turley joined in partnership with Dr. D. C. Peters, an Army surgeon also familiar with Kit, to write a biography based on the manuscript. The profits were to be shared among Turley, Peters, and Carson. Peters took the manuscript and, in collaboration with another author, published a biography of Carson in 1858.

John Gast's 1872 painting entitled "American Progress" gives graphic and metaphorical validation to the concept of Manifest Destiny that frontiersmen like Kit Carson ushered into the West.

Proceeds from the book reached $20,000, but none of this money ever made it to Turley or to Carson. The original manuscript disappeared, not to be found until the 1960s.

Kit Carson's dictated memoirs reflect much about his character that had been omitted from the frontier hero novels and sensational biographies. Though not page-turning reading, the autobiography reveals careful attention to detail and a good memory. Carson's unassuming prose reflects the memories of an unassuming man. He did not minimize the amount or ferocity of the Indian-fighting he took part in, and he celebrated deeds that he believed were proper retaliatory frontier justice. It is interesting that there is no mention of either of his Indian wives, Waanibe and Making Out Road. But Carson devoted much of the latter part of the manuscript to his position as an Indian agent for northern New Mexico, and he revealed great sympathy for the Indians' plight. He lamented that the government did not provide funds to build an agency on the Indian lands and that it was necessary to run the agency from his home in Taos. "They should not be allowed to come into the settlements," he declared, "for every visit an Indian makes to a town, it is of more or less injury to him." For Carson, the Indians' only chance to preserve traditional ways was to be moved to reservations as far from white settlements as possible. There they could be taught agriculture and be free of corrupting influences. Carson's views anticipated the federal government's policy dilemma of dealing with the subjugated tribes of the American West as the 1800s progressed. Kit Carson summarized his role as Indian agent in this way: "I frequently visit the Indians, speak to them of the advantages of peace, and use my influence with them to keep them satisfied with the proceedings of those placed in power over them."

Although regarded in lore as the rugged individualist, mountain man, and scout of the Wild West, Kit Carson had spent much of his adult life in public service. Since his days with Fremont, Carson had most frequently been a federal government contractor, employed as a guide, hunter, envoy, soldier, or scout. From 1854 to 1861, he held the position of Indian agent for the federal Bureau of Indian Affairs. Then, in 1861, this consummate public servant resigned that position to volunteer in the Union Army. With his extensive military experience in a sparsely populated part of the nation, Carson was commissioned as a lieutenant colonel in the First New Mexico Volunteer Infantry. Carson, who was born and raised in the slave states of Kentucky and Missouri (both border states in the Civil War), never wavered in his loyalty to the Union. New Mexicans generally had disdain for African-American slavery, a distaste that was deeply embedded in the culture of the Pueblos, the Spanish, and the Mexicans. Therefore, sentiments in New Mexico were generally pro-Union. Still, some Indians of the Southwest, realizing that white men were making war on one another, looked for ways to harm the Union cause and went on the warpath. The primary mission of the New Mexico volunteers was to secure New Mexico and Arizona territories from invasion by Confederates from Texas, and a secondary mission was to keep the Indians pacified. Hasty organizing and drilling began in Albuquerque. On Febuary 21, 1862, Colonel E. R. S. Canby led about 3,000 New Mexico Volunteers, including Kit Carson, against Confederate Brigadier General Henry H. Sibley, who had brought his force of 2,500 men across the Rio Grande River and up the east side of the river to the ford at Valverde, north of Fort Craig, New Mexico. After a brief but fierce frontal assault by the Confederates, Canby ordered his army to retreat. Both sides suffered heavy casualties, but this was a Confederate victory, and shortly thereafter, Sibley's army marched into Santa Fe. Four months later, following a Union victory in the Battle of La Glorieta Pass, the Volunteers forced them out of New Mexico. For his service in the Battle of Valverde, Kit Carson was brevetted to brigadier general.

The Civil War had extensive impact on New Mexico Territory. Aside from two major battles and increasing Indian unrest there, the war adversely affected the territory's importance in westward expansion. Before the war, the Santa Fe Trail combined with the Gila River Trail to connect East with West and California, rivaling the Overland Trail in importance. Moreover, the Butterfield Overland Stage Company began service from Saint Louis to San Francisco in the late 1850s, following a southern route through Indian Territory, Texas to El Paso, southern New Mexico Territory, Arizona Territory, San Diego, Los Angeles, and San Francisco. In 1858, Butterfield's horse-drawn coaches raced from Missouri to California in twenty-four days. "I congratulate you on the result," a proud President James Buchanan wired Butterfield. "It is a glorious triumph for civilization and the Union." When the war began, however, the Butterfield route was ordered north to follow the Overland and California trails. The United States Congress had debated the most feasible route for a transcontinental railroad line to California since the early gold rush days, but sectional issues had kept the ultimate decision deadlocked. Northerners demanded a northern route, while Southerners wanted the line to follow the southern Butterfield route. With the Confederate states in rebellion, the North began planning the northern route, leaving New Mexico isolated for decades to come.

Many wilderness veterans, like Carson's fur trade mentor Jim Bridger, eventually turned to new clients in the transport business. The frontier, almost by definition, receded as the transportation network advanced. Bridger, a beneficiary of the shift to northern transcontinental routes, helped the organizers of stagecoach lines and express companies find key routes in the country he knew so well. In the process, he left his name on western maps. The Bridger Trail ran north from the North Platte River and the Oregon Trail to the Yellowstone River and Bozeman, Montana. Bridger's Ferry took the Oregon Trail across the North Platte. As an all-weather alternative to that famous pathway, Bridger blazed a route from western Nebraska to northern Utah over Bridger's Pass. In 1861, along with Captain E. L. Berthoud and the Central Overland, California, and Pike's Peak Express Company, he laid out the Bridger–Berthoud Road west from Denver. And the South Pass–Green River–Salt Lake corridor that Bridger discovered in the early 1820s became the major east–west transcontinental route.

Because of sectionalism and the war, other new transportation ventures used the northern routes. The Pony Express team of daredevil horsemen carried the mail across the Overland Trail to California in just ten days during 1860 and 1861. In 1861, however, the time was cut to seconds when wires were joined on the first transcontinental telegraph, and the Pony Express quickly went bankrupt. The efficient transport of items heavier than paper and people awaited the railroads. The two decades before the Civil War saw track mileage in the United States leap from 3,000 to 30,000. When the Civil War eliminated consideration for a southern route, and federal subsidies made investments sufficiently attractive, the railroad plans were revived. In 1863 the Central Pacific began its push east from California. Generous grants of the public domain—which made the railroads the largest landowners in the West—and federal loans on a per-mile basis encouraged construction. In 1867 the Central Pacific's tracks extended across the Sierra. Meanwhile, the Union Pacific was advancing west from Omaha, Nebraska. The competition between the Central and Union crews resulted in rapid, if careless, construction, which reached the rate of ten miles per day over favorable terrain. The lines met on May 10, 1869, at Promontory, Utah.

The advent of the rapid, dependable, and relatively inexpensive transportation of heavy, bulky items helped make possible a series of economic bonanzas in the West. Like the fur trade, which had begun the process, each bonanza brought a wave of civilization surging westward across the Great Plains or eastward from California and Oregon. When the exploitable resource was depleted, the wave receded, but not without leaving a residue of permanent settlement. Second only to the trappers were the miners. After the great California gold rush of 1849, there were similar mineral booms in Nevada, Colorado, Arizona, Idaho, Montana, and Wyoming. Denver developed from gold strikes that attracted frontiersmen like bees to honey, and so did Helena, Montana, and Boise, Idaho. The richest concentration of gold and silver was struck on the eastern slope of the Sierra—the fabulous Comstock Lode. Thanks to the miners who flooded in, Nevada became a state in 1864. Life in all the mining camps was rough-and-tumble, with the usual frontier assortment of gamblers, prostitutes, and outlaws, but the need for a framework of law and order to protect the gains of the fortunate quickly spawned simple democracy, vigilante justice, and—in time—territorial status and statehood.

When the Confederate threat was eliminated from New Mexico by 1863, emphasis returned to Indian pacification. Kit Carson's next assignments included a series of negotiations, confrontations, and forced marches. In the fall of 1862, General James H. Carleton ordered Carson west to Fort Stanton in New Mexico Territory to put down an uprising by Mescalero Apaches. After successfully pacifying the Apaches, Carson was then ordered to the Navajo country of western New Mexico and eastern Arizona. The Navajos had recently begun an uprising against white settlements and military outposts in the region. General Carleton demanded a surrender by July 20. When this did not happen, he ordered Carson to advance about 700 men to "kill all Navajo men

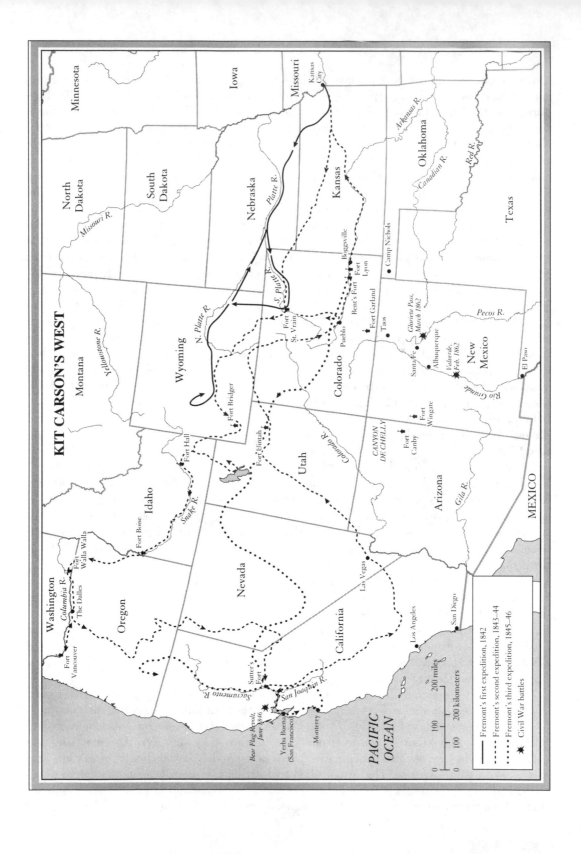

KIT CARSON'S WEST

Legend:
- Fremont's first expedition, 1842
- Fremont's second expedition, 1843–44
- Fremont's third expedition, 1845–46
- Civil War battles

able to bear arms and take all women and children as prisoners." What followed over the remaining months of 1863 darkened Kit Carson's reputation as a hero. Some Navajos did heed Carleton's order to surrender, but most divided into small bands that continued raiding. For several months, Carson's men launched counterraids deep into the Navajo country. Determined to break the Navajos' resistance, the Army burned crops and buildings and killed livestock. Carson, believing that the Navajos were making peaceful overtures, questioned Carleton's insistence on unconditional surrender, but to no avail. Carson's distaste for the regular army and this assignment was reflected also in several requests for leave during the campaign against the Navajos; the requests were rebuffed. Nonetheless, Carson carried out the scorched-earth war against the Navajos, reporting in January 1864: 23 killed, 34 captured, 200 voluntarily surrendered. Over the next few months, the Army displaced about 8,000 starving and homeless Navajos from their strongholds and force-marched them to Fort Canby and Fort Wingate. Next, Carleton ordered about 9,000 Navajos to be relocated to Fort Sumner, approximately 200 miles east. After a dismal failure in trying to teach the Navajos to farm in this new land, in 1868, the Army, under the orders of General William Tecumseh Sherman, escorted the Navajos back to their old country and their newly designated reservation.

Kit Carson did not live to learn of the Navajos' return to their homeland. The ordeal of the Navajo campaign had worn heavily on him, and serving in the regular army had not suited the mountain man. But it was an accident in 1860 that eventually led to his death. On a spring hunt in the San Juan Mountains, he was walking his horse when the horse fell, and Carson's legs got caught in the reins. None of his fellow hunters saw the accident, but Carson suffered a sprained shoulder and a serious injury to his chest. His recovery was long, and Carson began experiencing pain in his throat and chest that became worse with time. It is likely that the fall damaged his heart and led to a chronic heart condition. After the Navajo campaign, Carson participated in additional military activities against hostile plains Indians, including the Kiowas and Apaches. When he was assigned to command Fort Garland in south central Colorado in 1866, his wife joined him. Their family had grown; two more daughters had been born since 1864. It was here that Carson's health began to decline rapidly. Intense pain in his upper body made it difficult for him to ride a horse and do his job. In the next year, he resigned from the Army and was appointed superintendent of Indian affairs for Colorado Territory. In 1868 he made a painful journey to Washington to negotiate peace treaties for the Utes and to consult physicians about his medical condition. Despite his failing health, Carson carefully negotiated in the best interests of the Indians and also met with dignitaries for several photographs and gatherings.

Returning to his new home in Boggsville, Colorado, in April 1868, Carson witnessed the birth of another daughter, Josephine. Ten days later, however, his wife Josefa died suddenly, probably from complications of childbirth. Carson retired to Fort Lyon, Colorado, weakened and depressed. His doctor at the fort—as well as the doctors in Washington—diagnosed his condition as an aneurysm of the aorta, pressing on the pneumogastric nerve and causing spasms. There was no treatment for his condition. The doctors ordered him not to eat solid food, drink anything that would irritate his throat, or smoke. In great pain and grief-stricken at the loss of his wife, Carson made out his will. Each day his condition worsened, and he regularly coughed up blood. On May 23, 1868, Carson said he felt a bit better and asked for a meal of buffalo steak and coffee; he then asked for his tobacco pipe. A few minutes later Kit called out: "Doctor, compadre, Adios!" Blood gushed from his mouth and he fell silent. Kit Carson, the frontiersman whose extraordinary life marked one of the most memorable periods in the history of the American West, was dead at the age of fifty-eight.

Carson's grave illness is revealed in this, the last photograph taken of him, in March 1868.

Selected Readings

The Person

Carter, Harvey Lewis: *Dear Old Kit: The Historical Christopher Carson* (1968). Thoughtful biography built around Kit Carson's autobiography.

Dunlay, Tom: *Kit Carson and the Indians* (2000). Definitive and analytical study of the many aspects of Carson's relations with Native Americans.

Estergreen, M. Morgan: *Kit Carson: A Portrait in Courage* (1962). Well-organized and thorough biography.

Guild, Thelma S., and Harvey L. Carter: *Kit Carson: A Pattern for Heroes* (1984). Thorough biography with excellent maps.

The Period

°Bergon, Frank (ed.): *The Journals of Lewis and Clark* (1989). Well-edited version of the Corps of Discovery journals.

Billington, Ray A.: *Westward Expansion* (rev. ed., 1967). A good general treatment of America's frontiers.

Chittenden, Hiram M.: *The American Fur Trade of the Far West* (2 vols., 1935). An old but thorough account.

°De Voto, Bernard: *The Year of Decision, 1846* (1943). Examination of a pivotal point in the nation's history.

°De Voto, Bernard: *Across the Wide Missouri* (1947). The early history of the Far West.

Faragher, John Mack: *Women and Men on the Overland Trail* (1979). A comparative analysis of the experiences of men and women who left the Mississippi Valley region and traveled the Overland Trail.

°Gates, Paul W.: *The Farmer's Age* (1960). Agricultural history before the Civil War.

Goodman, George J., and Cheryl A. Lawson: *Retracing Major Stephen H. Long's 1820 Expedition: The Itinerary and Botany* (1995). Colorful account of Long's journey across the Great Plains to the Rockies.

Hart, James D.: *A Companion to California* (1987). Detailed encyclopedia of California history.

Mitchell, John G.: "On the Seacoast of Nebraska," *Audubon* (May 1989): 56–77. Colorful account of the migrations along the Platte River.

Myers, Sandra L.: *Westering Women and the Frontier Experience, 1800–1915* (1982). A broad account, based on hundreds of collections, revealing the diverse experiences of women on the western frontier.

Slotkin, Richard: *Regeneration through Violence: The Mythology of the American Frontier, 1600–1860* (1973). An imaginative interpretation of the forces affecting Carson's time and place.

°Smith, Henry Nash: *Virgin Land: The American West as Symbol and Myth* (1950). Explores the idea, as distinct from the reality, of the West as held by Americans in the eighteenth and nineteenth centuries.

°Taylor, George R.: *The Transportation Revolution, 1815–1860* (1951). An examination of the most important factor in the opening of the West.

For Consideration

1. Discuss the rendezvous system that the mountain men developed.

2. In what ways did frontiersmen like Kit Carson and the fur trappers epitomize Jacksonian America?

3. Analyze the importance of Missouri to the Mexican province of New Mexico.

4. Kit Carson went from Indian-fighter to Indian agent. Discuss this change in Carson's life in the context of the changing American West.

5. Mountain men found new ways of making a living after the fur business ended. What were some of those professions, and how did they symbolize the vanishing frontier?

°Available in paperback.

Chapter 8

Frederick Douglass

The tall teenaged boy had one foot on the stable loft ladder when he felt a hand close about his ankle. A quick pull brought him crashing to the floor. From a prone position, Frederick Douglass looked up at the grinning face of Edward Covey, professional slave breaker. The white man began to slip a noose over Douglass's legs in preparation for yet another session of the torture that had made the first six months of 1834 a nightmare of pain. Only two days before, Douglass had lain half dead in the woods near Covey's. It was the low point of his life. "I would have exchanged my manhood," he later recalled, "for the brute-hood of an ox." Now, lying on the stable floor, Douglass was seized by a blinding anger. Springing away from the noose, he grappled with the surprised Covey. For the better part of an hour the men struggled desperately. Finally, Covey staggered away. Douglass, by his own admission, was a changed man. The act of resistance "recalled to life my crushed self-respect and my self-confidence, and inspired me with a renewed determination to be a free man." Four years later he escaped to freedom. Four decades later he stood as the foremost spokesman of black America.

"Genealogical trees," Frederick Douglass wryly observed, "did not flourish among slaves." Few knew their ancestry or even their age. Douglass was no exception. He believed he had been born in 1817. His mother was black and a slave. He saw her only a few times. He supposed his father was white, and he was told that Indian blood also ran in his veins.

For his first seven years, Frederick Douglass lived a relatively comfortable life with his grandmother on a plantation in Maryland's Talbot County, east of Chesapeake Bay. Fishing and watching squirrels and playing on the dirt floor of his grandmother's cabin, he did not understand what it meant to be a slave. Gradually, however, his child's mind learned there was someone called Old Master. This vague figure, he found out, owned not only the land and the cabin, but his grandmother, his playmates, and him, too. It seemed inconceivable. The older slaves tried hard to shield the child from the full implications of his condition. Still, it was impossible to miss the involuntary shudder that invariably accompanied any discussion of Old Master. "Thus early," Douglass remembered, "did clouds and shadows begin to fall upon my path."

At about the age of seven, Douglass began a more intensive course of instruction in the meaning of slavery. On what he clearly remembered as a beautiful summer morning, he was taken from his grandmother's cabin to Old Master's plantation. The master in this case was Captain Aaron Anthony, who owned several farms and some thirty slaves. But Anthony also managed the slaves of Colonel Edward Lloyd. A power in eastern Maryland, Lloyd held twenty-five farms and more than a thousand slaves. And as it happened, Anthony made his personal residence on Lloyd's lavish plantation. There Douglass received a memorable impression of the Old South at its zenith.

The grandeur of the place astonished the boy. Like most large southern plantations of the 1820s, Lloyd's gardens and pastures, mills, and craft shops constituted a nearly self-sufficient economic unit. Old Master lived in "the great house," which was built of white-painted wood. Three spacious wings branched out from a broad front porch with its row of white columns. Leading from the porch to the gate a quarter-mile distant was a graveled driveway and a lush lawn planted with trees and flowers. In imitation of English nobles, Lloyd released rabbits, deer, and other game to roam the estate. To the rear of the great house another lawn ran down to the Wye River, Lloyd's chief artery of communication and trade. From his landing, the tobacco that sustained the plantation was shipped to market. A pleasure sloop, the Sally Lloyd, swung at its mooring, a rowboat trailing behind. Taking all this in, Douglass could not suppress a thrill at the "elaborate exhibition of wealth, power, and beauty." For him and his fellows, however, home meant one of the miserable slave huts scattered, half hidden, about the plantation. And Douglass quickly learned that beneath the genteel surface lay a tangled skein of brutality, passion, and blood. Shortly after his arrival at Lloyd's, an overseer had savagely beaten a young black woman who worked on another farm. The girl knew she belonged to Lloyd and, with blood streaming down her face and back, had dragged herself twelve miles to seek his protection. Douglass was there when she arrived. Lloyd refused to acknowledge her presence and turned the problem over to the chief overseer, Anthony. Up to this time, Douglass had entertained a favorable image of Anthony, who sometimes led him by the hand and patted his head in a paternal fashion. Now he saw the other side of the man. As Douglass recalled, Anthony cursed the bleeding girl and declared that " 'she deserved every bit of [the beating], and if she did not go home instantly he would himself take the remaining skin from her neck and back.' " Douglass realized that the girl had no alternative but to return the twelve miles to still more floggings. Absolute repression, he saw, was the keystone of the slave system.

In the next few years, Douglass's perspective on slavery expanded considerably. He saw mothers tied to trees and whipped to unconsciousness in front of their crying children. When his beloved grandmother became too old to work, Douglass later found out, she was left in a hut in the middle of the forest to die of starvation. He watched an enraged overseer shoot and kill a slave who dared to run from a threatened flogging. Maryland justice did not regard this deed as a crime. Douglass never knew a slave murderer to receive the slightest punishment. Rape of black women (sometimes for the purpose of breeding) was common but also outside the law. And Douglass noted that the offspring of such unions caused Old Master some embarrassment. Although the children were black, they were usually exempt from the punishment dealt other slaves, which led to problems. Lloyd was finally obliged to slip one of his troublesome black sons enough money to buy his freedom.

Douglass noticed that Lloyd's house servants always received preferential treatment on the plantation. In contrast to the field hands, these favored slaves rendered personal services in the great house. Many deliberately copied Old Master in dress, speech, and mannerisms and hardly condescended to associate with their brothers and sisters in the fields. But the house servants' social superiority was entirely self-assumed. The caprice of the slave owners could come crashing down on them as well.

The potential for atrocities, Douglass believed, made the slaveholder as well as the slave a victim of the system. There was no chance on either side for character development. "Reason," he wrote, "is imprisoned here, and passions run wild." The slave experience, he concluded, made livestock of human beings—indeed, the slaves had a worse fate. Old Master's "horses and dogs," Douglass maintained, "fared better than his men."

The slave system in which Frederick Douglass found himself mired in the 1820s had had its American origins in 1619, when the captain of a Dutch ship sold twenty bewildered Africans to the tobacco planters of Jamestown, Virginia. The slave trade was already well established. Portuguese and Spanish traders had carried human cargoes from West Africa's Gold Coast to Europe as early as the fifteenth century. Native black kings along the African coast made the trade possible by selling their own slaves or procuring them from the interior. Without exonerating whites for their role in slavery, we cannot ignore evidence that the profit motive that fed the trade existed irrespective of color.

The settlement of the New World opened new opportunities for slavery. Initial hopes centered on easy wealth from a paradisiacal land. Slaves had no role in this economy. But the dreams faded quickly under the impact of the New World reality: People would have to work for a living. However, the gentleman-adventurers who composed the first waves of settlers in the Caribbean and in England's southern colonies were not inclined to perform the hard field labor that the production of sugar, tobacco, and, later, cotton demanded. Moreover, it was difficult to convince immigrants from their own countries to be employees. In America, everyone wanted to be an employer. Slaves filled the resulting labor vacuum.

About ten million blacks came to the Americas in the three centuries of slave trade. The typical commercial pattern began with the shipment of liquor and manufactured goods from England or the North American colonies to Africa. The next leg, the middle passage, took slaves to the markets in the Americas. Hundreds of thousands of blacks died in the foul holds of crowded ships on the journey, but the profits in the business sustained it even if only half the cargo survived. Completing the economic triangle, sugar, tobacco, and cotton were then shipped in the slavers to the commercial centers of Europe and the northern colonies. Frederick Douglass's ancestors had reached America as a result of such exchanges.

The social status of the first black Americans was not immediately clear. There is some evidence that some African immigrants were regarded by their seventeenth-century contemporaries as indentured servants rather than as slaves. In other words, the blacks, like white servants, owed a certain amount of labor to the person who had paid their way to America, but they were not his property. They possessed the rights and immunities of human beings. In time, they could expect to earn their freedom. Their children, in any case, were free.

There is also evidence, however, that not all seventeenth-century servants were equal. The black ones had fewer rights from the beginning. In a very short time, their inferior status jelled into hereditary lifetime service, and they became property. The reason for this rapid hardening seems to have been a deeply rooted bias in the Anglo-American mind against blacks. Part of it stemmed from their color itself. In the eyes of whites, blacks were at once shocking, inexplicable, and frightening—associated, because of their color, with the powers of darkness. Given this bias, slavery seemed a way for white society to live with the disturbing strangers in its midst. Also significant in stamping slavery on the Africans was their social visibility. A white servant at least looked like everyone else. Taken from their place of servitude, they blended into society. They could thus reap the benefits of the fluid social and economic structure of a growing country. But blacks were marked by their color, which constantly testified to their menial origins. It was easy to pin on them the label *slave*. In any event, by 1700 it was clearly understood throughout the American colonies that slavery concerned blacks only. Slaves, as Frederick Douglass learned at a very tender age, had no humanity.

But the young Douglass also learned that there were varieties of slavery, some less brutal than others. While still a boy, he was sent from the Lloyd plantation to Baltimore and the home of Hugh Auld, a son-in-law of Captain Anthony. Specifically, Douglass was a gift to the Aulds' young son, Tommy. In this capacity, he lived a better life than he had thought possible. He had clean clothes, regular food, a bed, and a mistress who at first treated him more as a stepson than a slave. Mrs. Auld even began to teach Douglass to read. She made the mistake, however, of informing her husband of the boy's rapid progress. Auld became enraged and forbade the lessons. "Learning," he declared in Douglass's presence, "will spoil the best nigger in the world." If the boy learned to read the Bible, Auld continued, "it will forever unfit him to be a slave." Education, Auld concluded, could only make slaves "disconsolate and unhappy."

Frederick Douglass took this experience to heart. He sensed that the reason slaveholders opposed educating blacks was a fear that education would promote a desire for freedom. Douglass then redoubled his efforts to read and write. His teachers were the street society of Baltimore and a battered copy of Noah Webster's famous spelling book, which he somehow acquired and carefully hid. Instruction in writing came from copying the letters on the sides of shipping crates on Baltimore's docks. When he was thirteen, Douglass earned his first money blackening boots and used it, in the manner of Benjamin Franklin, to buy a book: *The Columbian Orator*. The volume contained stirring speeches advocating natural rights, and some of the orations even concerned the abolition of slavery. Exposure to such texts heightened Douglass's desire for freedom. No matter how kind his treatment, he knew he was someone's property, and the thought incensed him. Precisely as Auld had predicted, education and slavery were poor partners.

About the time he learned to read and write, Douglass left the Auld household to work in the shipyards of Baltimore. He thereby joined the ranks of a select group: the city slaves. These blacks constituted a substantial percentage of the slave labor force. They worked in the cities and towns of the South, but under conditions different from those of the plantation slaves. Normally, city slaves had their own quarters and the liberty to come and go in the town as they pleased. Their labor was frequently "hired out" to businessmen in the community, the wages accruing to the master. But occasionally, slaves would be permitted to work part of the time for themselves and in this way accumulate the funds to buy their freedom. Such self-freed blacks were not common in the South, but their presence constitutes evidence against the interpretation of American slavery as a completely closed, spirit-breaking system.

For a time in Baltimore, Douglass entertained hopes of being permitted to earn the money to buy himself from his master. His growing skill as a caulker of ships lent substance to this dream. But in 1833 Douglass's luck took a turn for the worse. The elder Aulds, who inherited Douglass from Captain Anthony's estate, died, and the resulting adjustments sent him back to a farm. Douglass was now the property of the Aulds' son, Thomas. Having tasted the liberal variety of slavery in Baltimore, resubmission to the harsher rural pattern was doubly hard. Douglass tried to maintain his dignity. He organized a Sunday school class for black children on the plantation but saw it disbanded by an angry mob of pious leaders of the local church. Moreover, Douglass's new owner warned him in no uncertain terms that such behavior would bring him to the same fate as Nat Turner.

Nat Turner was not just a name in the South in 1833 but the foremost symbol of the greatest horror a southern white could imagine—slave revolt. Try as they might, southerners could not

RAFFLE

Mr. Joseph Jennings respectfully informs his friends and the public that, at the request of many acquaintances, he has been induced to purchase from Mr. Osborne, of Missouri, the celebrated

DARK BAY HORSE, "STAR,"

Aged five years, square trotter and warranted sound; with a new light Trotting Buggy and Harness; also the dark, stout

MULATTO GIRL, "SARAH,"

Aged about twenty years, general house servant, valued at nine hundred dollars, and guaranteed, and

Will be Raffled for

At 4 o'clock P. M., February first, at the selection hotel of the subscribers. The above is as represented, and those persons who may wish to engage in the usual practice of raffling, will, I assure them, be perfectly satisfied with their destiny in this affair.

The whole is valued at its just worth, fifteen hundred dollars; fifteen hundred

CHANCES AT ONE DOLLAR EACH.

The Raffle will be conducted by gentlemen selected by the interested subscribers present. Five nights will be allowed to complete the Raffle. BOTH OF THE ABOVE DESCRIBED CAN BE SEEN AT MY STORE, No. 78 Common St., second door from Camp, at from 9 o'clock A. M. to 2 P. M.

Highest throw to take the first choice; the lowest throw the remaining prize, and the fortunate winners will pay twenty dollars each for the refreshments furnished on the occasion.

N. B. No chances recognized unless paid for previous to the commencement.

JOSEPH JENNINGS.

Slavery was essentially a form of livestock business, with institutions comparable to those associated with the management of cattle or horses. There were auctions (top), in which the merchandise was freely examined and sold to the top bidder. An advertisement for such an event (left) underscores the close association among white southerners of horses and slaves. Both kinds of livestock occasionally ran away, but the human fugitives proved much harder to catch.

deny the possibility of black insurrection. Slaves, after all, were not like other livestock. They could think, plan, organize, kill, rape, and plunder. And the slave system was not the benign, paternalistic welfare institution its apologists maintained. Behind the façade of moonlight, magnolias, and happy darkies singing for a beloved Old Master were force and fear. To understand the white viewpoint, it is necessary only to note that in many parts of the South, blacks outnumbered whites. Indeed, in the tidewater region where Douglass lived and in the Mississippi Valley, the ratio rose to as much as nine to one. If the blacks in these areas had rebelled, they could easily have crushed the white establishment. Whites knew this far better than blacks, and they exerted every effort to keep the South under tight control. American slavery was as much a means of social control as it was a method of economic exploitation. Any sign of slave resistance, especially organized group resistance, met with hysterical repression.

The pattern became clear as early as 1739, when one Cato led a group of South Carolina slaves on a rampage of killing and destruction. Reacting immediately, the white community crushed the revolt and slaughtered every black even remotely associated with the disturbance. In the 1790s, a full-scale racial war swept over the island of Hispaniola in the Caribbean. The leader of the blacks, Toussant L'Overture, eventually established political control. Frightened American slave owners took pains to keep news of the conflict out of southern newspapers and even out of southern conversation for fear of inspiring local blacks. But the American tradition of slave rebellion was extended by Gabriel's Revolt in 1801, the Denmark Vesey Conspiracy in 1822, and particularly by the Nat Turner Insurrection of 1831. It was the last that touched the life of Frederick Douglass.

Turner was a slave in Virginia. He knew how to read, studied the Bible, and found in it a justification for slaves turning against tyrannical masters. Turner was also a preacher with a considerable following in the black community of his region. In August 1831 he struck. A force of slaves descended on a series of plantations, knives in hand. In a short while, fifty-seven whites, mostly women and children, lay dead. Turner hoped his example would provoke a general slave revolt, but the whites retaliated with a crushing show of force. Two warships and three companies from Fort Monroe, Virginia, were sent to the town of Norfolk to quell the uprising. By the time this unit arrived, however, the rebellion was largely over. White vigilantes had organized to rout the slave army and, in retaliation, had killed more than a hundred blacks. Slaves who even looked suspicious were shot or hanged, and all that remained for the Army to do was to arrest any insurrectionists who survived. Turner was among twenty slaves who were captured and hanged. Throughout the South, terrified slave owners searched for the slightest indication of insubordination and met it with whips, guns, and rigid codes defining acceptable behavior. Nat Turner brought the fear latent in the slave system into the open.

The Turner revolt coincided with and contributed to a gradual hardening of southern attitudes toward slavery. To be sure, the "positive good" argument had been well established in 1820 at the time of the Missouri Compromise. But up to the 1830s, many southern whites were at least willing to weigh the advantages and liabilities of the system and to contemplate its eventual elimination. Indeed, before 1830 the American emancipation movement had centered in the South. Of 130 early antislavery societies in the country, 100 were southern. But after Nat Turner, southern criticism of slavery gradually stilled. Like Thomas Jefferson, many southern whites reached the conclusion that slavery might not be desirable but it was necessary. Others went still further, defending slavery as a positive good.

Economics, particularly the cotton boom, figured in this shift of attitude. So did the multifaceted proslavery argument that drew on sources as diverse as Scripture and physiology. Slaves, it was argued, had the minds of children and needed the protective guidance of masters. The upshot was the collapse of the colonization movement and with it the hope of sending freed slaves back to Africa or to the Caribbean. This collapse, in turn, killed southern emancipationism, the whole point of which had been to get blacks out of the South. Also influential in the closing of the southern mind regarding slavery was the marked increase in northern criticism of the institution. Self-criticism, they discovered, was one thing; outside denunciation of their system was something quite different and quite intolerable. Furiously, southerners pointed out that William Lloyd Garrison had begun publication of his rabidly antislavery newspaper *The Liberator* a few months before the Nat Turner Insurrection. The effect of such external criticism was to silence the internal kind. By the time Frederick Douglass was a teenager, slavery was untouchable, a topic on which objective discussion was impossible in the South. The need to keep a feared race permanently subordinated transcended all other considerations.

With the specter of Nat Turner seared into the southern mind, the emergence of Frederick Douglass as a literate, outspoken black with a taste for religion and a talent for leadership aroused instant suspicion. The consequence was a term at Edward Covey's slave-breaking establishment. But in this instance it was Covey who broke, and Douglass left his farm determined to be free. His first attempt to run away proved a dismal and almost disastrous failure, however. In 1836 Douglass and five fellow slaves laid plans to escape to the North by boat up the Chesapeake Bay. But one of the blacks disclosed the plans to his master. Douglass landed in jail with every expectation of being sold "down the river" to the cotton plantations of the Deep South. But almost miraculously, he received a reprieve from the Aulds, who recognized that slavery would be considerably safer without men of Douglass's spirit and intelligence. Thomas Auld arranged for Douglass to return to Baltimore and accumulate money as a hired-out laborer. He would be set free, Auld promised, at the age of twenty-five.

In Baltimore again, Douglass's life became entangled in the relationships of southern whites. The central fact here was that although slaveholders comprised a very small percentage (about 10 percent) of all white southerners, these same slaveholders were an elite that dominated the power structure of the region. They maintained their favored position only by resisting the challenge of the nonslaveholders. Sometimes the clash was direct, as in Virginia, where, in early 1832, the legislature debated a resolution abolishing slavery in that state. The tidewater planters lined up solidly against the proposal, but the nonslaveholding up-country farmers were just as solidly for it. The latter believed, with good reason, that their opportunities would be increased by the elimination of the slaveholding oligarchy.

The Virginia vote was surprisingly close, seventy-three to fifty-eight, and slave owners throughout the South took steps to protect their status. One step involved convincing the nonslaveholders that the perpetuation of slavery served their interests, too. The technique was to argue, according to Douglass, that "slavery was the only power that could prevent the laboring white man from falling to the level of the slave's poverty and degradation." In other words, without slavery, there would be several million blacks competing with whites for jobs and for status in the South. With slavery, even the lowliest southern whites had a social cushion securely beneath them. The planters also made it clear that if a black insurrection came, it would engulf all whites, not just slaveholders. The southern way of life was at stake, alleged the slaveholders, and they represented themselves as its champions and defenders. These arguments proved effective. By 1836 in Baltimore, the hatred of nonslaveholding whites for blacks, both slave and free, had been honed to a fine edge. When Douglass returned to work in the city's shipyards, he was met by a team of white workers, who beat him unmercifully as fifty of their fellows cheered.

The experience in the shipyards discouraged Douglass about the chances of earning freedom in the South, and once again his thoughts turned to escape. In addition, he had met a free black woman, Anna Murray, whom he wished to marry as a free man. On September 3, 1838, Douglass made his move. From a free black sailor of his acquaintance he borrowed a suit of clothes and a set of "protection," or "free," papers. Thus equipped, he boarded a train for Philadelphia and New York. In the course of the trip he encountered several white men whom he knew, but he remained unrecognized. His closest call came just south of the Mason-Dixon line, separating Maryland from Pennsylvania and slavery from freedom. In making a routine check, a conductor asked Douglass for his free papers. Comparison of the description of the rightful owner with Douglass's appearance would have revealed the subterfuge immediately, but the conductor only glanced at the papers, nodded, and moved on up the car. Frederick Douglass was a free man.

The North into which Frederick Douglass immigrated in 1838 was already fully aware of, and uneasy about, the South he had left. The tension generated by the Missouri crisis eighteen years earlier still lingered. Indeed, the intervening years had sharpened sectional consciousness. The election of 1824 found no fewer than five candidates, each with strong sectional ties, in the running. John C. Calhoun and William H. Crawford represented the South in their distrust of strong central government, high protective tariffs, and manufacturing. Henry Clay and Andrew Jackson drew the largest part of their support from the West and the more commercial Middle Atlantic states. The Northeast backed John Quincy Adams, who ultimately won the election after a widely criticized bargain that made Clay secretary of state.

During Adams's administration, the tariff continued to be a focus of sectional dispute. An analysis of congressional votes shows the South solidly against high tariffs, the Middle Atlantic states just as solidly for them, and New England mixed but shifting toward a pro-tariff stand as its stake in manufacturing increased. The climax came in 1828, when Congress enacted the highest tariff yet in American history. Southerners immediately branded it the "Tariff of Abominations." Led by Vice President Calhoun of South Carolina, they argued that the levy on foreign goods was, in effect, a tax on southern planters for the benefit of northern manufacturers. A high tariff had the effect of raising the price of the foreign goods southerners consumed. Many also believed that, by reducing the income of European textile manufacturers, the tariff prevented their buying more southern cotton. Moreover, the South saw Congress's power over the tariff as a bad omen for the future of other southern interests, particularly slavery. The extent of the South's displeasure became clear in Calhoun's 1828 essay "The South Carolina Exposition and Protest." In it he argued that a state that judged the federal government to have exceeded the powers granted under the Constitution of 1787 might nullify a federal act. This was the ultimate in states' rights, a political posture that became increasingly important to the South as its consciousness of its minority status in the nation increased.

The first chance to test the doctrine of nullification came in 1832, when Congress passed a new tariff bill that was unacceptable to the South. Led by Calhoun and Senator Robert Y. Hayne, famous for his debates with Daniel Webster over the nature of the federal union, the South Carolina legislature nullified the law, and Calhoun resigned as vice president. In a rage, President Andrew Jackson threatened to hang Calhoun and his supporters, dispatched a fleet of warships to

Charleston, and declared it his intention to lead an overland force against the rebels. For a few anxious months at the beginning of 1833, the fate of the union hung in the balance. But South Carolina's position was weakened by the fact that no other southern state came to its support, and on March 15 the legislature accepted a compromise engineered by Henry Clay. Fortunately, the tariff was an issue susceptible to compromise; one could easily find the middle ground between a duty of 50 percent and one of 30 percent. But there were other issues coming to the fore on which such compromises were impossible. As Frederick Douglass knew so well, human beings were either slave or free.

The exhilaration Frederick Douglass initially experienced on reaching New York quickly gave way to frustration and despair. In terms of the position of blacks, he found the city in many ways an extension of the South. Slave catchers, eager to return runaways to their masters, were everywhere. No one could be trusted. For a few dollars some blacks would even betray others. Moreover, the country was in the throes of a financial depression following the Panic of 1837, and jobs were scarce. For blacks it was worse. Just as in Baltimore, white laborers made sure that black ones were the last to be hired and the first to be fired. Douglass walked the streets for a few days until his money ran out. Then, in desperation, he turned to David Ruggles, a local black leader. Ruggles sheltered Douglass and arranged for his marriage to Anna Murray, who had arrived from Maryland. He also advised the newlyweds to leave New York for a safer location farther north.

Following Ruggles's suggestion, the Douglasses pushed on to New Bedford, Massachusetts. In this maritime center, the capital of the American whaling industry, Douglass hoped to find a chance to exercise his trade as a skilled caulker of ships. But on applying for a job, he learned that all the white workers in the yards would quit if a black one were hired. Douglass had to eke out a living sawing wood, shoveling coal, and sweeping chimneys. Anna served as a domestic when she was not caring for their two babies. Besides the economic struggle, there were other disturbing facts of northern life. Most of the churches refused to accept blacks as members of the congregation. Public transportation was also segregated. Douglass learned that even if he purchased a first-class train ticket, he was obliged to sit in the uncomfortable segregated car, reserved for blacks only. He concluded that northern society, lacking slavery, had been adept at finding alternative means to express its prejudice.

Still, there were reasons to take heart. A passion for reform flourished in the North at the time Douglass arrived. "In the history of the world," Ralph Waldo Emerson wrote in 1841, "the doctrine of Reform had never such scope as at the present hour." What Emerson had in mind was a series of interrelated ideas centered on the possibility of human betterment. The reformer of the 1830s and 1840s believed that every person was basically good. Strip away handicaps such as ignorance or lack of opportunity, and the innate goodness would shine through. No one was hopeless, no one beyond help. Each individual contained what Emerson and his fellow transcendentalists termed a "spark of divinity." It followed that the poor, the drunk, the insane, and the black were all susceptible to improvement—perhaps, the most enthusiastic reformers believed, even to perfection. Reform philosophy exuded a confidence stemming at once from the Enlightenment, romanticism, and the American sense of mission. As a celebration of individual potential, it was entirely consistent with American circumstances and ideals.

The abolition of slavery had a place of special importance in the galaxy of American reform crusades. In the abolitionist mind, both the slaveholder and the slave were ripe for improvement. Slavery, they believed, was a sin. Moreover, it was a blot on the American record of championing individual rights and freedoms, an embarrassing anomaly in a nation dedicated to liberty. By denying people control over their own destiny, slavery went against the grain of the entire New World experience.

Abolitionism as an organized reform movement had begun among the Quakers in the eighteenth century. At the time of the American Revolution, they did not hesitate to point out the contradictions between slavery and the ideals motivating American independence. There was some response: Most northern states declared slavery illegal before 1800. Some went further and agitated for national emancipation. Pennsylvania's antislavery society had Benjamin Franklin as its president in 1787. In the South, however, abolitionism was considerably less successful. Even blacks did not support it because of the plan for colonizing freed slaves in Africa that was invariably a part of southern abolition. Douglass, for instance, declared, "We are American citizens, born with natural, inherent and just rights; and . . . the . . . intolerable scheme of the American Colonization Society shall never entice or drive us away from our native soil." The more radical white reformers, believing that colonization was a poor substitute for full freedom for all in the United States, shared this opinion.

The debate over colonization came to a head in Baltimore at the very time Frederick Douglass was enslaved there. He did not know it, but Benjamin Lundy, a New Jersey Quaker, edited an antislavery newspaper entitled *The Genius of Universal Emancipation* in that city. Lundy believed in the gradual, compensated emancipation of slaves and their subsequent colonization in Africa. His coeditor disagreed violently, however. Indeed, violent disagreement was characteristic of William Lloyd Garrison. In sharp contrast to Lundy, he defended immediate, total, and uncompensated abolition; he rejected colonization; and he denounced the U.S. Constitution, which he regarded as proslavery, as "a covenant with death and an agreement with hell." Aggressive to the point of belligerence, convinced he was morally right, and driven by an obsession with becoming famous, Garrison broke with Lundy and went north to enter the abolition business on his own.

In 1831 Garrison launched a weekly antislavery newspaper, *The Liberator,* in Boston. Totally committed, he gave no quarter and asked none. "I will," he thundered in the first issue, "be as harsh as truth, and as uncompromising as justice. On this subject, I do not wish to think, or speak, or write with moderation. . . . I am in earnest—I will not equivocate—I will not excuse—I will not retreat a single inch—AND I WILL BE HEARD." Shortly after starting the newspaper, Garrison organized the New England Antislavery Society. Its agents fanned out and organized enthusiastically. They drew encouragement from the news that in 1833 the British abolition movement had borne fruit, with the emancipation of slaves in the British West Indies. By the time Douglass came to New England in 1838, about 2,000 local societies, with a membership of nearly 200,000, existed in the North.

Garrison and Wendell Phillips dominated the movement in New England, Gerritt Smith and the wealthy Tappan family in New York, and Theodore Dwight Weld in the Ohio Valley. Yet abolitionism was not universally popular in the North. Quite probably, a majority of northerners saw Garrison and his colleagues as irresponsible fanatics—revolutionaries who would tear the fabric of American political, social, and economic life in their intemperate zeal to end slavery. In 1835 Garrison was mobbed and beaten by his critics. He escaped lightly, however, compared with Elijah Lovejoy, who was killed in an encounter in Illinois two years later.

Frederick Douglass's first contact with abolitionism occurred early in 1839, a few months after his escape, when a copy of *The Liberator* fell into his hands. He had not known about Garrison before, but the position of the newspaper moved him so deeply that despite his poverty, he became a regular subscriber. "The paper became my meat and drink," Douglass later wrote. "Its sympathy for my brethren in bonds—its scathing denunciations of slaveholders . . . sent a thrill of joy through my soul." Douglass also joined the local abolition society in New Bedford and, in his words, "took right hold of the cause." By March 1839 he was addressing meetings of New Bedford blacks on the disadvantages of colonization. He also used these occasions to commend Garrison as a man "deserving of our support and confidence."

The first meeting between Douglass and Garrison occurred on August 9, 1841, when the abolitionist leader came to speak in New Bedford. "No face or form," Douglass acknowledged, "ever impressed me with such sentiments." Two days later the men were again together at an antislavery convention on the island of Nantucket. Friends persuaded Douglass to address the gathering, and at last he came forward—hesitant, embarrassed, and so nervous he could hardly stand. As Garrison remembered, Douglass's first words were apologetic. "Slavery," he said, "was a poor school for the human intellect." Then, drawing himself up to his full height of over six feet, he began to narrate his experiences as a slave. The audience was transfixed by the simple presentation. At its conclusion, Garrison himself arose to declare that "Patrick Henry . . . never made a speech more eloquent in the cause of liberty, than the one we . . . just listened to from the lips of a hunted fugitive." Capitalizing on the drama of the situation, Garrison next asked the assembly, "Have we been listening to a thing, a piece of property, or to a man?" A thousand voices responded, "A man! A man!" Would the audience allow Douglass to be taken back into slavery? "No!" came the roaring response.

Douglass spoke again at the evening session of the convention. By this time, Garrison and the other officers of the Massachusetts Antislavery Society were convinced that the young black with the deep voice might be one of the most potent weapons in their arsenal of persuasion. They offered Douglass a job as a lecturer on the antislavery circuit, at a salary of $450 a year. But the astonished Douglass accepted only a three-month appointment, convinced that he would be of limited value. As it turned out, he greatly underrated himself. The opportunity opened at Nantucket launched Frederick Douglass on a lifelong career as a liberator of his people.

The life of an antislavery lecturer, particularly a black one, was hardly dull. Many of the audiences Douglass faced were openly hostile and came armed with eggs and rotten vegetables. In 1843 Douglass and his colleagues were occasionally run off the stage and even beaten. It was during this sustained tour that people began to doubt Douglass's assertion that he was really an escaped slave. Sensing this reaction, his fellow abolitionists tried to persuade him to use more of the speech and mannerisms of the plantation. Douglass, they bluntly declared, was supposed to be an exhibit to accompany the presentations of the white speakers. But Douglass refused to hide his talents. In answer, he wrote his autobiographical *Narrative of the Life of Frederick Douglass: An American Slave.* Wendell Phillips advised him to burn the manuscript, since it could well lead to his capture and return to slavery. Douglass published his book in 1845, however, and watched with pleasure as sales quickly mounted to 30,000 copies. He did heed Phillips's advice to the extent of seeking temporary sanctuary in England, where for two years he enjoyed a huge success as a lecturer on a variety of reform subjects. Douglass returned to his family and country in 1847 with enough money to purchase his freedom. This was duly accomplished with the transmission of $710.96 to the Auld family in Baltimore. For the first time in almost a decade, Douglass emerged from the shadow of reenslavement.

Ambitious and determined after his sojourn abroad, Douglass decided to set his own course within the abolition movement. Late in 1847, he moved to Rochester, New York, and began publication of his own newspaper, *The North Star*. Many white abolitionists objected, but Douglass defended his venture as providing evidence of blacks' capability. Only by such independent participation in American life could blacks foster a sense of pride and self-reliance. His goal, he made clear, was not just freeing slaves but permitting a life of dignity for all black people throughout the nation. The newspaper, and plans for the education of free blacks that Douglass sponsored, contributed to this end. *The North Star* also aided Douglass in formulating and expressing his own reform philosophy.

For a decade, he was a Garrisonian. By the late 1840s, however, he had developed doubts about Garrison's rejection of political action as an abolitionist weapon. Garrison burned the Constitution, but in Douglass's opinion that document could be construed as a guarantee of freedom to *all* Americans, regardless of color. The problem was to allow everyone to share the liberties it defined. For this reason, Douglass felt, political action was needed, along with moral persuasion. Garrison stood on the principle of "no union with slaveholders." Douglass felt that southern institutions could be changed through the political process by pressure from the majority of Americans. It was essential, therefore, to extend the vote to all adults.

When Douglass called for extension of the vote, he had women in mind as well as blacks. In his eyes, these two social groups occupied a similar relationship to the white male establishment. They also constituted the majority of the population. Douglass believed that there was strength in unity, and he pressed for civil rights on both fronts. In fact, *The North Star* carried on its masthead the slogan "Right is of no sex—Truth is of no color." In 1848 Douglass proved the sincerity of his belief: He was the only man to take an active part in the Seneca Falls Convention, which launched the women's rights movement in the United States.

While Frederick Douglass labored in Rochester on the broad front of reform, the course of national politics once again brought sectional competition into prominence. The catalyst of the renewed tension was westward expansion. Both North and South knew that western resources, commerce, and votes were vital to achieving national dominance. At first, the South had enjoyed a major geographical advantage. The Appalachian Mountains, slanting northeast–southwest across the eastern United States, posed a major barrier to communication and trade between the North and the West. Southerners, on the other hand, were connected to the West by the Mississippi River. Places as widely separated as western Pennsylvania and northern Wisconsin could ship their products down the Mississippi to the port of New Orleans. But in the early nineteenth century, the Mississippi was a one-way street. Rivermen took their wooden flatboats down with the current, sold them for lumber, and walked back north along trails such as the Natchez Trace. In 1811, however, the first steamboat on the Mississippi enabled goods to move upstream. Commerce between West and South was possible, and political alliance seemed sure to follow.

The South's early success in the competition for the western trade and vote stirred the North to action. In 1825 New York completed the Erie Canal between Albany on the Hudson River and Buffalo on Lake Erie. This easy route west facilitated communication with the whole Great Lakes watershed. Moreover, the Erie Canal led to an excellent market and manufacturing center: New York City. New Orleans lacked these characteristics. In addition, the South and the West, both producers of raw materials, were not economically compatible. This became increasingly apparent after the opening of the Erie Canal. In 1838, the year Douglass came north, receipts at Buffalo exceeded those at New Orleans for the first time. It was a bad omen for the South. By this time, too, Pennsylvania's Main Line of canals and roads from Philadelphia to Pittsburgh was open for business. But the outcome of the North–South struggle for the West awaited the trans-Appalachian railroads in the 1850s. The systems developed by the New York Central, the Pennsylvania, and the Baltimore and Ohio railroads made it impractical to use the Mississippi except for passenger traffic and local trade. A revolution in technology and transportation left the South economically and politically isolated.

Nervous about this situation, southerners reacted angrily in 1846, when David Wilmot of Pennsylvania rose in the House of Representatives to propose that slavery be prohibited in any part of the territory to be acquired from the Mexican War. President James Polk attempted to soothe the South by suggesting that the land in question was unsuited to slavery for reasons of climate and soil. Cotton, tobacco, and slavery, he argued, had reached the natural limits of their expansion. Southerners were not so sure. In the first place, slave owners saw no reason why slaves could not be used for tasks other than picking cotton. Black bondspeople like Frederick Douglass had long worked effectively in cities, and their potential as miners, lumberjacks, and ranchers in the West was apparent. It was conceivable, John C. Calhoun argued, that slavery could become the normal institution for managing all labor in the United States. Furthermore, there was the question of property rights. Calhoun again led the way, a year after Wilmot's suggestion, in arguing that Congress had no authority to limit slavery and thus deprive citizens of their right to move where they pleased and take with them their property, slaves included. In effect, Calhoun was saying that the Missouri Compromise of 1820 (which prohibited slaves north of 36°30′) was unconstitutional.

The issue of slavery expansion became pressing in 1849, when California applied for admission to the union as a free (nonslave) state. The South objected strenuously and threatened secession. For a few anxious months at the beginning of 1850, the Union teetered on the brink of dissolution. But Henry Clay, Daniel Webster, and Stephen A. Douglas engineered a compromise in the Senate. As signed by President Millard Fillmore in September 1850, the series of acts admitted California as a free state, organized the remaining territory acquired from Mexico without restrictions on slavery, abolished the slave trade (but not slavery) in the District of Columbia, and strengthened the procedure for returning fugitive slaves to their masters.

For Frederick Douglass, the most important part of the Compromise of 1850 was the Fugitive Slave Law. Deliberately favorable to the slave owner, the measure was intended as a sweetener for an otherwise pro-North compromise. It was aimed at stopping the operation of the Underground Railroad. This shadowy volunteer organization assisted blacks fleeing slavery by passing them from hand to friendly hand until they were safe. In 1838 Frederick Douglass had received help of this kind in New York City from David Ruggles. Not really a railroad, the enterprise supposedly received its name from the complaint of a frustrated slave owner whose failure to trace his fugitives prompted him to remark that once in the free states, slaves vanished as if they had boarded a subterranean train. But the hunters often captured their quarry, and there were countless narrow escapes. A "conductor" on the Underground Railroad might awaken in the middle of the night to find a frightened fugitive in his or her yard and the owner's forces in hot pursuit. The "conductor" then had to hide the slave in an attic or secret stairwell. The following night the slave might be buried under a wagonload of hay and carried to the next "station."

In southern minds, such assistance to fugitive slaves was outright stealing—a violation of the natural law respecting the sanctity of property. The Fugitive Slave Law of 1850 reflected this viewpoint. Recapturing escaped slaves became a national rather than a state process. This policy bypassed the personal liberty laws with which many northern states had blocked the operation of earlier fugitive slave legislation. The new measure created commissioners who could issue warrants for the arrest of fugitives and who also served as judges in cases involving runaways.

LIBERTY LINE.

NEW ARRANGEMENT---NIGHT AND DAY.

The improved and splendid Locomotives, Clarkson and Lundy, with their trains fitted up in the best style of accommodation for passengers, will run their regular trips during the present season, between the borders of the Patriarchal Dominion and Libertyville, Upper Canada. Gentlemen and Ladies, who may wish to improve their health or circumstances, by a northern tour, are respectfully invited to give us their patronage.

SEATS FREE, *irrespective of color.*

Necessary Clothing furnished gratuitously to such as have "*fallen among thieves.*"

" Hide the outcasts—let the oppressed go free."—*Bible.*

☞For seats apply at any of the trap doors, or to the conductor of the train.

J. CROSS, *Proprietor.*

N. B. For the special benefit of Pro-Slavery Police Officers, an extra heavy wagon for Texas, will be furnished, whenever it may be necessary, in which they will be forwarded as dead freight, to the " Valley of Rascals," always at the risk of the owners.

☞Extra Overcoats provided for such of them as are afflicted with protracted *chilly-phobia.*

Despite newspaper notices and rewards, many escaped servants were never recovered. One reason was the existence of the Underground Railroad. This was actually a loose organization of northerners, both black and white, who assisted fugitives in their flight to freedom.

But there was no jury, and the testimony of blacks was not admitted as evidence. Finally, the Fugitive Slave Law provided that any white who aided fugitives (even by looking the other way as they passed by) was subject to fine and imprisonment and would be forced to reimburse the slave owner for the full value of the lost property.

Attitudes toward the Fugitive Slave Law differed sharply. Southerners and northern moderates regarded its operation as vital to the effectiveness of the Compromise of 1850 and consequently to the existence of peace and union. Extremists spoke openly of secession if the law was not obeyed. "Before God and man," a Raleigh, North Carolina, editorial warned, " . . . if you fail in this simple act of justice, THE BONDS WILL BE DISSOLVED." In antislavery circles, on the other hand, opposition to the law was equally intense. "This filthy enactment," declared the normally mild-mannered Ralph Waldo Emerson, "was made in the nineteenth century, by people who could read and write. I will not obey it, by God!" Frederick Douglass was quick to point out the effect of "this atrocious and shameless law" on free blacks: It subjected them to kidnapping. "The oaths of any two villains," Douglass observed, "were sufficient to consign a free man to slavery for life." Indeed, for several weeks following the passage of the Fugitive Slave Law, Douglass feared for his own safety. Friends posted guard around his house in Rochester. There was no trouble, but nearer to the South, a virtual border war ensued.

This tense atmosphere formed the backdrop for the most spectacular of the fugitive slave cases to occur after the Compromise of 1850. On September 11, 1851, a Maryland planter named Edward Gorsuch came to the tiny hamlet of Christiana in southern Pennsylvania, where, he had heard, several of his fugitive slaves were harbored. The runaways were indeed there, but so were a group of blacks and some white sympathizers determined to prevent their recapture. The inevitable confrontation came at the house of William Parker, the black leader. As the slaves cowered upstairs, Parker met Gorsuch at the door. "My property is in this house. I've come for it," the slave owner declared. Indignantly, Parker suggested that Gorsuch "go in the room . . . and see if there is anything there belonging to you. There are beds and a bureau, chairs and other things. Then go out to the barn; there you will find a cow and some hogs. See if any of them are yours." It was a case of right versus right; neither side would compromise principles that each considered sacred.

At last a mob of blacks charged Gorsuch, knocking him down. When he struggled to his feet, he received a shot in the chest and slumped in the dust—dead. Never before had an owner been a victim in the fugitive slave business, and Parker and his colleagues were suddenly struck by the sure consequences of their action. Before nightfall on September 11, they were en route to Canada via Frederick Douglass's house in Rochester. Douglass received the men warmly. "I could not look upon them as murderers," he wrote. "To me, they were heroic defenders of the just rights of man against manstealers and murderers." Acting swiftly before news of the Christiana Riot reached Rochester, Douglass hurried the blacks onto a steamboat bound for Toronto. Not until the gangplank had lifted did he return home, carrying as a memento from Parker the pistol of Edward Gorsuch.

Although such resistance to the Fugitive Slave Law delighted Douglass, it caused despair among moderates in the North and the South alike. They had hoped, desperately, that the Compromise of 1850 would be a final settlement of the sectional differences. But it seemed that the old belligerence had not died. Indeed, sectional polarization continued with renewed vigor in the 1850s. Indicative was the reception accorded *Uncle Tom's Cabin,* which appeared in 1852. A searing indictment of the slave system by Harriet Beecher Stowe of Andover, Massachusetts, the novel sold more than one million copies the first year. Stowe's novel told the story of the harsh treatment of a slave family at the hands of a vicious overseer, and it included daring escape and tragic death. Southerners attacked *Uncle Tom's Cabin* as a gross distortion—the product of an oversentimental woman who had no firsthand knowledge of her subject. Many in the North, however, were deeply moved. Frederick Douglass, whose own life testified to the truth of much of what Stowe had written, called her account "a work of marvelous depth and power."

After *Uncle Tom's Cabin,* opinion on both sides of the Mason-Dixon line hardened rapidly. Americans were increasingly less willing to discuss their differences and more inclined to fight to uphold their respective conceptions of "right." Once again, the question of westward expansion brought the competing moralities into direct confrontation. This time the issue was over the status of slavery in the unorganized territory beyond Missouri. Stephen A. Douglas, a dynamic senator from Illinois, triggered the controversy in January 1854, when he introduced a bill that made the fate of slavery in the territories of Kansas and Nebraska subject to local self-determination. Douglas's formula, known as *popular sovereignty* or *squatter sovereignty,* provided that the majority of residents of a territory, acting through their legislature, could vote slavery in or out before statehood. The Kansas-Nebraska Act, then, repealed the Missouri Compromise and its idea of a demarcation line between slavery and free soil. It made slavery at least a possibility in every part of the unorganized West. Frederick Douglass called Stephen A. Douglas's plan "perfidious," and many in the North agreed. As Horace Greeley put it, Douglas and President Franklin Pierce had "made more abolitionists in a month than Garrison and Phillips had made in a lifetime."

In Kansas itself, the result of popular sovereignty was civil war. Proslavery and antislavery partisans surged into previously uninhabited Kansas, each side set on becoming the determining majority. For two years they fought with ballots, but in 1856 they began to use bullets. Raiding parties from the slave state of Missouri attacked free-soil communities in Kansas. The free-soilers retaliated with "Beecher's Bibles," rifles collected by New England abolitionists at the suggestion of the Reverend Henry Ward Beecher, the brother of Harriet Beecher Stowe.

At this point, the enigmatic figure of John Brown strode onto the Kansas prairie. Frederick Douglass had met him a decade earlier and had been immensely impressed. "He was lean, strong, and sinewy," Douglass wrote, "of the best New England mould, built for times of trouble, fitted to grapple with the flintiest hardships." Brown hated slavery with the intensity of a fanatic. He told Douglass that the end of slavery justified any means. What Brown meant became apparent in Kansas. In May 1856, in the company of his sons (he had twenty children, though ten died in their infancy) and a few friends, Brown swooped down on the proslave settlements along Pottawatomie Creek. Arousing five settlers from their sleep, Brown proceeded to run them through with a sword in the name of the Lord. Afterward, he mutilated the corpses. Even Douglass called the act "a terrible remedy."

The shock waves emanating from "bleeding" Kansas were felt throughout the nation. Emotion took over, and both factions turned away from democracy in efforts to press their claims. Douglass noted "the display of pistols, bludgeons, and plantation manners in the Congress of the nation." In May 1856 Congressman Preston Brooks of South Carolina entered the Senate chamber and beat Massachusetts Senator Charles Sumner unconscious with a cane. Clearly, the cohesive forces holding the union together were weakening. The process was both reflected in and encouraged by the realignment of national politics. The Whigs succumbed to the slavery issue, and the Democrats split over it. In 1854 a new political coalition based on the principle of resistance to the expansion of slavery entered the lists under the name of the Republican party. By 1856, when Republican presidential nominee John Fremont ran a strong second to Democrat James Buchanan, it was evident that Republicans and northerners were increasingly one and the same. Slavery expansion had come to symbolize sectional economic and political dominance. But in the final analysis, it was the moral dimension of the issue that split the nation. As a rising Republican politician named Abraham Lincoln expressed it in a letter to a Georgian, "You think slavery is right and ought to be extended, while we think it is wrong and ought to be restricted. That I suppose is the rub."

The most disturbing event of the 1850s for Frederick Douglass was the Dred Scott decision of 1857. Scott was a slave whose master had taken him into the free-soil state of Illinois. Anxious to construct a test case, Scott and his supporters sued for his freedom. When the case reached the U.S. Supreme Court, the justices decided to press the case to its ultimate implications for slavery in the United States. By a vote of six to three, the Court sided with Chief Justice Roger Taney of Maryland in holding that as a slave, Scott was property and must remain so no matter where his master decided to live. In effect, this meant that Congress could not close a territory to slavery. The Missouri Compromise, already repealed by the Kansas-Nebraska Act, was now declared unconstitutional. The Taney Court went on to declare that slaves were not entitled to federal citizenship. Moreover, even free blacks—with the exception of those descended from people who had been citizens before 1787—lacked the rights of citizenship.

Taney's majority opinion maintained that Americans had always regarded blacks as "being of an inferior order," with "no rights which any white man was bound to respect." Frederick Douglass, who was barred from citizenship under the Dred Scott decision, was astounded. Taney had cut the bottom out of his campaign to win constitutional rights for blacks. On second thought, Douglass realized that the Supreme Court was "not the only power in the world. It is very great, but the Supreme Court of the Almighty is greater. Judge Taney . . . cannot change the essential nature of things—making evil good, and good, evil." Believing that the majority of Americans agreed with him rather than with Taney, Douglass took heart that the Dred Scott verdict might backfire by its very severity. He also knew that, after the Taney decision, "the portentous shadow of a stupendous civil war became more visible."

In 1858 the trails of John Brown and Frederick Douglass crossed again. With his work in Kansas completed (Kansans rejected the proslavery Lecompton Constitution in 1858), Brown came east bent on new assaults against slavery. For several weeks he lived under Douglass's roof in Rochester, and the men discussed Brown's plan for attracting fugitive slaves to forts in the mountains of Virginia and Maryland. Overlooking Brown's record of dishonesty and crime and a long history of insanity in his family, Douglass approved the idea. But when Brown abandoned guerrilla tactics in favor of capturing the federal arsenal at Harper's Ferry, Virginia, and starting a general slave insurrection, Douglass objected. The plan, he felt, was suicide. Undaunted, Brown persisted. On October 16, 1859, he and twenty-two others struck at Harper's Ferry and succeeded in capturing the arsenal. But as Douglass predicted, state and federal forces quickly hemmed in Brown and his men. John Brown's Raid ended October 17, when a force under U.S. Army Lieutenant-Colonel Robert E. Lee stormed the arsenal. Brown was captured, tried for treason, convicted, and sentenced to death by hanging (see pages 235–236). Northern pleas for leniency were rejected by a terrified and outraged South, which saw in the raid a threat to the whole fabric of southern life. According to Virginia's governor, the slave insurrection Brown desired struck at "life, law, property, and civil liberty itself." Such things were sacred. Those who challenged them deserved to die.

In antislavery circles, on the contrary, John Brown became a hero and a martyr. Many northerners thrilled to his last speech, in which he termed his raid "not wrong, but right" and welcomed the opportunity of mingling his blood with that shed by millions of slaves. Soon after his execution, a song appeared to commemorate the event. The second verse of "John Brown's Body" suggested that many in the North associated their cause with God's: "He's gone to be a soldier in the army of the Lord! His soul is marching on." Ralph Waldo Emerson simply said that Brown's gallows had become a cross. Douglass called Brown a "noble old hero" and made no apologies for his violence against slaveholders, who "voluntarily placed themselves beyond the laws of justice and honor." He had not joined the raiders, he explained, only because he disagreed with their means.

Just before John Brown's execution, the governor of Virginia summed up the cause for the furor and, incidentally, for the Civil War, in seven words. In speaking of the impossibility of pardoning Brown and of the radical divergence of opinion respecting him, the governor declared, "There is no middle ground of mitigation." The absence of such a middle ground greatly increased the probability of war. In other words, the nation had lost the consensus on fundamental definitions and values that holds a society together.

Soon after the capture of John Brown, Douglass learned that despite his disavowal of the raid, he had been implicated. Knowing he could expect no sympathy from the Buchanan administration, Douglass hurriedly packed and, once more a fugitive, left for Canada and later for England. On returning in the summer of 1860, he found a tense presidential campaign under way. The Democrats had convened in April in Charleston, South Carolina, but their party was fatally torn. Stephen A. Douglas had the support of northern Democrats, with his popular sovereignty formula for settling disputes over slavery. Southern Democrats believed that any restriction of the institution was illegal and would be the first step toward its abolition. The climax occurred when radical southerner William L. Yancey called on the convention to endorse a plank in the party platform stating "slavery was right." The reply came from an Ohioan: "Gentlemen of the South, you mistake us—we will not do it"—whereupon Yancey led the southern faction out of the convention hall. They later nominated John C. Breckinridge of Kentucky. Meanwhile, the northern Democrats chose Stephen A. Douglas. The schism virtually ensured the election of the Republican candidate, Abraham Lincoln.

Frederick Douglass was not happy with the Republican slogan for the 1860 campaign. He wished it to read "Death to Slavery" rather than "No More Slave States." But as the election approached, Douglass gave up his efforts on behalf of Gerritt Smith, the candidate of the Radical Abolition party, and took the stump for Lincoln. Douglass termed Lincoln's victory in November, with no electoral votes and very few popular votes from the South, a "glorious assertion of freedom and independence on the part of the North." The South was also prepared to assert its independence. South Carolina led the way on December 20, 1860, when a state convention unanimously approved an ordinance proclaiming the dissolution of the union between it and the other states. Within six weeks, five other states in the Deep South had also seceded, and in February 1861 they formed a new nation: the Confederate States of America.

The lame-duck Buchanan administration struggled to repair the crumbling nation. Senator John J. Crittenden of Kentucky advanced the idea of a compromise along the lines of the old Missouri and popular sovereignty formulas. Douglass regarded these proposals as evasions, but many in both camps favored them. After all, eight slave states had not seceded. Moderate southerners pointed out that President-elect Lincoln had promised not to interfere with slavery where it already existed, even if he did oppose its extension to the territories. And in the North, there was a widespread feeling that although slavery was bad, the breakup of the union was worse. A wave of anger rose against the abolitionists. Douglass personally experienced mob action. "The talk," he observed, "was that the blood of some abolitionist must be shed to . . . restore peaceful relations between the two sections of the country."

Many Americans in the winter of 1860–1861 simply could not conceive of civil war as a serious possibility. Someone would engineer a solution short of the battlefield, they thought. But there were many in both the North and the South who nodded in agreement when Lincoln applied to the United States the biblical warning that "a house divided against itself cannot stand." "I believe," Lincoln added, "this government cannot endure permanently half slave and half free." The issue, in other words, was not the extension of slavery, but slavery itself. And slavery—or, more precisely, the ethical conflict that the system engendered—was social dynamite.

Indicative of the presence of these deeper layers of conflict was the fact that the minor matter of provisioning federally owned Fort Sumter in Charleston harbor touched off the Civil War in early April 1861. "Thank God," Douglass sighed, grateful to have the issue come to a head at last. But the initial stages of the war were disappointing. On the field of battle, the disorganized Union forces suffered a humiliating defeat in the first major encounter of the war: the Battle of Bull Run in July 1861. A little over a year later, the Second Battle of Bull Run produced a similar outcome. The North fared better in its blockade of the southern coast and in the Mississippi River theater of operations, but by 1863 the Union had not achieved military advantage in keeping with its marked superiority in numbers, wealth, and industrial capacity.

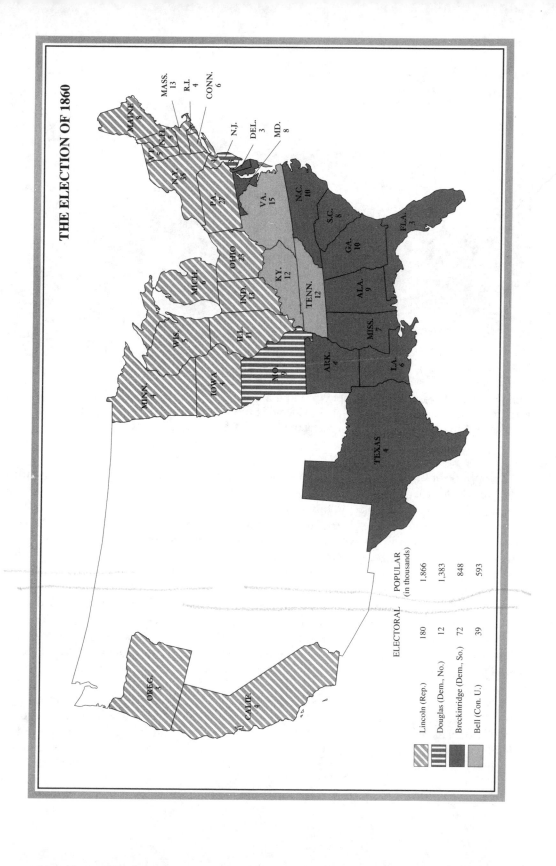

THE ELECTION OF 1860

MAINE
8

VT.
5
N.H.
5

MASS.
13
R.I.
4
CONN.
6

N.Y.
35

PA.
27

N.J.

DEL.
3

MD.
8

VA.
15

N.C.
10

OHIO
23

MICH.
6

IND.
13

KY.
12

TENN.
12

S.C.
8

GA.
10

FLA.
3

ALA.
9

WIS.
5

ILL.
11

MO.
9

ARK.
4

MISS.
7

LA.
6

MINN.
4

IOWA
4

TEXAS
4

OREG.
3

CALIF.
4

	ELECTORAL	POPULAR (in thousands)
Lincoln (Rep.)	180	1,866
Douglas (Dem., No.)	12	1,383
Breckinridge (Dem., So.)	72	848
Bell (Con. U.)	39	593

During the Civil War era, photography became a major source of historical documentation. This excellent print shows President Abraham Lincoln at the headquarters of the Army of the Potomac, October 3, 1862. Notice how the lanky Lincoln towers over his companions.

For people of Frederick Douglass's persuasion, the early stages of the Civil War were also frustrating on ideological grounds. President Lincoln steadfastly refused to define the conflict in terms of slavery. "My paramount object in this struggle," he wrote to *New York Tribune* editor Horace Greeley in 1862, "is to save the Union, and is not either to save or destroy Slavery." Douglass read these widely publicized words with a sense of profound discouragement. It was reinforced by Lincoln's initial refusal to accept black volunteers for the Union army and his revival of the old African colonization scheme. The fact was—and Douglass knew it well—that as much as Abraham Lincoln disliked slavery, he held no brief for blacks. The product of a self-made yeoman farming background, Lincoln feared the competition free blacks posed. And his prejudice ran deeper. In 1857 Lincoln had spoken of the "natural disgust" that "indiscriminate amalgamation of the white and black races" produced in the minds of "nearly all white people." A year later, he rejected the idea of political and social equality of the races on the grounds of a "physical difference." Lincoln candidly added that inasmuch as discrimination was necessary, "I am in favor of the race to which I belong having the superior position."

It was to Douglass's credit that he could overlook such expressions of prejudice in an attempt to understand and work with the president. Later, looking retrospectively at Lincoln's wartime record, Douglass remarked that in the first year of conflict, the faith of black Americans in the federal government "was taxed and strained to the uttermost." On "genuine abolition grounds," Lincoln seemed to Douglass to be "tardy, cold, dull, and indifferent." Yet measuring his conduct in terms of the sentiment of the country as a whole, Lincoln appeared "swift, zealous, radical, and determined." The president, Douglass came to see, acted as a barometer, carefully gauging and expressing the public mind. Lincoln knew that to move too quickly against slavery would be to lose support vital to the prosecution of the war. The question of border states like Maryland and Tennessee was particularly delicate. Union, then, provided safer grounds than slavery on which to launch an attack on involuntary black servitude.

Lincoln was a master of practical politics, and his strategy became clearer on September 22, 1862, when he issued a preliminary draft of the Emancipation Proclamation. Carefully timed in light of the process of the war, northern public opinion, and British relations with the Confederacy, the document stated Lincoln's intention to free the slaves in all areas not under control of the Union on January 1, 1863. Douglass realized that his policy did not really free any slaves, but it nonetheless gave freedom higher priority as a war goal.

The Emancipation Proclamation restored Douglass's confidence in Lincoln's and the North's ultimate purposes. "The first of January 1863," he remarked, "was a memorable day in the progress of American liberty and civilization. It was the turning-point in the conflict between freedom and slavery." Shortly thereafter, the War Department announced that it would accept black volunteers. Overjoyed, Douglass responded with a whirlwind of activity. Too old to fight personally, he traveled thousands of miles, pleading with northern blacks to enlist. The Fifty-fourth and Fifty-fifth Massachusetts Regiments, which included two of Douglass's sons, were the result.

But it soon became clear that prejudice extended into the military. Not only were black regiments discriminated against in pay, equipment, and courts-martial, they were regularly given

Frederick Douglass helped enlist black soldiers like these for the Union cause in the Civil War. Although they were victims of blatant discrimination on the part of the white troops, the black regiments distinguished themselves on numerous occasions. By 1865 blacks made up almost a fifth of all Union troops.

preference over white troops for suicidal missions. Word came to Douglass in July 1863, for instance, that the Massachusetts Fifty-fourth, exhausted from eight days of frontline service and forced marching, had been ordered to storm a Confederate stronghold. Although the Fifty-fourth fought bravely, 42 percent of its men were killed. Furious, Douglass stopped recruiting black soldiers and requested an interview with the president. Lincoln, who knew of Douglass's work, received him warmly, listened to his complaints, and responded—honestly, Douglass felt. Just the existence of black soldiers, Lincoln pointed out, was a gain. The remaining inequities would take time to eradicate. Disappointed as he was by such procrastination when blacks were paying the ultimate tribute to their nation on the field of battle, Douglass still campaigned in Lincoln's successful bid for reelection in 1864.

Frederick Douglass received news of the collapse of the Confederacy in 1865 with mixed emotions. Speaking at a celebration in Boston's Faneuil Hall on April 4, 1865, he rejoiced in the fall of the slave power but questioned whether his compatriots, North as well as South, were prepared to accept blacks as citizens in the reconstructed United States. Douglass at first believed that the best policy was to let the four million ex-slaves alone. "Do nothing with them," he advised white society, "mind your business and let them mind theirs." All blacks needed was "simple justice, and an equal chance." Obtaining it was not simple, however. While the war was still in progress, Lincoln had proposed a plan of reconstruction that restored citizenship to southerners who pledged loyalty to the Constitution and who supported a Thirteenth Amendment, abolishing slavery. When 10 percent of the voters in a state met this requirement, it would be readmitted to the Union. Douglass opposed the plan. Nothing in it guaranteed blacks the right to vote or any of the other privileges of citizenship.

Debate on the merits of Lincoln's plan ended abruptly on April 14, 1865, when John Wilkes Booth, a southern fanatic, assassinated the president. Douglass hoped the resulting wave of northern anger would encourage a harder line toward the South, but Vice President Andrew Johnson's reconstruction policy was, if anything, more lenient. The new president refused to support black suffrage on the grounds that it would cause racial war; and in response to demands for black equality, he suggested African colonization. By the end of 1865, all the Confederate states except Texas were ready to be readmitted under Johnson's plan. Former slaveholders had regained political dominance. Black Codes had been adopted that made it a crime for a black to be unemployed. The ex-slaves, of course, had no work. Once arrested, they were hired out to their former masters to pay off their fines. Douglass, who had had personal experience with such a hiring-out arrangement, loudly protested it as thinly disguised slavery. It appeared that freedom would make little difference to the southern black. Abandoning plans to retire at the age of fifty, Douglass resumed his crusade for black dignity.

The attitude of northern whites was crucial to the success of Douglass's effort. Some, like William Lloyd Garrison, ended their efforts on behalf of blacks when the Thirteenth Amendment was adopted in December 1865. As an abolitionist, Garrison maintained, his work was done. Douglass insisted it was just beginning. Fortunately for Douglass, the Radical Republicans shared his viewpoint. These northern congressmen, led by Thaddeus Stevens of Pennsylvania and Charles Sumner of Massachusetts, favored harsher treatment of the defeated South. Their motives stemmed from political and economic ambitions for their party and region as well as from a humanitarian concern for blacks. Moreover, they believed that Congress, not the president, should control the reconstruction process.

By 1866 a civil war existed in the government; presidential vetoes and congressional overrides were the weapons. Douglass, by now a national figure, took to the lecture circuit to denounce Johnson as "a traitor to the cause of freedom." The congressional elections of 1866 suggested that many Americans agreed. Emboldened, the Radical Republicans pushed their own plan of reconstruction over Johnson's veto. The plan rejected all existing state governments in the South and divided the region into five military districts. A guarantee of black citizenship and suffrage (subsequently embodied in the Fourteenth and Fifteenth Amendments) was set as a precondition for readmission to the Union.

Douglass applauded this toughened federal policy toward the South, but he also realized the importance of economic assistance at the grassroots level. Without the much discussed "forty acres and a mule," ex-slaves were destined to descend into the quasi slavery of tenant farming and sharecropping. In the summer of 1867, Douglass had a chance to help when President Johnson offered him a position as head of the Freedman's Bureau. Although tempted by the power of this federal welfare agency, Douglass did not accept the post that he correctly interpreted as an insincere gesture to ward off political criticism. Praise for Douglass was widespread and lavish. "The greatest black man in the nation," wrote one editor "did not become a tool of the meanest white." Douglass looked even better when, a few months after his refusal, a movement to impeach the president came within a single Senate vote of success. But the impeachment trial was only symbolic. Ulysses S. Grant had already won the election of 1868, with the crucial assistance of a half million black voters. The Republicans' desire for black suffrage was not entirely altruistic.

Here, former slaves are registering to vote in Macon, Georgia, under the supervision of the Union army. The date is September 1867. Two years later, Congress proposed the Fifteenth Amendment (ratified in 1870), with the intent of guaranteeing black suffrage. But left to southern whites, rather than the Army, black voting rights quickly turned into a travesty.

Radical Reconstruction proved less advantageous for the ex-slaves than Douglass had hoped. Changing southern laws was one thing, changing behavior quite another. The promised military protection was largely on paper. In practice, the ex-slaves were victims of systematic repression and terror. Southern whites found ways to minimize the black vote by keeping the site of the polls secret or by falsely arresting hundreds of blacks on election day. Plantation owners joined in a resolution not to sell land to any black. When a freedman managed to establish himself as an independent farmer, his farm was subjected to raids and vandalism. White terrorist groups such as the Pale Faces, the Knights of the White Camellia, and the Ku Klux Klan appeared throughout the South. Nominally, these were rifle clubs, but Douglass well knew the nature of their favorite target. Other "club" activities consisted of burning the schools, churches, and homes of blacks who did not keep their white-defined place. In truth, however, there was surprisingly little desire among the ex-slaves to challenge the traditional social order. Many of them continued voluntarily in the old ruts of servility. Slavery, it appeared, had left scars on the black personality that were not quickly or easily erased.

By the 1870s, Douglass had sensed that the nation was tiring of the black problem. For half a century it had been wracked with controversy over race and section. People of all parties yearned for peace and the chance to settle down to the business of business. Northern investors had a special desire for a final settlement of the sectional animosity. Despite its agricultural past, the South possessed the potential for an urban industrial economy. If the tense, unsettled atmosphere of military Reconstruction could be ended, northern money might combine with southern managerial talent to build a "New South" of mines, mills, railroads, and cities.

This line of reasoning argued for returning control over southern affairs to southern whites. The gradual withdrawal of Union troops from the South in the early 1870s marked the beginning of this process. It ended in 1877, when the last troops departed after an informal agreement among sectional politicians: Rutherford B. Hayes, the Republican, would be awarded the presidency in the disputed election of 1876; he, in turn, would terminate Reconstruction. The treatment of southern blacks was tacitly understood to be a regional problem rather than a national one. In effect, this meant the end of all black rights except freedom from slavery.

For Frederick Douglass, now old in the service of his people, the postwar abandonment of blacks was a bitter pill. The Fourteenth and Fifteenth Amendments still stood, but in practice, black Americans were second-class citizens. When the U.S. Supreme Court declared the Civil Rights Act of 1875 unconstitutional, Douglass realized the full extent to which the federal government had turned its back on blacks. Now a black could not even sit as an equal with whites on public conveyances or dine with them at public inns. The era of the "Jim Crow" laws had begun. Douglass angrily attacked the decision as "a further illustration" of a "malignant, vulgar, and pitiless prejudice" in the United States.

Douglass devoted the closing years of his life to the problem of how such prejudice could be overcome. Resuming his old vocation as an editor, he launched *The New Era*. Its motto was "Free men, free soil, free speech, a free press, everywhere in the land. The ballot for all, education for all, fair wages for all." Education was especially important in Douglass's eyes, even though he had achieved his personal successes (climaxed by his appointment as minister to Haiti in 1891) without a single day of formal schooling. Reviving a plan he had discussed in the 1850s with Harriet Beecher Stowe, Douglass called for an "industrial college" for blacks. Remarkably well conceived, his plan rested on his conviction that black Americans were not sufficiently prepared to benefit from regular high schools and colleges. Anticipating the philosophy of Booker T. Washington and his Tuskegee Institute (founded in 1881), Douglass declared that his people "needed more to learn how to make a good living than to learn Latin and Greek." On the other hand, Douglass was not prepared to accept vocational education alone. A compromise was possible: Blacks should be taught "to use their hands as well as their heads."

The most powerful weapon in Douglass's possession during the 1880s was his persistent agitation of the American conscience. The man who had delivered thousands of lectures summoned the energy to give hundreds more. His last talk, at a women's rights meeting, took place just a few hours before his death on February 20, 1895. He also led by example—simply refusing to accept discrimination when he encountered it in his personal life. On many occasions, Douglass deliberately challenged Jim Crow laws and then patiently explained his viewpoint to irate whites. Sometimes he convinced them. On one occasion when he did not, he held onto his seat so tightly that, when he was finally ejected, the chair went with him.

In 1884, eighteen months after the death of Anna, Douglass quietly married his secretary, Helen Pitts, a middle-aged college-trained woman. The fact that she was white raised eyebrows and voices in both the white and the black communities. Helen answered them simply by saying, "I was not afraid to marry the man I loved because of his color." Douglass, more philosophical, pointed out that the marriage was in keeping with his teachings of a lifetime. Color, he had always insisted, was an artificial issue raised to degrade and repress blacks. As for intermixing races, Douglass saw nothing unusual about what had been a fact of American life for 250 years. Glancing with a smile at his own bronze skin, he liked to squelch his critics with the observation that his first wife "was the color of my mother, and the second, the color of my father."

Selected Readings

The Person

Blight, David W.: *Frederick Douglass' Civil War: Keeping Faith in Jubilee* (1989). Traces Douglass's activities in the 1850s and through the war itself.

Chesebrough, David B.: *Frederick Douglass: Oratory from Slavery* (1998). Skillful compilation of Douglass's speeches recalling his time as a slave.

°Douglass, Frederick: *Life and Times of Frederick Douglass*. Originally published in 1892 and subsequently rewritten several times. The most convenient edition is that edited in 1962 by Rayford W. Logan.

Douglass, Frederick: *Life and Times of Frederick Douglass: His Early Life as a Slave, His Escape from Bondage, and His Complete History: An Autobiography* (1993). Detailed account of his life from childhood, through the Civil War, and after.

Huggins, Nathan Irvin: *Slave and Citizen: The Life of Frederick Douglass* (1980). A good recent interpretation; a short, but readable, addition to the *Library of American Biography Series*.

°Lampe, Gregory D.: *Freedom's Voice, 1818–1845* (1998). Details Douglass's activities as an antislavery orator.

McFeely, William S.: *Frederick Douglass* (1991). A narrative history that places Douglass at various geographic settings during his lifetime.

Preston, Dickson J.: *Young Frederick Douglass: The Maryland Years* (1980). A careful study of Douglass's roots in eastern Maryland and the experiences of his youth.

°Quarles, Benjamin: *Frederick Douglass* (1948). A frequently laudatory early life.

°Available in paperback.

°Quarles, Benjamin (ed.): *Frederick Douglass* (1948). A sampling of Douglass's writings, along with opinions of him by representative figures of his time and later.

Sundquist, Eric J. (ed.): *Frederick Douglass: New Literary and Historical Essays* (1990). Scholarly analyses of Douglass's work and his times.

Williamson, Scott C.: *The Narrative Life: The Moral and Religious Thought of Frederick Douglass* (2002). Divides Douglass's life into narrative epochs reflecting recent interpretations.

The Period

David, Paul A., et al.: *Reckoning with Slavery: A Critical Study in the Quantitative History of American Negro Slavery* (1976). A collaborative response to the claims of Fogel and Engerman's *Time on the Cross*.

Davis, David Brion: *The Problem of Slavery in Western Culture* (1966). A definitive study of slavery in the American context.

°Elkins, Stanley: *Slavery* (3d ed., 1976). An imaginative but controversial interpretation that Douglass's life does not support.

Engerman, Stanley L.: *The Reinterpretation of American Economic History* (1971). An analysis of the economics of slavery. See also Engerman's collaborative work with Robert Fogel, *Time on the Cross: The Economics of American Negro Slavery* (1974).

°Genovese, Eugene D.: *The Political Economy of Slavery* (1965). A Marxist interpretation. See also Genovese's *Roll, Jordan, Roll: The World the Slaves Made* (1974).

Gougeon, Len, and Joel Myerson (eds.): *Emerson's Antislavery Writings* (1995). An informative introduction followed by some of Ralph Waldo Emerson's best essays.

Gutman, Herbert G.: *The Black Family in Slavery and Freedom, 1750–1925* (1976). A good social history of the slave experience.

Jordan, Winthrop: *White over Black* (1974). The symbolic and emotional components of the bias Douglass spent his life resisting.

Litwack, Leon: *Been in the Storm So Long: The Aftermath of Slavery* (1980). An analysis of the meaning of freedom for black men and women.

°McPherson, James M.: *The Struggle for Equality: Abolitionists and the Negro in the Civil War and Reconstruction* (1964). Social as well as political history.

Patterson, Orlando: *Slavery and Social Death* (1982). An examination, by a black sociologist, of the meaning of slavery in the United States and sixty-five other societies throughout history.

°Stampp, Kenneth M.: *The Peculiar Institution* (1956). A balanced history of slavery in the United States.

Stauffer, John: *The Black Hearts of Men: Radical Abolitionists and the Transformation of Race* (2002). An analysis of abolitionists, including John Brown and Frederick Douglass.

°Woodward, C. Vann: *Origins of the New South, 1877–1913* (1951). The story of the South's recovery from the Civil War.

For Consideration

1. What were some of the unusual circumstances of Frederick Douglass's early years that heightened his desire to escape slavery?

2. Trace Douglass's experiences in the North up to his publication of *A Narrative of the Life of Frederick A. Douglass*.

3. How did Douglass view President Lincoln's actions in the early years of his administration with regard to ending slavery? What actions changed Douglass's views?

4. Douglass's opinions regarding reconstruction underwent some transformations. What were they, and why did Douglass change his views?

5. Late in life, Frederick Douglass married a white woman, a rare event in the late 1800s. Douglass explained the marriage in philosophical terms, while his wife spoke more emotionally. Analyze their statements in the context of Douglass's life.

Chapter 9

Robert E. Lee

It was an unusually warm and muggy Palm Sunday, that April 9 of 1865. At exactly one o'clock in the afternoon, the three men sitting quietly in the small courthouse meeting room heard the sound of approaching horses. For the Confederate commander of the Army of Northern Virginia, Robert Edward Lee, the wait, lasting the better part of two hours, had seemed an eternity. He had exchanged occasional comments with his staff member and the Union general who had escorted them there, but Lee had spent most of the time sitting silently, reliving the triumphs, disasters, and ironies of the past few years. Not only had Lee spent thirty-one years in the U.S. Army, which had just defeated the Confederacy, but he would soon be surrendering to a fellow West Pointer who had earlier been dismissed from the service for habitual drunkenness. Casting his lot with the South, Lee had joined the Confederacy and taken up arms against his former colleagues in defense of his native state of Virginia. But some of the fiercest combat had taken place in Virginia, and much of his homeland lay in ruins.

Lee's private lamentation was interrupted by the entry of Ulysses S. Grant, the general-in-chief of the Union's Army of the Potomac. Dressed in an ill-fitting private's tunic rigged with a general's shoulder straps, puffing on a soggy black stogie, dusty and disheveled, Grant stood in stark contrast to the soldier who rose to shake his hand. The tall, lean man with noble features and deep brown eyes set off by a silver beard and gray uniform surely aroused a sense of awe in Grant. After all, Lee had held off Grant's army for almost two years with forces outnumbered at least three to one, and they were short of food, clothing, and ammunition the entire time.

After shaking hands, the two men sat down to work out an agreement. Grant, sympathetic to Lee and the Confederacy—and elated to have the madness of this war of American against American over—said simply, "The officers and men surrendered [were] to be paroled and disqualified from taking up arms again until properly exchanged." In other words, Lee suddenly realized, the Confederates could simply lay down their arms and go home. When Lee asked if the men could keep their horses, Grant said he insisted on it. Moments later, Robert E. Lee signed the document of surrender that soon ended the savage bloodshed of the most costly and deadly conflict in American history.

When asked to trace his family tree shortly after the Civil War ended, Robert E. Lee required two pages just to list those members who had lived in Virginia. The Lee family had been in America since the mid-1600s, and creative genealogists could trace a lineage back to William the Conqueror. Richard Lee, the first of the family to come to the New World, had settled in the northern part of the Virginia colony and had become British Governor William Berkeley's secretary of state. Two members of the Lee family, Richard Henry and Francis Lightfoot, had signed the Declaration of Independence. And although Charles Lee had served as President George Washington's attorney general, another family member, Richard Bland Lee, had become one of Virginia's most active Federalists.

Robert's father, General Henry "Light-Horse Harry" Lee, had been a celebrated cavalryman in the American Revolution. Light-Horse Harry's eagerness for adventure had earned him the title "Virginia's favorite young soldier" at the war's conclusion. His heroics, first in action on the northern front and later against British troops in South Carolina and Georgia, had also earned him the high praise and favor of General Washington. Henry Lee used this fame—and his family's wealth and prestigious record of public service—to secure a position as governor of the state of Virginia in 1791. During the Revolutionary War, Henry had courted and married his cousin Matilda Lee. After having four children, Matilda died in 1790. On her death bed, she exposed a tragic flaw in her husband by placing the estate of Stratford Hall and all the other land that she had inherited into a trust for their children. Matilda feared that Henry would squander her family's fortune in the same kind of speculative schemes that had consumed his own inherited wealth.

After Matilda's death, Henry Lee faced the prospect of an austere future. He had no money left of his own and was denied access to his wife's estate. Lee solved this problem temporarily when he married Anne Carter, daughter of one of Virginia's wealthiest landholders. For a brief time Henry Lee was contented with this marriage. But, ignoring his duties as Virginia's governor, he was soon back to his old tricks of speculation in a series of land deals. His political fortunes waned not only because of his poor performance, but also because the Jeffersonian Republicans were fast winning power away from the Federalist party.

Henry Lee's declining political fortunes led him to act irrationally, and he spent his family into debt. By the time of Robert E. Lee's birth in 1807, the family's stately home at Stratford Hall was almost devoid of furniture, and the front doors were chained to keep law enforcement officers from serving legal papers. By Robert's second birthday, Henry had served two sentences in debtor's prison. One of his sons by his first marriage, Henry Jr., came into possession of Stratford when Robert was an infant. Thereafter, Anne and the four children could remain in the home only as guests of her stepson. For two years they lived off the grace of the young squire, while Light-Horse Harry, penniless and propertyless, served another term in jail. During this time, Robert, a bright, handsome child, experienced the unforgettable gentility and elegance of the fabulous mansion. But on Henry's release from prison, the family moved to a small, sparsely appointed home in Alexandria.

Because of his Federalist views, ranging from suppression of the Whiskey Rebellion to opposing war with Britain in 1812, Henry became further estranged from the prevailing political climate. After being beaten by a mob while defending the office of an antiwar newspaper in 1812, Henry left the country for a self-imposed exile in Barbados. Robert was only six years old when his father left the country, and Henry had spent half of those years in jail. Robert's first cognizant years were spent in fear of the creditor and the sheriff, both of whom were frequent visitors to the Lee home. Robert never forgot the shame of his father's life; his mother would not allow him to. Although she was careful not to promote feelings of hatred for Henry among her children, she

Robert's mother, Anne Carter Lee (left), is portrayed before her marriage to the dashing general Henry "Light-Horse Harry" Lee (right). The inscription on the cameo pinned to Anne's dress reads, "George Washington to his dear Anne." Washington was a close friend of the wealthy Carter family.

instilled values that were diametrically opposite those of her husband. As often as possible, she took her children from their modest home in Alexandria to visit the staid grandeur of her parents' Shirley estate. At Shirley the Lee children saw opulence and also the example of wisely spent money. Robert and his siblings grew to maturity with a powerful sense of duty, economy, forbearance, and austerity. Hard work, consistency, loyalty, and the highest moral conduct guided the Lee family after their father's departure. None of the children took these lessons to heart better than Robert who, at age twelve, after his mother became an invalid, took charge of running the family affairs.

Despite being forced to assume adult responsibilities at this early age, Robert still managed to enjoy Alexandria as a child of the local aristocracy. The Lee name still garnered prestige and position throughout Virginia, and the Carter side of the family literally dominated Alexandria society. Robert had many friends and relatives and was growing into a handsome and gregarious young man who mixed well in social circles. It was in Alexandria (a town of about 7,000) that Lee developed a deepening love for his Virginia homeland; he spent his leisure hours playing with friends, swimming in the Potomac River, horseback riding, hunting, and socializing with relatives. His happiness during this part of his life is not surprising when one considers the setting: Robert E. Lee lived at the pinnacle of southern society in a prosperous community.

Like so many of his class, Lee grew to overlook the glaring inequity of human bondage in his society. Both the Carter and Lee families owned slaves. But if there were degrees of depravity

The grandeur of the Virginia planter aristocracy into which Robert was born here at Stratford Hall soon vanished for the Lees. Light-Horse Harry went bankrupt and eventually left his wife and children to fend for themselves.

in that institution, the upper South practiced the least malevolent form. Slaves in Virginia—especially in the urban setting in which Robert came of age—often occupied less arduous positions as personal servants, skilled laborers, or artisans. This was in stark contrast to the torturous chain-gang labor systems of the Cotton South, where slaves were often worked to death. In the 1810s, it was possible for a young man like Robert E. Lee, living in Alexandria, to overlook the injustice of what Virginia constitution-framer George Mason had branded "the peculiar institution."

Though Mason had predicted as early as the 1780s that slavery would eventually bring disaster to the Union, many patrician whites in the upper South viewed slavery as not only a "positive good" for blacks but also a natural and proper way of life. Others rejected Mason's gloomy prophecy, believing that the institution would simply die out because of declining profitability. In the 1820s, Virginia's ratio of whites to blacks was about two to one, while in other parts of the South, blacks outnumbered whites. Young southerners of Robert Lee's age therefore grew up surrounded by blacks in bondage, and to them slavery undoubtedly seemed normal. Slaves were treated reasonably well on the tidewater plantations Robert visited, and the "genteel gentlemen-planters" living in the rich tradition of Washington and Jefferson at Stratford and Shirley helped him grow comfortable with the master–slave relationship.

Alexandria offered quality private schooling, and Robert Lee proved to be an excellent student. But the family income, based solely on the investments that Henry had not squandered, was sufficient only to maintain the household and keep Robert's siblings in school. Robert had expressed an interest in studying medicine, but his mother could not afford to send him to medical school. Robert had also enjoyed studying the classics at Alexandria Academy. His youthful experiences on the Lee and Carter plantations had given him a taste of the charmed life of a "country gentleman," who managed the affairs of an estate while studying the great works of literature at his leisure. Of course, Robert had neither the money nor the land to lead such a life.

With such limitations on a career choice, Robert decided to pursue a practical occupation in the U.S. Army. He had studied military history and strategy in his reading of the classics, and a military education was particularly appealing because those admitted to the national military academy at West Point, New York, attended school without paying tuition. Although a military career did not lead to wealth, West Point offered stable, even exciting prospects. Although West Point admitted only 250 out of several thousand applicants each year, Lee was admitted in 1824 on the basis of solid academic achievement and strong recommendations from his teachers.

The West Point that Lee entered in 1825 was actually a school of engineering, reflecting the strategic value of military construction. During the American Revolution, General Washington had recognized the need for engineers to fortify strategic sites, and he appointed Colonel Richard Gridley as the first chief engineer of the United States. Gridley's well-designed earthen fortifications protected the American marksmen who thwarted the British siege at Bunker Hill. When the turmoil of war and revolution in Europe had posed a threat to Atlantic ports in the 1790s, President Washington established a permanent Army Corps of Engineers to build forts and revetments along the eastern seaboard. Washington had also authorized the creation of an engineering school at West Point, New York, on the Hudson River that opened during Jefferson's presidency. Expanded and refined in technical curriculum over two decades of American war and territorial conquest, the West Point that Lee entered in 1825 was easily the most advanced engineering school in the nation—if not the world.

Lee progressed through the highly disciplined four-year program without a blemish on his record. His academic forte was mathematics, but he distinguished himself as both a soldier and a student. While visiting his ailing mother in Alexandria, Lee attracted the attention of many of the young ladies of the town. His noble demeanor and his family's checkered past loomed behind the laughing eyes and clever witticisms. Lee's charm and good looks soon earned him the nickname "the marble model."

Lee graduated with highest honors in 1829, but his triumph was tempered by the news that his mother was gravely ill. Journeying to her residence, he found the fifty-four-year-old woman wracked by the struggles and illnesses of a difficult life. Robert felt an outpouring of compassion for this woman to whom "he owed every thing." For a short while after leaving West Point, Robert tended to his mother's needs. But her health continued to decline, and on July 10, 1829, Anne Carter Lee died, with her closest child, Robert, at her side. Lee, then twenty-two, would never forget the pain. Even four decades later, on entering the same room at the Carter family's Ravensworth estate, he said, "It seems but yesterday."

Awaiting his first assignment, Lee frequently visited the Arlington estate of George Washington Parke Custis, set majestically on a hill overlooking the Potomac River near Alexandria. Custis was the grandson of Martha Custis, who married George Washington after her first husband died. Upon their marriage, George Custis became the first president's adopted son. After his grandmother's death, George Custis left Mount Vernon and used the family money to build the Arlington estate as a shrine to Washington. Memorabilia of the legendary "Father of the Country" were everywhere at Arlington, and Lee reveled in the greatness of the Virginia planters' aristocracy whenever he visited the mansion. Courtship was Lee's primary purpose for visiting, however. The eccentric Custis had only one daughter—Mary Anna Randolph Custis, an attractive but terribly indulged woman of twenty-one. Because the other Custis children had died in infancy, Mary had been spoiled and pampered by her parents and the servants. Robert grew enamored of Mary, who was actually his distant cousin. Mary felt the same, and soon they were thinking of marriage. Before Robert had the chance to propose, however, his first assignment came. In November 1829 he arrived at Cockspur Island, Georgia, to assist in building a fort just south of Savannah.

Cockspur Island, Lee soon discovered after his arrival in November 1829, was a poor place to build a fort of any kind. The swampy lowland soil severely tested Lee's engineering training, as he and his men slogged through mud and rain trying to find a solid area on which to build. Absence made Lee long for Mary Custis. He wrote to her often and grew more certain that he wanted to marry her.

When mosquitoes and heat put an end to summer work on Cockspur Island, Lee ventured to Arlington, ready to ask Mary for her hand. Because of a recent sex scandal involving Lee's half-brother, however, and because Lee had no wealth and could expect little as a career army officer, George Custis at first opposed the marriage. But Lee was charming enough to win the favor of Mary's mother and at least make her father regret that there was no wealth or property in his family. By the end of that summer of 1830, Robert and Mary were certain they wanted to be married. That Robert Lee and Mary Custis never really looked outside their families for a spouse reflected the insularity of the Virginia society of their time. Steeped in European tradition, the Virginia planters imitated the aristocratic custom of marrying within the family line to protect property and title. To be sure, the Virginia planters believed they were the American aristocracy. Thus, on June 30, 1831, Robert and Mary were married in a grand ceremony at Arlington.

Shortly after the wedding, the Lees went to Fort Monroe. Mary was exceedingly unhappy on the Army post—living in a small second lieutenant's quarters—and constantly longed for the pampered life she had lived at Arlington. Her parents had mourned her leaving, and after the couple came to Arlington a few months later, only Robert returned to Fort Monroe. Mary, who was pregnant with their first child, remained at Arlington. This was a portent of things to come. For most of Robert's Army career, Mary remained at Arlington with her parents and children. She hated Army life and refused to socialize with other wives at the post. At first, Robert was crushed by her desire to remain "the child of Arlington," but he gradually grew to accept the situation. His correspondence throughout those years, however, reflects a sadness and, eventually, grief over the separation of his family. Loneliness and homesickness for Virginia followed Lee throughout his Army career.

After the completion of his engineering duties at Fort Monroe, Lee was transferred to headquarters in Washington, D.C. When the Lees could not find suitable housing in the District, they decided that Mary and their son, George, would stay at Arlington while Robert commuted back and forth daily. When their second child, Mary, was born, Mary Custis Lee suffered a pelvic infection that prevented her from walking for nearly a year. Thereafter she walked with a slight limp, and the affliction gave her recurring problems for the rest of her life. After 1835 Mary and her children stayed at Arlington under her parents' care, while Robert assumed the vagabond status of an Army "lifer." Over the next decade, Lee was stationed in Saint Louis and New York City, in charge of engineering projects planned to aid navigation of the Mississippi River and New York Harbor. During those years, the Lee family grew to include six children, all of whom lived with Mary at Arlington. Robert grew increasingly frustrated by his career and life and began to regard himself as a failure. Although he had proved himself an exceptionally competent engineer and officer, he had attained only the rank of captain by 1845. The Lees believed that this slow advancement stemmed from Robert's refusal to aggrandize himself to his superiors.

This portrait of Mary Anna Randolph Custis Lee was painted in 1831, the same time as the portrait of Robert on page 224. The great-granddaughter of Martha Washington, Mary Custis Lee was the sole heir to her father's 13,000-acre Arlington estate.

He entertained thoughts of leaving the Army for more lucrative private engineering work—his loneliness and isolation compounding his depression and making him melancholy and often morose.

Lee was on the verge of resigning from the military when, on May 13, 1846, word came that the United States had declared war on Mexico. President James K. Polk's declaration of war marked the culmination of years of controversy concerning the territory of Texas. Although a dispute with Mexico over the southern boundary of Texas, which had been admitted to the Union in 1845, was the obvious cause of war, the issue of American imperialism, or "Manifest Destiny," was at the heart of the conflict. Critics of the war charged that the expansion of slavery into new territories was Polk's real motive in initiating hostilities. Indeed, Polk was a pro-slavery Democrat and viewed some Mexican lands as potential slave territory for the production of cotton, as the fertile plains of eastern Texas already demonstrated. Still, he argued that most of the land in question was not suited for cotton production.

The expansionism leading to war with Mexico was not met with unanimous support in the South. Of all the residents of the South, Virginians had the least to gain from the economic designs of those in the cotton-growing states. In contrast to the other slaveholding states, Virginia had a diverse economy, with extensive roads, turnpikes, and railroads. Cotton, the driving force behind slave expansion by the 1830s and 1840s, was not an important crop there. Some Virginia planters were freeing their slaves, and the state's healthy economy had led many of its citizens to hope for an end to the institution. For the most part, Virginians had closer commercial and cultural ties to the eastern seaboard than to the new southern states, where the plantation system was on the rise. Lee, for example, was an avid reader of northeastern newspapers, and as a West Pointer and Army officer he had strong connections with the North. Yet he and other Virginians felt themselves being drawn into a compact with other slaveholding states, largely because of the abolitionist press and the "outside influences" promoting slave rebellion. Meanwhile the "slave bloc"—the plantation owners, who doggedly maintained the institution—grew stronger by exploiting white southern fears of such a revolution.

By the 1840s, Virginians were inevitably drawn into what by then was clearly the sectional issue of slavery. Southern congressmen had agreed to limit slavery geographically in the 1820 Missouri Compromise, hoping that a Democratic lock on the presidency, control of the U.S. Supreme Court, and a balance of slave and free states in Congress would protect their interests. But by the mid-1830s, economic and political alignments had coalesced into regional alliances for and against slavery. Landless southerners had left the eastern seaboard to settle the new lands west of the Appalachians. Many of those who built homes north of the Ohio River resented the wealthy planters who dominated in the East and were repelled by slavery. In southern Ohio, Indiana, and Illinois, neither slavery nor blacks were welcomed. When farmers from these states, opposed to what they termed the "unfair competition" of slavery, joined with the industrialists and manufacturers of the Northeast and the Middle Atlantic states, the peaceful resolution of the slavery issue was further complicated.

The annexation of Texas, engineered by Secretary of State John C. Calhoun in 1844, anticipated the controversy over war with Mexico. Despite Mexican President Santa Anna's warning that annexation would mean war, and against strong opposition by abolitionists and prominent members of the Whig party, the annexation went forward. Congressional voting on the annexation resolution revealed the divisiveness of the Texas question. The House of Representatives approved the measure by 120 to 98, and it passed by only two votes in the Senate. Public opinion also demonstrated the controversial nature of annexation and impending war with Mexico. Defending the desire of Texans for admission to the Union, the *New York Morning News* editorialized in May 1845: "An unalienable right of man [*sic*] is to institute for themselves that form of government which suits them best, and change it when they please." But what expansionistic Americans really wanted—"unalienable" rights aside—was the land. The force of Manifest Destiny had thus joined hands with that of slave expansion in supporting Texas statehood. Meanwhile, abolitionist Senator Salmon P. Chase of Ohio complained that the government was, in fact, acting "to extend the peculiar institution." Other abolitionists identified the annexation as a function of "the Slave Power," and farmers in the Northwest grew more wary that slaveholding territory might extend all the way to the Pacific Ocean. Such alignments over the annexation of Texas signaled that sectionalism was approaching a crisis, and the battle lines for civil war had been drawn even then.

Regardless of his own opinions about Texas, Lee was excited when war broke out with Mexico. Here was the chance for an engineer moving slowly up the ranks to break through the bureaucracy and fight in a war. As soon as word came that President Santa Anna had rebuffed the American ambassador to Mexico, John Slidell, and that Polk had signed a declaration of war, Lee requested a transfer to active field duty in Mexico. On August 19, 1846, Lee, approaching his fortieth birthday, was ordered to join General John Wool in Mexico.

After taking care of affairs at Arlington, including writing a will, Lee caught steamers bound for New Orleans and Port La Vaca, Texas, then journeyed to San Antonio by horse. Wool's army was soon ordered to join the main force, headed by Zachary Taylor, in northern Mexico. The mop-up adjunct force that Lee joined saw little action. Taylor's troops had routed the poorly equipped Mexican forces all the way to the disputed Rio Grande River border some months before. The fact that about 1,700 Americans easily defeated some 7,500 Mexican troops was a portent for the entire Mexican War. For Robert Lee, the opportunity for good service and heroism arose early in 1847. With fellow West Pointers George McClellan, Joseph E. Johnston, George Meade, and P. G. T. Beauregard, Lee was chosen for the first Engineering Battalion of the U.S. Army. The unit would join General Winfield Scott in an expeditionary force to the Mexican capital. Scott's army sailed down the Gulf Coast en route to a descent on Vera Cruz. The force of 10,000 easily took control of that city. From there, they pushed toward Mexico City. Robert Lee distinguished himself several times along the way, volunteering as a scout and bringing back vital information on the terrain ahead and enemy locations. For his service, Lee received commendations and the favor of General Scott.

Lee learned several lessons in military strategy on the Mexico City campaign. He served as Scott's chief adviser on the tactics of assailing the Mexican capital and learned the importance of bold and "audacious" strategic measures. In each battle, Scott gave the Mexican army no chance to retreat and regroup. Relentlessly, his forces pushed the enemy force back toward Mexico City, leaving it exhausted, disorganized, and ready for surrender. Lee saw the value of fortification and flanking maneuvers. And he learned the importance of an efficient military hierarchy, wherein field generals were allowed to carry out the master plan of their chief with great autonomy. In short, Lee experienced effective military organization, as the U.S. Army carved up the Mexican army at will.

After the war, Lee did a brief tour at Baltimore Harbor, three years as superintendent of West Point, and then transferred to the West again. When he arrived in Texas in April 1855, politics were unavoidable anywhere in America. In the aftermath of the Mexican War, the Whigs had won the 1848 presidential election by running Mexican War hero Zachary Taylor. Upon his death in 1850, Millard Fillmore of New York had taken over. When California had attempted to enter the Union as a free state, the precarious balance maintained since the Missouri Compromise was again threatened. The "Great Compromiser," Henry Clay of Kentucky, had made one last bid to preserve national unity. His Compromise of 1850 provided for the admission of California as a free state, the organization of New Mexico territory without provisions concerning slavery, the abolition of slave trade in the District of Columbia, and the legal obligation of all citizens to assist in returning fugitive slaves (see also pages 209–211).

Slave states now numbered one fewer than free states, and southern Democratic attempts to provide popular sovereignty (the ability of new territories to decide on slavery by popular vote) in Kansas and Nebraska territories gave rise to the formation of a new and powerful party devoted to ending the expansion of slavery into the West. Affiliates of the recently organized Free-Soil party, northern Whigs, and disaffected antislavery northern Democrats organized the Republican party in 1854. Republicans challenged the Fugitive Slave Law and the Kansas-Nebraska Act of 1854, which nullified the Missouri Compromise's prohibition of slavery north of the 36°30′ line and provided for popular sovereignty. The Republican party adopted the principles of the defeated Wilmot Proviso (1846), which stated that "neither slavery nor involuntary servitude shall ever exist" in any part of the territory acquired from Mexico. The narrow 1856 victory of Democrat

James Buchanan over the first Republican presidential candidate, John C. Fremont, suggested that the era of compromise was ending.

At remote Camp Cooper on the Brazos River in central Texas, Lee and his colleagues often discussed sectional politics. Soldiers from the North and the West attacked slavery with increasing vigor, while those from the South defended the institution. Lee, too, adopted the position of the slave owners, but without actually endorsing slavery. By defending their right to own slaves, he and his southern colleagues brought themselves in line with the slavocracy. Lee had a lifetime of ambivalence about slavery. He had grown up around it, and he enjoyed the lavish existence it gave to those who owned human property. But again and again he expressed his moral opposition to the institution, hoped it would end peacefully, and feared the extremism he was seeing among the soldiers in Texas. "Mr. Buchanan, it appears, is to be our next President," he wrote to Mary before the 1856 election. "I hope he will be able to extinguish fanaticism both North and South, cultivate love for the country and Union, and restore harmony between the different sections."

Like others from the South, Lee espoused the tenacious "positive good" thesis when he commented that "blacks are immeasurably better off here than in Africa. . . . The painful discipline they are undergoing, is necessary for their instruction as a race, and I hope will prepare and lead them to better things." While Lee disliked slavery, calling it a "moral and political evil," he believed that its end was in the hands of "Providence." Leaving things in the hands of Divine Providence was often Lee's way of dealing with problems. His career discontent was resolved through the view that it was God's will that it be that way. Lee grew fatalistic and, by this time, had come to believe that death brought relief to those who suffered in life. The idea that death was a merciful blessing arose numerous times in his correspondence—so often that some of his relatives believed he was obsessed with it. When his country was being rocked over slavery, Lee's ambivalence led him to look again to Providence for the answer. He believed that the end of slavery was in God's hands, and northerners had no right to interfere.

In 1857 Lee himself became a slaveholder. On the death of Mary's father, Lee became executor of an Arlington estate that was in utter disarray. George Washington Custis had been eccentric to the point of ignoring the management of the plantation and, in his will, ordered the freeing of the 196 slaves on the estate within five years of his death. Lee would have been happy to free them, but Custis had also left the estate more than $10,000 in debt—and in terrible disrepair. Worse still, Lee returned from Texas to find his wife a near invalid, crippled by her pelvic ailment and spreading arthritis.

Burdened by such problems, Lee asked for an extended leave to care for his wife and get the estate out of debt. He rented out the most able-bodied slaves, organized others into a work force to repair the estate, sold off most of the livestock, and planted wheat and corn in the fields that his father-in-law had allowed to lie fallow for years. Though he grew to love the Arlington estate, Lee found his role as a slave owner depressing. Beyond the distaste he felt for being a "master," Lee was troubled that the Arlington slaves, except for the domestic servants, were almost completely unskilled. Accustomed to working with disciplined Army personnel, he was anxious to restore Arlington to profitability and be done with the "unpleasant legacy" left him by Custis. Not only did Lee free all the Arlington slaves by the five-year deadline, but he also found suitable work for all of them after their manumission. For several years thereafter, Lee supported one of the freed families in New York City while they sought work. Meanwhile, he restored the Arlington estate to its former grandeur.

The kind of gradual emancipation exercised at Arlington did not satisfy abolitionists, who demanded an immediate end to slavery. Pennsylvania Democrat James Buchanan hoped to avoid

Two individuals who in very different ways inflamed sectional tensions during the 1850s were Harriet Beecher Stowe and John Brown. Stowe published the powerful antislavery novel *Uncle Tom's Cabin* in 1852, and Brown carried out a deadly abolitionist raid in "bleeding Kansas" in 1856. In 1859, Brown and his followers seized the federal arsenal at Harper's Ferry, Virginia, before being captured, tried, and hanged.

national conflict during his administration by appeasing the proslavery forces. But his support of slaveholding in Kansas thoroughly enraged the abolitionists. Equally galling to antislavery advocates was the 1857 Supreme Court decision in the case of *Dred Scott v. Sandford.* The court ruled against Scott, a slave whose master had taken him from the slave state of Missouri into Illinois and Wisconsin Territory. Scott asserted that his time in free territory made him a free man. But the Supreme Court, headed by conservative southerner Roger B. Taney, disagreed. Not only did this decision deny freedom to Scott, but it also classified all slaves as property, thus giving slave owners the right to take their human belongings anywhere—even to free territory— and keep them (see also pages 212–213).

The troubled times became even more volatile when John Brown, a messianic abolitionist who had clashed with proslavery forces in Kansas, raided the federal arsenal at Harper's Ferry, Virginia, on October 16, 1859. With a band of twenty-two black and white supporters, the force killed four men and took several others hostage. Brown and his men then barricaded themselves in a fire engine house near the arsenal. That evening, Lieutenant J. E. B. Stuart called on Robert E. Lee at Arlington. Lee agreed to lead a group of marines to Harper's Ferry and bring Brown and his small group to justice. Suppressing Brown's uprising in the name of the president, Lee used restraint in taking the abolitionist into custody. In questioning Brown, Lee concluded that his plan to start a general slave rebellion in Virginia was the "attempt of a fanatic or a madman." He dismissed the raid as the work of "rioters." But the event sent shock waves throughout the

South. Southern fears were heightened by abolitionist press releases from the North, which both praised Brown as "Saint John the Just" and called for more violence to end slavery. If ever there was any chance that southerners would initiate gradual emancipation to end slavery, it ended with John Brown's raid. Whether they owned slaves or not, most southerners thereafter viewed northerners as enemies. The North's apparent willingness to promote violence in the crusade against slavery brought southern anger to a fever pitch. The greatest fear among white southerners, a general slave rebellion, now seemed to have the full approval of northerners. With their social order endangered and the threat of murder by slave mobs hanging over their heads, southerners became resolute in their hatred of the North.

On December 3, 1860, one year and one day after John Brown was executed, outgoing President Buchanan announced in his State of the Union address: "The different sections of the Union are now arrayed against each other, and the time has arrived, so much dreaded by the Father of his Country, when hostile geographical parties have been formed." Both the Whig and the Democratic parties, which had been able to quell sectional radicalism for decades, were in decline. The Whigs had fared poorly in 1852, with Winfield Scott as their candidate. Daniel Webster was dead, and Henry Clay was aging and ailing. Bitter factional parties, such as the Know-Nothings (championing anti-Catholicism and anti-immigration planks) and the single-issue Prohibitionists, diluted the national character of the Democratic and Whig parties. As a result, a new two-party system had emerged: the Republicans in the North and the Democrats in the South. Those who had so long advocated nationalism were now forced to support parties with regional interests.

Indeed, Buchanan, who had warned the year before of impending civil war, stood as president of a nation on the verge of collapse. Southern extremists in the Democratic party had turned their backs on Stephen Douglas of Illinois for his less-than-hard-line proslavery attitude. Instead, they formed the National Democratic party and nominated John C. Breckinridge of Kentucky for president in 1860. Douglas complained bitterly, and correctly, that some supporters of the Breckinridge candidacy were "disunionists" intent on splitting the Democratic vote, thereby permitting the election of an antislavery candidate and forcing a general secession of the South. Southern fears that a strong antislavery candidate would appear on the 1860 ballot were confirmed when the Republican party, maintaining its steadfast opposition to the expansion of slavery into the territories, nominated Abraham Lincoln, a congressman from Illinois. Lincoln's opposition to the Kansas-Nebraska Act and the *Dred Scott* decision was well known from his 1858 senatorial debates with Stephen Douglas. His refusal to discuss the slave issue or to be conciliatory toward white southerners after his nomination for the presidency reinforced his image as a "black Republican." After Lincoln's nomination, a group of nationalistic Whigs, fearing the consequences of a sectional Republican victory, nominated John Bell of Tennessee as the candidate of the Constitutional Union party. They hoped to restore the old alliance between Whigs and Democrats. The four-way race gave the Republican Lincoln a clear victory in the electoral vote. A party opposed to slavery was finally in the White House, and the decades of compromise were at an end. In the wake of the election, secession fever swept the South. South Carolina, where secession zealots like William Barnwell Rhett had the ear of the people, officially withdrew from the Union only two weeks after Buchanan's foreboding speech.

The tumultuous events of 1860 occurred after Robert E. Lee had returned to duty in Texas. After Lincoln's election, talk of secession swept through the state. Lee deeply regretted the move toward secession. He disapproved of what the "Cotton States" were doing and argued that "secession [was] nothing but revolution." But he also sympathized with white southerners, who were caught up "in a convulsion" of terror. Fearing what war would do to the country, Lee told his son Custis that he would "easily lay down [his] life for its safety. . . . I wish for no other flag than the 'Star spangled banner' and no other air than 'Hail Columbia.' " If war came, Lee might have to choose sides, North or South. He hoped that day would never come. But on February 4, 1861, the Confederate States of America (including South Carolina, Georgia, Alabama, and Florida) were a reality, and the new nation was busily preparing for war. When Texas seceded, state militia forces seized the federal installation where Lee was stationed. General D. E. Twiggs, the commandant, was a southerner, who actually arranged the surrender by refusing to fire on the Texas militia. The federal troops, including Brevet Colonel Lee, were ordered back to Washington.

On April 11, 1861, Confederate guns fired on federally occupied Fort Sumter in the harbor of Charleston, South Carolina. In response, President Lincoln ordered the formation of a 75,000-man force to crush the rebellion. The Civil War had begun, but Virginia had not yet seceded. Lee held a faint hope that he could remain neutral in the impending conflict. Virginians were ambivalent about secession. The state legislature had, for example, held a peace convention in February 1861, aimed at avoiding war. Twenty-one states had been represented, and the convention had passed a series of resolutions resembling those of the Crittenden Compromise, which had failed in Congress a few months before. Like Senator John C. Crittenden of Kentucky, delegates to the peace convention hoped to placate the southerners by extending the 36°30′ boundary between slave and free states all the way to California and by protecting slavery where it existed. Prominent Virginians such as former president John Tyler urged the assembly to preserve the Union "our godlike fathers created," while another speaker pleaded to "arrest the progress of this country on its road to ruin." Virginia's leaders hoped to use whatever influence they had as descendants of the Founding Fathers to prevent civil war. However, with the states of the lower South absent and secession fever sweeping the region, the peace convention failed, a signal that the secession of the upper South was imminent.

As Virginia debated secession, Lee was pondering his future with the U.S. Army. In a series of meetings, President Lincoln, General Scott, and Lincoln's adviser, Francis Blair, made it known that they wanted to place Lee in command of the army being mobilized to put down the rebellion. Lee's frustration over slow promotion would be resolved; he would become a general. A thirty-year career would be fulfilled. But if Virginia seceded, what would Lee do?

By a vote of eighty-eight to fifty-five, the Virginia legislature seceded from the Union on April 17. Lee learned of the decision while on his way home to Arlington. "I must say that I am one of those dull creatures that cannot see the good of secession," Lee confessed to his pharmacist when he stopped in to pay a bill. He had only twenty-four hours to take the Union position or resign. He could not remain neutral and stay in the U.S. Army. Lee talked briefly with his wife that evening, already knowing her horror regarding a "Yankee invasion" of Virginia. He then retired to his study to write his fateful letter of resignation. "Though opposed to secession and deprecating war," Lee later wrote, "I could take no part in an invasion of the Southern States."

The following day, Lee rode into Washington to submit his resignation. Winfield Scott, one of Lee's champions, took the news with disappointment. Scott had thought so highly of Lee that he had earlier recommended that the government insure Lee's life for $5 million per year in the event of war with Britain. Now Lee was lost to the Army. Accepting the resignation, the doleful Scott remarked, "Lee, you have made the greatest mistake of your life, but I feared it so."

Many other U.S. military officers from the South faced the same dilemma as Lee. Some, who remained in the Union, were disowned by their families. Others, like Lee, hoped they could retire and remain neutral in the war. With fighting all around him, it is unlikely that Lee would have been able to sit out the conflict quietly at Arlington. He undoubtedly would have been branded a coward and traitor by both Confederate and Union presses. Leaving the country was another option, but one the Lees were not disposed to undertake.

Two days after resigning, Lee accepted a commission in the Army of Northern Virginia. He had opposed secession to the last moment, but he was now a Confederate general. To refuse to fight for the Union was one thing, but to take up arms against the United States quite another. What had happened? Lee had broken his oath of allegiance to defend the Constitution and had taken up the states' rights cause of the Confederacy. No one really knows what went through Lee's mind in those days, but his obsession with providential intervention provides a possible explanation. Perhaps it was God's will now for him to fight for the South. Had Virginia not seceded, Providence might well have guided a different course for Lee.

Lee's decision had a profound impact on the progression of the Civil War. As a seasoned military strategist at the age of fifty-four, he brought the most comprehensive, technologically advanced knowledge of warfare to bear against his own former army. Moreover, he took a fledgling, ragtag, poorly equipped, and generally disorganized military force and instilled in it the discipline and leadership necessary to put up a good fight. Lee's resolution to pour his energy into the Confederate cause contributed substantially to the fact that four long years of bloody and destructive conflict ripped through the country.

The hastily organized Confederacy chose Richmond as its capital after Virginia's secession. The day before Lee arrived on April 22, 1861, excited citizens of that city held an all-night "secession parade." Homemade "Stars and Bars" flags of the Confederacy flew everywhere in the festive city, strains of "Dixie" rang out from small bandstands, and ebullient officials beamed as Lee, their "tower of strength," accepted his commission somberly on April 23. As he looked about the capital of the Confederacy, Lee well knew there was little cause for joy. Hordes of would-be soldiers poured into Richmond. Ad hoc drills were taking place, with the drilling hardly resembling anything military. Aside from its disorganized government, the Confederacy was utterly unprepared to defend itself in the face of impending war. And because Lee knew of the North's plans to preserve the Union through invasion if necessary, he could only lament while others reveled.

In an ominous letter, he warned his wife, "War is inevitable, and there is no telling when it will burst around you. . . . You have to move and make arrangements to go to some point of safety. The war may last ten years." Shortly thereafter, Mary and her family left Arlington, but not before she placed a warning on the front door: "Northern soldiers who profess to reverence Washington, forbear to desecrate the home of his first married life, the property of his wife, now owned by her descendants." The notice was signed, "A Granddaughter of Mrs. Washington." A few days after her departure, Union troops occupied Arlington, built fortifications, and turned the estate into officers' quarters. The conversion of Arlington served as both symbol and substance to the traitorous Robert E. Lee.

Although President Lincoln promised in his inaugural speech not to tamper with slavery where it existed, he flatly rejected secession of the southern states. Lincoln had come to office determined to preserve the "last, best hope for the world"—the experiment in American democratic government. Born in the slaveholding border state of Kentucky, Lincoln had seen the institution firsthand. He had actually married into a slaveholding family, but this only served to heighten his distaste for bondage. Moving to the free state of Illinois, Lincoln made a political career of espousing compassion and rights for all people. He was nonetheless a shrewd politician, and his successful presidential bid was based on preserving the "perpetual union" and taking a very cautious stance on slavery. Lincoln was not an abolitionist. Instead, like Lee, he was an emancipationist who supported the idea of colonizing freed blacks in the West Indies or Africa. As a result, he won the support of the important Free-Soil wing of the Republican party, which feared a mass migration of blacks to the Midwest upon emancipation.

Although Lincoln was amenable to compromise and gradual emancipation, reactionary southern presses steamed after the election of the "black Republican." Responding to fears that the North would "Brown us all" after Lincoln's election, Confederate president Jefferson Davis prepared the new nation for a northern invasion. Southerners were optimistic that they could fight a defensive war successfully and that, when push came to shove, European nations needing their raw materials would surely come to their aid. But for practical people like Lee, such hopes were political wishful thinking—and in his view, politicians had brought this crisis about in the first place. His role was to figure out how to fight a war. How could northern naval power be neutralized? How could the Confederacy generate enough revenue to fight a protracted war? How would the army enlist and train competent troops in a matter of weeks? How would the South acquire arms and supplies and move troops efficiently? In short, Lee asked the questions that overzealous southerners had not asked in their haste to secede. How would a decentralized, agricultural region of about 6 million whites and 3.5 million black slaves, with few roads and even fewer railroads, no industry, and no currency, hold its own against an industrialized, well-linked nation of 21 million, which already had a large and well-equipped army and navy? Resolutely accepting the challenge, Lee said, "I devote myself to the service of my native state, in whose behalf alone will I ever again draw my sword."

In his first action as a Confederate general, Lee participated in establishing the military infrastructure that would organize the army along the same pattern as the army from which he had just resigned. Considering that the Confederacy was attempting to build an army from a few decentralized state militia, the organizational challenge was daunting. The Confederates controlled the Harper's Ferry arsenal, so there was a foundry and a ready supply of weapons. In charge of protecting the Atlantic shoreline, Lee transferred cannon to the coastal defense fortifications on the Potomac, York, and James rivers, not far from those he had built for the Federals at Fort Monroe thirty years before. Next, Lee supervised the formation of an army for the defensive war ahead.

Lee's first military campaign, the defense of western Virginia during the summer of 1861, was a failure. Forced to concentrate his efforts on building up defenses around Richmond, Lee was unable to place more than a minimal detachment of state militiamen in northwest Virginia. When a Union force of Ohio volunteers led by General George B. McClellan marched into the region from southern Ohio, they surprised the Confederate contingent in the middle of a May night and sent them running. Confederate leaders, including Lee, had underestimated the strength of the long-standing hatred that western Virginians harbored for the tidewater part of the state. The Confederates did not plan an elaborate defense of the region bordering the Ohio River, and they were surprised to learn—in the wake of McClellan's successful march—that western delegates had met and had chosen to defect from Virginia and join the Union. The de facto creation of West Virginia in June 1861 forced President Davis to send troops in to recover the lost western counties. On the way to West Virginia, Lee recalled in a letter to his wife that he had traveled the same road twenty years before en route to Saint Louis. He told her that if anyone then had told him the reason for which he would next travel that road, he would have "supposed him insane."

In this campaign, Lee undoubtedly felt he was working with the insane. His assignment was to coordinate operations, but he was not granted full authority over the other three brigadier generals leading detachments on the campaign. W. W. Loring, an army career soldier and a non–West Pointer, was a stubborn and insubordinate man who resented Lee's position of superiority. Henry A. Wise and John B. Floyd were both former governors of Virginia with no military experience. Against the wishes of most southern military strategists, wealthy or politically important men who sought adventure were sometimes granted strategic positions in the Confederate army. Not only were Wise and Floyd unfamiliar with military operations, but they also conducted an ongoing personal feud in which embarrassing the other often took priority over defeating the Federals. Lee was appalled by the lack of discipline among Loring's men and the filth and squalor of their camp. Wise's and Floyd's detachments, mostly poorly trained volunteers, were even less capable of fighting efficiently. As Lee prepared to meet the Federal army, under the command of William S. Rosecrans, he despaired over the bickering of his generals and the ineptitude of this army of civilians. Late summer deluges of rain in the Blue Ridge Mountains only exacerbated an already difficult situation for the Confederates.

Amid the rain, mud, and chaos, the Confederate offensive in West Virginia failed in September 1861. When the combined units of Floyd and Wise retreated shortly after Loring's forces had been defeated, Lee decided to give up the campaign. Lee's caution might have stemmed from an initial lack of will to fight or the fact that as a "gentleman," he had failed to assert his authority sufficiently. But conflicting orders from superiors and internecine squabbles among field commanders also helped doom the campaign. Poor supply lines, another problem that only worsened as the war progressed, also hampered the campaign in West Virginia. "We have only lived from day to day," Lee wrote his son Custis, who was also in the Confederate army, "and on three-fourths rations at that. It is the want of supplies that has prevented our advancing, and up to this time there is no improvement." To Mary he wrote, "It is so difficult to get our people . . . to comprehend and execute the measures required. . . . The measles are prevalent throughout the whole army." The realities of war fell heavily on the Confederates during the campaign for West Virginia.

Certain that the Yankees were holding West Virginia as an armed camp, southern newspaper editors attacked Lee for having "extreme tenderness of blood" during the campaign. Branding him "Granny Lee," many demanded his removal from active military duty. But Jefferson Davis disagreed. Like Lee, this former West Pointer and Mississippi senator had long opposed secession, but he was a staunch defender of states' rights and, in a fiery resignation speech before the Senate, had supported the Mississippi cotton bloc after Lincoln's election. Arrogant, inflexible, temperamental, and prone to support cronies, Davis in many ways hampered the Confederate effort throughout the war. Nonetheless, Davis supported Lee's retreat in West Virginia and had continuing faith in his judgment.

Following the West Virginia campaign, Lee was sent to organize the defense in South Carolina and Georgia. The state governors there had refused to relinquish control of their state militias to the Confederacy. Loath to give up any power, the governors were convinced that each southern state should handle its own defense with its own troops. As a result, more than 20,000 state policemen and volunteers were scattered about the southern seaboard states, haphazardly awaiting a northern offensive. Lee and Davis believed that such disorganization had been responsible, in large part, for the fall of several coastal forts to the Federal navy in recent months. Using steam-powered warships and shell guns that fired longer-range and more accurate bullets, the Federal navy had maneuvered outside the range of Confederate artillery at Point Royal Sound between Charleston and Savannah. Meanwhile, the agile ships had bombarded the southern fortresses until surrender came on November 7, 1861, the day of Lee's arrival. The fall of Point Royal was critical. Now the Federal navy could prevent supplies and warships from passing through to most of the Confederate Atlantic seaboard. The capture of Point Royal also left southern inland cities vulnerable to naval attack via the wide rivers of the tidewater South. Lee knew he had to secure those entry points rapidly.

After the experience in West Virginia, Lee believed he had to assume a greater role as commander. He found the governors, who were stunned by their recent military defeats, far more acquiescent than his fellow generals had been in West Virginia. In less than six months, Lee abandoned all of the nonessential coastal outposts that could not be protected from the Federal navy. He then moved inland, built obstructions at strategic river inlets, and moved in artillery to repel the Federal fleet. Next, he set up defenses for the key coastal city of Charleston, South Carolina. Finally, he coordinated the armies of the Carolinas and Georgia into a unified fighting force of 25,000.

After his brief duty in the coastal states, Lee returned to Richmond at the behest of Jefferson Davis—and despite the outcries of politicians and newspaper editors who maintained that Lee was "a better engineer than a general." As Lee assumed his new role as strategic military adviser to Davis, the Confederacy was experiencing success in several campaigns. Except for the loss of West Virginia, the South had had an early series of victories and only light casualties. These successes had boosted morale greatly and lent credence to the optimistic view that a few southern boys could whip any ten Yankees.

Yet Lee believed such victories would be short-lived if the Confederacy did not change its overall military strategy. It would be impossible, Lee maintained, to continue to fight a defensive war—the prevailing southern plan of repelling Union invasions throughout Confederate territory. The Confederacy could not defend all of its borders, which included an Atlantic coastline hundreds of miles long, the Mississippi River, and the mountains of western Virginia. By the spring of 1862, Confederate troops were in steady retreat in their attempts to protect the Mississippi River area from Union assault, and Federal forces were massing for a major attack on Richmond. In light of these events, Lee called for a concentration of Confederate military strength. Only then, he told Davis, can we "hope to win any decisive advantage." Instead of a purely defensive strategy, Lee advocated an "offensive-defensive" strategy, wherein the Confederates could attack the Union army at a chosen point with strength and concentration and prevent the enemy from attacking everywhere. And after a strategic battle victory, the Confederate army would withdraw to defend its own territory.

As Lee devised his strategy, Abraham Lincoln was experiencing difficulties with his supreme commander, thirty-four-year-old George McClellan. McClellan was a brilliant strategist and student of military history. After his successful leadership of the Ohio volunteers in western Virginia, Lincoln chose him to succeed Winfield Scott as general-in-chief. McClellan was highly successful in combining the operations of the Federal army and navy. He also developed a grand strategy to defeat the Confederacy based on disrupting the rail lines running from the Mississippi River to the eastern seaboard and down the Atlantic Coast.

Despite all of his positive attributes, McClellan proved to be unsatisfactory to Lincoln. The "Napoleon of the North" had supreme confidence in his own judgment and generally ignored the advice of others. Moreover, as a Democrat, he often quarreled with Lincoln and his cabinet and actually made unsolicited political recommendations to the president. But McClellan's overly cautious command decisions irked Lincoln the most. While moving his huge Army of the Potomac down Chesapeake Bay from Washington to Yorktown, Virginia, in April 1862, McClellan hesitated in attacking Richmond when he met with minor Confederate resistance. With 80,000 men ready to strike and many more in reserve, an all-out attack might have captured the poorly defended Confederate capital. When Lincoln wired a protest of the delay, McClellan condescendingly dismissed it.

McClellan's delay proved costly. It allowed Lee and other Confederate strategists, Joseph E. Johnston and Thomas "Stonewall" Jackson, to retreat and regroup. When heavy spring rains left McClellan's troops in disarray, Johnston attacked at the town of Seven Pines, hoping to catch the Union army off guard and halt its movement toward Richmond. In two days there were more than 10,000 casualties on both sides, and Johnston himself was seriously wounded. The following day, Robert E. Lee took command of the Army of Northern Virginia. "I wish [the command] had fallen upon an abler man," Lee wrote his daughter-in-law, "or that I were able to drive our enemies back to their homes." Regardless of his modesty, Lee soon won the respect of his men by the example he set. By his mere presence he inspired the troops. He carefully avoided rebuking his subordinates and kept morale high with support and encouragement.

Morale and encouragement were sorely needed as soldiers on both sides witnessed the horror of war at Seven Pines. "Long lines of ambulances . . . toiled slowly along," a veteran of the battle recalled, "the long torturing way marked by the trail of blood that oozed drop by drop." The ferocity of former countrymen now fighting as enemies amazed most who witnessed or participated in the battle at Seven Pines.

Although it was a tactical victory, Seven Pines failed to accomplish Confederate goals. Johnston's troops had dazed the Army of the Potomac, but it remained menacingly close to Richmond—so close that Union soldiers could hear the church bells of the capital. When Lee gave up the Johnston-devised assault, the *Richmond Examiner* lamented "Evacuating Lee's" ascension. Ignoring such jibes, Lee made plans to remove McClellan's army from Richmond's doorstep. He spent most of the month of June 1862 fortifying the lines protecting the capital. When Lee persuaded Jefferson Davis to order the army to dig trenches to protect Richmond from Federal attack, he was derisively nicknamed "the King of Spades." But Lee could only lament the Confederacy's choice of Richmond (only 100 miles from Washington, D.C.) as its capital and try to draw McClellan away from it.

Lee's first step was to dispatch General J. E. B. Stuart's cavalry on a reconnaissance mission. After encircling McClellan's army, Stuart reported back that its northern flank was weak. Meanwhile, Lee sent another division on a diversionary march through the Shenandoah Valley, supposedly bound for unprotected Washington, D.C. When Lincoln realized this, he ordered McClellan to send 20,000 troops after the division, despite his general's protest that it was a trick. Dispatching Stonewall Jackson's division to attack the vulnerable northern flank, Lee then split his own troops, sending part of them to join the northern assault and the other part to attack McClellan's army head-on, beginning on June 26. In what became known as the Seven Days' Campaign, Lee surprised the Union troops with his "audacious maneuvers" at several locations on the peninsula of southeastern Virginia. The Confederate losses were heavy: 3,200 dead and 17,000 wounded or missing, compared to only 1,700 dead and 8,000 wounded for the Federals. The ferocious assault nonetheless succeeded in pushing McClellan's army away from Richmond and also in the capture of more than 30,000 muskets and dozens of artillery pieces from the retreating Union army. Thereafter, southern presses changed their opinion of "Granny Lee." He now became known as "one of the great military masters" and was hailed as "Uncle Robert."

Lee himself was disappointed that his troops, because of poor communication and lack of tenacity, had failed to do more damage to McClellan's army, which he believed "should have been destroyed." His assistants had not followed his orders to pursue the enemy relentlessly in retreat, as Winfield Scott's army had done in Mexico. Lee's plans depended on the rapid converging of well-coordinated divisions of the army, which did not transpire. On the first day of the battle, for example, at a village called Mechanicsville, A. P. Hill attacked the weak northern flank without the anticipated assistance of Stonewall Jackson's troops, which were late in arriving. As a result, Hill's assault did not inflict the damage Lee had hoped for, and it had also removed the element of surprise from the flank attack. Six days of head-on battles followed, with the eventual retreat of McClellan's army.

Rare to show temper publicly, Lee raged after the victory of the Seven Days' Campaign. Lee's son Rob, who saw him after the battle, said, "The great victory did not elate him." For Lee, it was no victory, because the offensive-defensive strategy had not been fulfilled. The Seven Days' Campaign could have but had not been the killing blow, the one that would make Union leaders realize invasion was impossible. Lee saw little reason to celebrate this blown opportunity of a successful concentrated offensive. In his view, there would be few more such opportunities.

Despite the celebrated removal of McClellan from the outskirts of Richmond, the war was taking an ominous turn for the South by the summer of 1862. In the West, the southern strategy remained largely defensive. Attempting to protect Tennessee and Kentucky with too few resources led Confederate strategists in that region to indecision intermingled with a few ill-timed offensives.

Meanwhile, Union General Ulysses S. Grant—a West Point graduate who had taken to drinking while on assignment in Oregon Territory and was forced to resign—had found a second military life with the coming of the Civil War. Grant oversaw the western strategy of securing the Mississippi River and isolating Arkansas and Texas. When Commander David Farragut captured New Orleans in April 1862, the Confederacy's western trade artery was closed to all but internal commerce. Next, the Union sought control of the river from its mouth to its confluence with the Ohio River.

In keeping with McClellan's strategy of disrupting Confederate rail lines, Grant's 40,000-man army pushed south from Illinois into western Tennessee toward the rail center at Corinth, Mississippi. In the long run, the constant Union presence in this region would bedevil the South and turn the tide of the war, but the immediate result was the bloody stalemate at the Battle of Shiloh on April 6–7, 1862. The fierce two-day battle began when Confederate forces, led by Albert Sidney Johnston and P. G. T. Beauregard, launched an all-out attack near Shiloh Church in southern Tennessee. Their goal was the recovery of all the territory recently won by Grant, and the attack did surprise the Union troops. Johnston mismanaged his advantage, however. His frontal assault allowed Grant's rifle corps to take a frightful toll. Union losses were greater among the total of 23,000 casualties (dead, wounded, and captured), but on the second day, Grant's army stopped the Confederate advance and forced a retreat. Less than two months later, Union forces captured Corinth.

In the eastern theater, meanwhile, Robert E. Lee became known as a master military strategist. Taking outnumbered and outsupplied forces, Lee won several victories through bold surprise attacks. With Richmond safe for the moment after the Seven Days' Campaign, Lee was ready to strike somewhere in northern territory. By this time, he had convinced Davis that this

In this painting of Jefferson Davis and his Confederate cabinet at Richmond, probably done in 1862, General Robert E. Lee outlines the southern strategy.

was the South's only plausible strategy. A successful strike and occupation might win European diplomatic recognition and thus persuade the North to let the Confederacy go. As Lee knew, this was the only way to end the war on favorable terms for the South. Otherwise, the Confederacy would be forced to surrender or would be crushed amid devastating casualties and destruction.

Because of George McClellan's unpopularity in Lincoln's cabinet and his actions in the Seven Days' Campaign, Lincoln had replaced him as general-in-chief with Henry Halleck. In August 1862, Lee's forces defeated Halleck's subordinate, General John Pope, twice—at Cedar Mountain, and then at Bull Run, near the town of Manassas, some twenty miles west of Washington, D.C. In both battles, the Confederacy's best generals—Stonewall Jackson, Jeb Stuart, James Longstreet, and A. P. Hill—served under Lee. Second Bull Run (also known as Second Manassas) was a decisive victory. Lee's offensive-defensive strategy had been better coordinated than in the Seven Days' campaign. Attacking Pope's flank at two points, with divided armies led by Jackson and Longstreet, caused initial panic. Then Lee attacked the disorganized Federals with full force, causing another retreat back to Washington.

With these victories, the Army of Northern Virginia had completely routed the Union army out of Virginia. The Army of the Potomac, which months earlier had posed a threat to Richmond, was now busily building earthen barriers to protect the nation's capital. Still, the victory had come at a great cost to the Confederates. Lee lost 19 percent of his soldiers at Second Manassas, and Pope's losses amounted to 13 percent. The supply shortage reached crisis proportions just as

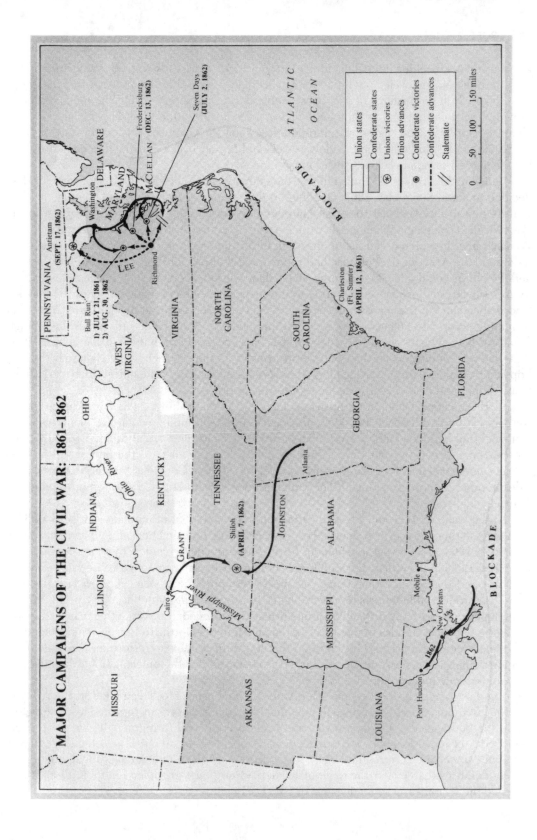

MAJOR CAMPAIGNS OF THE CIVIL WAR: 1861–1862

ATLANTIC OCEAN

Legend:
- Union states
- Confederate states
- ✳ Union victories
- —— Union advances
- ⊙ Confederate victories
- – – – Confederate advances
- // Stalemate

0   50   100   150 miles

BLOCKADE

PENNSYLVANIA

OHIO

INDIANA

ILLINOIS

MISSOURI

WEST VIRGINIA

KENTUCKY

TENNESSEE

VIRGINIA

NORTH CAROLINA

SOUTH CAROLINA

GEORGIA

ALABAMA

MISSISSIPPI

ARKANSAS

LOUISIANA

FLORIDA

DELAWARE

MARYLAND

Washington

Ohio River

Antietam (SEPT. 17, 1862)

Fredericksburg (DEC. 13, 1862)

Seven Days (JULY 2, 1862)

McCLELLAN

LEE

Richmond

Bull Run
1) JULY 21, 1861
2) AUG. 30, 1862

Charleston (Ft. Sumter) (APRIL 12, 1861)

Atlanta

JOHNSTON

GRANT

Shiloh (APRIL 7, 1862)

Cairo

Mississippi River

Mobile

New Orleans

Port Hudson

1862

BLOCKADE

Lee's army was reaching its peak fighting efficiency. Lee knew that his army was ill equipped to penetrate the North, even though the timing was right. Lee told Jefferson Davis that his troops lacked "much of the material of war, [was] feeble in transportation . . . and the men are poorly provided with clothes and in thousands of instances are destitute of shoes." Concerned also about the perilously low stock of ammunition, Lee knew the Union army's current state of disarray would not last for long. Food ran low as well, and Lee advocated moving into the North during the harvest season to help satisfy his men's hunger.

Believing his army could "inflict injury upon our adversary" despite the lack of supplies, Lee decided to act in September 1862. Dividing his 60,000-man army into several contingents, Lee sent Stonewall Jackson's unit to retake Harper's Ferry, which the Confederates had lost in the West Virginia campaign. When another force moved as far north as Hagerstown, Maryland, near Pennsylvania, Lee directed all his troops north into Union territory. Unfortunately for the Confederates, the Army of the Potomac had intercepted a dispatch of Lee's plans. Before Jackson and the others could rejoin Lee, George McClellan, who had been reinstated because of his ability to motivate soldiers, moved his army to intercept Lee's. Lee probably knew of the massing troops ahead and of the impossibility of destroying the Federal army at this juncture. Instead of retreating across the Potomac, however, he determined to face McClellan's forces. Lee's judgment was flawed by his absolute fixation on striking a decisive blow in the North and by his view that time was running out for the Confederate army to accomplish such a task. He also had a faint hope that a major victory in slaveholding Maryland would convince state officials there to join the Confederacy and further legitimize the southern secession.

In the ensuing battle along Antietam Creek near Sharpsburg, Maryland, 75,000 Union soldiers clashed with about 40,000 Confederates. Lee's outnumbered forces, many of whom were fighting barefoot, battled McClellan's army to a standstill. Several times, Lee's army was on the verge of collapse, but timely reinforcements held the lines. At the end of the two-day battle, some 5,000 men lay dead, approximately 2,700 of them Confederates. Casualties on both sides numbered more than 26,000. The Union army was badly stunned, but the invasion of the North had failed.

In the wake of Antietam, President Lincoln, more confident of ultimate victory, issued his own devastating blow to the South. His Emancipation Proclamation announced that as of January 1, 1863, all slaves in the rebellious territories would be free unless those states ended the rebellion. Lincoln knew that the ultimatum would probably have no impact on ending the two-year war and that its immediate effect on slavery was purely symbolic. The proclamation was more the product of his efforts to placate the factions within the Republican party and impress foreign powers, especially Britain. While abolitionists continued to advocate their cause, the border states balked at the idea of free blacks streaming into the North. To Lincoln, "emancipation" still meant recolonization, and he admitted that if it were possible to restore the Union without freeing a single slave, he would do so. But he also believed that the proclamation would damage the Confederate military cause.

Lee hastily returned to Virginia after Antietam, and again McClellan allowed the Army of Northern Virginia to escape. Instead of pursuing Lee, McClellan's army returned to Washington, while the bedraggled Confederates scurried back to Richmond to regroup. This time Lincoln removed McClellan for good. His replacement, Ambrose Burnside, resumed the siege of Virginia and forced Lee's retreating troops to again defend the Confederate capital. Fighting a mostly defensive battle near the town of Fredericksburg on December 13, 1862, Lee's troops repelled the Union attack, inflicting almost 13,000 casualties on the Federals.

Early in 1863, Lee was forced into further defensive action. Because the Federal navy forced him to send part of his troops into North Carolina, Lee was unable to prepare for the next offensive. In the meantime, a new Union commander, Joseph Hooker, was moving the Army of the Potomac toward Richmond again. Circumventing Lee's fortifications around Richmond, Hooker moved his forces through a forested area called the Wilderness near Charlottesville. Hooker made a critical mistake by boxing his army between a dense forest and the Rappahannock River. Aware of the Federals' position, Lee dispatched Stonewall Jackson and his men to attack Hooker with a flanking maneuver, followed by an all-out frontal assault by Lee's army. Chaos ensued among Hooker's men, who panicked and retreated north across the Rappahannock River on May 5 and 6.

Because the battles of Fredericksburg and the Wilderness were defensive in nature, Lee found little comfort in the victories. The campaigns inflicted heavy casualties on the Confederates, including the loss of Lee's most trusted ally, Stonewall Jackson, who was mistakenly shot by his own men. While Confederate newspapers grew more confident with the victories, the political and military leaders knew the reality. The Confederacy was running out of money and supplies. Food rations were cut continually; shoes and clothing grew scarcer. And after Antietam and the Emancipation Proclamation, European governments showed even less willingness to aid the Confederate cause—which now appeared to be a bad financial risk.

Much of what Lee had feared when he put on a Confederate uniform was coming to pass by late 1863. Angrily, he told his son Custis of the meager food rations and inadequate supplies at the camp near Charlottesville. Lee feared his men would be "unable to endure the hardship of the approaching campaign." In addition to the other woes, scurvy, influenza, and measles were running rampant through the camp. Lee understood the causes of the current Confederate plight. Britain and France had been of little help despite the secessionists' early predictions, and the Union blockade of Atlantic ports was taking its toll on the delivery of arms, military supplies, and commercial goods. Southern businessmen were literally going broke. The hastily formed Confederate political structure, based on state sovereignty, provided little support for the war effort because of its inability to generate desperately needed capital. Through infighting and power mongering, southern governors and Confederate congressmen hampered any coordination of the loosely based nation. The defensive strategy in the West was failing by mid-1863, and Jefferson Davis suggested that some of Lee's force be transferred to Mississippi and Tennessee. Lee insisted, however, that Virginia was the focus of the war, partly out of parochialism but also because he believed the West could not be defended successfully. As supplies ran low and the economic blockade tightened, southern strategists had little choice but to give Robert E. Lee one more chance to win a decisive victory in the North.

The Army of Northern Virginia broke camp near Charlottesville on June 6, 1863, and set out for Pennsylvania. Given the circumstances, Lee's strategy had become purely offensive. He hoped to move the fighting as far from Richmond as possible and engage the Army of the Potomac on its own territory. James Longstreet, one of Lee's adjutant generals, urged an attack on Washington, D.C. but Lee was more interested in drawing the army into the open and defeating it than in besieging the well-fortified city. If the Confederates could march to a large northern city unopposed by the Federal army, Lee would then consider an occupation of Washington, Baltimore, or Philadelphia—but he doubted that the Army of the Potomac would remain in Washington. Lee hoped for a major engagement with a stunning victory. Before leaving, however, Lee warned Jefferson Davis of the dire situation in his army: "Our resources in men are constantly diminishing, and the disproportion in this respect between us and our enemies . . . is steadily augmenting." If this plan, desperate as it was, did not work, Lee told Davis to be prepared for an all-out invasion.

As Lee's army pushed through Maryland and into Pennsylvania, partisan Union women met them with waving American flags and jeers. When the general himself rode by, however, the taunts usually stopped. The "marble model," now distinguished by a gray uniform and a gray beard, struck an impressive figure riding on his stallion, Traveller. One woman who saw him ride by was said to have stopped waving her flag, dropped the banner, and exclaimed, "Oh, I wish he was ours!" And a Pennsylvania woman who went to Lee's camp to ask the Confederates for flour also requested the general's autograph. "Do you want the autograph of a rebel?" Lee asked. "General Lee," she responded, "I am a true Union woman, and yet I ask for bread and your autograph." Lee gave her both, and she remembered him as a gentleman, "with strength and sadness on his face."

On June 28, Lee learned that the Army of the Potomac had crossed into Maryland and was marching to intercept the Confederates in Pennsylvania. His plan had worked thus far, and the opportunity was at hand to win a climactic military victory. When the Blue and the Gray stood across a small valley between two ridges just south of the town of Gettysburg, Pennsylvania, on June 30, 1863, more than 150,000 men had massed for what was to be the deciding battle of the war in the East. The Army of the Potomac had yet another commander, George Meade, whom Lincoln had just chosen to replace Hooker.

Though early fighting favored the South, the tide of the three-day bloodbath eventually turned against the Army of Northern Virginia. Lee's ambitious plan depended on absolute coordination, absolute fearlessness on the part of his men, and a good knowledge of the battle terrain. But fighting on the road in unfamiliar territory proved more difficult than fighting in Virginia. The hastily prepared encampments provided Lee's men with no protection from Union assault. Lee's response, based on his objective of decisive victory, was to attack. Determined to smash through the Union line on Cemetery Ridge, Lee directed General George Pickett to lead a "charge," which succeeded only briefly in penetrating the line before relentless rifle fire restored it. Lee had underestimated the impact of placing his troops in long lines exposed to rifle fire, and Pickett's division was cut to ribbons by the Union batteries and sharpshooters in the "bloody angle" between Seminary Ridge and the Little Round Top. Longstreet, too, added to the ghastly Confederate losses by deciding to rest his exhausted division before moving it to the front line.

The creeks around Gettysburg ran red with the blood of Americans during the climactic third day of battle, when "Pickett's Charge" raged, but ultimately the Union defenses held. Lee, who recognized the risky nature of a frontal assault, believed he had no choice but to attack while the ammunition supplies held out. He also maintained later that if Stonewall Jackson had been there, the Confederates would have won the Battle of Gettysburg. But Lee had placed all Confederate hopes in this campaign, and he had asked too much of his men to carry out the plan. After a week of hard marching in midsummer, Lee sent his outnumbered, unrested, and ill-supplied forces into full attack—an attack that lasted three days. During the battle, Lee tried desperately to outflank the long Union line, with no results except to thin his own forces. His order to charge the front line on the third day was ill conceived, since it put Pickett's men directly in the line of sharpshooters using accurate rifles. Even if Lee had cracked the Union lines and declared victory, his army would have been isolated in the North, its ammunition and supplies exhausted. On his retreat, Confederate casualties numbered more than 20,000, while Union losses were more than 23,000. Still, the North had held firm. The second Confederate invasion into the North had been halted, and the war in the East was essentially over. Although Meade did

Innovations in photography during the 1850s provide graphic pictorial coverage of the Civil War. Above, Union soldiers pose near Yorktown, Virginia, in 1862. The artillery shown could launch shells thirteen inches in diameter. Below, clusters of dead Confederate soldiers lie near Gettysburg in July 1863. The poor condition of their shoes and clothing tells the story of an undersupplied army.

not pursue and inflict a "killing blow" on Lee's army, it was now only a matter of time. The North could and would replace its casualties with fresh troops; the South could not.

A thousand miles to the west, the tide was also turning, as General Grant completed his mission of taking control of the Mississippi River in the Battle of Vicksburg. The Union had made steady gains in the West since Shiloh (April 1862). Union detachments headed by William Rosecrans and Don Carlos Buell roved through Tennessee and Kentucky, while Grant's army moved down the Mississippi toward Vicksburg. The successful siege of this Mississippi town, beginning in late 1862 and ending on July 4, 1863, affirmed Grant as an able strategist. Using a minimum of manpower, and eschewing the idea of a decisive battlefield victory, Grant cut off the Confederate fortress protecting the Mississippi River by leaving the river and setting up encampments on dry land to the east. His actions confused the Confederates, and when he did attack toward the end of the siege, the surrender was won with fewer than 5,000 Union casualties, while the Confederates had 12,000. The Union now controlled all water routes in the Mississippi Valley; Arkansas, Texas, and Louisiana had been isolated and neutralized. Vicksburg was a crushing logistical defeat for the South, and Grant's success compelled Lincoln to choose a new person for the job offered to Robert E. Lee only three years before.

Grant's strategy as general-in-chief was simple: to grind the South down militarily and force surrender. Taking command of all the Union armies, Grant ordered General William Tecumseh Sherman's forces in the West to march east to the Atlantic port city of Savannah, Georgia. Grant's and Sherman's mighty armies, each more than 100,000 strong, were growing more powerful each day. Grant's army chased Lee's retreating troops in a series of battles that included the Wilderness campaign, Spotsylvania, and Cold Harbor. These skirmishes ended in a ten-month siege of Petersburg, Virginia, only forty miles from Richmond. Here Lee staged a vigorous defense, keeping the huge army at bay for nearly a year. Some of Lee's advisers had warned that Grant, unlike his predecessors, would not withdraw his army after one defeat. Grant was determined to crush southern resistance by an invasion of Richmond, and casualties were heavy on both sides during 1864 and 1865. Such losses forced the Confederates to enlist boys and old men to carry on the fight. Unlike Lee, Grant had neither the desire for, nor much faith in, the impact of a decisive battle. Such victories had been important in Napoleon's time, but rifles (those with spiraled etchings inside the barrels, affording greater accuracy) had made the cost of the frontal assault greater than the benefit. Grant realized that technology had changed the strategy of war, and Lee did not. Of course, Lee did not have the luxury of superior numbers, transportation, and resources. There was also the liability of Lee's avowed necessity for an offensive strategy and a decisive military victory. In contrast, by 1864, Grant was contented to win without any major victories; instead, he would exhaust the enemy in Virginia.

Meanwhile, General Sherman and the other western commanders who joined him cut a five-mile swath of destruction from Chattanooga, Tennessee, to Savannah, Georgia, in his "March to the Sea." Sherman's scorched-earth policy, which including the burning of Atlanta, was simple: Destroy everything that could be used by the rebels to make war. This included railroad tracks, depots, water towers, livery stables, and general stores. By early 1865, Sherman's troops were carving up South and North Carolina on their way to Richmond.

Even though Lee was given command of the entire Confederate army in January 1865, he could do little more than outmaneuver Grant in a desperate attempt to protect Richmond. In late March, Union forces broke through the lines at Petersburg. Days later, Richmond was reduced to ashes by Union artillery fire, and the Confederate government fled further inland.

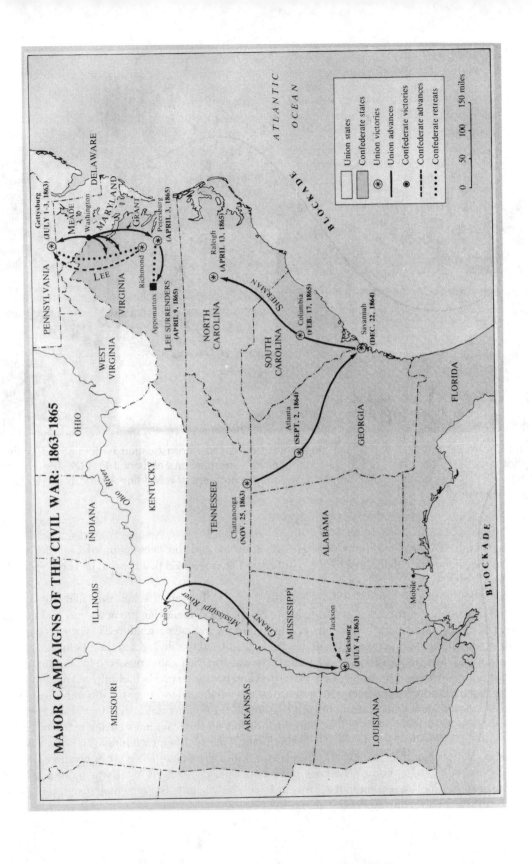

MAJOR CAMPAIGNS OF THE CIVIL WAR: 1863–1865

Legend:
- Union states
- Confederate states
- Union victories
- Union advances
- Confederate victories
- Confederate advances
- Confederate retreats

Scale: 0 50 100 150 miles

ATLANTIC OCEAN

BLOCKADE

PENNSYLVANIA — Gettysburg (JULY 1–3, 1863)
MEADE — Washington — MARYLAND — DELAWARE
GRANT — Petersburg (APRIL 3, 1865)
LEE — Richmond
Appomattox — LEE SURRENDERS (APRIL 9, 1865)
VIRGINIA — WEST VIRGINIA

OHIO — Ohio River — INDIANA — ILLINOIS — MISSOURI

KENTUCKY

NORTH CAROLINA — Raleigh (APRIL 13, 1865)
SOUTH CAROLINA — Columbia (FEB. 17, 1865)
SHERMAN
TENNESSEE — Chattanooga (NOV. 25, 1863)
GEORGIA — Atlanta (SEPT. 2, 1864)
Savannah (DEC. 22, 1864)
ALABAMA — Mobile
MISSISSIPPI — Jackson
GRANT — Mississippi River — Cairo
ARKANSAS
LOUISIANA — Vicksburg (JULY 4, 1863)
FLORIDA

BLOCKADE

The enormous physical, social, and intellectual task called Reconstruction is dramatized in this photograph of Charleston, South Carolina, after its surrender on February 18, 1865. The end of the Civil War was less than two months away, but the problem of rebuilding American society was just beginning.

With the fall of Richmond, news of Sherman's success, and the decimation of Lee's forces—outnumbered by more than three to one—Jefferson Davis realized that the end had come for the Confederacy.

On the morning of April 9, 1865, General Robert E. Lee approached the village of Appomattox Courthouse surrounded by Confederate troops still disbelieving the news they had heard. They ran to Lee's side when he rode up, crying, "General, are we surrendered?" Vowing to go on fighting, the underfed and unpaid Confederate soldiers tried to rally behind their beloved leader. Lee stopped his horse, looked all about at the dirty, war-torn faces, and reflected for a moment on the last four years before speaking. Lee was a tired and beaten man. He had suffered a mild heart attack shortly before Gettysburg, and a heart attack would indeed take his life only five years later. Moreover, during the last months of the conflict, Lee's mental health had also appeared questionable; he was tempted, at least once, to ride out on the front lines during battle to end it all. Two of his sons had fought for the Confederacy. One had been wounded; the other was a prisoner of war. Mary Lee was living with relatives out of the war zone—a bitter invalid who had been uprooted from her home. The Lees had lost all their possessions in the war, including their Washington heirlooms. Arlington itself was in Union hands and, as a crowning insult, had been turned into a cemetery for Federal soldiers.

Lee would spend the last five years of his life a melancholy and depressed man, prone to delirium and to justifying the southern cause. His decisions to quit the army, to join the Confederacy, and to persuade Jefferson Davis to follow an offensive strategy undoubtedly haunted him. Although he maintained to his dying day in 1870 that he had acted in the only way he could, Lee must have lamented his resignation from the Union army and the loss of his career, home, and stability. Robert and Mary Lee were never allowed to return to Arlington. Far more haunting was his prevailing offensive strategy, aimed at gaining the decisive victory he had never attained—a strategy that had sent thousands to die on both sides during the bold Confederate frontal assaults. Perhaps this had been the only viable southern strategy, but Lee's outcries during nightmares as his health failed indicated that he was a deeply troubled man.

Lee had made a decision that had changed him from an honored military officer to a rebel. But once decided, he had taken an unorganized military force and given it an inspiration and prowess that struck the awe of the "Rebel yell" into Union soldiers. He had given the Confederacy a strategy for victory, and however flawed it might have been, he had provided a focus and a will among his troops to support him. Lee's aggressive strategy had only delayed the inevitable Union victory, however, and actually had made it more complete. His beloved Virginia lay in ruins, as well as much of the rest of the South. Slavery had been abolished in the South by Lincoln's Emancipation Proclamation, but it had taken the fury of all-out war to convince southerners of the fact. Lincoln's determination to preserve the Union had prevailed. The states were not as "sovereign" as the secessionists had believed; the American nation was supreme. Secession was not permitted, even at the cost of 600,000 lives.

Lee pondered some or all of these matters as he rode into the courtyard. To his soldiers who had gathered around him on that Palm Sunday morning he said, "Men, we have fought the war together, and I have done the best I could for you." And with those words, Lee dismounted from his horse and walked slowly into Appomattox Courthouse.

Selected Readings

The Person

Bowden, Scott, and Bill Ward: *Last Chance for Victory: Robert E. Lee and the Gettysburg Campaign* (2001). Exhaustive study of the battle of Gettysburg.

Bradford, Gamaliel: *Lee: The American* (1912). A good example of adulatory historians' attempts to lionize Lee.

Connelly, Thomas L.: *The Marble Man: Robert E. Lee and His Image in American Society* (1977). An account of the hero building of Lee after his death and into the twentieth century.

Davis, Burke: *The Gray Fox: Robert E. Lee and the Civil War* (1956). An account of Lee's Civil War history, with lengthy war correspondence.

Dowdey, Clifford: *Lee* (1965). A thorough, overall historical account of Lee's life and times.

Flood, Charles Bracelen: *Lee: The Last Years* (1981). Chronicles Lee's experiences after Appomattox, when he was president of Washington University in Virginia.

Gallagher, Gary W.: *Lee the Soldier* (1996). Essays by scholars with widely differing views on Lee's military decision making.

Harwell, Richard: *R. E. Lee: An Abridgment of the Four-Volume R. E. Lee by Douglas Southhall Freeman* (1961). A skillful condensation of Freeman's 1934 multivolume definitive biography.

Jones, J. William: *Personal Reminiscences, Anecdotes, and Letters of Gen. Robert E. Lee* (1874). An adulatory commentary, but valuable for the hundreds of letters and remembrances it contains.

Marvel, William: *Lee's Last Retreat: The Flight to Appomattox* (2002). Day-to-day accounts of the last days of the Civil War in the East.

McCaslin, Richard B.: *Lee in the Shadow of Washington* (2001). An exploration of Lee's self-comparison to General George Washington.

McKenzie, John D.: *Uncertain Glory: Lee's Generalship Re-Examined* (1997). Calls into question the quality of Lee's decisions as head of the Army of Northern Virginia.

Nolan, Alan T.: *Lee Considered: General Robert E. Lee and Civil War History* (1991). An analytical revision of the Lee "American hero" thesis.

Palmer, Michael A.: *Lee Moves North: Robert E. Lee on the Offensive* (1998). Readable accounts of action in Maryland and Pennsylvania.

Sanborn, Margaret: *Robert E. Lee: A Portrait, 1807–1861* (1966). A good account of the Lee family and Virginia.

Thomas, Emory M.: *Robert E. Lee* (1995). Well-researched biography balancing recent revisions of Lee's character.

Wheeler, Richard: *Lee's Terrible Swift Sword: From Antietam to Chancellorsville, An Eyewitness History* (1992). A lively account of Lee's defense of Virginia.

The Period

Beringer, Richard E.: *Why the South Lost the Civil War* (1986). Examines the social, political, and military factors that brought southern defeat.

Catton, Bruce, Charles P. Roland, David Donald, and T. Harry Williams: *Grant, Lee, Lincoln and the Radicals: Essays on Civil War Leadership* (2001). Updated, revised, and edited version of the 1964 classic.

Faust, Patricia (ed.): *Historical Times Encyclopedia of the Civil War* (1986). Thorough work, full of names, places, dates, battles, technology, and interpretations.

°Foner, Eric: *Free Soil, Free Labor, Free Men: The Ideology of the Republican Party before the Civil War* (1970). Traces the groups and interests that made up the Republican party.

Hattaway, Herman, and Archer Jones: *How the North Won: A Military History of the Civil War* (1983). A dynamic account of interpretations of Civil War strategy and military history.

Johnson, David E.: *Douglas Southall Freeman* (2002). Life and times of the preeminent Lee biographer.

Kelley, Robert: *The Cultural Pattern in American Politics: The First Century* (1979). Traces the rise and fall of political parties from colonial America until 1900.

°Merk, Frederick: *Manifest Destiny and Mission in American History: A Reinterpretation* (1963). Analyzes the rise of American imperialism and its impact on westward expansion, especially concerning Mexican territory.

°Randall, James G., and David Donald: *The Civil War and Reconstruction* (2d ed., 1969). A complete, scholarly, and concise account of these events.

Reed, Rowena: *Combined Operations in the Civil War* (1978). Interpretations of military operations in the Civil War, focusing on combined army and navy strategies.

°Available in paperback

Sifakis, Stuart: *Who Was Who in the Civil War* (1988). Biographical sketches of most of the important figures in the Civil War.

Weigley, Russell F.: *The American Way of War: A History of United States Military Strategy and Policy* (1973). Analyzes strategies of American military leaders during wars from the Revolution to Vietnam, including accounts of Lee and Grant.

For Consideration

1. How was Robert E. Lee tied to the Virginia planter aristocracy and the Founding Fathers?

2. As a Virginian and a U.S. Army officer, Lee's views on slavery and emancipation differed from many pro-slavery Southerners. Discuss those differences.

3. Describe Lee's dilemma when offered command of the Federal army in 1861.

4. Contrast the initial Confederate strategy with that of Lee's as he took command of the Army of Northern Virginia in 1862.

5. Judging from Lee's experiences and the state of the Confederacy, was there ever a chance the South could have won the war?

Credits

We gratefully acknowledge the use of photographs from the following sources:

Chapter 1:
Page x: Bridgeman Art Library; Page 5: Narrative and Critical History of America, Winsor, Houghton Mifflin, New York; Page 7: New York Public Library Special Collections; Page 9: © The British Museum; Page 10: Reprinted with permission of the Macmillian Company from *Columbus* by Langstrom; Page 11: Giraudon/Art Resource, New York.

Chapter 2:
Page 22: Courtesy, American Antiquarian Society; Page 30: Courtesy of the John Carter Brown Library at Brown University; Page 32: Old Academy Museum, Wethersfield, Connecticut; Page 42: Art Resource, New York; Page 46: New York Public Library, Special Collections.

Chapter 3:
Page 50: Brown Brothers; Pages 58 and 68: Library of Congress; Page 59: The Huntington Library, Art Collections, Botanical Gardens, San Marino, CA/SuperStock; Page 62: Royalty-Free/Corbis; Page 73: Philadelphia Museum of Art, Gift of Graeme and Sarah Lorimer in memory of their granddaughter, Mary Caroline Morris.

Chapter 4:
Pages 78 and 86: Massachusetts Historical Society; Page 85: Culver; Page 93: New York State Historical Association; Page 95: The Historical Society of Pennsylvania (HSP), Second Sreet from Market Street with Christ Church, Philadelphia drawn and engraved by William Birch [Bd 61 B531.2 Plate #15].

Chapter 5:
Page 102: White House Historical Association (The White House Collection) (55); Pages 109 and 130: Library of Congress; Page 110: Bettmann/Corbis; Page 114: Virginia Conservation Commission, Richmond, Virginia.

Chapter 6:
Page 136: Field Museum of Natural History, #A93851c; Page 144: Collection of The New York Historical Society; Pages 147 and 150: The Granger Collection, New York; Page 154: Parks Canada Agency, Fort Malden National Historic Site of Canada.

Chapter 7:
Pages 160, 188, and 194: Courtesy Taos Historic Museums; Page 165: The Walters Art Museum, Baltimore, Maryland; Page 172: Huntington Library, San Marino, California; Page 179: General Research Division, The New York Public Library, Astor, Lenox and Tilden Foundations; Page 184: Library of Congress; Page 189: Museum of the City of New York.

Chapter 8:
Page 196: Samuel J. Miller, "Frederick Douglass," 1847–52. Major Acquisitions Centennial Endowment, 1996.433. Reproduction, The Art Institute of Chicago; Pages 201 (top), 216, and 217: Library of Congress; Page 201 (bottom): from *The Western Citizen*, July 13, 1844.

Chapter 9:
Pages 224, 227 (left), and 231: Washington-Custis-Lee Collection, Washington and Lee University, Lexington, Virginia; Pages 227 (right) and 228: Virginia Historical Society, Richmond Virginia; Page 235: (left) The Schlesinger Library, Radcliffe Institute, Harvard University (A102–439–1z); (right) Ohio State Historical Society; Pages 244 and 249: Library of Congress; Page 252: National Archives.

Index

Note: Italicized page numbers indicate illustrations